ONE ~~~~OLOGY
COMPANION

THE CRITICAL CRIMINOLOGY COMPANION

Editors

Thalia Anthony
Chris Cunneen

Hawkins Press
2008

Published in Sydney by:
    Hawkins Press
    An imprint of The Federation Press
    PO Box 45, Annandale, NSW, 2038
    71 John St, Leichhardt, NSW, 2040
    Ph (02) 9552 2200 Fax (02) 9552 1681
    E-mail: info@federationpress.com.au
    Website: http://www.federationpress.com.au

National Library of Australia
Cataloguing-in-Publication entry

    The Critical Criminology Companion
    Editors Thalia Anthony; Chris Cunneen.

    Bibliography.
    Includes index.
    ISBN 978 1876067236 (pbk)

Criminology – Australia, Criminology – New Zealand, Crime – Australia, Crime –New Zealand,
Crime Analysis – Australia, Crime Analysis – New Zealand.

364

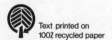

Text printed on
100% recycled paper

Typeset by The Federation Press, Leichhardt, NSW.
    Printed by Ligare Pty Ltd, Riverwood, NSW.

Contents

PART V
FUTURE DIRECTIONS IN CRITICAL CRIMINOLOGY

Contributors

Thalia Anthony is a Lecturer at the University of Sydney Faculty of Law. Her research focuses on the relationships between colonisation, Indigenous people and law. Currently she is working with Northern Territory Indigenous communities on compensation for stolen wages. Thalia has devised university courses in Crime and Society and organised the Australasian Teaching Critical Criminology Conference 2007. Her publications include research on the application of criminal law to Indigenous communities and colonial legal history.

Chris Cunneen is NewSouth Global Chair in Criminology at the University of New South Wales. Previously, he was Director of the Institute of Criminology. Chris has worked with a number of Australian Royal Commissions and Inquiries. He has published widely in the area of juvenile justice, policing, and Indigenous issues including the following books: *Juvenile Justice, Youth and Crime in Australia* (2007), *Indigenous People and the Law in Australia* (1995) and *Conflict, Politics and Crime* (2001).

The editors would like to thank the University of Sydney Faculty of Law for its financial assistance and Sarah Gavaghan for her outstanding research and editorial work.

Dorothea Anthony is completing her research thesis in psychology examining the relationship between social consciousness and social personality as well as studying for a Master of Law and Legal Practice at UTS Sydney. She has a Bachelor of Arts, a Diploma of Science (Psychology) and was awarded the University of Sydney Wentworth Medal. Dorothea has lectured on Criminology and Psychology at Macquarie University and the University of Sydney. Her academic interests include psychosocial studies and the philosophy of psychology and law.

Harry Blagg is Director of Studies at the Crime Research Centre at the University of Western Australia. He has worked on projects including monitoring the recommendations of the Royal Commission into Aboriginal Deaths in Custody, policing Indigenous youth, and family violence. Harry has published widely on these issues as well as critiques of restorative justice as it impacts on Indigenous people. From 2001 to 2005 he was Research Director on the West Australian Law Reform Commission's project, *Aboriginal Customary Laws*.

David Brown is a Professor in the Law Faculty at the University of New South Wales where he has been teaching since 1974 in the area of criminal law, criminal justice and criminology. He is co-author of *Rethinking Law and Order* (1998); *The*

Prison Struggle (1981); and the leading text *Criminal Laws* in four editions (1990 to 2006). David was a co-editor of *The Judgments of Justice Lionel Murphy* (1986); *Death in the Hands of the State* (1988); *Prisoners as Citizens* (2002); and *The New Punitiveness* (2005).

Mark Brown is a Senior Lecturer in Criminology at Melbourne University. His primary teaching and research interests lie in the areas of penality, corrections and colonial penal history. Mark has written extensively on the subject of dangerousness and legislative measures to deal with serious offenders. He has co-edited with John Pratt *Dangerous Offenders: Punishment and Social Order* (2000) and is a co-editor of *The New Punitiveness: Current Trends, Theories, Perspectives* (2005).

Bree Carlton is a Lecturer in Criminology at Monash University. Her interests include histories of punishment, high-security and supermax prisons, and the impact of criminal justice institutions and state practices on individuals and communities. Her book, *Imprisoning Resistance: Life and Death in an Australian Supermax*, was published in 2007.

Kerry Carrington is Professor of Sociology at the University of New England, co-editor of the *Journal of Sociology*, and Editorial Board member of *Public Space: the Journal of Law and Social Justice*. She is the co-author of *Policing the Rural Crisis* (2006); author of *Offending Girls: Sex Youth & Justice* (1993); *Who Killed Leigh Leigh* (1998); and co-editor of *Critical Criminology* (2002); *Travesty! Miscarriages of Justice* (1991) and *Cultures of Crime and Violence* (1995).

Janet Chan is Professor of Social Science and Policy at the University of New South Wales. Her research interests include criminal justice policy and practice, sociology of organisation and occupation, and social organisation of creativity. Janet is internationally recognised for her contributions to policing research, especially her books on police culture and socialisation: *Changing Police Culture* (1997) and *Fair Cop* (with Devery and Doran 2003), and other publications on police reform, police accountability, police use of information technology and the legal regulation of police discretion.

Garry Coventry is the Coordinator of Criminology Programs at James Cook University and was appointed in 2005 as the University's first criminologist to develop a unique program focused on tropical Australia. His career over 30 years includes positions in various universities and research institutes in Australia and the United States. Garry has been an active researcher in a broad range of criminology areas including crime prevention, innovative criminal justice system programs, social justice and the prison.

Mark Findlay is a Professor in the Faculty of Law at the University of Sydney and the Deputy Director of the Institute of Criminology. Mark is Chair in International Criminal Justice at the University of Leeds. He has worked as a research consultant for international agencies, governments and private consortia. Mark's books include

The Globalisation of Crime (2000), *Problems for the Criminal Law* (2001), *Introducing Policing* (2003) and *Transforming International Criminal Justice* (2005). *Governing through Globalised Crime* is due for release in early 2008.

Michael Grewcock recently completed a PhD at the University of New South Wales, where he also teaches criminology and criminal law. Prior to commencing his PhD, he worked as a solicitor and researcher in London for 13 years, including for three years as the legal policy officer for the Howard League for Penal Reform.

Scott Guy is a Lecturer in Law at Griffith University. He completed his PhD in the area of legal theory/constitutional law at the University of Queensland Law School. He has published articles in the area of legal theory in such journals as the *Federal Law Review, Current Issues in Criminal Justice, Australian Journal of Family Law* and the *Bond Law Review*.

Mark Halsey is a Senior Lecturer at the School of Law, Flinders University of South Australia. From 2005 to 2007 he taught criminology at the University of Melbourne. Since 2004, Mark has examined pathways into crime, experiences of confinement, and the challenges of release from the perspectives of young men in custody. Key themes and issues arising from this research can be found in *Journal of Criminal Law and Criminology, Probation Journal, Punishment and Society*, and *Imaginary Penalities* (forthcoming, edited by Pat Carlen).

Barbara Ann Hocking is Associate Professor in the Faculty of Law at the Queensland University of Technology. Barbara is also Honorary Research Assistant at the Riawunna Centre, University of Tasmania. Before joining QUT, she worked as a researcher with the Australian Law Reform Commission, the University of Sydney Faculty of Law, the Queensland Law Society and the Queensland Teachers' Union. Most recently, Barbara worked as an academic at Griffith University from 1989 to 1994. Barbara's publications include *Liability for Negligent Words* (1999).

Russell Hogg teaches in the School of Law at the University of New England. He is co-author with David Brown of *Rethinking Law and Order* (1998) and co-author with Kerry Carrington of *Policing the Rural Crisis* (2006). Russell's recent work is on terrorism and Australia's anti-terror laws.

Gail Mason is Associate Professor in the Faculty of Law at the University of Sydney. Prior to this she was a lecturer in Gender Studies. She is the author of *The Spectacle of Violence: Homophobia, Gender and Knowledge* (2002) and has published widely in *Social and Legal Studies, British Journal of Criminology* and *Hypatia*. Gail's current research centres on the contribution of emotion or affect to the constitution of 'hate crime' as a concept and legal category.

Jude McCulloch is an Associate Professor in Criminology at Monash University. She has researched on police shootings, crime and the media, women and policing, family violence, policing dissent, paramilitary policing, counter-terrorism, globalisation and the 'war on terror'. Jude published *Blue Army: Paramilitary Policing in Australia* (2001). Jude is currently investigating Community Policing and Culturally Diverse Communities as part of an Australian Research Council Linkage grant with the Victoria Police. She is also examining measures relating to the suppression of financing terrorism.

Pat O'Malley is Professorial Research Fellow in Law at the University of Sydney. His work over the last 10 years has focused on risk and neo-liberalism, especially as these affect criminal justice. His recent publications include *Risk, Uncertainty and Government* (2004) and an edited collection with Kelly Hannah Moffat on *Gendered Risks* (2007). His latest book, *The Currency of Justice* – due for release late 2008, examines the use of fines and monetary damaged as regulatory techniques in consumer societies.

Darren Palmer is a Senior Lecturer and Convenor of Criminology at Deakin University. He is a member of the editorial committees *Crime Prevention and Community Safety* and *Police Practice and Research*. Darren has previously taught criminology at La Trobe University. His research interests centre on techniques of governing policing practice. Darren's current research is focused on police governance and crime and policing with a particular emphasis on rural and regional Victoria.

Sharon Pickering is Associate Professor at Monash University and teaches in Criminology. She teaches and researches in the field of refugee law and policy, criminology and human rights. Sharon's books include *Global Issues, Women and Justice* (2004) and *Refugees and State Crime* (2005). Her book *Counter-terrorism Policing* is due for release in 2008.

Scott Poynting is Professor in Sociology at Manchester Metropolitan University. His research interests include the sociology of ethnicity; immigration and racism; racialisation and criminalisation; the sociology of youth, and the intersections of ethnicity, masculinity, and social class. Scott is co-author of *Bin Laden in the Suburbs: Criminalising the Arab Other* (2004) and *Kebabs, Kids, Cops and Crime: Youth, Ethnicity and Crime* (2000); and co-editor of *Outrageous! Moral Panics in Australia* (2007).

John Pratt is Professor of Criminology at the Institute of Criminology, Victoria University of Wellington. He has taught and lectured at universities in the United Kingdom, continental Europe, North America and Australia. John has undertaken extensive research on the history and sociology of punishment in modern society. His four books include *Punishment and Civilization* (2002) and *Penal Populism* (2007). He has co-edited three, including *The New Punitiveness* (2005) and has published more than 100 journal articles and book chapters.

Elizabeth Stanley is a Senior Lecturer at Victoria University in Wellington. She was previously a lecturer in Critical Criminology at the Centre for Studies in Crime and Social Justice in the UK. Elizabeth's research interests are in state crime, human rights, transitional justice and social justice. She has undertaken studies on rights and detention in New Zealand and the UK, and her work in South Africa, Chile and Timor-Leste has focused on truth commissions and court processes.

Julie Stubbs is Professor of Criminology in the Faculty of Law, University of Sydney. Her research focuses on violence against women and her publications address domestic violence law reforms, intimate homicide, battered woman syndrome, a critical appraisal of restorative justice, post-separation violence and child contact, sexual assault, and cross-cultural issues in the legal system. Julie has served on several inter-departmental committees concerning violence against women and an international expert panel on domestic violence.

Stephen Tomsen is Professor of Criminology at the University of Western Sydney. His research fields include hate crime, masculinities and crime, policing and public order, and access to legal services. Stephen's recent publications include *Violence, Sexuality and Prejudice* (2008), *Crime, Criminal Justice and Masculinities* (2008), *Lawyers in Conflict* (2006) and *Hatred, Murder and Male Honour* (2002). He is currently conducting an Australian Research Council-funded study of the policing and regulation of night-time economies.

Robert van Krieken is Associate Professor of Sociology at the University of Sydney, where he recently helped establish a program in Socio-Legal Studies. His areas of research include the stolen generations, cultural genocide, liberalism, legal reasoning and family law. Robert is author of *Children and the State* (1992) and *Norbert Elias* (1998), and the lead author of *Sociology: Themes and Perspectives* (2005).

Rob White is Professor of Sociology in the School of Sociology & Social Work at the University of Tasmania. He has written extensively in the areas of youth studies and criminology, and among his publications are books such as *Crime & Criminology* (2005), *Youth & Society* (2004), *Controversies in Environmental Sociology* (2004), and *Juvenile Justice: Youth and Crime in Australia* (2007). Rob's book, *Crimes Against Nature: Environmental Criminology & Ecological Justice*, is due for release in 2008.

Alison Young is Professor of Criminology in the School of Political Science, Criminology and Sociology at the University of Melbourne. She is the author of *Judging the Image* (2005), *Imagining Crime* (1996) and *Femininity in Dissent* (1990), in addition to numerous articles on the intersections of law, crime and culture. Alison is currently completing a book, *Crime Scenes*, on spectatorship, cinema and violence, and is carrying out an Australian Research Council-funded study of street art.

INTRODUCTION

Thalia Anthony and Chris Cunneen

The idea behind this collection of chapters developed over many years, and has several purposes. First, we wanted to put together a book that represented a range of critical voices in Australian and New Zealand criminology. There are several books available that specifically address criminology in the local ANZ context, but they struck us as being somewhat pedestrian in their outlook, and did not represent what we thought were some of the more exciting, and politically engaged intellectuals. With a few exceptions, the authors in this collection will not be found in other Australian criminology collections. In part it was the absence in mainstream texts of some of the most theoretically sophisticated and politically committed criminologists that drove this collection. So this book is partly about showcasing the intellectual breadth and depth of critical and radical criminology. To our mind, the writers represented here are broadly representative of critical work in Australian and New Zealand criminology. Many of the contributors to this book are internationally renowned scholars and widely published in their particular areas of interest.

Secondly, we wanted a book that could be used to teach criminology, particularly as an introduction to the themes, ideas and concerns that engage and motivate critical intellectuals and activists in their daily work. In this sense the book is about providing a space for something which is more than simply descriptive or administrative criminology. We wanted to say something that is important to us as engaged intellectuals, rather than simply rehearse a number of standard themes that typically represent the 'introduction to criminology'.

We do not attempt a single definition of critical criminology. Critical criminology seeks to locate and understand the reasons for crime within wider structural and institutional contexts. These contexts may be conceived of in various forms including socio-economic, class-based, cultural, racialised or gendered. Critical criminology stresses the co-production of crime and crime control, neither of which can be divorced from the wider contexts within which they are situated. We do not privilege one context over another.

Yet we believe that this book remains true to a broad notion of critical criminology which seeks to 'advance a progressive agenda favouring disprivileged peoples' (Schwartz & Freidrichs 1994: 221). It draws attention to possibilities for developing progressive alternatives to the institutional mechanisms and social experiences of crime (Simons 2004: 299; Muncie 2003: 151). Accordingly, this book does not provide one perspective on what is 'critical criminology'. It is based on multifaceted standpoints for understanding crime and crime control. Theoretically it interprets criminology from a range of positions that expose the dominant crime discourse and interests it represents. In our view this is criminology – politicised explorations of the role of crime and crime control in society.

Sitting next to this book on the bookshop shelf will be a collection of different criminology texts. Those books will provide the questions and answers as to what criminology is, does and should do. This book – as a collection of radical discourses – is not simply what criminology isn't, doesn't and shouldn't do. Rather, it seeks to delve into debates about the positivist questions criminology poses and provide them with a context, critique and alternative policy position. And it attempts to do this from theoretically informed positions.

We do not take for granted the 'crime problem' or present a 'what works' approach to crime policy. We question why certain groups are defined as criminals, terrorists or outsiders; why police need more coercive power; why military inter-vention and torture become targeted at internal civilian communities; who decides crime policy and what assumptions they hold. The concern with 'policy' is within the overriding aim of critical criminology to deconstruct the privileged meanings and discourses which frame the reality of crime and control and to draw attention to the possibility for (more) inclusive and liberating interpretations (Pavlich 2000: 331). For us the central questions should not be 'what works' but 'what liberates', 'what diminishes oppression', what 'maximises human potential', and 'what respects human dignity'.

In order to address these issues, you may find that by the end of this book you know more about so-called 'orthodox criminological issues' because you have the tools for understanding them, rather than taking their apparently neutral assumptions about crime, the criminal and crime problem for granted. Part I considers the theo-ries and methodologies that underpin traditional criminologies within various critical frameworks. In Chapter One, Julie Stubbs unpacks the process of doing critical criminology theory and research. She emphasises the challenge to positivism, engagement with social context and broader sociological theory and politicisation of research. Stubbs introduces a number of criminologies that endeavour to produce critical criminologies, including feminist, postmodern and poststructural approaches.

In engaging critical research, Alison Young in Chapter Two looks at the relationship of crime to culture. Young explores the cultural fascination with crime as depicted in the media and popular culture. Rob White in Chapter Three interrogates the relationship between class and criminality. The 'classist' nature of crime policy and orthodox criminology are examined with a view to rejuvenating class analysis in critical criminologies. In regarding traditional psychological understandings of crimi-nality, Thalia Anthony and Dorothea Anthony in Chapter Four point to the Frankfurt School's psychoanalytic alternative. The School treats criminality as a product of state impulses to criminalise, rather than individual wrong. Continuing the focus on state policy, Chapter Five by Pat O'Malley addresses the role of risk. The malleable constructions of risk are posited for political ends. Chapter Six by Robert van Krie-ken rounds out the theory by raising alternative approaches to explaining shifts in criminal justice systems of 'late' or 'post' modern societies.

Part II covers a range of issues that present critical theory in action. Kerry Carrington's Chapter Seven surveys and critiques the trends in feminist crimi-nologies. The issue of masculinity and crime is unpacked by Stephen Tomsen in Chapter Eight, with a view to exposing essentialist understandings of male offending in orthodox criminology. Critical theory in action is most vividly portrayed in Mark Halsey's critique of 'the chase' in Chapter Nine. Halsey reveals the experience of the chase for the offender and police in the paradigm of masculine cultures. Just as revealing is Scott Poynting's critique of the popular connection between crime and ethnic minorities in Chapter 10. Poynting suggests that critical criminologists must not only refute this connection in their research, but also probe the ideologies that produce this mythic connection. The final chapter in this Part, Chapter 11, is by Harry Blagg, who confronts the damaging disjuncture between the criminal justice system and Aboriginal law. He points to the importance of self-determination, especially through the recognition of customary law, to address the disjuncture.

Part III takes for granted that there are no inherent definitions of crime. To enrich and broaden understandings of crime, this Part embraces alternative notions of offending, offences and offenders. To begin, Michael Grewcock conceptualises the state as a criminal actor in Chapter 12. Elizabeth Stanley illuminates processes of torture and terror as criminal acts in Chapter 13. The criminalisation of individuals who are defined by international law as refugees and asylum seekers is examined in Chapter 14 by Sharon Pickering. She classes these people as the new and undeserving criminals. Gail Mason then looks at attacks by dominant social groups on marginal ones, known as 'hate crime'. In Chapter 15 she claims that 'hate crime' needs to be defined with caution to avoid enforcing and legislating difference. The approach by Barbara Hocking and Scott Guy in Chapter 16 supports more regulation of criminality in terms of corporate offenders. They critique the under-criminalisation of violence and manslaughter in the workplace.

Part IV is dedicated to various aspects of crime control. The chapters in this Part consider the official responses, particularly in terms of policing and imprisonment. Jude McCulloch raises in Chapter 17 the modes and manifestations of police power, including through selective policing, discriminatory law enforcement and police abuse of power. She points to the legalising of these modes with counterterrorism policing, and the need for a popular response. In Chapter 18, Janet Chan considers the notion of police culture and argues that it should not be engaged too simplistically. The complexities of police culture need to be accounted for if policy responses are properly directed.

Turning to the prison system, David Brown in Chapter 19 conveys the denial of citizenship rights to prisoners. However, he provides a glimmer of light with the recent High Court decision that limited the curtailment of prisoner rights. Prisoners themselves express resistance to the denial of their rights, as Bree Carlton's Chapter 20 brings to life. Her study of Jika Jika High-Security Unit in Victoria reveals the intense prisoner responses to highly coercive institutions. Chapter 21 by Mark Brown examines the punitive regimes that have developed in late modernity within the lens of Hannah Arendt's critique of the fascist state. These themes are further developed by John Pratt in Chapter 22. Pratt discusses the role of penal populism in law and order policy developments.

Part V looks to future directions in critical criminology. Law and order is examined by Russell Hogg in Chapter 23 in terms of resistance and contestation. Hogg conceives the age of law and order as also characterised by accountability and democratic forces, as well as the emergence of a human rights framework. Chris Cunneen in Chapter 24 elucidates restorative justice in terms of its capacity to overcome limitations in the criminal justice system. However, he also raises the limited potential of restorative justice where it becomes wedded to dominant institutions. Garry Coventry and Darren Palmer consider in Chapter 25 how to constitute a rural critical criminology. They emphasise the need to depart from rural criminology's parochial roots, and shift towards a contextual understanding of remote communities, with regard to punitive policy, marginalisation of Indigenous people and globalisation.

Finally, in Chapter 26, Mark Findlay examines the international criminal justice scene and the convergence of globalised crime and governance. The consequences are 'a reduction in civil liberties, a denial of plurality, and a marginalisation of civil society'. The consequences implore a resurgence of critical criminology.

The chapters in this collection provide up-to-date debates and policy alternatives to punitive and authoritarian regimes. However, the political clout of critical criminology only gathers momentum in its reflexive process, ongoing critique and active engagement.

Thalia Anthony
Chris Cunneen

Sydney
January 2008

References

Muncie, J 2003, 'Critical Criminology: Issues, Debates and Challenges', 23 *Journal of Social Policy* 151.

Pavlich, G 2000 'Just Promises: Tracing the Possible in Criminology', 11 *Current Issues in Criminal Justice* 327.

Schwartz, M & Friedrichs, D 1994, 'Postmodern Thought and Criminological Discontent: new metaphors for understanding violence', 32(2) *Criminology* 221.

Simons, G 2004, 'Critical Criminology at the Edge: postmodern perspectives, integration and applications', 23 *Contemporary Sociology* 599.

PART I

THEORIES AND METHODOLOGIES OF CRITICAL CRIMINOLOGY

1

CRITICAL CRIMINOLOGICAL RESEARCH

Julie Stubbs

Introduction

The detailed consideration of research practices is often confined to methods courses and seen as technical matters separate from theory. Yet research and how knowledge is constructed are fundamental to what we do as criminologists and especially to the perspectives described as criminal criminology. For instance, there is 'no ontological reality of crime' since crime is a moral and political construct; this has theoretical and methodological implications that challenge the very notion that there might be a discipline of criminology (Young 2002: 254; Barton et al 2007: 207). While this is acknowledged and given weight in some criminological traditions it is ignored by others.

This chapter can provide only a limited account of the large, diverse and fluid field of critical criminological research. In doing so it risks suggesting greater consistency and uniformity than the field contains and will necessarily gloss over key debates, tensions and controversies in what is a continually unfolding area.

Theory and research

Theory and methods are commonly taught as separate domains. Social science methods courses too often present theory 'as a set of variables to be measured or applied in data interpretation, or as an hypothesis to be falsified or verified', while theory courses typically portray it as 'one of many perspectives on the world, a description of social objects or events, or as a school of thought' (Frauley 2005: 245-246). Theory is reduced to something to 'be made reference to' rather than as 'conceptual work'. For Frauley (2005: 246), learning to think theoretically, and to do theory, is integral to social science enquiry and criminology. The dualism of theory and practice is false; 'all theory is connected with the empirical (although variably in terms of the level of abstraction), otherwise it would not qualify as 'social theory' in the first place' (Bottoms 2000: 18, citing Layder 1998: 4).

The relationship between theory and research is understood in various ways within criminology. Bottoms (2000) provides a useful account. Simply put, classicism was engaged mostly with normative theory, and their empirical assertions were largely untested. Positivism adopts a hypothetico-deductive approach based on a version of the natural sciences, which assumes that theory-neutral facts can be collected, and theory in the form of an hypothesis is tested to verify or falsify the theory

(Bottoms 2000 26-28). By contrast, ethnographic research typically eschews positivism's natural sciences model and emphasises that humans act on the basis of the meanings the social world has for them; qualitative methods tend to focus on the specific context of behaviours with less concern for generalisation. Inductive reasoning is used to build theory from an understanding of the social situation (Bottoms 2000: 30). Critical criminological approaches typically conceptualise theory and research as inherently linked; theorising and processes of knowledge formation are often subjects of critical inquiry (Jupp 1989: 23).

Characteristics of critical criminology and their implications for research

The label critical criminology(ies) has been applied to various established and emergent theoretical perspectives that differ in significant ways, with diverse origins and political allegiances (Carrington 2002). The perspectives commonly include Marxism, abolitionism, feminisms, peacemaking, poststructuralist and postmodernist approaches. Sometimes included are Left Realism, Constitutive Criminology, Cultural Criminology and Restorative Justice. However, some writers challenge the attempt to apply any unifying category or label. Instead they emphasise the differentiation of such approaches and mark the fragmentation, fracturing or plurality of criminology (Ericson & Carriere 1994). But is there some value in reflecting on shared elements; if so what are they and what are their implications for research?

Some features of critical criminology/ies predate the common usage of that term and are shared with or borrowed from allied disciplines. Common elements include an orientation *against* – the mainstream, official definitions and statistics, positivism, and so on – and an aspiration *towards* – social justice, human rights, and so on. Indeed according to Cohen (1988: 18), critical criminology 'emerged because the spurious scientific claims of traditional criminology had served to remove crime from politics'. Currie (2002: viii) sees critical criminology as attempting to realise a criminological imagination 'able and willing to break free of old constraints and look at the problems of crime and punishment with fresh eyes'. He invokes C Wright Mills' (1959/1973) classic work, *The Sociological Imagination*, which sought to link the individual with social structure and history (Barton et al 2007). Such an integration of individual, structural and historical levels requires careful methodological attention.

Characteristics commonly seen as typical of critical criminology/ies, or related categories, include some or all of the following:

- transgressing mainstream criminology;
- challenging official definitions and statistics of crime and crime control;
- rejection of positivist methodologies;
- rejection of correctionalism;
- disavowal of the criminologist 'as neutral scientific expert';
- a critical posture towards agents, systems and institutions of social control;
- preference for sociological theories over individualistic theories;
- emphasising the effects of social power and inequality as underlying offending, victimisation and criminalisation;

- drawing on a wider body of social theory;
- engaging with normative questions;
- recognising that research and knowledge are political;
- a desire for social and political change, social justice or human rights;
- political engagement, allegiances with social movements and 'turning cases into issues';
- valuing the 'view from below'; and,
- reflexivity concerning research and criminology (summarised from Carrington & Hogg 2002: 2-3; Carlen 2002; Bottoms 2000: 33; Hudson 2000: 189; Loader 1998; Scraton 2002).

Critical approaches have been valued for 'opening up new frameworks for inquiry', generating 'often fruitful dialogue with a host of cognate disciplines', emphasising 'that crime and crime control are matters of political rather than just technical disputation' and recognising that 'criminological enquiry cannot be pursued adequately without posing some fundamental questions about order, power, authority, legitimacy and social justice' (Loader 1998: 201).[1] However, critical criminology/ies have also attracted a range of criticisms. Some variants have demonstrated 'the dangers of theoreticism' (Loader 1998; Brown 2002; Carlen 2002), a 'predilection for critique over reconstruction' (Loader 1998: 201; Carlen 1998, 2002), insufficient normative engagement (Loader 1998), putting political goals above 'the search for truth' (Bottoms 2000: 33-35) or devising theory in the service of politics (Carlen 2002: 245). Brown (2002: 92) reminds us that early versions were Eurocentric, and Carrington (2002: 129) detects 'a deep lingering tension between feminism and radicalism over the legitimacy of the experience of victimisation'.

Challenge to the mainstream

Critical criminology is defined in part by what it opposes. This includes the 'historically predominant' conception of criminology in instrumental terms which presumes that 'criminology provides a set of techniques capable of generating reliable, scientific knowledge concerning crime and its causes, knowledge that can contribute to effective policy making' (Loader 1998: 192-193) and that takes official measures of crime at face value. Criminologists challenging the mainstream have long questioned definitions of crime, urging the decriminalisation of some behaviours, and moving beyond narrow constructions of crime to include a wider range of objects of inquiry such as human rights, abuses of state power, racialised and gendered violence, or a focus on the transnational and the global. Others wish to reorient research and theory away from crime to concepts such as ordering, harm, or to transcend the discipline altogether (Barton et al 2007).

One manifestation of mainstream criminology is what Loader labels 'jobbing criminology', which in the United Kingdom is most aligned with institutional settings such as the Home Office and Scottish Office, which has a 'dependent relationship to official crime control agendas' (Loader 1998: 193-194; see also Walters 2007). The Home Office is described as wedded to 'a set of empiricist epistemolo-

---

1   Loader's commentary refers to 'anticriminology' following Stan Cohen (1988), but the theoretical approaches he lists are consistent with critical criminology.

gical assumptions as to what constitutes 'good' research', such as an outmoded reliance on quasi-experimental design, and fails to recognise 'the methodological pluralism that now characterises the wider sociological and criminological field' (Loader 1998: 193). He acknowledges that 'jobbing criminology' can nonetheless challenge 'political wisdom' and is not reducible to being simply the servant of its master, but the approach is deficient in that it typically resorts to 'neutral, technical language' which does not articulate the ethics and politics at hand (1998: 193) and pursues 'a limited range of explanatory avenues, structuring enquiries largely around the question "what works?"'(1998: 197). The challenge to criminology associated with government institutions is particularly sharp in the United Kingdom (see further below, Walters 2007). However, in Australia the debates are less fraught and the distinctions between the critical and the mainstream are less clear. That is not to suggest that there are no differences in approach, or no conflicts between protagonists pursuing different approaches. However, as Brown (2002: 86) has observed 'in the Australian context there is not a monolithic 'mainstream' criminology' and, that in certain contexts it might be important to utilise mainstream approaches and 'enter alliance with its practitioners' in public debate and struggles.

Engagement with broader social theory

Theorists from outside criminology have had considerable impact on research within the field both historically and in recent times. For feminist criminologists engaging with broader theory has been productive and necessary, since criminology was late to acknowledge feminism and indifferent or even hostile to its concerns. Critical criminologists commonly draw on social theory to analyse behaviours or practices with reference to social structure and in historical context. The chapters in this collection provide numerous examples of critical criminologists' engagement with broad social theory.

Hudson (2000: 178) identifies three approaches as having been particularly influential in critical criminology; they shared focus on 'research which contributed to the emancipation of those who are repressed by existing social and power relations'. First is the critical theory of the Frankfurt School, which 'concentrated on culture and ideology in authoritarian societies, drawing on Marxist and psychoanalytic concepts'. The second is '"discourse" research using the ideas and methods associated with Michel Foucault' (Hudson 2000: 178), 'investigat[ing] the exercise of power in liberal societies, foregrounding the development and influence of the human/social sciences'. The third is standpoint research 'replac[ing] the centrality of concepts such as 'class' and 'liberalism' with patriarchy and gender divisions' (2000: 178). Others identify Gramsci as having been very influential in the emergence of critical criminology, especially in the United Kingdom; his work promoted the creation of 'an alternative "counter-hegemonic" discourse infused with socialist values and principles, that reconceptualized the organization of society' (Barton et al 2007: 4).

Challenge to positivism (and phenomenology)

Critical criminology and critical research generally have been shaped in part in reaction to positivism and to a lesser extent phenomenology. C Wright Mills argued that 'abstracted empiricism' damaged sociology by the 'methodological inhibition' associated with its appeal to a limited version of the philosophy of the natural sciences. For Mills, 'the kinds of problem that will be taken up and the way in which they are formulated are quite severely limited by the Scientific Method. Methodology in short seems to determine the problems' (1959/1973: 67). The enduring influence of positivism in criminology and other disciplines has been lamented by many but has been bolstered by the rise of new forms of positivism in the guise of crime science (Walters 2007: 19-22).

Walklate (2000) provides a contemporary example of the 'stranglehold' of positivist oriented work on criminology and victimology. She describes how 'the commitment to the use and deployment of the criminal victimization survey' has 'significantly defined the parameters of the fear of crime debate' such that fear and risk have been so commonly linked (2000: 198), even to the point of calibrating whether fear is commensurate with risk and thus 'rational'. Her own use of the same technique, informed by critical victimology and a commitment to examining how people understood risk and fear, challenged the dominant perspective. She used both qualitative and quantitative methods, ensured that the crime victimisation survey was attuned to the local context, and moved across levels comparing lay and professional perceptions with formal policy processes. She developed a more nuanced understanding of the victim and how that label was 'embraced' or 'attributed', or not, and she discovered that 'trust' had more to offer in understanding community dynamics than risk or fear (Walklate 2000: 198).[2]

Phenomenology perhaps had greatest influence in North America. It is associated with the construction of social reality and gives emphasis to consciousness and perception; 'the social world is constituted by rules of description and classification' (Downes & Rock 1988: 202). It has a focus on the everyday and the micro-social. Phenomenological research was central to challenging realist conceptions of crime statistics. Once crime rates were seen as produced, like other phenomena, 'by interpretative work and social organization … [t]he solid facts of crime seemed to melt into a rather fluid and unreliable subjectivity' (1988: 207). Phenomenology continues to be influential in some forms of critical criminology such as constitutive criminology but its micro-social focus does not sit easily with others (Jupp 1989: 119-120).

Reflexivity

Reflexivity is a key feature of critical research with several meanings. It acknowledges that theory is developed within a social and political context, and requires researchers to reflect on their research practice and make adjustments accordingly (Harvey 1990: 10-11). Reflexivity involves considering the validity of research findings and the question 'what counts as knowledge?' (Jupp et al 2000: 169). It can also refer to a method of research that entails 'reflecting upon, analyzing and challenging dominant ideological positions in society' (Jupp et al 2000: 172; Hudson

---

2   Hollway and Jefferson (2001) introduced a more complex subjectivity to this debate in a methodologically innovative way drawing on a critical realist epistemology (see Poynting this volume). As socio-legal theorist Alan Norrie (2005: 164) describes: 'critical realism agrees that experience of the real world is possible and necessary, but against it, insists that this is not a sufficient basis for scientific understanding. Knowledge requires active theory building and testing in order to provide depth explanations of the stratified reality that underlies the surface forms given to experience'. Neither idealist approaches, nor empiricism are adequate.

2000). Reflexivity encourages questions about criminology and its relationship to power and crime control (Hudson 2000: 176). Lisa Maher's book, *Sexed Work* (1997), provides an excellent example of reflexive ethnographic work that is theoretically and methodologically sophisticated, engaging multiple methods and levels of analysis.

The politics (and political effects) of research

Critical criminology recognises the politics and political effects of research. While positivism has shown 'deep suspicion' of 'political or moral engagement', this is untenable when crime is avowedly a political and moral construct and 'doing research and theory in criminology is itself inevitably linked to the political landscape' (Bottoms 2000: 33). Foucault's (1977) account of power/knowledge is a profound challenge to the assumption within mainstream research that knowledge is neutral and outside power relations. As Hogg (1998: 152) demonstrates:

> [T]echniques of modern criminological thought ... especially statistics, do not simply measure problems as if they constituted some pre-existing reality ... they are the means of bringing them within the domain of knowledge and government.

This highlights criminology's 'dangerous relationship to power'; 'the categories and classifications, the labels and diagnoses and the images of the criminal produced by criminologists' legitimate crime control and 'have implications for the life-chances, for the opportunities freely to move around our cities, and for the rights and liberties, of those to whom they are applied' (Hudson 2000: 177). But what are the implications for critical research? For Hudson (2000: 177) the answer is not to withdraw from research due to its moral and political risks, but to engage in 'critical research which exposes the political contexts in which criminological knowledge production is embedded'. And of course Foucault's body of work has generated a multitude of new objects and sites for empirical research.

Critical criminology is not free of institutional constraints. For instance, academic research has been commodified as universities seek to supplement inadequate budgets by promoting funded research and as they submit to government research measurement exercises like the Research Quality Framework (Australia) or Research Assessment Exercise (United Kingdom). Funding bodies set research agendas. In most jurisdictions there are few avenues for independent research funding not tied to government schemes or agencies, or corporate interests. The Australian Research Council (ARC) has National Research Priorities,[3] which are not an easy fit with critical criminology, although critical researchers have secured ARC funding for some projects. Several United Kingdom commentators have analysed the consequences of funding that prioritises research aligned with the harsh agenda of New Labour. For instance, Walters (2007: 28-32) identifies government research as ignoring crimes of the powerful while endorsing the regulation of the poor, and corporate research as motivated by profit. He calls for a boycott on government-funded and corporate contract research; criminologists should instead 'embrace diverse knowledges of resistance' (2007: 30; but see Loader 1998).

Challenging dominant constructions of knowledge is central to critical criminology and has been a strong focus for feminists (Naffine 1997). This builds on

---

3 See <www.arc.gov.au/pdf/DP08_FundingRules.pdf>.

11

theoretical traditions that have sought to challenge the 'hierarchy of credibility' (Becker 1967), 'appreciate the deviant' (Matza 1969); to give voice to the excluded, and to value the 'view from below'. Standpoint epistemology is associated with a particular feminist approach (see below) but has a wider meaning that Hudson traces to the Frankfurt School. Objective, value-free knowledge is unattainable, and thus, 'since standpoint is inevitable, it had better be overt' (Hudson 2000: 184). Standpoint is commonly used in two contradictory ways: to found claims to a superior epistemology or politics, or to denigrate another's work as arising from an interested standpoint (Nelken 1994: 23). Nelken (1994: 24) sees standpoint epistemology as useful for comparative criminology in recognising 'the limitations of culturally shaped standpoints' as in ethnocentrism, and in analysing how culture shapes 'conceptions of crime and responses to crime' and 'the discipline of criminology itself'.

Normative engagement

Normative research is consistent with critical criminology's aspirations for social change but is often overlooked in discussions of criminological research, perhaps because of the tendency to separate research and theory. Normative research differs from explanatory research and seeks 'a rational and principled explanation of the moral/political justifications for a given course of action' (Bottoms 2000: 48). Loader (1998: 207) argues for greater normative engagement to ensure that 'doing criminology … always entails reflection upon questions of order, justice, authority and legitimacy' and articulates 'ethically informed models of alternative institutional arrangements'. In the context of security, Zedner (2007: 271) promotes empirically grounded normative theorising in order to 'elaborate and defend a conception of justice apposite to the potential and problems of security society'. She sees restorative justice as one of few contexts in which criminology has 'develop[ed] a constructive theory of change' (2007: 270).

Critical social research

Critical social research has a long history outside criminology. It has an epistemological foundation, or theory of knowledge, that sees knowledge as 'structured by existing sets of social relations' that are oppressive (Harvey 1990: 2). Critical social research typically seeks to establish what underlies the surface appearance of a phenomenon, to reveal the oppressive nature of social relations and to inform social change. This often means working between different levels of analysis, to connect the specific with 'the structures, processes and ideologies that underpin them' (Jupp et al 2000: 19; Hudson 2000). It may involve theoretical triangulation, that is, working with multiple theories that address different levels and connecting criminological analysis with general social theory (Hudson 2000). Critical researchers initially focused primarily on class; attention to race or gender based oppression arose only from about the 1970s. Since then critical scholarship has engaged with other forms of social relations (heterosexism, disability discrimination, religious oppression, and so on), with questions related to imperialism and colonisation (Harvey 1990: 2-3), and more complex conceptions of these categories begun to consider intersections between social categories. Postmodernist and poststructuralist work has also had an important influence on critical social research.

Within critical research 'knowledge and critique are intertwined'; critique is not something appended to 'an accumulation of 'fact' or 'theory' gathered via some mechanical process, rather it denies the (literally) objective status of knowledge … Knowledge is a dynamic process not a static entity' (Harvey 1990: 3). But does critical social research imply any particular research method? It is important to distinguish between epistemology, methodology and method. Epistemology is a theory of knowledge that entails 'the presuppositions about the nature of knowledge and of science that inform practical inquiry' (1990: 1). Methodology is 'the interface between methodic practice, substantive theory and epistemological underpinnings', and 'makes explicit the presuppositions that inform the knowledge that is generated by the enquiry'. Method is 'the way empirical data are collected' (1990: 1-2).

It is not the method that designates an approach as critical; critical researchers use a diverse range of methods, and methods are not 'inherently positivist, phenomenological or critical' (Harvey 1990: 1). Critical research is shaped 'at the level of methodology' (1990: 201). Some areas of critical criminology do have an orientation towards a particular method or methods, with a strong tendency towards qualitative approaches such as participant observation or in-depth interviews. However, debates about the relative merits of qualitative and quantitative research commonly express epistemological or methodological differences. At the level of methods, multimethod approaches (method triangulation) commonly employ both qualitative and quantitative methods that have different strengths. For critical criminology, as for other traditions, the appropriate method depends on the research objectives.

Similar methods are used in markedly different ways. For instance, crime victimisation surveys have been used differently by researchers aligned with Positivist, Left Realist and Critical Victimology perspectives and various Feminist approaches.[4] Researchers adopting different epistemological and methodological frameworks understand official crime statistics differently. From an interactionist perspective,[5] official statistics reflect the practices of the agencies that produce them (Jupp 1989: 92-97). Radical perspectives see crime statistics as 'reflect[ing] structurally induced' patterns of crime and criminalisation, demonstrating the 'outcome of class relations' (1989: 99). While unmasking positivist claims to objective and value-free knowledge might be seen to require a rejection of official statistics per se, critical researchers can and do engage with official statistics including by exposing the conditions and social context which shaped them.

Feminist criminological research

Early critical criminology showed little interest in feminist concerns (Carrington 2002: 123; Naffine 1997). Thus, feminist scholars such as Maureen Cain saw the need 'to be transgressive of the discipline of criminology and its ideological and methodological assumptions' (Carrington 2002: 118) and some feminists saw feminism and criminology as irreconcilable (Smart 1990). Nonetheless feminist criminology has been a vital part of critical criminology (see Carrington this volume).

---

4   However, Left Realism has been challenged for 'a latent slippage into positivism' for its use of this method (Walklate 2000: 187-8; Smart 1990).

5   Interactionist perspectives emphasise that policies and practices which generate crime statistics 'are expressed in interactions with potential offenders and involve the application of social meanings, definitions and labels by law enforcement personnel' (Jupp 1989: 94).

Like critical research generally, feminist research is not defined at the level of methods but by epistemological and methodological commitments (Harding 1987). Feminist criminology initially focused on challenging theories that ignored gender, or treated it in limited or stereotyped ways, and undertaking empirical research on women's experiences of crime and the criminal justice system (Daly & Maher 1998: 2). This work made an important contribution by documenting women's experiences and opening up new areas of inquiry. However, it often used a feminist empiricist approach that had serious epistemological shortcomings; while it sought to improve scientific knowledge by making women subjects of criminology, it did not question the underlying premises of science (Naffine 1997: 30-37). By contrast, other feminists used standpoint epistemology 'to place women as knowers at the centre of inquiry' (1997: 46), to value subjugated knowledge and to give emphasis to women's experience. Some versions of standpoint feminism saw women's knowledge as more complete in that the 'view from below' added to and challenged dominant perspectives (1997: 45-60). However, standpoint feminism has attracted criticism especially for essentialism, that is, for presenting a singular account that ignored differences between women, and commonly was based on a white, middle class, heterosexual standard (Naffine 1997: 53; Carrington 2002: 119).

Second phase feminist criminological work was influenced by earlier criticisms and by developments within criminology and beyond such as critical race theory, postmodernism and poststructuralism. Daly and Maher (1998: 3) summarise that work as concerned with: 'problematizing the term women as a unified category', 'acknowledging that women's experiences are, in part, constructed by legal and criminological discourses', rethinking 'the relationship between sex and gender' and 'reflecting on the strengths and limits of constructing feminist 'truths' and knowledge'. However, they identify a tension in recent developments between studies of 'real women' and those concerned with 'women of discourse'. The first metaphor describes research that 'explores women as agents in constructing their life worlds including their lawbreaking and victimization', while the second sees women as 'constructed in and by particular discourses'. Daly and Maher (1997: 4) argue that both strands of feminist work are necessary, but they demonstrate that they are not easily reconcilable because they have 'their own theoretical referents and specialised vocabularies'. A recent example of feminist research that successfully integrates poststructural theory and empirical research is Gail Mason's (2002) study of homophobic violence.

Postmodernism and poststructuralism

It is difficult to map the many ways in which some critical researchers have engaged with postmodernism or poststructuralism. The terms have been used in multiple ways, sometimes interchangeably. Postmodernism is commonly associated inter alia with the rejection of grand narratives, the unitary subject and science as the means to truth (Carrington 2002; Daly & Maher 1998). Poststructuralism typically denotes an approach that challenges 'hierarchical binary oppositions in language' and analyses the role of discourse in 'shaping subjectivity, social institutions and politics' (Daly & Maher 1998: 3). These positions have unsettled taken-for-granted assumptions and provoked a rethinking of theory and practice among some critical theorists.

For instance, Carlen (1998: 71) sees value in a form of poststructuralism that 'both recognises and denies structuralism'. She accepts 'the effectivity of the structures of social process and consciousness' but also adopts a poststructuralist stance to deny that they have any unitary meaning, or 'that they always and already have perennial applicability to any specific society, social formation or individuated subjectivity'.

Critical criminological projects that draw on postmodernism or poststructuralism have adopted or adapted various methodologies and methods. For instance, deconstruction[6] is commonly used by researchers to examine claims to truth within criminological, legal and related psychological discourses. Cultural criminology, with roots in symbolic interactionism and subcultural theory (see Young this volume), also draws on postmodernist approaches and methodologies associated with cultural studies, media studies and interpreting 'the visual' (Ferrell 2003). Some projects focused on subjectivity have turned to psychoanalysis. For instance, Hollway and Jefferson (2001) have developed a psychosocial conception of the subject that connects the psychoanalytic with the discursive; they have adapted a narrative interview method as the best fit with their methodological commitments.

Some concluding thoughts

Critical criminology/ies are diverse and subject to ongoing development likely to be influenced by borrowings from and dialogue with allied disciplines, and innovations generated by inter-disciplinary work. Like criminology generally, critical criminological research confronts conceptual and methodological challenges arising from factors such as: transnational and global developments in the social order; the shift to a 'pre-crime society' as conceived within crime control and scholarship in the domain of security (Zedner 2007); reconsidering subjectivity; and constructions of and responses to difference.

I share Freidrichs' (1996: 123) preference for a progressive pluralist critical criminology that: aspires to 'a more egalitarian, humane and authentically democratic society'; 'acknowledges the endless complexity, contradictions, and conundrums characterizing the totality of social existence', has a 'skepticism toward exclusive 'truth' claims' and recognises 'that many different perspectives (and methods) can advance our understanding of facets or dimensions of social reality'. The plurality, complexity and lack of a shared origin among critical criminology/ies, and the ongoing predominance of positivism within criminology offer significant pedagogical challenges. Students need to engage in a kind of multiple shift. The concern to link specific analysis with historical context and social structure necessitates moving between levels in analysis, which in turn suggests the need for more complex and considered methodological approaches than typical of single level analysis. Doing theory and research as critical scholars fully literate in the discipline requires being conversant with and having the capacity to critically engage those positions that are being challenged. However, it also offers an enormous range of possibilities.

---

6   Deconstruction involves 'a careful reading and de-coding of text (written or spoken) … to unveil the implicit assumptions and hidden values … embedded within a particular narrative' (Arrigo 2003: 48). Deconstructive approaches are not confined to postmodern or poststructuralist theoretical perspectives.

References

Arrigo, B 2003, 'Postmodern Justice and Critical Criminology: positional, relational and provisional science', in Schwartz, M & Hatty, S (eds), *Controversies in Critical Criminology*, Anderson Publishing, Cincinnati.

Barton, A, Corteen, K, Scott, D & Whyte, D 2007, 'Introduction: developing a criminological imagination', in Barton, A, Corteen, K, Scott, D & Whyte, D (eds), *Expanding the Criminological Imagination: critical readings in criminology*, Willan Publishing, Cullompton.

Becker, H 1967, 'Whose side are we on?', 14(3) *Social Problems* 239.

Bottoms, A 2000, 'The Relationship Between Theory and Research in Criminology', in King, R & Wincup, E (eds), *Doing Research on Crime and Justice*, Oxford University Press, Oxford.

Brown, D 2002, '"Losing my Religion": reflections on critical criminology in Australia', in Carrington, K & Hogg, R (eds), *Critical Criminology: issues, debates, challenges*, Willan Publishing, Cullompton.

Carlen, P 1998, 'Criminology Ltd: the search for a new paradigm', in Walton, P & Young, J (eds), *The New Criminology Revisited*, Macmillan Press, Houndmills.

Carlen, P 2002, 'Critical Criminology: in praise of an oxymoron and its enemies', in Carrington, K & Hogg, R (eds), *Critical Criminology: issues, debates, challenges*, Willan Publishing, Cullompton.

Carrington, K 2002, 'Critical Criminologies: an introduction', in Carrington, K & Hogg, R (eds), *Critical Criminology: issues, debates, challenges*, Willan Publishing, Cullompton.

Carrington, K & Hogg, R 2002, 'Feminism and Critical Criminology: confronting genealogies in Australia', in Carrington, K & Hogg, R (eds), *Critical Criminology: issues, debates, challenges*, Willan Publishing, Cullompton.

Cohen, S 1988, *Against Criminology*, Transaction Publishers, New Brunswick.

Currie, E 2002, 'Preface', in Carrington, K & Hogg, R (eds), *Critical Criminology: issues, debates, challenges*, Willan Publishing, Cullompton.

Daly, K & Maher, L 1998, 'Crossroads and Intersection: building from feminist critique', in Daly, K & Maher, L (eds), *Criminology at the Crossroads: feminist readings in crime and justice*, Oxford University Press, New York.

Downes, D & Rock, P 1988, *Understanding Deviance: a guide to the sociology of crime and rule breaking*, Second edition, Clarendon Press, Oxford.

Ericson, R & Carriere, K 1994, 'The Fragmentation of Criminology' in Nelken, D (ed), *The Futures of Criminology*, Sage, London.

Ferrell, J 2003, 'Cultural Criminology', in Schwartz, M & Hatty, S (eds), *Controversies in Critical Criminology*, Anderson Publishing, Cincinnati.

Foucault, M 1977, *Discipline and Punish: the birth of the prison*, Peregrine, London.

Frauley, J 2005, 'Recasting Theory and Theorising in Criminal Justice Studies: practising theory considered', 13 *Critical Criminology* 245.

Friedrichs, DO 1996, 'Critical Criminology and Progressive Pluralism: strength in diversity for these times', 7(1) *Critical Criminology* 121.

Harding, S 1987, 'Introduction', in Harding, S (ed), *Feminism and Methodology: social science issues*, Open University Press, Milton Keynes.

Harvey, L 1990, *Critical Social Research*, Unwin Hyman, London.

Hogg, R 1998, 'Crime, Criminology, Government' in Walton, P & Young, J (eds), *The New Criminology Revisited*, Macmillan Press, Houndmills.

Hollway, W & Jefferson, T 2001, *Doing Qualitative Research Differently: free association, narrative and the interview method*, Sage, London.

Hudson, B 2000, 'Critical Reflection as Research Methodology', in Jupp, V, Davies, P & Francis, P (eds), *Doing Criminological Research*, Sage, London.

Jupp, V 1989, *Methods of Criminological Research,* Unwin Hyman, London.

Jupp, V, Davies, P & Francis, P (eds) 2000, *Doing Criminological Research,* Sage, London.

Loader, I 1998, 'Criminology and the Public Sphere: arguments for utopian realism', in Walton, P & Young, J (eds), *The New Criminology Revisited,* Macmillan Press, Houndmills.

Maher, L 1997, *Sexed Work: gender, race and resistance in a Brooklyn drug market,* Clarendon Press, Oxford & New York.

Mason, G 2002, *The Spectacle of Violence: homophobia, gender, and knowledge,* Routledge, New York.

Matza, D 1969, *Becoming Deviant,* Prentice-Hall, New Jersey.

Mills, C Wright 1959/1973, *The Sociological Imagination,* Penguin, Harmondsworth.

Naffine, N 1997, *Feminism and Criminology,* Allen & Unwin, Sydney.

Nelken, D 1994, 'Reflexive Criminology?', in Nelken, D (ed), *The Futures of Criminology,* Sage, London.

Norrie, A 2005, *Law and the Beautiful Soul,* Glasshouse, London.

Scraton, P 2002, 'Defining "power" and challenging "knowledge": critical analysis as resistance in the UK' in Carrington, K & Hogg, R (eds), *Critical Criminology: issues, debates, challenges,* Willan Publishing, Cullompton.

Smart, C 1990, 'Feminist Approaches to Criminology or Postmodern Woman meets Atavistic Man', in Gelsthorpe, L & Morris, A (eds), *Feminist Perspectives in Criminology,* Open University Press, Milton Keynes.

Walklate, S 2000, 'Researching victims', in King, R & Wincup, E (eds), *Doing research on crime and justice,* Oxford University Press, Oxford.

Walters, R 2007, 'Critical Criminology and the Intensification of the Authoritarian State', in Barton, A, Corteen, K, Scott, D & Whyte, D (eds), *Expanding the Criminological Imagination: critical readings in criminology*, Willan Publishing, Cullompton.

Young, J 2002, 'Critical Criminology in the 21st Century: critique, irony and the always unfinished', in Carrington, K & Hogg, R (eds), *Critical Criminology: issues, debates, challenges,* Willan Publishing, Cullompton.

Zedner, L 2007, 'Pre-Crime and Post-Criminology?', 11(2) *Theoretical Criminology* 261.

2

CULTURE, CRITICAL CRIMINOLOGY AND THE IMAGINATION OF CRIME

Alison Young

Introduction: crime in popular culture

Like most disciplines, criminology possesses a preferred domain of objects of analysis. This domain of objects tends to be limited or static, privileging the phenomenon of interpersonal crime, fear of crime, and trends in crime prevention and punishment. Many issues and approaches have been marginalised through the maintenance of this preferred domain. Consequently, the relationship of crime to culture has received little attention until relatively recently.

What is strange about this omission is, first, that the question of cultural representation and its interpretation has exercised a range of other disciplines (notably social theory, feminist studies and cultural studies) over the past three decades while criminology has more or less ignored it; and, secondly, that media representations of crime constitute a mainstay of cultural consumption.

To borrow from Sparks' (1990: 123) analysis of television crime drama, cultural images of crime are enduringly popular because they offer 'a set of stories which address certain social anxieties in its audience', and are able 'to render the messy and troubling complexities of law enforcement pleasurable by assigning them to the ancient simplicities of crime and punishment'. The prevalence of popular cultural images of crime is apparent when we consider the diversity of cultural forms in which such representations are found: literature, advertising, art, film, newspapers, television news, and television crime drama.

The reliance of the news media on crime stories has been well documented (see Cohen & Young 1981; Jewkes 2004; Mason 2006; Peelo 2006; Soothill & Walby 1991) and fictional stories about crime and criminal justice are a staple of both cinema and television drama. On Australian television there can be found reality TV shows about police, documentaries and current affairs programs such as *Four Corners*, *Sixty Minutes*, and *Insight* about crime and criminals, and, most significantly, a large range of crime drama series. On free-to-air television channels, at least one crime drama can be viewed every night of the week. Australian television currently features series predominantly from the United Kingdom (such as *The Bill*, *Life on Mars*, and *Judge John Deed*) and the United States (such as *Law & Order*,

C.S.I., *Without a Trace*, and *Boston Legal*). When Australian pay television is included, crime dramas such as these and others (for example, *Spooks*, *The Sopranos*, *The Wire*, and *The Practice*) can be viewed at any hour of the day or night. No other genre of drama features so prominently.[1]

In cinematic terms, crime stories are comparably widespread, arising in genres such as the thriller, the police procedural, the crime film, the action movie, and the conspiracy movie, as well as a host of less conventional ones (think of *Thelma & Louise*, which combines the genres of road movie, chick flick and crime story, or *Fun with Dick and Jane*, which marries a crime story to screwball farce). Whether presented as a direct narrative involving crime, police and criminal justice or as a less explicit and more allegorical investigation of justice, images of crime and justice can be found on the cinema screen throughout the year.

Popularity obviously connects to prevalence: that viewers enjoy crime dramas would seem to be borne out not just by audience ratings (which often show crime dramas to be in the top 10) but also by the proliferation of certain shows into spin-offs or multiple versions (*Law & Order* and *C.S.I.* being the prime examples of this phenomenon), since networks will not continue to invest in a series which cannot sustain an audience.

The prevalence and popularity of popular cultural images of criminal justice together point to a critical issue for criminology: since it is a criminological given that crime is 'bad' (giving rise to fear, or anger, to social decline, to economic, physical or psychological suffering), why is it that so much of our entertainment involves crime stories? Despite the taken-for-granted condemnation of crime as a social phenomenon, individuals in large numbers choose to spend their leisure time consuming media stories about crime – stories which often present victimisation in graphic and confronting detail. Critical criminological research therefore needs to investigate responses to crime not just as an event but also *as an image*, by thinking through the implications of the cultural fascination with crime.

Culture, crime and criminology: sub-culture and style

The field of inquiry that is often called 'cultural criminology' is still an emerging one, with many lacunae and elisions. Two main perspectives can be identified within cultural criminology. The first approach, which can be called 'sub-cultural criminology', was more or less inaugurated by the publication of Ferrell and Sanders' collection of essays, *Cultural Criminology* (1995). Ferrell and Sanders' (1995: 5) innovation was to interpret sub-culture as a sub-*culture*, with a concomitant focus upon questions of style: 'the shared aesthetic of the sub-culture's members', arguing that 'subtleties of collective style define the meaning of crime and deviance for sub-cultural participants, agents of legal control, consumers of mediated crime images, and others'.

Ferrell and Sanders (1995) are explicit about cultural criminology's connection to sub-cultural studies of crime, evoking the Chicago School's emphasis on the 'motives, drives, rationalisations and attitudes' of members of a criminal sub-culture (Sutherland & Cressey 1978: 80). The antecedents of contemporary sub-cultural

---

1   Note also that crime and justice issues also feature as sub-plots within television series whose main narrative has other concerns (for example, *Lost*, *Desperate Housewives*, *The West Wing*, *McLeod's Daughters*, *All Saints*, and so on).

criminology therefore range through Sutherland and Cressey, Stuart Hall, Howard Becker, Stan Cohen, Dick Hebdige and Paul Willis.

Cultural criminology built on Sutherland and Cressey's (1978: 80) emphasis on ways that members of a criminal sub-culture might develop shared 'motives, drives, rationalizations, and attitudes' for sub-cultural behaviour (1978: 80). It endorsed the views of Hall and the Birmingham School that the mass media played a highly significant role in both the labelling and communication of deviant sub-cultural identity (Hall et al 1978) and also sought to incorporate Becker's (1963) argument about the intertwined relations of that which is labelled deviant or criminal and those social, political and legal institutions with the power to label. Obvious resonance is found between Stan Cohen's (1972) early work on moral panics and cultural criminology's interest in the consequences of labelling for sub-cultural members. Cultural criminology's respect for its subjects derives also from the work of Hebdige (1979) and Willis (1977) who argued that marginalised or criminalised groups engage in sub-cultural activities with deliberation and symbolic purpose.

Although sub-cultural criminology's infancy was located in symbolic interactionism's radical rejection of positivist and administrative tendencies in criminology, subsequent elaborations of the paradigm constitute more of a nostalgia for radicalism in place of any wholesale theorisation of culture as signifying process and the imagination of crime. Thus, contemporary sub-cultural criminological writings tend to fall into one of two genres: first, the ethnographic documentation of a sub-cultural group, event or activity (for example, Miller 1995; Tunnell 2004); and, secondly, the manifesto, in which terrain is staked out and terms of engagement specified. In an example of the latter, Hayward and Young (2004: 259) state:

> [Cultural criminology] is the placing of crime and its control in the context of culture; that is, viewing both crime and the agencies of control as cultural products – as creative constructs. As such, they must be read in terms of the meanings they carry. Furthermore, cultural criminology seeks to highlight the interaction between these two elements … Its focus is always upon the continuous generation of meaning around interaction; rules created, rules broken, a constant interplay of moral entrepreneurship, moral innovation and transgression.

Several key conceptual difficulties are buried within this statement. 'Crime' and 'its control' remain the primary terms, with culture reduced to a 'context' (on a par with, say, 'history', or 'society'). Crime and its control are therefore constructed as transcendental or metaphysical concepts, transferable from location to location. 'Cultural criminology' is construed as an act under the control of the criminologist, who 'places' crime and its control in the cultural context for analysis. And there is a whiff of 'old wine in new bottles', in the emphasis on interaction: indeed, sub-cultural criminology retains both interactionism's emphasis on the motivations and beliefs of deviant actors, and its recognition that deviant labels tend to confirm deviant identities. To that extent, sub-cultural criminology is in many ways simply a revised form of interactionism, with 'cultural' substituting for 'symbolic'.

In another manifesto for sub-cultural criminology, Presdee's *Cultural Criminology and the Carnival of Crime* (2000), further problems of conceptual structure become apparent. First, Presdee (2000: 4) focuses upon the emotional dimension of criminal behaviour, or what he calls 'the world of emotions'. Each of the activities of the everyday (going to school, going to work, going out for a drink or going dancing) is shot through with emotional attachments. Thus, the story of the everyday becomes a story of how the self loves or hates its relationships with others. More specifically, the criminal becomes a subjective consciousness which moves through the urban spaces of the everyday, *emoting*. Thus Presdee (2000: 4-5) writes:

> The way that we enjoy violence, crime and humiliation and hurt is part of the equation and needs to be examined and thought through … Indeed, crime is as much about emotions – hatred, anger, frustration, excitement and love – as it is about poverty, possessing and wealth … Rage, anger and hatred are commonplace characteristics in the performance of crime.

Presdee (2000: 3), like many sub-cultural criminologists, draws on the work of Jack Katz (1988), taking seriously Katz's contention that criminal acts produce a 'delight in being deviant' and a pleasure in being shamed, arguing for 'an attempt to put some pieces of the puzzle of crime, violence and transgression together to help us make sense of what goes on around us'. Here violence becomes a synecdoche for crime; crime becomes a synecdoche for transgression. There are obvious empirical and definitional difficulties here: not all crime is violent; not all crime is transgressive; not all transgression is violent, and so on, and thus sub-cultural criminology risks practising a version of the exclusionary practices that it so abjures (see Young, J 1999). Other definitional difficulties relate to the fact that many of the activities described by sub-cultural criminologists are not criminalised (or even on occasion regarded as particularly deviant) by either the media or law, which should make us question sub-cultural criminology's insistence upon their inclusion. Does criminology need to designate more criminals and deviants?

More fundamentally, what is the thread that sutures together the signifying chain linking crime, violence and transgression in a unitary category? For sub-cultural criminology, as for Katz, *emotion* knits these three terms. Criminal behaviour may have varying emotions attached to its performance – anger, jealousy, and so on – but it is the fact of emotion that is construed as significant for the subject. Furthermore, it is this emotionally subjective 'I', or self, which is outlawed in the figure of the criminal. As this emotional subject performs its various transgressive acts, a labelling process takes place. Presdee (2000: 7) states, 'The response by authority to the unfathomable is to outlaw and to criminalise'. The 'unfathomable' is transgressive desire and the result is 'the criminalisation of everyday life' (2000: 15).

This result is an effect of:

> a cultural process whereby those with power come to define and shape dominant forms of social life and give them specific meanings … [I]t is the way that the powerful have the ability to define both how and what we see, and therefore what is deemed deviant and what is deemed criminal (Presdee 2000: 17).

The outlaw, then, is a figure produced by the cultural constructions of the socially powerful. And it is a *literal* figure: in sub-cultural criminology outlaws are joyriders, sadomasochists, hillbillies, urban trash scroungers, gang members, young people at raves, persecuted artists, neo-Nazi skinheads, goths, the homeless, graffiti writers, skateboarders, punks, and more (see Presdee 2000; and the essays in Ferrell & Sanders 1995; and Ferrell et al 2004).

The outlaw is deemed to move through the spaces of the everyday as a self-absorbed body of experience. It is a subject without ethics, a body of desires colliding with other bodies along its teleological route. This sub-cultural subject lacks an ethical body in part because of the conception of the everyday as a series of idiosyncratic symptoms, emotional performances, and collisions between desiring and violent bodies. Thus criminal and criminalised behaviours become rendered as a set of lifestyle choices: masks adopted, costumes donned and poses held by knowing subjects. Everyday life thus consists of the choice between attending a rave or going to the opera, between joyriding or taking the bus, between mass eco-cyclist demonstrations and driving one's car.

The subject in this conceptualisation is an active, desiring subject, continually participating in dozens of micro-choices, which accumulate into a sort of lifestyle, some of which is subject to the criminalisation process by powerful people who see something threatening in such behaviours. As in interactionism, the emphasis is on the asymmetrical flow of (labelling) power: despite its argument that style has constitutive force not only for criminal sub-cultures but also for 'the broader social and legal relations in which these sub-cultures are caught' (Ferrell & Sanders 1995: 5), sub-cultural criminology has on the whole tended to focus primarily on an accumulation of criminal sub-cultures, with little sense of a subject whose self-determination is thwarted by others, whose experience of the everyday is stratified by the desires of other subjects, whose choices are countermanded by a discursive economy of subordination.

Thinking through the image of crime: criminological aesthetics

The second perspective engaging with crime's relationship to culture can be termed 'criminological aesthetics', and its starting-point is that 'crime's images are structured according to a binary logic of representation. Oppositional terms (man/woman, white/black, rational/irrational, mind/body and so on) are constructed in a system of value which makes one visible and the other invisible' (Young, A 1995: 1). The notion of a system of value, structured through the logic of binary oppositions and subject to varying shifts in the social economy of representation, moves the criminological theorising of culture away from a framework which constructs acts as having symbolic meaning (in an epiphenomenal relation to their literal effects) and individuals as actors arrayed around the social field at a greater or lesser distance from the dominant centre. A criminological aesthetics emphasises practices of interpretation over the generation of meaning (which tacitly relies on a conception of truth, authenticity or actuality), processes of signification rather than symbolisation (which posits a zero sum relation between meaning and image), and affect instead of emotion. The imagination of crime is an affective process, which does things to the bodies of individuals (whether criminals, the agents of criminal justice, victims, judges, or the cinema audience) as much as it has effects in the evolution of practices of criminal justice or paradigms of criminological thought.

The concept of affect has only recently been given serious attention within criminological scholarship (see De Haan & Loader 2002; Karstedt 2002). However, there is a tendency for criminologists to confuse affect and emotion. Affect, as can be seen from the work of Massumi (1992), who draws on such authors as Spinoza and Bergson as well as Deleuze and Guattari, derives from the tradition of post-Deleuzean social theory. Massumi (1992: 93) writes that affect is akin to the 'ways in which the body can connect with itself and with the world', and, as such, has to do with *intensity* rather than identity (which is the touchstone of sub-cultural criminology's approach). Where sub-cultural criminology builds from its Katz-derived fixation upon emotion to ask of criminal actors 'what does it feel like to commit a crime?', the deployment of affect as a key concept in criminological aesthetics broadens the interlocutive possibilities to ask questions also of those who name or respond to crime in various ways (what affect arises from an encounter with crime? What affect arises from an encounter with an image of crime? How does such an affective encounter relate to the politico-cultural and legal factors that limit what it is possible to say and do about a particular image?). It allows questions to be asked of these subjects on the understanding that one is never just 'a criminal', or 'a victim', or 'a police officer', or 'a fan of action movies', so much as locales of potential whose subjectivities are made and remade according to the images ascribed to them.

To emphasise affect, then, rather than emotion is to admit that crime connects bodies known and unknown through the proliferation of images. The connection might be a minor or substantial interruption to one's sense of the proper, or a reinforcement of one's view of 'the state of society today', or an experience of the exhilaration of illicit behaviour. Whatever the case, *crime as image connects bodies*.[2]

A number of convictions underlie the research that has been done in the name of criminological aesthetics (see for example, Biber 2007; Hutchings 2001; Jewkes 2004; Lippens 2004; Phillips & Strobl 2006; Scott Bray 2006; Valier 2003; Valverde 2007; Young, A 2007). First, the affective and effective force of the image: a spectator can be impelled to violence by an artwork (see the examples described in Young, A 2005), or disturbed by a story of murder and trauma (on Pat Barker's novel *Border Crossing*, see Valier 2002), or moved by the characters in a television series (for example, on *Buffy the Vampire Slayer*, see MacNeil 2006). The relation between an image and its spectator or reader is a profound one. Looking at an image or reading a story requires an acknowledgement on the part of the individual that representation exists in the world, that appearance has a place and a force within society. Criminological aesthetics attends to the matrix of intersections between the spectator, the image and the context of reception, with perhaps the most important factor in any instance being the possibility that the subject – including the legal institution as well as the individual – feels *addressed* by the image and thus bound up in a relation with it.

Criminological aesthetics, as the term implies, acknowledges the manifest ubiquity of images of *crime* (the criminological *telos* of the approach) and the centrality of the image to contemporary life (the framing of that question as one of aesthetics). That images of crime and justice abound has been noted by others; however, the aesthetic dimension (that is, its implication of the spectator in a relation with the image) of that abundance also has the potential to mark out a new terrain of political inquiry for criminology. As bell hooks (1995: 124) puts it:

> We need to place aesthetics on the agenda. We need to theorize the meaning of beauty in our lives so that we can educate for critical consciousness, talking through the issues: how we acquire and spend money, how we feel about beauty, what the place of beauty is in our lives when we lack material privilege and even basic resources for living, the meaning and significance of luxury and the politics of envy.

---

2   For a detailed discussion of such an approach in the context of graffiti, see Halsey & Young (2006).

Part of that agenda, for critical criminology, must include a reflexive consideration of the process of interpretation of images of crime – a process of entanglement
and implication. The image does not exist in isolation from the spectator (or from
law, or from the institutions of criminal justice). Looking and interpreting has dynamism; responses are, by definition, responsive. In this co-implication, we find the traces of a politics: underlying criminological aesthetics is a conviction that we must
add to the politics of social change and legal transformation the significance of an
ethics of visual interpretation, which responds to the project of signification and
values the manifold instances of the imaginary in contemporary criminal justice.

Crime in and as the image: doing cultural analysis

To demonstrate the concerns of a criminological aesthetics, it is worth briefly
examining a case study – the Columbine High School shootings in 1999 in Littleton,
Colorado, when Eric Harris and Dylan Klebold killed 13 people. In the aftermath of
the event, the news media quickly posited a series of explanations for Harris and Klebold's actions: including insufficiently regulated access to guns, inadequate parenting, bullying in the school, and the possible impact of computer games such as
Doom and the music of Marilyn Manson. It was widely surmised that Harris and Klebold, despite being under-age, had purchased guns directly (they had in fact done so
through an adult straw buyer), that they were members of a group known as the
'Trenchcoat Mafia' (whereas they in fact were not associated with this group, but had
simply worn long coats to school to hide the rifles they carried), that they were isolated loners subjected to bullying (they had in fact a number of friends within the
school), and that the cultural products they consumed had influenced their actions
(although the boys did play computer games, their purported liking for Marilyn Manson was entirely inaccurate – they favoured harder rock music such as that of Ram-
mstein).[3]

Some criminological commentary exists on the search for explanations in the
wake of the Columbine shootings (see Muzzatti 2004). However, criminological
aesthetics takes this analysis further than the trading of sociological explanations, by
examining also the way in which an event which was claimed to arise out of the
impact of the image upon two vulnerable individuals has also both been reconfigured as an iconic event itself (whereby the very name 'Columbine' now signifies
a school shooting) and has also been used as a means through which to demonstrate
the impossibility of explaining the inexplicable.

In respect of the latter concern, a film by Gus Van Sant, *Elephant* (2003),
restages the Columbine shootings in a high school in Portland, Oregon, and takes up
the notion of the search for an explanation, by including an array of explanatory narratives in some flashback scenes depicting Eric and Alex as they prepare for the

---

3   In the wake of such media surmises, there were a number of cultural consequences. Marilyn Manson
     became the object of media criticism and was forced to issue public statements condemning violence;
     he also features in Michael Moore's film *Bowling for Columbine*. When it transpired that Harris
     hated Manson and in fact was a fan of the rock band, Rammstein, the band had to issue statements
     distancing their music from actual violence. The boys' purported membership of the 'Trenchcoat
     Mafia' led to New Line Cinema's attempt to withhold *The Basketball Diaries* from video and DVD
     circulation. And the boys' enjoyment of computer games produced a widespread increase in
     regulatory attention to such games (including, for example, the withholding from release or revision
     of classification for games such as *Grand Theft Auto* and *Getting Up*, a graffiti-related game).

shootings. The boys are shown watching a documentary about Nazism on television; their parents are either absent, or depicted only up to shoulder height (the missing parent or a body with absent head or face making literal the idea of inadequate parenting). They order guns from the internet and peruse weapons sites online; one plays a computer game involving the shooting of individuals in the back; Alex is shown being bullied at school by 'jocks'; the two boys are shown kissing in the shower. However, these purported 'explanations' simply appear and are given no diegetic function within the film. Indeed, the film's surfeit of possible explanatory narratives points out the impossibility of arriving at an explanation and leaves the shootings an inexplicable enigma.

Narrative content, however, is only one aspect of the analysis that a criminological aesthetics carries out. Equally significant is form – neither understood as a question of film style (which constructs it as epiphenomenal to film content) nor in binary opposition to content. Rather, cinematic form (that is, how a film constructs its images) is irrevocably *intertwined* with cinematic narrative (that is, the story told by a film). The point made above, that Van Sant not only refuses to provide an explanatory narrative but actually uses the film to show how the search for an explanatory narrative is doomed to failure, is only a starting-point. The way in which the cinematic image of *Elephant* addresses the spectator cannot be separated from the story told within the film. Thus, it would be correct to state that *Elephant* is a highly realist film, but it both undercuts its realism and problematises the criminological search for explanations through a number of formal devices. It has, for example, a fragmented temporality, taking place almost entirely within one day and composed for the most part of mundane events, typical for any high school (gym class, science class, having lunch in the cafeteria, reporting to the principal's office, chatting with friends, walking down corridors from one classroom to another). Some of these events are shown more than once, filmed from different camera angles to denote the perspective of different characters, or the story they would narrate of the event if they could. For example, we see the two killers arrive at the school three times over (and filmed as part of different characters' 'stories'). There is no suspense as to 'whodunnit'; the first time we see 'Eric' and 'Alex' arrive at the school, wearing military clothing and weighted down with bags, is early in the film, and the repetition of this scene dispenses with uncertainty as to the identity of the killers but works instead to build an increasing sense of dread in the viewer.

Such dread is compounded by the withholding of the shootings until the last third of the film. The spectator knows that the shootings will occur, but neither when nor who will be the boys' victims. Each character in the film may therefore be death-bound; each mundane occurrence is freighted with the significance of being potentially the last moment before violent death. The actors are non-professionals; characters are denoted by the first name of the individual who plays each role. The film contains inter-titles, cutting from the visual action to a black screen displaying in white typeface the name of a character or characters. Such a device acts to distance the viewer from the events on screen, disrupting the illusion of a continuous relation between spectator and screen that is key to realist cinema.

Much of the film plays out with no soundtrack other than the characters' conversations and the ambient sounds of the school. When sound effects are used, they are deployed to increase the sense of the uncanny: wind-like noises, birdsong, running water, and the piano music of Beethoven (especially 'Für Elise', the piano piece perhaps more associated with high school than any other). The occasional use of slow-motion filming lends certain scenes a dream-like quality, but, unlike action films which rely on slow-motion to convey, paradoxically, a sense of speed (for example, characters diving to safety during gun battles or explosions in films such as *Face/Off*, *Lethal Weapon*, or *Die Hard*, and most famously, the bullets dodged by Neo in *The Matrix*), *Elephant* eschews any such effects during the scenes in which Eric and Alex shoot their classmates and principal. Slow-motion is reserved for casual encounters and moments of reverie; the violence occurs in 'real time' and with no music soundtrack.

Expectations drawn from other genres (such as the crime film or the action movie) are frequently confounded in *Elephant*. Heroism in this film, for example, does not lead to narrative conclusion. Once the shootings have begun, a character named 'Benny' is introduced. He is tall, athletic, appears calm where others are fleeing the school in panic. On discovering a girl who is so traumatised that she has been unable to escape, he helps her to climb from a classroom window, but does not take that route himself, instead returning to the corridors to help others. He is, therefore, portrayed as a heroic character. He comes upon Eric, standing over the school principal. The film shows him approaching Eric steadily, slowly from behind, in order, we assume, to disarm him or at least to save the principal. A single trumpet note plays on the soundtrack (heraldic, hopeful, but also ominous). However, Eric hears Benny's approach, and simply shoots him dead at close range, thereupon shaking his head and saying, flatly, 'fuck! … '. And after pretending to allow the principal to escape, Eric then shoots him dead. It is just as the spectator begins to hope for a heroic intervention in the dreadful events on display (thanks to our saturation with tropes of heroism in the standard action movie or thriller), that hope is almost immediately quashed. The heroic character gets no second chances (once Eric hears him, his fate is sealed); salvation is achieved at random in just the same way that violent death is delivered.

The film's dominant and much-remarked cinematic trope relates to its lengthy tracking shots, as the camera, sitting just behind a character's shoulder, follows individuals around during the school day. One sequence has the camera sitting, static, on a playing field, as cheerleaders rehearse in the distance, girls jog past in the foreground, and boys play football in medium range. Characters simply run in and out of shot, as Beethoven's 'Moonlight' Sonata plays, for almost two minutes. As one character, 'Nathan', puts on his sweatshirt, the camera, seemingly at random, follows him off the playing field and then, for a further four minutes, into the school and down a series of corridors. Nothing happens; there seems no reason to pick this boy to observe. Such randomness operates as a visual premonition of the randomness that will occur once Eric and Alex start shooting people: the characters' fates are determined simply by chance. Nathan features in the film's final scene, as Alex happens to come upon Nathan and his girlfriend Carrie hiding in a meat locker in the school kitchen. The film ends abruptly as Alex recites 'eeny meeny miney mo', implying that one, or even both, will be shot according merely to the haphazard but inexorable logic of a child's nursery rhyme.

Conclusion: critical criminology and the imagination of crime

The above case study shows that criminological aesthetics is no simple matter of interpreting secondary cultural data divorced from the primary matters of crime and justice in everyday life. Events such as the Columbine shootings, or the attacks of 9/11, or the murder of two-year-old James Bulger in the UK, provide particularly acute examples of the ways in which crime and its images are incapable of straight-forward separation, but they should not be regarded as anomalous. Rather they serve to highlight the ways in which everyday life is lived in the imaginary. Imagination – the process by which we make images of crime – evokes the drive of spectatorship: the desire to see which in turn touches upon the desire to be seen.

The aesthetics of crime engages with the processes by which crime is imagined: 'the linguistic turns and tricks, the framing and editing devices in and through which crime becomes a topic, obtains and retains a place in discourse' (Young, A 1996: 16). As Derrida's (1981: 91) reading of Plato reminds us, representation is always the scene of a crime. While representing the crime, images also constitute or legislate the event, mediating and framing its actors and affects, and facilitating the flow of response and responsibility. It should be no wonder, then, that despite claims of lawlessness and disorder, of the ineffectiveness of the criminal justice system, and of our disapproval of criminality, that crime has got under our skins and is keeping us enthralled.

A criminological aesthetics grapples with processes of identification *with*, *in* and *as* law and *against* crime and disorder. It does not advocate identification with the criminal or the deviant as a matter of course; it asks rather how we live through our images of crime, victimage, justice and punishment. It investigates how, following Biber (2007: 105):

> the image is dangerous for a society that has invested it with meaning and power. When we surrender to the image our capacity for truth, justice and fantasy fulfil-ment, we separate ourselves from our own capacities for judgment and ethical choice.

Such capacities are not lost in the imagination of crime, but rendered contingent. Images can offend, move, disgust, sadden, condemn, and, as *Elephant* shows, can also both invite judgment while simultaneously show us the impossibility of its achievement. All the more reason, then, to continue to struggle with the image and imagination: to trace the translation of affect into law, into judgment and punishment.

References

Becker, HS 1963, *Outsiders: studies in the sociology of deviance*, The Free Press, New York.

Biber, K 2007, *Captive Images: race, crime, photography*, Glass House Books, London.

Cohen, S 1972, *Folk Devils and Moral Panics*, MacGibbon & Kee, London.

Cohen, S & Young, J 1981, *The Manufacture of News*, Constable, London.

De Haan, W & Loader, I 2002, 'On the Emotions of Crime, Punishment and Social Control', 6(3) *Theoretical Criminology* 243.

Derrida, J 1981, *Dissemination*, Chicago University Press, Chicago.

Ferrell, J, Hayward, K, Morrison, W & Presdee, M (eds) 2004, *Cultural Criminology Unleashed*, Glass House Books, London.

Ferrell, J & Sanders, C (eds) 1995, *Cultural Criminology*, Northeastern University Press, Boston.

Hall, S, Critcher, C, Jefferson, T, Clark, J & Roberts, B 1978, *Policing the Crisis: mugging, the state, and law and order*, MacMillan, London.

Halsey, M & Young, A 2006, '"Our Desires are Ungovernable": writing graffiti in urban space', 10(3) *Theoretical Criminology* 275.

Hayward, K & Young, J 2004, 'Cultural Criminology: some notes on the script', 8(3) *Theoretical Criminology* 259.

Hebdige, D 1979, *Subculture: the meaning of style*, Methuen, London.

Hooks, B 1995, *Art On My Mind*, The New Press, New York.

Hutchings, P 2001, *The Criminal Spectre in Law, Literature and Aesthetics: incriminating subjects*, Routledge, London.

Jewkes, Y 2004, *Media and Crime*, Sage, London.

Karstedt, S 2002, 'Emotions and Criminal Justice', 6(3) *Theoretical Criminology* 299.

Katz, J 1988, *Seductions of Crime: moral and sensual attractions of doing evil*, Basic Books, New York.

Lippens, R 2004, 'Introduction: Imaginary. Boundary. Justice' in Lippens, R (ed), *Imaginary Boundaries of Justice*, Hart Publishing, Oxford.

MacNeil, WA 2006, *Lex Populi: the jurisprudence of popular culture*, Stanford University Press, Palo Alta.

Mason, P 2006, 'Lies, Distortion and What Doesn't Work: monitoring prison stories in the British media', 2(3) *Crime, Media, Culture* 251.

Massumi, B 1992, *A User's Guide to Capitalism and Schizophrenia: deviations from Deleuze and Guattari*, The Massachusetts Institute of Technology Press, Cambridge.

Miller, JA 1995, 'Struggles Over the Symbolic: gang style and the meaning of social control', in Ferrell, J & Sanders, C (eds), *Cultural Criminology*, Northeastern University Press, Boston.

Muzzatti, SL 2004, 'Criminalising Marginality and Resistance: Marilyn Manson, Columbine and Cultural Criminology', in Ferrell, J, Hayward, K, Morrison, W & Presdee, M (eds), *Cultural Criminology Unleashed*, Glass House, London.

Peelo, M 2006, 'Framing Homicide Narratives in Newspapers: mediated witness and the construction of virtual victimhood', 2(2) *Crime, Media, Culture* 159.

Phillips, ND & Strobl, S 2006, 'Cultural Criminology and Kryptonite: apocalyptic and retributive constructions of crime and justice in comic books', 2(3) *Crime, Media, Culture*.

Presdee, M 2000, *Cultural Criminology and the Carnival of Crime*, Routledge, London.

Scott Bray, R 2006, 'Enduring Images and the Art of Remembering: Book Review of *City of Shadows: Sydney Police Photographs 1912-1948* (Peter Doyle with Caleb Williams) and Exhibition Review of *City of Shadows: Inner city crime & mayhem 1912-1948* (Curator Peter Doyle)', 18(2) *Current Issues in Criminal Justice* 376.

Soothill, K & Walby, S 1991, *Sex Crime in the News*, Routledge, London.

Sparks, R 1990, 'Dramatic Power: television, images of crime and law enforcement' in Sumner, C (ed), *Censure, Politics and Criminal Justice*, Open University Press, Milton Keynes.

Sutherland, E & Cressey, D 1978, *Criminology*, 10th edition, Lippincott, Philadelphia.

Tunnell, KD 2004, 'Cultural Constructions of the Hillbilly Heroin and Crime Problem', in Ferrell, J, Hayward, K, Morrison, W & Presdee, M (eds), *Cultural Criminology Unleashed*, Glass House, London.

Valier, C 2002, 'Punishment, Border Crossings and the Powers of Horror', 6(3) *Theoretical Criminology*.

Valier, C 2003, *Crime and Punishment in Contemporary Culture*, Routledge, London.

Valverde, M 2007, *Law and Order: images, meanings, myths*, Glass House Books, London.

Willis, P 1977, *Learning to Labour*, Columbia University Press, New York.

Young, A 1995, *Imagining Crime: textual outlaws and criminal conversations*, Sage, London.

Young, A 2006, *Judging the Image: art, value, law*, Routledge, London.

Young, A 2007, 'Images in the Aftermath of Trauma: responding to September 11th', 3(1) *Crime, Media, Culture* 30.

Young, J 1999 *The Exclusive Society: social exclusion, crime and difference in late modernity*, Sage, London.

3

CLASS ANALYSIS AND
THE CRIME PROBLEM

Rob White

Introduction

This chapter proceeds from the premise that one of the key missing elements of contemporary critical criminology is class analysis. Class is at the core of criminality, marginalisation and criminalisation under the conditions of contemporary global capitalism. Present day social inequalities and social oppressions are manifestations of deep class divisions and class conflicts, now being played out on a world scale. Yet, very few critical criminologists actually utilise class analysis in their work. Indeed, many do not even refer to classes at all, except in elliptical ways, for example through reference to categories such as the socially disadvantaged, the poor or the excluded. Class has tended to be embedded *implicitly* within critical work, in ways that assume what in fact often needs to be explained. Alternatively, class analysis has tended to be marginalised in the light of other strategic emphases (for example, analysis of gender) and conceptual emphases (for example, analysis of risk).

Where do class and class analysis fit within the relatively short history of Australian criminology? To answer this we have to appreciate the difference between critical criminology in the 1970s and early 1980s, and criminology in the 21st century. For example, the work of left wing criminologists in the 'radical era' was largely informed by two key influences. First, many critical criminologists were directly engaged with and had practical ties to social reform movements such as prisoner action groups, feminist collectives and Indigenous rights activists (see Brown 2002). Secondly, and this is crucial to the present discussion, many likewise were members of or fellow travellers with, militant socialist organisations – including the Communist Party of Australia (CPA), the Socialist Workers Party, and the International Socialists through to the Socialist Left of the Labor Party. Importantly, 'socialism' was not merely a slogan; it was often and usually linked to education in the basic concepts and principles of Marxism. This was not simply an academic exercise. It involved reading the works of Marx, Lenin, Gramsci, Mao and Trotsky, and discussing the relevance and significance of revolutionary leaders and movements for understanding and acting within the Australian context. The detachments from its working class and activist base and the transfer of Marxism into the academy (and its institutional career structures) may have been in train (see Anderson 1979), but the separation between socialist academic and socialist movement was not quite complete.

By the late 1980s and into the 1990s, intellectual life took on a different character in the academy. The failures of Stalinisation, and the rise of neo-liberalism, took their tolls within the socialist movement generally. The subsequent demise of the CPA and its publication *Tribune*, once a staple diet for the Left on campus (whatever a person's specific party affiliation), left a huge hole in radical politics and radical education. In its heyday the CPA had well over 30,000 active members, trained and educated militants in the struggle for a new society. Socialist parties of the Left, such as the CPA, were important in socialising a whole generation of activists into using the concepts of class analysis and learning the lessons of revolutionaries throughout history and across the globe.

The fall of the Berlin Wall and the demise of the Soviet Union in 1989 underscored the failure of Soviet-style communism. Importantly, it ideologically reinforced the neo-liberal campaign discrediting Marxism and its proposed alternatives to capitalism, as evidenced in popular proclamations at the time that neo-liberal capitalism constituted the 'end of history'.

Meanwhile, there were intense discussions on the Left about the transformative possibilities and reformist pitfalls of the new social movements. In practice, many activists got bogged down in a kind of lowest common denominator politics, one that subsumed 'class' and 'socialism' into a melting pot of conflicting ideals and social interests (such as 'environmentalism'). The diminished presence and influence of Left radical parties and party factions generally was further reinforced by the intellectual left-culture wars involving 'postmodernism' and Marxism in academic circles. In both cases, the retreat from class was thereby accelerated.

The consequence of these trends is that very few in academia today learn 'class' in the same way that it was learned in the previous era. It is not that class has gone away (although there have been changes in actual class relations); but our basic understanding of class and class analysis has been altered. In its stead there developed approaches that more often than not were antagonistic to Marxist class analysis, or that wished to sever any connection with the class politics of socialism.

Critical criminology badly needs a reassessment and re-substantiation of the importance – indeed, the centrality – of class analysis. This is not to denigrate or belittle the consciousness of complexity in contemporary social analysis, especially in the light of 30 or more years of theorising *intersections* (the acknowledgment that there are complex relations between gender, class, race and ethnicity, among other features of social life). However, too often the mode of intersection analysis itself ends up striving to achieve an equality of concepts, rather than reflecting the hegemony of class structure in our lives. It is this that determines the basic material resources that underpin what we do, when we do it, with whom, and how we do it. Class as a lived relation predominantly *shapes* as well as interacts with other key facets of our social being.

While 'race' or 'gender' oppression cannot be reduced to explanations which subsume this oppression simply under 'class exploitation', it needs to be acknowledged that the class structuring of gender, ethnicity and race at the level of lived experiences is central to an understanding of economic and social inequality. The

31

various dimensions of sexism and racism are inextricably intertwined with the development and extension of capitalism on a world scale. The economic, ideological and political relations of oppression are thus inseparable from the context of capitalism within which they exist. By extension, patterns and manifestations of criminality likewise flow from the complex determining matrix of class and class economy that frames and shapes its dimensions. Acknowledging this, means that, for critical criminology, class analysis ought to occupy an analytically central working place within our investigations and interventions.

Theorising class and crime

Abstractly conceived, class refers to specific relationships of people to the means of production in a society (White & van der Velden 1995). That is, it describes how and where individuals fit into the overall mode of production in any particular social formation. In a capitalist society, the defining classes are the capitalist class and the working class, although these are not the only classes that are present. In any class society, the fundamental classes are the class of direct producers and the ruling ownership class that appropriates the social surplus of the direct producers. In the more concrete terms of historically existing class societies, however, there is always some 'slippage' at the boundaries of class, insofar as individuals can occupy positions that shade into or oscillate between more than one class situation (see Meiksins 1986). Nevertheless, it is the specific predominant class relations that we enter into that are central from the point of view of shaping material interests and structural position. Class is fundamental to how people access societal resources, whether these are economic, social, cultural or political.

A distinction can be made between class description and class analysis. Most contemporary discussions of class within criminology have relied on descriptive characterisations of 'social class'. As such they have provided indications of 'class effects', not 'class structuring'. For instance, the focus has been on the empirical situation of selected population groups variously described in terms of 'disadvantage', 'poverty' and 'social exclusion'. Such descriptive work has been a feature of positivist as well as critical criminologists, as indicated for example in research that examines the link between unemployment (and/or poverty) and crime at the local neighbourhood level (see Weatherburn & Lind 2001; Lee 2006; Vinson 2007).

While social analysis is provided in this sort of research, it generally is not analysis of *class* as such. Class is used as a shorthand descriptor by which to explore issues pertaining to blocked opportunities and the social, economic and criminological impact of inequality on the poor, the disadvantaged and the excluded. The focus of attention is on the plight of those at the bottom end of the class structure. But there is no inherent or necessary interest in understanding the dynamics of domination and subordination accompanying class division. The question may well be 'what is to be done?', but this is framed in terms of 'what to do about or to the poor?' (an effect of class inequality), rather than the structures that generate poor and rich to begin with (a structural relation of class exploitation). As Jamrozik (2001: 271-272) puts it:

> Many of the issues that are commonly regarded as 'social problems' are indeed normal conditions in a free-market society. For example, unemployment, poverty,

inequality and law-breaking are normal conditions, directly related to and stemming from particular political, economic and social arrangements. ... The activities that are provided to ostensibly remedy or alleviate the given problem serve, first and foremost, to legitimise the situation and at the same time alleviate public consciousness by demonstrating that the government cares and aims to remedy the situation. The outcome is usually a demonstration of an inadequacy or fault of the affected population – it is indeed an activity creating a 'blaming the victim' syndrome.

In addition to relational accounts that see impoverishment and wealth accumulation as 'normal' features of class society, class analysis is interested in how 'social being determines social consciousness' (Marx 1977). This is basically a viewpoint that says class has a profound shaping influence in the lived experiences of people. For example, the capitalist class cannot be understood only in terms of who actually comprises it (predominantly wealthy white men), but in terms of the relations it embodies (ownership, control and exploitation of non-owners). If we see things this way, then the issue becomes one of how particular social relations are produced and reproduced – including crime and criminality.

To discern the nature of crime and criminality under capitalism, therefore, analysis ought to examine patterns of activity as shaped by class position and class relations. Class situation is linked to specific types of criminality. Thus, where you are located in the class structure will influence the kinds of criminal activity you engage in, the propensity to engage in such activity, and the intensity of that involvement (and, of course, whether it will be identified by the state as criminal, and whether it will be policed or punished). The next part of this chapter outlines in concise form the class patterns of criminality in capitalist society.

Capitalist criminality

We begin with capitalist criminality. The capitalist class is comprised of the owners of capitalist enterprises and those who control and manage the capital accumulation process on their behalf (who themselves overwhelmingly own shares in the enterprises they manage). It is the dominant class economically, but the smallest numerically (van der Velden & White 1996). The initial difficulty in determining criminality within the capitalist class is that state laws reflect the very interests of the capitalist ruling class that controls the state. As such, many types of social harm may not be incorporated into the criminal law if to do so would go against capitalist interests generally. Making this transparent and specific should be a central focus of critical criminology.

State-defined crimes applicable to the capitalist class incorporate white-collar and corporate crimes that have significant structural effects in terms of deaths and financial losses. However, because such crimes are usually directed in the first instance against other capitalists or against the rules governing the marketplace, they are rarely accorded the same ideological and political weight as street crime by the criminal justice system, by capitalist political parties and by the mainstream press. Consequently, little in the way of capitalist criminality is specifically perceived by the general public to be of special interest to them personally (except in the case of events such as preventable workplace deaths – industrial homicide).

33

Types of crimes	Examples
Economic	Breaches of corporate law, environmental degradation, inadequate industrial health and safety provisions, pollution, violation of labour laws, fraud, embezzlement
State	Police brutality, government corruption, bribery, violation of civil and human rights, misuse of public funds

Motivations	Examples
Maximising profit	Structural imperative to minimise costs and maximise economic returns in a competitive capitalist market environment
Augmenting wealth	Attempts to bolster one's own personal position in the economic and social hierarchy
Social control	Violation of privacy and of human rights is justified in the name of national interest, and whatever legal, coercive and propaganda means are necessary will be used to ensure public order, to quell dissent and further private economic interests

Criminalisation	Examples
Shaping definitions	Capacity to influence what is defined as harmful, and the definition of certain acts as being civil or criminal harms, thus limiting police involvement and coercive state intervention generally
Protecting interests	Capacity to mobilise best legal assistance and intricate knowledge of the law
Sentencing	Use of stereotypes and criminal histories to mitigate against harsh punishments due to the nature of the offence (not seen as serious) and offenders (upstanding citizens)

Working class criminality

The working class (wage-labour) consists of those who live by selling their labour power to those who own capital, but also the majority of workers in various state apparatus, including high- and low-waged, skilled and unskilled, full-time and part-time workers. It is the largest class numerically. The working class also includes a pool of not-employed workers whose position within the (global) labour market constitutes a reserve army of labour (van der Velden & White 1996). In periods of general or sectoral reduction in labour reserves, capital either reconstructs the reserve army (for example, the immigration mechanism) or capital itself migrates to areas where the surplus labour arrangement (and hence price) is more favourable to accumulation.

Street crime is the bread-and-butter of mainstream criminology, even though the extent of economic, social, environmental and physical harm is much less than that provided by capitalist criminality. This is because crime, as crime, has generally been constructed in terms of working class criminality. Such crimes tend to be more visible and transparent than capitalist crime. They also have their greatest impact within and upon the working class itself.

34

Types of crimes	Examples
Economic	Street crime, workplace theft, low-level fraud, breach of welfare regulations, prostitution, drug dealing
Socio-Cultural	Vandalism, assault, rape, murder, resistance via strikes and demonstrations, public order offences, workplace sabotage, gang fights

Motivations	Examples
Subsistence	Gaining illegal income to meet basic income needs, attempting to supplement low wages and income relative to subsistence levels
Alienation	Separation of people from mainstream social institutions such as education and work, and a structural and economic sense of powerlessness
Exhilaration	Gaining worth, value and excitement by transgressing the ordinary rules and norms of bourgeois society

Criminalisation	Examples
Limited means to effect crime	Reliance on limited resources, including the body, to carry out the crime
State intervention	Key target for state surveillance, detection, investigation and intervention, few resources to protect interests within law and court
Sentencing	Harms codified in criminal law, certain crimes subject to harsher sentencing regimes via mandatory sentencing

Petty bourgeois criminality

The petty bourgeoisie is a diverse class grouping that traditionally is made up of small-scale owners of capital (for example, family farmers, small landlords, small business), self-employed professionals (for example, doctors, lawyers), and now also includes new middle layers of employment at the management and technical levels of capitalist enterprises and various apparatuses of the state (van der Velden & White 1996). The petty bourgeoisie form an intermediate layer poised between the capitalist class and the working class proper. It constitutes a relatively advantaged class grouping compared with the working class, but does not hold decisive social or economic power.

Class is directly associated with economic, social and political power, and is evident in how laws are framed, institutions are organised and societal resources are distributed. For the petty bourgeoisie there is the constant threat of downward mobility as well as the possibility of an upward climb, depending upon everything from changes in tax rules, discovery of new market niches through to income reporting requirements. Survival is very much dependent upon self-reliance, and this is in turn constructed around whatever it takes to stay afloat or to get ahead.

Types of crimes	Examples
Economic	Price gouging, violating labour laws, tax violations, discrimination, fraud, selling unsafe products, alternative illegal crops
Regulatory	Violation of professional codes of conduct, ignoring regulations relating to standards and service provision

Motivations	Examples
Maximising profit	Cutting corners due to market pressures, precarious position vis-à-vis subsistence and profit margins
Augmenting wealth	Material rewards of corruption of systems and processes, using social status to extract surplus profits
Alienation	Comparing plight of small business with advantages given to big business thus justifying tax and other workplace related fiddles

Criminalisation	Examples
Variable capacity	Type of crime is dictated by scale of operation, resources available, contingent opportunities, link between legal and illegal markets
Protecting interests	Variable capacity to protect oneself from prosecution, depending upon collective structures (for example, professional associations) and nature of state regulation (for example, regulatory capacities of agencies such as health and safety)
Sentencing	Depends upon the specific nature of the crime (growing cannabis versus service fraud), immediate resources, and definition of harm as criminal or civil

Underclass criminality

The underclass strata is equivalent to the traditional but archaic term 'lumpen-proletariat'. These more marginalised layers of the surplus population consist of those who have an extremely residual and virtually inactive reserve labour role and whose economic and social conditions have, as a consequence, sunk well below that of the average member of the working class. Members of the underclass strata generally lie outside the normal boundaries of the labour market as permanently discarded, injured, obsolete, or unusable labour power or, as a consequence of not having any foreseeable opportunity to commodify their labour power, have socially and culturally removed themselves from the parameters of capitalist production relations (van der Velden & White 1996).

While linked to the working class, the underclass is structurally and behaviourally separated from it, a separation that may be reinforced by the social reproduction of exclusion due to social factors relating to family, religious, ethnic and racial background. When professionalised and organised, underclass crime can take on the structural form of petty bourgeois and even capitalist criminality – the relations of production and exploitation can thus mirror those of legitimate large-scale enterprises and small business operations.

Types of crimes	Examples
Economic	Drug dealing, protection rackets, robbery, prostitution, black market
Socio-Cultural	Vandalism, assault, rape, murder, collective fighting

Motivations	Examples
Subsistence	Gaining illegal income to meet basic income needs, reliance upon the informal economy, welfare and charity, exclusion from formal labour market
Socialisation	Intergenerational reproduction of unemployment, poverty and illegal means of subsistence, sense of territoriality, wealth generation as part of professional or organised crime
Resistance	Protection and valorisation of ethnic/racial identity

Criminalisation	Examples
Limited means to effect crime	Reliance on limited resources to carry out the crime, but may be organised into criminal collectives
State intervention	Periodic target for state surveillance, detection, investigation and intervention, some limited capacity to protect interests through use of bribes and threats
Sentencing	Harms codified in criminal law, certain crimes subject to harsher sentencing regimes via mandatory sentencing, street credibility may be linked to experience of imprisonment

The social impact of capitalist expansion and restructuring is manifest in dynamic structural tendencies of immiseration of large numbers of people and polarisation of income, nationally and globally. One aspect of this is the expansion of the truly disadvantaged, especially in the backward and emerging sectors of the global economy. Another is the advent of the super-rich.

Class control and the capitalist state

The criminalisation industries of the state and the media reflect concern about the growing reality of subsistence criminality driven by an expanding layer of poor and unemployed which has emerged out of global political-economic restructuring. Thus, a key site of contemporary class struggles is that of 'law and order'. On the one hand, deprived individuals, families and communities will organise their own means and forms of subsistence and enjoyment. They will especially do so under circumstances in which they are excluded from desirable areas in which to live and separated from opportunities to find paid work. Moreover, even if work is there to be had, illegality may be far more rewarding, secure and satisfying as a source of income than the insecurities and exploitations of precarious employment in the formal sectors of the economy.

On the other hand, the ideological representation of the poor and deprived as an irresponsible 'underclass' is built into the policy apparatus of the state in relation to both welfare and criminal justice. Unemployment and any resistance to enforced participation in poor workplace situations are reduced to 'bad attitudes' and 'bad families'. The response therefore is to impose varying forms of mutual obligation on the poor – below poverty line benefits and inadequate services in return for work search obligations and imposition of training and employment programs. For those who do not play the game, there is exclusion from state support. For those who ignore the game and make a living through alternative means, there is state coercion – in the form of increased policing, harsher sentencing and greater use of imprisonment.

The crux of state intervention is how best to manage the problem of disadvantaged groups (their presence and activities), rather than to eradicate disadvantage – for to eradicate it would require action to reverse the polarisations in wealth and income, to pit the state directly in opposition to dominant class interests.

Most Australian justice systems deal predominantly with offenders from working class backgrounds (including Indigenous and ethnic minority people), and thereby reflect the class biases in definitions of social harm and crime, as well as basing responses on these biases. In so doing, they reinforce the ideological role of law and order discourse in forging a conservative cross-class consensus about the nature of social problems (White & van der Velden 1995; Parenti 2000). The reinforcement of this discourse also unwittingly enhances the legitimacy of coercive state intervention in the lives of working class people, even if under the rationale of 'repairing harm' as in the case of restorative justice. At a social structural level, such processes confirm the role of 'crime' as the central problem (rather than poverty, unemployment, racism), neglecting or avoiding entirely the roles of class division and social inequality.

The way in which the state deals with conventional (working class) and corporate (capitalist) criminality is, of course, very different. The problem for criminologists in trying to tackle corporate crime is that virtually every act of the corporate sector is deemed, in some way or another, to be 'good for the country'. This ideology of corporate virtue, and the benefits of business for the common good, is promulgated through extensive corporate advertising campaigns, capitalist blackmail (vis-à-vis location of industry and firms) and aggressive lobbying. Anything which impedes business is deemed to be unreasonable, faulty, bad for the economy, not the rightful domain of the state, to undermine private property rights, and so on. In other words, the prevailing view promulgated by government and business is that, with few exceptions, the 'market' is the best referee when it comes to preventing or stopping harm and potential harm. Powerful business interests (which, among other things, provide big financial contributions to mainstream political parties) demand a 'light touch' when it comes to surveillance of, and intervention in, their activities. The state should not, therefore, play a major role in regulation of corporate activities beyond that of assisting in the maintenance of a general climate within which business will flourish.

In effect, recent years have seen the 'disappearance' of specifically defined corporate crime. As Snider (2000) points out, this has occurred through a combination of de-criminalisation (repeal of laws defining corporate activity as criminal in nature), de-regulation (repeal of measures that formerly restricted corporate activities) and downsizing (destruction of the state's enforcement capability). This has been accompanied by a major ideological offensive on the part of capital in support of 'free market' policies that directly challenge anti-business forms of state intervention, and includes massive green-washing campaigns that legitimate destructive environmental practices (Beder 1997; Snider 2000). There has been a major shift away from use of state coercion (in virtually any circumstance) in dealing with corporate wrongdoing and specific instances of social and environmental harm. Instead, the preferred method of corporate regulation has been varying forms of 'self-regulation' and an emphasis on use of gentle state persuasion, rather than government command.

The 'naturalness' of corporate crime – the way in which social harms, economic exploitation and environmental destruction is built into the fabric of everyday, ordinary life as a 'normal' feature of how we produce and consume – makes it that much more difficult to challenge. This is compounded by the fact that much of what occurs does so in a fully 'legal' way, regardless of actual harm. Moreover, where external controls (materially and ideologically) on profit maximisation are weakened, then we can reasonably expect to see an increased incidence in illegal corporate activity and, more generally, greater propensity for social harm regardless of legal definition.

To address corporate criminality, then, requires a political understanding of class power, and a rejection of formally legal criteria in assessing criminality and harm. It is therefore from beginning to end a political process. As such, it implies conflict – over definitions of behaviour and activity (for example, as being good or bad, harmful or not so harmful, offensive or inoffensive), over legitimacy of knowledge claims (for example, media portrayals, expert opinion), and over the role and use of state instruments and citizen participation in putting limits on corporate activity (for example, via regulations, public access to commercial information).

The contrast between how governments respond to street crime and to crimes of the powerful alerts us to the class dynamics underpinning the criminalisation process – from defining harm through to responding to specific offences and offenders. These class dynamics are also relevant in any discussion of explanations for corporate criminality as a social phenomenon. In other words, the basis for such criminality lies within the social structure itself, in the very nature and imperatives of capitalist forms of production, consumption and distribution.

Crime and class struggle

From the point of view of critical criminology, analysis of class and the application of class analysis inevitably leads to examination of class struggles (defined here as the constant struggle over distribution of social surplus) and the balance of social forces within particular capitalist social formations and, indeed, globally. Accordingly, if class analysis is to be relevant, consistent and activist in orientation, it needs to link up to the mass resistance to neo-liberal agendas and practices, to develop counter-hegemonic discourses to those of law and order, and to forge alliances with those who challenge capitalist criminality in its diverse forms.

As regards working class and underclass criminality, different types of consideration and intervention are required. There is nothing romantic, productive or progressive about street crime. Such crime:

> divides the working class against itself, deepens the divisions between employed and unemployed, sharpens racial antagonism, confirms ethnic stereotypes, and depreciates the quality of life in working-class neighbourhoods. It helps to recruit

'respectable' residents into campaigns for tougher 'law and order' measures. Even if crime can be seen to be precipitated by conditions of poverty, marginalization and 'super-exploitation', it provides no solution to these problems (Hall & Scraton 1981: 485).

All of this and more we have seen in recent times in Australia, particularly in regards to the events at Cronulla beach in December 2005 as well as crimes involving ethnic minority groups (see Poynting & Morgan 2007; Poynting this volume).

Members of the working class who engage in crime may do so because of the necessities imposed by capitalism, but crime in and of itself generally constitutes little more than an accommodation to the existing order (Hirst 1975). The exception to this is when the marginalised become politically organised. For example, progressive movements have occasionally been born out of the crucible of gang life. The Black Panthers in the United States emerged out of such formations. It is important to note how youth gangs in the USA, when given a voice, have emphasised the systemic processes of exclusion from mainstream educational, economic and social life that have made them what they are (see Davis 1990). In the Australian context, the persistent marginalisation and scapegoating of young Arab-background and Muslim people in Western Sydney likewise opens the door to explicit political organising around progressive themes. Many of the young men in these 'gangs' have sought to valorise their ethnicity (and masculinity) through anti-social forms such as territorialism and aggressive masculinity (see Collins et al 2000). Yet the seeds are there for the formation of specifically political responses to negative police interventions and social inequalities.

The place of the underclass in assessing the politics of crime deserves specific mention. The underclass has a dual character: it is spawned by its conditions of life under capitalism, but it is simultaneously open politically to reactionary movements and thuggish street activities. It can include neo-Nazi warriors and fundamentalist jihadists, and members of the underclass basically prey upon other sections of the working class, and, for many, 'their highest forms of political action are mob agitation and street fighting' (Hirst 1975: 216). Indeed, the work of anti-racist and anti-hate crime activists amongst the ranks of critical criminologists is frequently directed at combating the terror wrought by reactionary sections of the working classes. Such criminal elements only comprise a tiny fraction of the overall industrial reserve army and surplus population, but they can have a great impact.

Exceptional acts and exceptional groupings can also come to dominate the law and order landscape. Thus, the rape by a few can be used to smear the reputations and community standing of the many; the riots of the disenchanted used to extol the social dangers of the permissive and the hand-out (see Poynting & Morgan 2007). If those from the most economically and socially marginalised communities can be portrayed as 'deviant' and inherently criminal and evil, then people will be less willing to consider the fact that they constitute the social groups with the highest rates of unemployment and poverty.

It is important to politically organise around criminal justice issues, as much as anything because violence and crime 'drive the victims of capitalism, racism and sexism into the arms of a racist, pro-business, sexist state. In short, crime justifies state violence and even creates popular demand for state repression' (Parenti 2000: 43). But, as this chapter has also tried to indicate, the relationship between class and crime precludes adopting conventional criminal justice tactics and strategies to tackle what is essentially a political and economic problem.

Conclusion

The doing of criminology itself ought to be scrutinised from the point of view of class analysis. Almost by definition, the role of criminology has been to work within and on behalf of the state apparatus to grapple with the social disorder within capitalist order. Criminology is generally class-blind, in the sense that issues and interventions are rarely framed in terms other than street crime and the 'crime problem'. The structural relations underpinning the social order and the class structuring of communal power and resources are simply not on the agenda, which remains largely one of social control. For critical criminology, this raises big issues about how debates should be framed and the class politics of what it is that we do. Affecting this, too, is the class situation of the criminologist within government or the academy. Careerism today demands forms of work that are ideologically safe (or irrelevant) and/or that are based around commercially productive research projects. Where does the doing of class analysis fit into this overall picture?

Crime is immediately implicated in and a manifestation of wider class processes. It is symptomatic of basic divisions in society that at their core revolve around the private ownership and control of the means of production. For critical criminology, class analysis means acknowledging that capitalism *ipso facto* equates to a society that is necessarily divided by class interests, and that is ultimately transformed through class struggle. The task of critical criminology, therefore, is to contest the terms upon which the crime problem is debated, and to rejuvenate the socialist vision – including notions such as 'from each according to capacity, to each according to need'. Reiterating such ideas may well find increasing public resonance in a world so obviously beset by gross inequality and environmental crisis.

References

Anderson, P 1979, *Considerations on Western Marxism*, Verso, London.

Beder, S 1997, *Global Spin: the corporate assault on environmentalism*, Scribe Publications, Melbourne.

Brown, D 2002, '"Losing My Religion": reflections on critical criminology in Australia', in Carrington, K & Hogg, R (eds), *Critical Criminology: issues, debates, challenges*, Willan Publishing, Cullompton.

Collins, J, Noble, G, Poynting, S & Tabar, P (eds) 2000, *Kebabs, Kids, Cops & Crime: youth, ethnicity and crime*, Pluto Press, Sydney.

Davis, M 1990, *City of Quartz: excavating the future in Los Angeles*, Vintage, London.

Hall, S & Scraton, P 1981, 'Law, Class and Control', in Fitzgerald, M, McLennan, G & Pawson, J (eds), *Crime and Society: readings in history and theory*, Routledge & Kegan Paul in association with Open University Press, London.

Hirst, P 1975, 'Marx and Engels on Law, Crime and Morality', in Taylor, I, Walton, P & Young, J (eds), *Critical Criminology*, Routledge & Kegan Paul, London.

Jamrozik, A 2001, *Social Policy in the Post-Welfare State: Australians on the threshold of the 21st century*, Pearson Education Australia, Sydney.

Lee, M 2006, 'Public Dissent and Governmental Neglect: isolating and excluding Macquarie Fields', 18(1) *Current Issues in Criminal Justice* 32.

Marx, K 1977, 'The German Ideology', in Marx, K & Engels, F, *Selected Works,* Vol 1, Progress Publishers, Moscow.

Meiksins, P 1986, 'Beyond the Boundary Question', 157 *New Left Review* 101.

Parenti, C 2000, 'Crime as Social Control', 27(3) *Social Justice* 43.

Poynting, S & Morgan, G 2007, *Outrageous! Moral Panics in Australia,* ACYS Publishing, Hobart.

Snider, L 2000, 'The Sociology of Corporate Crime: an obituary (or: whose knowledge claims have legs?)', 4(2) *Theoretical Criminology* 169.

van der Velden, J & White, R 1996, 'Class Criminality and the Politics of Law and Order', in Kuhn, R & O'Lincoln, T (eds), *Class and Class Conflict in Australia*, Longman, Melbourne.

Vinson, T 2007, *Dropping Off the Edge: the distribution of disadvantage in Australia*, Catholic Social Services, Melbourne.

Weatherburn, D & Lind, B 2001, *Delinquent-Prone Communities*, Cambridge University Press, Cambridge.

White, R & van der Velden, J 1995, 'Class and Criminality', 22(1) *Social Justice* 51.

4

PSYCHOLOGISING CRIMINALS AND THE FRANKFURT SCHOOL'S CRITIQUE

Thalia Anthony and Dorothea Anthony

Introduction: a broader view on psychology's contribution to criminology

The birth of criminology and psychology as scientific pursuits in the mid-19th century drew together the two disciplines (Hollin 2002: 147). Institutional criminologists, the courts[1] and popular culture[2] have maintained their fascination with and reliance on psychological models to explain criminal behaviour. They assume that the individual's psychology is the cause of crime and that psychotherapy can be relevant in the eradication of crime. But despite this focus on the individual criminal or act of crime, psychology has a broader tradition in criminology, including in critical criminologies. Notably, the Frankfurt School engaged neo-Freudian psychoanalysis to provide a political critique of the criminal justice functions of the authoritarian state. Such an approach tends to be overlooked by those who associate psychology with positivism.[3]

This chapter will examine models of crime that serve to explain criminal behaviour of the individual, originating with the psychobiological studies of Cesare Lombroso and the personality theories of Sigmund Freud. These approaches are seen as reductionist by nature and as such ignore context and critique (Hudson 2000: 179).

The chapter goes on to argue that the contribution of psychologists to criminology should be elucidated in its entirety. There is a tendency among criminologists to only refer to the psychological contribution in its positivist or clinical form (Hollin 2002; Hayward 2005). They sideline the group of neo-Freudian scholars, known as the Frankfurt School, who interrogated the state's urge to criminalise and paved the way for critical criminology. In criticising the contemporary fascist regime of the 1930s, the Frankfurt School redirected attention from the deemed individual criminal actor to the authoritarian state. By combining the sociology of Marx with the psychology of Freud, one of the School's leading advocates, Erich Fromm (2000b),

---

1   See *Roper v Simmons* (2005) 543 US 551.

2   See Hayward (2005: 110).

3   Taylor et al (1973: 11) characterises positivism primarily as the 'insistence of the unity of scientific method'. In doing so, it tends to maintain the status quo of society.

posited that punishment is not about reducing 'crime' but channelling the masses' anti-state and anti-ruling class impulses. Criminal justice is a 'cruel and irrational system' that 'serves as a major source of legitimation for the dominant classes' (Fromm, cited in Anderson 1998: 693). While the Frankfurt School focused on uncovering the legitimating role of criminal justice processes for fascism, we will argue that orthodox psychobiological approaches have also legitimated the state's role. Diagnosing the inherent flaws of individual 'deviants' has long justified state intervention.

The Frankfurt School's radical reformulation of criminology nonetheless was limited by its therapeutic recommendations, which reverted attention to individual treatment. Social change could only occur through psychotherapy and social (re-)learning of the masses. This prognosis trumped the School's Marxist persuasion towards reconfiguring the state and society. However, this did not limit the School's lasting influence on critical criminology, which drew on the School's inter-disciplinary engagement, ideological analysis, and its critique of state control. Indeed, by condemning the injustices of authoritarianism, the Frankfurt School set the parameters for a new criminological inquiry.

Lombroso's psychobiology and positivism

Early developments in the direction of psychological reductionism (often referred to as 'psychologism') came from psychobiological research that postulated that the size of the brain was a determinant of criminality. These studies opposed contemporary notions that crime was a product of free will and that physical punishment would deter criminal choices (van Swaaningen 1997: 31). Socrates in the fourth century BC wrote in his work *On Justice* that those who partake in crime do so 'unwillingly' through 'lack of knowledge and wisdom inherent in some human constitutions' (cited in Plato 1997: 1692). However, not all groups of individuals were predisposed to criminality. Slaves were more inclined to display attributes associated with crimi-nality. This marked the beginning of justifications for selective law enforcement based on the so-called 'inherent' limitations of identified (powerless) groups. The selection would become based on racial criteria with the emergence of criminology in the 19th century.

In 1876 Cesare Lombroso's (2006) *Criminal Man* launched criminology as a coherent discipline and informed its positivist tendencies; in doing so, the striking prejudices of Lombroso's studies were rationalised. Lombroso studied what he referred to as 'born criminals' by identifying prisoners' physical appearance and brain capacity. He asserted the ape-like atavism of 'born criminals' was evidenced *inter alia* by their darker skin and smaller brains. These features resulted in crimi-nals having 'primitive behaviour' and lacking remorse, moral indifference and indolence.

Lombroso's ideas were a product of the power relations on the 19th century world stage and the ensuing ideological scene that divided the world along racial lines. Imperialism had taken full flight and social Darwinist ideas served as the scientific justification for capitalism in the West to extend its civilisation to peoples deemed to have a lower evolutionary development. With the nominal abolition of slavery, the new targets of law enforcement were members of the emerging working class, and especially its ethnic sub-set. It is no surprise, therefore, that in Lombroso's (2006) studies of the physical characteristics of prison inmates, he found that distinctly ethnic groups were highly represented (especially marginalised Italians from Southern Italy: van Swaaningen (1997: 32)). Lacan (1996: 18) referred to Lombroso's biologism as fulfilling the 'satisfactions' of the 'dominant class'.

Lombroso (2006) explicitly sought to demonstrate that the characteristics of European criminals were akin to those of Indigenous people in distant colonies. Rather than explain this by virtue of discriminatory criminal justice processes, he used a 'scientific methodology' to legitimise their criminalisation and conceal systemic biases. Lombroso (2006) stated that uncivilised and primitive atavistic traits among European criminals were also present among Indigenous people in the colonies. For Lombroso (2006: 223), this explained 'why [European] convicts mix so easily with primitive peoples in the penal colonies of Australia and French Guyana, adopting their customs, including cannibalism'. Animalistic tendencies in Australian Aboriginal habits, including mothers killing their babies to avoid feeding them, were identified by Lombroso (2006: 178) to prove his connection between European murders and primitive people. In describing European criminals, Lombroso's (2006: 57) reference to Australian 'aborigines' is again overt:

> Prognathism, thick and crisp hair, thin beards, dark skin, pointed skulls, oblique eyes, small craniums, overdeveloped jaws, receding foreheads, large ears, similarity between the sexes, muscular weaknesses – all these characteristics confirm the findings from autopsies to demonstrate that European criminals bear a strong racial resemblance to Australian aborigines and Mongols.

Embedded in Lombroso's 'science' is a policy agenda in support of the death penalty – aimed at European criminals as well as primitive people in uncivilised populations. Those who commit crimes due to their animalistic instincts can only be addressed through eradication (Lombroso 2006: 180). Their criminal biologism could not be dealt with through rehabilitation or punishment with a view to deterrence. The social Darwinist thrust of this policy is lucid:

> To claim that the death sentence contradicts the laws of nature is to feign ignorance of the fact that progress in the animal world, and therefore the human world, is based on a struggle for existence that involves hideous massacres. Born criminals, programmed to do harm, are atavistic reproductions of not only savage men but also the most ferocious carnivores and rodents. This discovery should not make us more compassionate toward born criminals (as some claim), but rather should shield us from pity, for these beings are members of not our species but the species of bloodthirsty beasts (Lombroso 2006: 348).

Therefore, Lombroso's positivist approach (studies of prisoners' physical characteristics) is steeped in support for a coercive and colonial state regime. Staples (1975: 15) argues that criminology's race models, including Lombroso's, serve as a form of oppression against Indigenous people and 'black' people. It regulates the colonial relationship by legitimating subordination of these groups (1975: 15). This would manifest in draconian colonial policies and selective law enforcement within the colonising world, including through racial profiling that attempts to highlight physical attributes of minority ethnic and Indigenous groups in the search for 'criminals' (Norris 2006: 11; del Pozo 2001).

Lombroso's approach had a direct bearing on psychology's original studies of criminals. Neuroscience researchers conducted, and continue to conduct, inter-racial investigations correlating brain size with anti-social behaviour and intelligence (for example, Herrnstein & Murray 1994). It was not until Freudian psychoanalysis, learning theory and social psychology of the 20th century that observations in relation to inherent racial features took a backseat to identifying learned behavioural characteristics. However, even with this transition, criminology's positivist assumptions would remain intact and support a targeting of groups whose upbringing did not conform to western morality.

Freud's psychoanalysis and other psychological approaches

The enormous influence of Sigmund Freud's personality studies in the 1920s prompted a realigning of the quest in criminology – away from 'nature' explanations of criminal cognition and neuroscience (for example, Raine 1993) and towards the 'nurture' foundations of the criminal personality (although not completely excluding the psychobiological emphasis). Freud (1957) developed an understanding of the personality as constituted by different forces: *id* (the instincts in the unconscious mind that seek gratification, such as aggressive and sexual urges/libido – referred to as the 'pleasure principle'); *ego* (the conscious mind that keeps *id* in check – known as the 'reality principle'), and the *superego* (constituting moral norms and values – providing the guilt function). These forces interact dynamically – competing against each other, and against social norms. Personality is the outcome of these struggles. The interaction – and specifically the development of the *superego* – is particularly crucial in the early years of the individual, therefore making parenting vital.

Criminal personality, according to Freudian criminology, can result, on the one hand, from an inability of the mind to adequately harness *id*, leading to the over-expression of instinctive behaviour. On the other hand, a repressed or under-expressed *id* can lead to neurosis and forms of crime aimed at overcoming feelings of inadequacy and emotional insecurity. In the latter instance, the *ego* may overstep its limits, with a narcissistic need to 'prove oneself' through crime. Or else the *superego* can flourish as an 'unconscious sense of guilt' (Freud 1961: 52). A causal factor of criminal behaviour, therefore, is an individual's need to be punished as a result of an over-developed *superego* and sense of guilt. Yochelson and Samenow (1976: 80) claim that some criminals take risks so they can get caught, which amounts to 'self-punishment'. Crucial to the neutralisation of *id* is parenting that encourages discipline and conformity, that is, fostering a 'healthy' *superego* and *ego*. Neglectful parenting will lead to an over-developed *id*; whereas indulgent parenting will lead to an under-developed *superego*.

Having discerned these dynamics of the criminal personality, the Freudian approach (true to its scientific underpinnings) was focused on putting right the dysfunction. Criminal personality could be treated with psychoanalytic therapy. This movement has been referred to as the genesis of the 'treatment ideal' (Hollin 2002; 148) or the 'what works' model (for example, MacKenzie 2006).

In some respects Freudian criminology has become synonymous with the so-called 'enlightened' or 'humanist' rehabilitation program for criminals, which informed the penal 'welfarist' reforms after WWII and saw the proliferation of 'mental hygiene' institutions for offenders (see Garland 2001; Hale 1995: 87-92). Freud himself wrote in 1931 that the prison system was 'an expression of the brutality and lack of judgment that govern our civilization today' (cited in Anderson 1998: 673). Freudian prison psychiatrist Aschaffenburg (1913: 252, 263) scorned the 'pathetic' doctrine of retribution that underpinned punishment, and evidenced its failure by pointing to the high levels of recidivism among former prison inmates. These approaches are embedded in an assumption that criminals were 'sick'/neurotic individuals. But Freud's contribution is not to be confused with that of the humanist psychologists, including Carl Rogers (1951), who have a metaphysical concept of self-enlightenment, based on the development of empathy and 'self-actualisation' rather than resolving complex conflicts in the criminal mind. Rogers proclaimed that social harmony is achieved when individuals show 'unconditional positive regard' for one another.

Freudian-inspired interventions have been criticised for replacing incarceration with another form of institutionalisation and control (Anderson 1998: 670-671). These 'healing' institutions have been exposed by critics like Goffman (1961) and Foucault (1965) as exerting as oppressive and destructive power over the human person as the penitentiary (also see Furedi 2004). Other criticisms put forward by Anderson (1998) are that the psychoanalytic school was preoccupied with the characteristics of the offender rather than the broader social environment, and the 'neurotic' came to be used so indiscriminately or inconsistently that it became virtually meaningless.

In other respects, Freudian analysis would provide a new rationale for categorising certain individuals as inherently criminal, such as those who do not conform to western notions of good parenting. In particular, suspicion was cast on children who experienced 'maternal deprivation' (Bowlby 1969-1980) as a result of their 'broken homes' (Aichhorn 1936) – which served to criticise divorced couples and single parents, but also the institutionalisation of children (Rutter et al 1998: 15, 185-186). In these environments, children were under-socialised, leading to 'latent delinquency' where the *id* manifested in criminal urges (Aichhorn 1936). Criticisms of neglectful parenting have been appropriated by governments to legitimise state intervention. Notably, the Australian government draws heavily on the alleged over-representation of child neglect in Indigenous communities to justify intervention in the Northern Territory (Brough 2006; also see Richardson 2005).

Over time, criminologists would focus not only on parenting as core to the developmental factors behind criminal behaviour, but also on sociological conditions. These learned behaviour theories, developed instrumentally in Sutherland's (1947) differential association theory, are much more on a par with criminology's contemporary focus on environmental influences, but were not entirely divorced from cognitive understandings of human conduct (see Dotter 2005). Representative of the social learning approach are the experiments conducted by Berkowitz and LePage (1967) where participants who were made angry by a provocateur, were told to administer electric shocks to that provocateur. Half of the participants were in the presence of a shot gun and revolver, while the other half were exposed to badminton racquets. The results showed that significantly more electric shocks were administered in the presence of guns. While this reveals that the environment is an important behavioural factor, it does not consider why this conduct is criminalised. What social learning approaches fail to dissect, which Gorecki (1974: 473) highlights, is the process of criminalisation within a particular society: 'The sweeping theories – in Lombroso's, Freud's and Sutherland's style – provide for explanations which are comprehensively general, parsimonious, and apparently universal'. Moreover, contrary to the Frankfurt School's approach, these theories are unable to grasp the role of the state in the criminalisation process.

The Frankfurt School's politicisation of psycho-criminology

When the Frankfurt School of Social Research, a group of neo-Freudian psycho-analysts, emerged in the late 1920s, they sought to wed a dynamic analysis of the individual to an analysis of the specific condition of society at the time and its criminal tendencies. The School was overtly anti-fascist and developed its critique from this standpoint. Accordingly, it pointed to the impossibility of objective analysis where political bias in the criminal justice system prevails. The School claimed that the psychology of the state was infected by concepts of authoritarianism. Punishment, therefore, is no more than an irrational response to an irrational act; it answers an affect with an affect, despite all pretensions to judge the motives of a criminal act as if it were a normal part of the legal discipline. Punishment, the School posited, does not become rational just because it is studied by scientists (Reiwald 1949).

Researching at a time when fascism was building strength in Western Europe, the School sought to unravel the punitive urges of the state. A Swiss member of the School, Paul Reiwald (1949: 278), stated that not only crime but also criminal justice finds its roots in aggressive and destructive urges. Criminal law has developed 'counter-aggression as justified, formalised and partially subliminated against the unjustified, formless and primitive aggression of the a-social' (1949: 278).

One of the School's leading theorists and a practising psychoanalyst (see Funk 2000), Erich Fromm, expressly demoted the grand criminological question – *How can crime be reduced*? Fromm made this inquiry redundant because the unconscious motives of deemed criminals were unchangeable (Fromm 2000a: 124). Based on this premise, and given that policy-makers were aware of the ineffectiveness of crime measures, Fromm (2000a: 124) asked, *Why do governments persist with their punitive agenda?* This question would structure the School's social critique and the field of critical criminology. The Frankfurt School would address this question with reference to a Freudo-Marxist theoretical framework that looked to social (or societal) personality as a means of understanding state force.

The School sought to demonstrate that 'authoritarianism' is a condition of state legitimacy (see Adorno et al 1950). The authoritarian state would control the social position of individuals. At the same time, through a dialectical process, the authoritarian personality would legitimise the authoritarian state. Fromm (1941: 8) stated, 'to understand the dynamics of the social process, we must understand the dynamics of the psychological processes operating within the individual, just as to understand the individual we must see him in the context of the culture which moulds him'. With Nazi Germany as a backdrop, Adorno (1950: 3) explained fascism with reference to the 'ideological framework of anti-Semitism' and 'an individual's susceptibility to this ideology [which] was based primarily upon his psychological needs'.

The School viewed society historically, as a developing living organism tantamount to an individual. It had a psychological character – driven by instincts and impulses – as well as a socio-economic character. Society would reinvent itself with changes to its 'libidinal economic base' (Jay 1996) that would inform the dominant personality type or 'social personality'. The Frankfurt School attributed to capitalism the *authoritarian* social personality, and its complement, the *conformist* social personality. The criminal justice system embodies capitalism's authoritarian tendencies, but these tendencies also emerge militarily in times of war. Often the excesses of the criminal justice system and war go hand in hand, such as in Nazi Germany, and reflect a society giving into its basic instincts. In *Escape from Freedom*, Fromm (1941) observed conformism, authoritarianism and destructivism as reactions to the isolation, alienation, and bewilderment in society.

In his criminological writings from 1930-1931, which have only recently been published in English, Fromm (2000b: 145) claimed that punishment and deterrence is not focused on 'the potential criminal'; but has a 'sociopsychological' function. Criminal justice is an 'important agent of legitimation', whereby the state imposes itself as a 'father figure to the mass of the population' (cited in Anderson 1998: 680). The authority of the criminal justice system instils in the unconscious of the masses that 'existing social relations are necessary' and 'grounded in the superior insight and wisdom of the rulers' (Fromm 2000a: 125). The father confronts the child with fear of his physical and mental superiority, which leads to tension and conflict, but 'frequently the child makes the best of his situation when he succeeds in transforming into admiring worship his aversion toward the forbidding father' (Fromm 2000a: 125). This is the very attitude 'that the state desires and considers necessary among the great mass of its citizens' (Fromm 2000a: 125). Therefore, the criminal justice reproduces both physically and psychologically the father's punitive role (cited in Anderson 1998: 684).

The legitimising function of the criminal justice system also serves the propertied ruling class. According to Fromm (2000b: 145), the punitive fatherly state would internalise the masses' fear, such that it could be transferred to obedience to the 'ruling class'. This was necessary for the preservation of 'social stability in class society' (Fromm 2000b: 145). Thus the criminal justice system legitimises state power and social relations as a whole.

Moreover, punishment gratifies the 'sadistic impulses' of the masses (Fromm 2000a: 126) and thus diverts mass anger away from the state and ruling classes. The criminal becomes the target of the masses' pent-up rage; a rage that stems from the masses' sexual and economic deprivation. In seeking to explain this hostility to the powerless, Adorno et al (1950: 971) claim that 'a basically hierarchical, authoritarian, exploitative parent-child relationship' leads to 'a disdainful rejection of whatever is relegated to the bottom'. Lynn Chancer (1992) picks up on Fromm's ideas in explaining the mass psychology of crime: 'individuals often acquiesce to the powerful in a masochistic fashion and then act in a sadistic fashion towards the powerless'. This is echoed in Garland's (1990: 238) argument that modern society has 'an emotionally laden fascination with crime and punishment and sometimes a deep susceptibility for the rhetorical appeals of authoritarian penal policies'.

The inquiry of the Frankfurt school has been carried on in branches of critical criminology research (see Stubbs this volume), and manifests specifically in the studies of Arendt (1951) and Mark Brown (this volume). However, its call for social change and its humanist legacy has often been forgotten.

The humanist legacy of the Frankfurt School

Although critical criminology shies away from a 'what works' approach (preferring to question 'what does not work'); the psychoanalytic background of the Frankfurt

School predisposed it to considerations of treatment. The School sought to cure the neurosis of capitalism in terms of its authoritarian personality. This societal character could be humanised by treating the supporters of the regime – particularly through social learning. On the one hand, freedom of expression and individuality should be promoted (Reiwald 1949) above the domination of markets and repression (Lasch 1979; Fromm 1941). On the other hand, parents should be taught to bring up their children with humanist values (Adorno et al 1950). These changes would harness *id* and discipline the *superego*'s humane morality. The eventual outcome perceived by the Frankfurt School would be a peaceful and harmonious society free of crime and violence.

In a circular argument, Reiwald (1949: 302) proclaimed that the authoritarian personality could be abandoned with the renunciation of punitive measures. Reiwald (1949: 303, quoting Auguste Forel) stated, 'the future of criminal law lies in its abrogation; that is, in the removal of any right to punish'. The penal (ir-)rationale fosters the authoritarian personality and is therefore the enemy of democracy (Reiwald 1949). Similarly, Fromm (1963: 103) claimed that capitalism's 'sick, diseased and neurotic' personality could be made into a 'sane society' with humanist psychoanalysis. The abolition of alienation, loneliness and helplessness, and the formation of 'socialist humanism' would enable individuals to realise their inner potential, such that they would not need to sadomise the 'criminal'. Fromm supports a society guided by maternal love rather than paternal punishment (Radosh 2000: 78). Some feminists have criticised this approach for essentialising women (Mills 1987), while others have praised its 'humanistic values' (Radosh 2000: 79). Christopher Lasch (1977, 1979) alternatively identifies an increase in maternalism in middle-class families, and the relative decline of strong support and guidance offered by paternal care-givers. This phenomenon is said to have played a decisive role in the emergence of a culture of emotionally 'empty' and inward looking individuals. For Lasch (1977: 156), the authoritarian personality of early capitalism has been superseded by the narcissistic personality of advanced capitalism.

The Frankfurt School's arguments for social change face an inherent obstacle: how do humans free themselves from their authoritarian personalities if such personalities stem from 'unconscious' psychology within the authoritarian context? (Salov 1974). Moreover, how does a sick, diseased society arrive at or realise the idea of a sane society? (Dobrenkov 1976: 141). These contradictions reveal the psychologistic origins of the School that preclude a sociological analysis of change beyond the individual.

Adorno et al (1950: 12), in their empirical treatment of the authoritarian personality, also entertained humanist ideas. Based on interviews, clinical techniques and questionnaires with 'potentially antidemocratic individuals', their research concluded: 'All that is really essential is that children be genuinely loved and treated as individual humans' (1950: 975). This would involve educating parents on modern theories regarding the 'correct' upbringing with values compatible with an ideal society. It would mark a departure from adults' tendency to ethnocentrism and authoritarianism (1950: 973). However Adorno et al (1950: 975) admitted that parents would 'exhibit in their relations with their children much the same moralistically punitive attitudes that they express towards minority groups' and thus 'the modification of the potentially fascist structure cannot be achieved by psychological means alone'. This problem 'requires the efforts of all social scientists'.

These conclusions have attracted criticisms that the School's hypothesis is lacking 'concrete, praxical forms that could help sociologists, criminologists, politicians and practitioners to adopt critical practices in the criminal justice system' (Hall 2002: 183). Marxists such as Brecht condemned the School's education remedies that promote tolerance and harmony, for overlooking the need for revolutionary change to the economy and culture (cited in Jay 1996: 227; also see Brown 1974: 72; Wells 1963: 103).

Moreover, the Frankfurt School's vision of 'social humanism' and notions of a 'sane human consciousness' have been criticised for its 'speculative abstraction' (Hall 2002: 183). The lived experiences of individuals are overshadowed by these social forces (Tucker & Treno 1980; Valadez & Clignet 1987; Bell 1960). The expression of social personality can also be viewed as predicated on a unitary notion of the state that excludes multiple agencies and *governmentalities* (see Rose et al 2006: 85).

The vision of the Frankfurt School towards a humanitarian society, nevertheless, is a clear call for the abandonment of authoritarianism at a time when complicity would have been a less daring position. The renunciation of society's coercive apparatus was a pressing concern of the Frankfurt School who were experiencing the excesses of Nazi Germany. They did not hide behind their anti-fascist standpoint, but used it to expose the brutalities of the criminal justice system and develop a critical theory for which the authoritarian state could be understood. The School's critical approach is timely in our contemporary climate. This is a climate where governments increasingly exercise authority in the realm of criminal law.

Conclusion: the Frankfurt School's ongoing impact on critical criminology

This chapter has considered the development of psychological theories of crime from Lombroso to the neo-Freudians. What becomes clear, in light of the Frankfurt School, is that the School's predecessors in psychology actually legitimised the state's crime function through their inquiry into individual criminal fault, causes and cures. These classic psycho-criminologies reinforce the scientific understanding of criminals that makes the state's punitive response appear rational.

The Frankfurt School draws on psychology to traverse a different path. They use it to question the significance of the criminal justice system: why does the state criminalise? This question amounted to renouncing the assumptions that the state was fulfilling a rational role of reducing crime by exercising force. The Frankfurt School consciously sought to reduce this force by replacing fascism with a humane society. Only with social change could violence and force, which was associated with the authoritarian personality, be removed from society.

The Frankfurt School's critique of positivism and state control laid the foundations for critical criminology, which would go on to interrogate the state and corporations as criminals in their own right (see Stanley, Grewcock and Hocking & Guy this volume). While the Frankfurt School may be seen as limited by the concept of psychoanalytic treatment of social personality (based on treating one individual at a time) rather than restructuring socio-economic institutions, its inquiry is nonetheless dramatically different to orthodox criminology. It replaces the classic question of 'why does the individual commit crime?', with the critical questions of 'why does the state punish?' and 'why does the individual condone the punitive state?'. These questions were not posed with neutrality, but with a conscious objection to the authoritarian state.

References

Adorno, TW, Frenkel-Brunswik, E, Levinson, DJ, & Sanford, RN 1950, *The Authoritarian Personality,* Vol 1 & 2, Harper Books, New York.

Aichhorn, A 1936, *Wayward Youth,* with foreword by Freud, S, Meridian Books, New York.

Anderson, K 1998, 'The Young Erich Fromm's Contribution to Criminology', 15(4) *Justice Quarterly* 667.

Arendt, H 1951, *The Origins of Totalitarianism*, Schocken Books, New York.

Aschaffenburg, G 1913, *Crime and its Repression,* translated by Albrecht, A, Little & Brown, Boston.

Bell, D 1960, *The End of Ideology: on the exhaustion of political ideas in the fifties,* Free Press, Glenncoe.

Berkowitz, L & LePage, A 1967, 'Weapons as Aggression-Eliciting Stimuli', 7 *Journal of Personality and Social Psychology* 202.

Bowlby, J 1969-1980, *Attachment and Loss,* 3 vols, Basic Books, New York.

Brough, M 2006, *Communique – Safer Kids, Safer Communities*, 26 June, <www.facsia.gov.au/internet/minister3.nsf/content/safer_kids_communique_Jun06.htm>

Brown, P 1974, *Toward a Marxist Psychology*, Harper Colophon Books, New York.

Chancer, L 1992, *Sado-Masochism in Everyday Life*, Rutgers University Press, New Brunswick.

del Pozo, B 2001, 'Guided by Race: an ethical and policy analysis of racial profiling in law enforcement decision-making', 19 *QUT Law and Justice Journal* 266.

Dobrenkov, VI 1976, *Neo-Freudians in Search of 'Truth',* translated by Judelson, K, Progress Publishers, Moscow.

Dotter, D 2005, 'Developing the Criminal Self: Mead's social psychology and Sutherland's differential association', 25(4) Sociological Spectrum 379.

Foucault, M 1965, *Madness and Civilization*, Random House, New York.

Freud, S 1957, 'Civilization and its Discontents', in Strachey, J (ed), *The Standard Edition of the Complete Psychological Works of Sigmund Freud,* Vol XXI, Hogarth, London.

Freud, S 1961, 'The Ego and the Id', in Strachey, J (ed), *The Standard Edition of the Complete Psychological Works of Sigmund Freud*, Vol XXIX, Hogarth, London.

Fromm, E 1941, *Escape from Freedom*, Farrar & Rinehart, New York.

Fromm, E 1963, *The Dogma of Christ and other Essays on Religion, Psychology and Culture*, Routledge & Kegan Paul, London.

Fromm, E 2000a, 'The State as Educator: on the psychology of criminal justice (1930)', in Anderson, K & Quinney R (eds), *Erich Fromm and Critical Criminology: beyond the punitive society*, University of Illinois Press, Urbana.

Fromm, E 2000b, 'On the Psychology of the Criminal and the Punitive Society (1931)', in Anderson, K & Quinney R (eds), *Erich Fromm and Critical Criminology: beyond the punitive society*, University of Illinois Press, Urbana.

Funk, R 2000, 'Erich Fromm's Life and Work', in Anderson, K & Quinney R (eds), *Erich Fromm and Critical Criminology: beyond the punitive society*, University of Illinois Press, Urbana.

Furedi, F 2004, *Therapy Culture*, Routledge, London.

Garland, D 1990, *Punishment and Modern Society: a study in social theory*, Clarendon, Oxford.

Garland, D 2001, *Culture of Control: crime and social order in contemporary society*, Oxford University Press, Oxford.

Goffman, E 1961, *Asylums*, Doubleday, New York.

Gorecki, J 1974, 'Crime Causation Theories: failures and perspectives', 25(4) *The British Journal of Sociology* 461.

Hale, NG 1995, *The Rise and Crisis of Psychoanalysis in the United States: Freud and the Americans, 1971-1985*, Oxford University Press, New York.

Hall, S 2002, 'Erich Fromm and Critical Criminology: beyond the punitive society – book review', 76 *Capital and Class* 182.

Hayward, K 2005, 'Psychology and Crime: understanding the interface', in Hale, C, Hayward, K, Wahidin, A & Wincup, E (eds), *Criminology*, Oxford University Press, Oxford.

Herrnstein, RJ & Murray, C 1994, *The Bell Curve,* Free Press, New York.

Hollin, CR 2002, 'Criminological Psychology' in Maguire, M, Morgan, R & Reiner, R (eds), *Oxford Handbook of Criminology,* Oxford University Press, Oxford.

Hudson, B 2000, 'Critical Reflection as Research Methodology', in Jupp, V, Davies, P & Francis, P (eds), *Doing Criminological Research,* Sage, London.

Jay, M 1996, *The Dialectical Imagination: a history of the Frankfurt School and the Institute of Social Research 1923-1950,* University of California Press, Berkeley.

Lacan, J 1996, 'A Theoretical Introduction to the Functions of Psychoanalysis in Criminology', translated by Bracher, M, Grigg, R & Samuels, R, 1(2) *Journal for the Psychoanalysis of Culture and Society* 13.

Lasch, C 1977, *Haven in a heartless world: the family besieged*, New York, Norton.

Lasch, C 1979, *The Culture of Narcissism: American life in an age of diminishing expectations,* Norton, New York.

Lombroso, C 2006, *Criminal Man*, translated by Gibson, M & Rafter, NH, Duke University Press, Durham.

MacKenzie, DL 2006, *What Works in Corrections: reducing the criminal activities of offenders and delinquents*, Cambridge University Press, Cambridge.

Mills, P 1987, *Women, Nature and Psyche*, Yale University Press, New Haven.

Norris, G 2006, 'Criminal Profiling: a continuing history', in Petherick, W (ed), *Serial Crime: theoretical and practical issues in behavioral profiling*, Elsevier & Academic Press, Burlington.

Plato 1997, 'On Justice', in Cooper, JM & Hutchinson, DS (eds), *Plato: complete works*, Hackett, Indianapolis.

Radosh, PF 2000 'Gender, Social Character, Cultural Forces, and the Importance of Love: Erich Fromm's theories applied to patterns of crime', in Anderson, K & Quinney R (eds), *Erich Fromm and Critical Criminology: beyond the punitive society*, University of Illinois Press, Urbana.

Raine, A 1993, *The Psychopathology of Crime: criminal behavior as a clinical disorder*, Academic Press, San Diego.

Reiwald, J 1949, *Society and its Offenders*, translated by James, TE, Heinemann, London.

Richardson, N 2005, *Child Abuse and Neglect in Indigenous Australian Communities*, Australian Institute of Family Studies, <www.aifs.gov.au/nch/pubs/sheets/rs10/rs10.html>.

Rogers, C 1951, *Client-Centered Therapy: its current practice, implications and theory*, Constable, London.

Rose, N, O'Malley, P & Valverde, M 2006, 'Governmentality', 2 *Annual Review of Law and Social Science* 83.

Rutter, M, Giller, H & Hagell, A 1998, *Antisocial Behaviour by Young People*, Cambridge University Press, Cambridge.

Salov, V 1974, 'Psychoanalysis and History', 5 *Social Sciences* 177.

Staples, R 1975, 'White Racism, Black Crime, and American Justice: an application of the colonial model to explain crime and race', 36(1) *Phylon* 14.

Sutherland, E 1947, *Principles of Criminology*, JB Lippincott, Philadelphia.

Taylor, I, Walton P & Young J 1973, *The New Criminology: for a social theory of deviancy*, Routledge, London.

Tucker, K & Treno, A 1980, 'The Culture of Narcissism and the Critical Tradition: an interpretive essay', 24 *Berkeley Journal of Sociology* 341.

Valadez, J, & Clignet, R 1987, 'On the Ambiguities of Sociological Analysis of the Culture of Narcissism', 28 *The Sociological Quarterly* 455.

van Swaaningen, R 1997, *Critical Criminology: visions from Europe*, Sage, London.

Wells, HK 1963, *The Failure of Psychoanalysis: from Freud to Fromm*, International Publishers, New York.

Yochelson, S & Samenow, SE 1976, *The Criminal Personality, Vol 1: a profile for change*, Jason Aronson, New York.

5

NEO-LIBERALISM AND RISK IN CRIMINOLOGY

Pat O'Malley

Introduction: the risk society thesis

The 'risk society' is a concept that crosses many academic disciplines. It is a vision of the present times in which risk consciousness pervades society. According to this concept, risk management becomes increasingly central as a technique used to govern all manner of problems. The development of risk in the health field for example is hard to ignore as we are constantly bombarded with information about risks in our diet, the need to examine family histories for risk factors, the importance of exercise in health risk reduction and so on. Statistical evidence is gathered, correlations between 'risk factors' and harmful outcomes are identified, and emphasis is placed on intervening to prevent the occurrence of the harm. Much the same is true for transportation, where, for example, armies of crash test dummies are sacrificed in the name of vehicle risk reduction. Sport, finance, industrial safety, the education system and crime control have all become shaped by risk reduction techniques. As this chapter will reveal, in Australia and New Zealand – and to a lesser extent the United Kingdom – the governance of illicit drugs may be dealt with in terms of the risks that drug use represents and, in theory at least, this focus may subordinate the more generally accepted resort to criminal justice, or even displace it where justice interventions are seen to heighten risks to the user or to others.

In the most influential account, Ulrich Beck (1992, 1997) has argued that the risk society is created by the development of 'modernization risks'. These are created by the unholy marriage of science and capitalism that drives innovation forward before we can consider its full implications. Typified by the threat of nuclear contamination, global warming, global financial meltdown in the networked economy, holes in the ozone layer and possible terrorist attacks on the infrastructure of whole cities, these new risks are catastrophic in their impact. At the same time – ironically for the 'risk' society – they are not statistically predictable. Put simply, because these are non-recurring events, or events that unfold so quickly or invisibly that we cannot gather data on them beforehand, they cannot be predicted using statistical risk techniques. Because of the global scale of risks, institutions such as the family, trade unions and national governments – including the welfare state that is itself based on risk management – begin to lose their functions. Thus while risks grow, individuals are thrown back upon their own resources more and more. In this environment, people become more conscious of the riskiness of life, and demand more information about the risks they face. Risk techniques develop in pace with this demand, but this only breeds more insecurity as new risks are discovered all the time. This, says Beck, is the risk society.

Some criminologists have picked up on this theory in order to understand major changes that have been occurring in the field of crime control. The most influential of such accounts has been Ericson and Haggerty's (1998) *Policing the Risk Society*. They see in the present a fundamental shift in the work of police. Police have always been recorders of information relating to security, but Ericson and Haggerty see this role as becoming police forces' *central* task. They take as a key point of departure Beck's depiction of the risk society as the 'information society' – a society in which increasing demands for security create ever increasing needs for information. Clearly police are a pivotal agency of security. Consequently, they argue, police adopt a strategic position as security-knowledge brokers: gathering risk-related information, sorting and interpreting such knowledge, and forwarding it to relevant institutions.

Most police work is now focused *neither* on crime control (probably it never was), *nor* on order maintenance and social service, but on informational transactions concerned with risk. Central to this work is the filling in and processing of forms, and the entering of these data into computers, all of which represent tightly structured 'communication formats'. Such communication formats are fundamental to understanding the change in policing, it is argued, for they serve to define the relevant dimensions of policed (or governed) events. Report sheets, for example, increasingly are structured around issues of risk, thus shaping the information that can be recorded: other information cannot be registered (Ericson & Haggerty 1998: 356-412). Risk becomes the way problems are coded. Police and crime are thus restructured in the risk society.

From risk society to neo-liberalism

Despite the enormous impact of Ericson and Haggerty's (1998) book, comparatively few criminologists have deployed the full-blown Beck theory of the risk society when attempting to interpret current developments in crime control. One reason for this, is that Beck's (1992, 1997) theory itself is rather all-encompassing, a grand theory that reduces complex phenomena (well beyond the world of crime) to effects of one grand contradiction. As well, by implication under such a theory any effort to resist or change what is going on has to address the global order, in particular the nexus between capitalism and science that Beck sees as driving this process. This seems a rather massive and long-term process, when many criminologists are more concerned to consider and deal with specific changes in crime control associated with risk frameworks. A closely linked problem is that some criminologists find the theory too abstract to explain the specific nature of changes in risk that are taking place. That is, while the rise of risk may be vitally important, criminologists may be more concerned with the particular ways in which risk is used – and to understand this we need more specific theoretical tools than a theory of a catastrophic change in the world order. For such reasons, increasing attention has been paid to the ways in which risk has been promoted and shaped by more immediate political processes.

Beginning in the early 1990s, criminologists began to interpret many changes across the domain of crime control as reflecting the ascendancy of neo-liberalism. Broadly speaking, neo-liberalism is said be distinguished by a series of central concerns, which may be summarised as follows:

- an attack on state-centred governance, expounding a view that the interventionist state crippled economic dynamism by over-regulation, and by diverting potentially profitable activities into non-profit state agencies;
- an assault on the welfare state and on the welfare expertise that is seen as generating a culture of dependency rather than activity and independence, and as destroying individual freedom and responsibility by inserting technocratic governance into all walks of private life;
- the advocacy of the market as a model for most social order (including most surviving 'state' operations), advocacy of the business enterprise as a model for organisational and individual activity, and idealisation of the entrepreneur as the model for preferred individual self-governance;
- promotion of business-like relations, especially the formation of contractual and quasi-contractual relationships such as 'partnerships' between state and non-state agencies;
- an emphasis on cost-effective, pragmatic, results-based government, coupled with accountability at all levels, and especially a desire to make government accountable for expenditure and productivity;
- the reaffirmation of individual responsibility and of the responsibility of families and communities for the government of their own affairs; and
- an affirmation of 'freedom of choice', including choice in relation to consumption as a market-provided reward for success.

Critical criminologists in Australia and elsewhere noted that from the 1980s these neo-liberal principles could be detected in reforms of policing, sentencing and penal practice. Police, for example, had to introduce new managerial principles that reflected a business environment. These were associated with outsourcing many tasks such as transporting prisoners and operating red light cameras, performing security work under contract in order to increase income, and becoming more responsive to their 'customers' through public audits and a 'service' mentality (O'Malley 1997; O'Malley & Palmer 1996).

The criminal justice sector was swept by an array of prison privatisations, and the wider-spread privatising of services such as institutional catering. Competitive tendering was introduced as a means of ensuring its own efficiency even where privatisation was not required (O'Malley 1994). Many sanctions changed to reflect this political environment, with the appearance of behaviour 'contracts' between justice agencies and young people (and often their parents), 'enterprising prisoner' schemes where offenders were given responsibility for their own improvement, and reparation schemes whereby offenders compensated victims for harms caused (O'Malley 1999). Greater stress was placed on the individual responsibility of offenders. The centrality of 'welfare' therapeutic issues in sentencing and corrections began to be changed in favour of more retributive sanctioning that regarded offenders not as the victims of pathology or social inequality, but as rational choice actors who should be held to account for their misdeeds. Linked with this, a more critical stance was taken with respect to whether such therapeutics had ever succeeded in reforming prisoners, leading to greater stress on more 'cost effective' models of imprisonment as simple incarceration (O'Malley 1992).

While neo-liberals often argued that they were in favour of a 'small state' and less 'state intervention', the process was far more complex. While certain 'services' were privatised and outsourced, and while community involvement and private security were developed, there was no diminution in the state sector of crime control. Rather, crime control has been refocused in terms of 'stronger' and more 'efficient' state agencies responsive to populist demands.

In this environment, perhaps it was not surprising that criminologists began to pay attention not simply to the spread of risk in criminal justice, but also to the fact that this process was strongly characterised by developments that reflected neo-liberal political rationalities. Perhaps the first shift of this sort was the changing prominence and nature of crime prevention.

Risk techniques in crime prevention

Crime prevention before the 1970s had been a relatively marginal exercise as far as crime control was concerned. For police, it was largely regarded as a by-product of police patrols and the deterrent effect of successful detection, arrest and conviction. Police resisted the formation of specialist crime prevention officers even though the insurance industry, for example, had long pressed for this (O'Malley & Hutchinson 2007). More broadly, crime prevention appeared more or less buried within the array of welfare state interventions, as part of long-term programs to address 'social problems' including the causes of crime, notably understood as inadequate socialisation and disrupted families, poor education, socio-economic disadvantage and community breakdown. This latter field of crime prevention reflected a mainstream criminology that was well entrenched not only in academic departments – where it had become the norm – but also in the welfare state. Here it sat well with the social and psychological experts and practitioners who strongly influenced state policy and practice at the time. In other words, criminologists were key players in what passed for crime prevention as well as for much practice in the criminal justice system.

During the 1980s, both of these approaches to crime prevention began to change. On the one hand, police became much more focused on crime prevention, commonly suggesting that this was a response to rising crime rates. As the then Victorian Police Commissioner said, police have increasingly 'moved away from simply trying to catch crooks' and now are 'trying to stop people becoming crooks in the first place' (*The Age*). In this respect, the Victoria Police, like the other Australian police forces travelling the same road, was not so much innovating new solutions, as following in the footsteps of United Kingdom policing developments. There, police resistance to crime prevention had been marked, partly because it did not fit with the masculine-heroic culture of modern policing. But eventually this was overcome by neo-liberal governments insisting on such changes as part of a raft of reforms making police more responsive to community demands and business needs emphasising prevention over 'cure' (O'Malley & Hutchinson 2007). Perhaps seeing the writing on the wall, Australian police followed suit, and adopted forms of crime prevention that reflected such neo-liberal concerns.

As suggested, neo-liberals were convinced that there was a need for individuals and communities to take over increased responsibility for their own governance. At the most general level the claim was made that police had been delivered responsibilities for crime minimisation that were never 'traditionally' their duty. Communities and individuals were urged to become 'active' on their own behalf, and (in another example of business ideologies) to form 'partnerships' with police in crime prevention (Vicsafe 1992; Victorian Coalition 1992). Neighbourhood Watch was a particularly favoured model, as were Police Community Consultative Committees, because they localised protection. By implication, 'communities', whether spatial 'neighbourhoods' or more dispersed units such as the 'small business community', were not so much existing social networks as deliberately created entities that were an implement of neo-liberal governance (Rose 1996b).

What was clear to critical criminologists was the nexus between community governance and neo-liberal politics. In the neo-liberal vision, those communities and individuals that mobilised most effectively on their own behalf would achieve the best protection against crime risks. At the same time, in line with the same ethos, police shifted their role (at least in theory) from being simply the guardians of civil society to 'empowering' citizens by providing them with information, advice and support. In short, the shifts were associated with specific political arguments that individuals were morally obliged to protect themselves and that the most effective protection would result where individuals partnered or cooperated with the state and police while acting on their own behalf.

Such developments pushed risk to the foreground, in the process also decentering offenders and promoting victims to a central place in crime control. In marked contrast to social welfare crime prevention, where offenders' problems and pathologies were the focus, here the offender merely appears as the abstract 'other' to be guarded against. One of the characteristic features of the time was the development of 'victimology' to take its place alongside criminology, complete with its own journals and conferences. In this victim territory, neo-liberal concerns with the customers of justice, and the concerns of certain critical criminologists such as Left Realists and some feminist criminologists converged (Matthews & Young 1992a, 1992b; Stanko 1990). The result, it should be stressed, was not always that intended by these critical voices. For example, as Stanko (1996) was to point out, crime prevention 'advice' for women rendered them responsible for their own security while at the same time providing them with gender-biased risk information that both restricted their freedom of movement in public places, and ignored the risks associated with women's safety and security in the domestic environment.

Strengthening the tide against 'welfare' concern for offenders, 'situational crime prevention' increasingly emphasised practices such as 'target hardening' (redesigning houses and streetscapes to minimise crime risks, installation of security hardware etc). Here, the focus is not at all on the offender, for he or she merely appears as an abstract rational choice actor who will (mimicking the neo-liberal hero of the entrepreneur) take opportunities for enrichment wherever they occur. As one of the array of contemporary criminology texts advocating crime prevention in Australia argued:

> A situational approach to crime prevention has rational choice theory as its basis. That is, it rests on the assumptions that offenders freely and actively choose to commit crimes; that the decision to commit crimes is made in response to

immediate circumstances and the immediate situation in which an offence is contemplated; and the motivation to offend is not constant or beyond control, ie it is dependent on a calculation of costs and rewards rather than being the result of inheriting or acquiring a disposition to offend (Geason & Wilson 1988, see also Buchanan & Hartley 1992).

Neo-liberal ideas, in other words, were not simply influencing crime control, but also some of the leading criminologists who were engaged with it – for this orientation was heavily promoted by the Australian Institute of Criminology (see also Geason & Wilson 1989). Indeed this sort of development undercut almost all modern criminology, whether of the positivist sort that focused on social and psychological causation, or of the various more radical types that examined the role of offenders' interpretations and motivations, and the role of class, race and gender inequality. By turning crime into a question of risk-related situations, rational choice offenders and risk-bearing potential victims, this pattern of change in crime prevention had profound implications for the development of criminology and its cognate policy areas (Garland 1996).

Such influences on criminology were reinforced by other interventions of incoming neo-liberal governments. Of significance here was the subjection of the esoteric and mutually disputatious human sciences to the 'transparent' calculative regimes of accounting and management (Rose 1996a). This rendered the disputing disciplines and professions of the welfare state – sociology, psychology, psychiatry, social work and so on – governable and accountable in terms of market-like criteria. Particularly important were cost benefit analyses and related forms of evaluation (Potas et al 1989). Such techniques of accountability – themselves also promoted at the time by the Australian Institute of Criminology – were not likely to support wide-ranging and long term social interventions of the sort favoured by sociological forms of criminology (O'Malley 1992). In quite a large measure this has remained the case, especially as risk techniques have been applied as a means of measuring cost effectiveness: only if interventions reduced the risk of offending over a measurable period of usually no more than a year or so, could they be sustained or even expanded. On the negative side this meant that all criminologically guided and reformist measures came under the regime of risk reduction. The overtones of social welfare rationales that inhabited such measures for at least 60 years were short circuited – at least in theory.

However, there is a danger of exaggerating the change towards neo-liberal risk techniques and unifying its problematic implications. On the positive side what this *did* permit was the continued operation and development of other kinds of disciplinary intervention that had been characteristic of welfarism. Take the example of developmental crime prevention. The characteristic approaches of much criminology in the era of social welfare were modelled primarily in terms of social and individual pathologies requiring intervention by experts who took over responsibility for the problem. In neo-liberal visions, as noted, emphasis is on the danger of such interventions producing powerlessness, apathy and passivity among their clients. Instead, the emphasis is to be on 'accessibility', 'assistance', 'help', 'support' and especially 'empowering'. Such discourses in Australia and elsewhere have emerged in current versions of developmental crime prevention. Thus, with respect to the 'crime risk factor' of abuse, it is stressed that:

The professional focus on the medical model popularised in the 60s' has changed. Now, the notion of community and neighbourhood services to *assist* vulnerable families with child rearing in order to diminish abuse is gathering momentum ... The thrust of our work has been maximising the empowerment of families (Tolley & Tregeagle 1998: 6-8).

Despite these rhetorical shifts, the 'empowering' practices of this born again discipline bear a very strong family resemblance to the interventions of the welfare era – involving 'family support, early intervention, and home visiting programs' (National Crime Prevention 1999a: 17). Likewise, developmental psychology's list of crime-risk factors – 'family isolation', 'inadequate parenting', 'single parents', 'attachment difficulties', 'low self-esteem', 'poor social skills', 'poor cognitive skills' and so on, is seemingly identical with the lists of causes of crime with which such criminologists worked under the welfare state. The preventative and rehabilitative agendas of the former era are thus reintroduced under the sign of risk, ironically, among much fanfare welcoming them as a 'new' approach to crime prevention (see for example, Homel 1998).

In addition, much developmental crime prevention of late has begun explicitly to identify as risk factors the kinds of 'social conditions' identified under welfare programs, social justice and social criminology. Consider the following:

> Children experience different levels and combinations of risk. Social and economic disadvantage, however, bring a host of associated risk factors for children and families. Conditions of poverty contribute to poor health and nutrition and increased levels of family stress. Children born into poverty are also at greater risk of experiencing discrimination and victimization ... While there is much that children and families can accomplish by working together, additional financial resources and supports from governments and communities are necessary to reduce poverty and create environments that promote safety, gender equality and freedom from discrimination (National Crime Prevention of Canada 1997: 10).

The report goes on to recommend that a comprehensive crime prevention strategy provides 'educational, social and health services', and urges that it 'is essential that this strategy address child poverty' (1997: 11). Perhaps this example is unusual in that it specifically discounts self-help and community governance, but the general tenor of its argument is not at all uncommon. Thus, the [Australian] National Crime Prevention (1999b: 13) lists 'socio-economic disadvantage', 'population density and housing conditions', 'lack of support services' and 'social or cultural discrimination' among its crime-related 'cultural and community factors'. The agenda, although situated within a risk discourse gives expression to the welfare-social rationalities, and in so doing begins to hint at social justice and certainly of the kinds of socially – rather than individually – ameliorative programs that were associated with the welfare state.

Still, it cannot simply be assumed that whatever is associated with neo-liberalism is somehow reactionary. I have already indicated that some quite diverse political voices were appropriated into this politics, and some effects have been quite positive. In the drug field, for example, the Australian Government since the 1980s had opposed the American model of the War on Drugs, and promoted instead a drug harm minimisation policy. This risk-based framework focused on harms rather than illicit drugs as such – one effect being that alcohol and tobacco appeared as even more problematic than heroin or cocaine. In this light, drug *use* appeared problematic whether licit or illicit. Discourses of 'drug abusers' and 'drug addicts' were marginalised partly for this reason. More important, however, was that these discourses were seen as demonising illicit drug users and thus increasing risks. On the one hand demonisation rendered users less likely to access treatment, and more likely to engage in risky practices, for example using unhygienic places to administer drugs. On the other, casting drug users as immoral and irrational, 'abusers' and 'addicts' meant that they could not be enlisted into the risk-reduction program. However, by recasting them as rational choice actors in a generalised national culture of drug use, illicit drug users could participate in risk reduction (see generally O'Malley 2004). Indeed, under the aggressively neo-liberal Kennett government in Victoria, criminologists appointed to state drug commissions pushed forward such progressive proposals as increased medical and residential support for users, needle and syringe exchanges, and selective legalisation of drugs (Premier's Drug Advisory Council 1996).

Criminology thus needs to recognise not only that neo-liberalism shapes risk, but equally that this does not in itself necessarily close off any avenues toward optimistic risk-based programs of governance. This is an issue because David Garland's highly influential but unremittingly pessimistic vision of *The Culture of Control* (2001) sees risk as a major tool in the abandonment of the program of penal modernism. He completely focuses on the ways in which risk techniques promote mere control rather than the optimistic reformism of the welfare era, and subject any surviving therapeutic of social amelioration to sustained erosion. In light of the above, this pessimism can be queried, and a more politically thoughtful approach adopted. As Lucia Zedner (2002) has urged, there are great dangers in promoting exaggerated dystopian accounts of this kind. Such 'criminologies of catastrophe' are dangerous (O'Malley 2000). A whole generation of criminologists is being educated and trained in the shadow of such pessimism, whereas it can be argued that the terrain of crime control is a good deal less stable and more optimistic than would be supposed from such interpretations.

The intention is not to suggest that social criminology and welfare programs have returned to dominance in crime prevention – nor even to suggest that mere restoration of the welfare state is a solution to all ills. Tying crime prevention programs to demonstrable and cost-effective risk reduction undoubtedly has changed the general ethos and character of the whole field of crime prevention. Returning power to technocratic expertise is no less dangerous than in the 1960s. But the fields of developmental criminology and of drug harm minimisation can also be thought of as examples of successful struggles against negation. They are points of possible transition in which seemingly discarded elements of therapeutic and constructive offender-oriented policy and knowledge are brought back by resistant disciplines and agendas to re-'socialise' risk. The space for resistant politics, in other words, has to be left open in a critical criminology. This is one of the key implications of studying risk in terms of neo-liberalism *as a contestable political rationality,* rather than envisioning changes as part of a sweeping global transformation to the risk society. This point needs to be pursued in a slightly different way in relation to risk and criminal justice.

Restricting risk in the criminal justice system

As indicated already, by the early 1990s, the assault on welfare therapeutic practices in the criminal justice system was well underway. Criminological accounts of offending that stressed social breakdown and advocated social assistance and therapeutic aid, implied a reduction of emphasis on the moral accountability of criminals. However, while the neo-liberal preference for individually 'responsibilising' 'just desserts' and more punitive penal reforms was well understood by critical criminologists, in the United States alarming tendencies were detected that married such shifts to the rise of risk-based sanctioning. In a series of influential arguments, Feeley and Simon (1992, 1994) argued that a new 'actuarial justice' was forming. In this 'new penology', sometimes typified by 'Three Strikes and You're Out', sentencing increasingly was shifting away from the traditional model of proportionality with offence toward one that made sentences proportionate to the risk represented by the offender. Long sentences would be handed down where even relatively trivial offences formed part of an offender's profile that made them a risk to society. Coupled with this, the content of the sentence shifted from therapeutic reform toward simple incarceration or incapacitation. The logic as Feeley and Simon (1992, 1994) saw it was one of 'pure risk' – the function of prison or similar sentences such as house arrest and electronic monitoring was not to reform offenders but to render them neutral from a risk point of view. The impact of such reform was to contribute substantially to the soaring rates of imprisonment in the US.

One view is that this 'new penology', as the form of justice consistent with the risk society, will sweep other forms of justice to one side. There is a sense in which risk's advance is inexorable. Thus, a number of Australian States during the 1990s, including Victoria, Queensland, Western Australia and Tasmania, legislated to impose indefinite sentences on offenders convicted of violent crimes – not on the basis of proportionality with the offence, but on the basis of the risk posed to the community.[1] However, such changes have largely been restricted to such offences, which, while serious, are a very small part of the overall pattern of sentencing dispositions. As well, even with respect to such sanctions the response has not been a resort to 'prison warehousing'. Rather, prisoners under incarceration are exposed to a wide array of correctional and therapeutic programs ranging from anger management therapy to group counselling on sexuality. Likewise, while it was argued that risk would sweep aside professional decision-making with respect to parole, this has not happened. In the United Kingdom, for example, the outcomes of risk assessment are just one factor taken into account in decisions to release prisoners on parole: such decisions are still made in the last instance on the basis of professional judgement rather than risk scores. Much the same is true for the deliberative processes of the Adult Parole Board of Victoria, for example. For this Board 'potential risk to the community and/or the individual offender' is estimated along similar clinical and individual-case based lines – while even this bowdlerised 'risk' procedure is only the fourth-mentioned of a dozen factors considered in making decisions. Most of the remaining criteria are made up of the traditional considerations of offender history, professional reports and evaluations from psychiatrists, psychologists and other professionals, as well as representations by the offender or other stakeholders. In short, even in parole contexts – where Pratt (1998) has suggested risk is most likely to become influential in Australasia – the model remains primarily one of individual justice shaped around judicial consideration and the clinical expertise of the human

---

1   *Sentencing Act* 1991 (Vic) s 6A; *Penalties and Sentences Act* 1992 (Qld) s 163; *Sentencing Act* 1995 (WA) Part 14; *Sentencing Act* 1997 (Tas) s 19.

sciences. Criminologies and penologies of the social era have not simply been swept away by neo-liberal risk.

Finally, in this respect, as Arie Freiberg (2001) has mapped out in detail, the Australian judiciary has deployed many effective defences against the encroachment of risk-based sentencing agendas. These range from court sentencing principles of individual justice and of proportionality to the offence, to tactics such as the strict construction of statutes in order restrict their impact.[2] Even in the United States, where actuarial sentencing would appear to be most advanced, Simon and Feeley (1995) were soon forced to retract their dire forecasts and work back toward a vision in which risk has had a much more restricted effect. In keeping with what has already been suggested about the complexities of neo-liberalism, as John Pratt (1998: 178) observed some years ago:

> [T]he emphasis on 'rights' and due process of law at the expense of utilitarianism and broader social defence philosophies, during the development of neo-liberalism, seems likely to ensure that there is very little space for [risk-based sentencing and sentences] to be developed as a significant tactic of control in this space for the foreseeable future.

Criminologists have to beware of uncritically accepting catastrophic forecasts in which justice will be completely transformed in the risk society. Among other things, neo-liberalism itself has a more complex relationship to risk than such accounts suggest. To the extent that neo-liberalism has been the ascendant political rationality through which changes in the direction of risk have been mediated, then it is to this politics, rather than to complete transformations of modernity that criminologists might rightly wish to turn.

Conclusions

It is important for criminologists to recognise that risk is never simply a statistical or predictive category driven by objective correlations. The moment risk is deployed as a technique for governing any problem, it must immediately be given shape by selecting which variables to attend to: determining which risks are to be reduced and which ignored; establishing 'unacceptable' levels of risk and acceptable ways of reducing risks; evaluating who should bear risks, and who risk should protect. These decisions are always political, even if they are depoliticised due to neutral language of risk. As Floud and Young (1982) predicted more than 20 years ago, the current wave of risk-based policies in crime control have shifted the burden of risk from victims to offenders. I have argued that this process, in general and in detail, reflects the change from welfare-social politics toward a neo-liberal political rationality. At the same time, I have also stressed that this fact renders risk an object of politics and political resistance in which criminology is itself involved. As seen, while social and psychological criminology were integrated with the policies and practices of social welfare approaches to crime, and have sometimes resisted the negative impact of neo-liberalism, there was no shortage of those who shifted the nature and content of the discipline in the direction of an approach that regarded offenders as rational

---

2   For example, in relation to the meaning of 'prior convictions' to be considered as grounds for risk-based sentencing. Such resistance is not new, and these struggles have been dated by Glaser (1962) back to the 1920s.

choice actors and victims as the rightful subjects of a new defensive social science. Nor was this always 'a bad thing', as drug harm minimisation perhaps suggests.

While this can be seen as reflecting the rise of neo-liberalism, nevertheless left and feminist critics played some role in this transition. This does not imply that they were either complicit or dupes. Rather, it reflects the point raised by Nikolas Rose (1996a) that what emerged as neo-liberalism itself was constituted out of critiques of welfare liberalism raised from both sides of the political fence. This is one reason why it has been so easy for some theorists to argue that these politics now are 'beyond left and right'. But we should also recognise that this same point has meant that neo-liberalism is a rather abstract rationality capable of considerable inter-pretation. We can and should recognise that labour parties around the world have been promoters of the doctrines identified as neo-liberal: notably the Keating Labor government in Australia in the 1990s, and the Blairite New Labour in Britain. In these regimes, social democratic strains as quite visible, as well as neo-liberal themes. We can and should recognise that the formation of the New Right under the Thatcher and Reagan governments, which established neo-liberalism in the English-speaking world, were themselves constituted by uneasy alliances of free-market libe-rals and social authoritarian neo-conservatives. It is out of these regimes that the War on Drugs emerged. The governmental regimes of the 'post-social' world that has emerged since the 1970s exhibit a political diversity as broad as those of the sup-posedly golden era of the welfare state (Rose 1996b). For this reason, the politics of crime control in the past few decades have often taken on a 'volatile and contra-dictory' character that is hard to reconcile with a narrow vision of neo-liberals as free market individualists (O'Malley 1999). Boot camps, the death penalty, the War on Drugs and chain gangs exist in this environment as do 'enterprising prisoner' schemes, restorative justice, drug courts and drug harm minimisation programs. Placing the rise of risk in crime control and criminology within the framework of neo-liberalism – rather than within the context of a 'risk society' – centres politics and its complexities, and highlights the possibility that things can be otherwise. Such a focus helps us see not only how neo-liberal politics shapes risk, and how there is nothing inevitable about the nature and trajectory of risk, but also to see that the con-temporary neo-liberal polity remains a field in which political diversity and political contests are as vital as ever.

References

Beck, U 1992, *Risk Society*, Sage, New York.

Beck, U 1997, *World Risk Society*, Polity Press, London.

Buchanan, C & Hartley, P 1992, *Criminal Choice: the economic theory of crime and its impli-cations for crime control,* Centre for Independent Studies, Canberra.

Ericson, R & Haggerty, K 1998, *Policing the Risk Society,* Clarendon Press, Oxford.

Everingham, S 1998, 'Benefits and Costs of Early Childhood Interventions', in Parliament of NSW (ed), *Crime Prevention through Social Support,* Parliament of NSW Legislative Council, Sydney.

Feeley, M & Simon, J 1992, 'The New Penology: notes on the emerging strategy of cor-rections and its implications', 30(4) *Criminology* 449.

Feeley, M & Simon, J 1994, 'Actuarial Justice: the emerging new criminal law', in Nelken, D (ed), *The Futures of Criminology,* Sage, London.

Floud, J & Young, W 1982, 'Dangerousness and Criminal Justice', 22 *British Journal of Criminology* 213.

Freiberg, A 2001 'Guerillas in our midst? Judicial responses to governing the dangerous', in Brown, M & Pratt, J (eds), *Dangerous Offenders: punishment and social order,* Routledge, London.

Garland, D 1996, 'The Limits of the Sovereign State', 36(4) *British Journal of Criminology* 445.

Garland, D 2001, *The Culture of Control,* Oxford University Press, Oxford.

Geason, S & Wilson, P 1988, *Crime Prevention: theory and practice,* Australian Institute of Criminology, Canberra.

Geason, S & Wilson, P 1989, *Designing Out Crime: crime prevention through environmental design*, Australian Institute of Criminology, Canberra.

Glaser, D 1962, 'Prediction Tables as Accounting Devices for Judges and Parole Boards', 8 *Crime and Delinquency* 239.

Homel, R 1998, 'Pathways to Prevention' in Parliament of NSW (ed), *Crime Prevention Through Social Support*, Parliament of NSW Legislative Council, Sydney.

Matthews, R & Young, J (eds) 1992a, *Rethinking Criminology: the realist debate*, Sage Contemporary Criminology Series, London.

Matthews, R & Young, J (eds) 1992b, *Issues in Realist Criminology*, Sage Contemporary Criminology Series, London.

National Crime Prevention 1999a, *Pathways to Prevention,* National Anti-Crime Strategy, Canberra.

National Crime Prevention 1999b, *Hanging Out: negotiating young people's use of public space*, National Anti-Crime Strategy, Canberra.

National Crime Prevention of Canada (NCPC) 1997, *Preventing Crime by Investing in Families*, NCPC, Ottawa.

O'Malley, P 1992, 'Risk, Power and Crime Prevention', 21 *Economy and Society* 252.

O'Malley, P 1994, 'Neo-Liberal Crime Control: political agendas and the future of crime prevention in Australia', in Chappell, D & Wilson, P (eds), *The Australian Criminal Justice System, The Mid 1990s,* 4th edn, Butterworths, Sydney.

O'Malley, P 1997, 'Policing, Politics and Postmodernity', 6 *Social and Legal Studies* 363.

O'Malley, P 1999, 'Volatile and Contradictory Punishment', 3 *Theoretical Criminology* 175.

O'Malley, P 2000, 'Criminologies of Catastrophe? Understanding Criminal Justice on the Edge of the New Millennium', 33 *Australian and New Zealand Journal of Criminology* 153 (Special Millennium Number).

O'Malley, P 2004, 'The Uncertain Promise of Risk', 37 *Australian and New Zealand Journal of Criminology* 323.

O'Malley, P & Palmer, D 1996, 'Post Keynesian Policing', 25 *Economy and Society* 137.

O'Malley, P & Hutchinson, S 2007, 'Reinventing Prevention: why did crime prevention develop so late?' 47(3) *British Journal of Criminology.*

Potas, I, Vining, A & Wilson, P 1989, *Young People and Crime*, Australian Institute of Criminology, Canberra.

Pratt, J 1998, *Governing the Dangerous,* Federation Press, Sydney.

Premier's Drug Advisory Council (PDAC) 1996, *Drugs in Our Community*, Government Printer, Melbourne.

Rose, N 1996a, 'Governing Advanced Liberal democracies', in Barry, A, Osborne, T & Rose, N (eds), *Foucault and Political Reason,* UCL Press, London.

Rose, N 1996b, 'The Death of the "Social"? Refiguring the territory of government', 25 *Economy and Society* 327.

Simon, J & Feeley, M 1995, 'True Crime: the new penology and public discourse on crime', in Blomberg, T & Cohen, S (eds), *Punishment and Social Control: essays in honor of Sheldon Messinger,* Aldine, New York.

Stanko, E 1990, 'When Precaution is Normal: a feminist critique of crime prevention', in Gelsthorpe, L & Morris, A (eds), *Feminist Perspectives in Criminology,* Open University Press, Milton Keynes.

Stanko, E 1996, 'Warnings to Women. Police Advice and Women's Safety in Britain', 2 *Violence Against Women* 5.

The Age 1992, *New directions for police*, 13 November.

Tolley, S & Tregeagle, S 1998, *Children's Family Centres' Integrated Support Services to Prevent Abuse and Neglect of Children,* Barnardos Australia, Sydney.

Vicsafe 1992, *Practical Crime Prevention*, Victoria Ministry of Police and Emergency Services, Melbourne.

Victorian Coalition 1992, *A Safer Victoria*, Liberal National Coalition, Melbourne.

Zedner, L 2002, 'Dangers of Dystopias in Penal Theory', 22 *Oxford Journal of Legal Studies* 341.

6

CRIME AND SOCIAL THEORY

Robert van Krieken

Introduction

In his foreword to one of the books that launched critical criminology, *The New Criminology*, Gouldner (1973: ix) observed that the book's 'reorienting power' was not just that it drew on bodies of social theory otherwise neglected in criminology, or theorisations of crime overlooked in social theory. What made it important was 'its ability to demonstrate that all studies of crime and deviance, however deeply entrenched in their own technical traditions, are inevitably also grounded in larger, more general social theories which are always present (and consequential) even as unspoken silences'.

It remains, then, an ongoing question how middle-range theories and conceptualisations explain a particular 'technical' criminological problem within a broader understanding of how crime comes about, its relationship to the structuring of social relations, modes of inequality and forms of power, as well as its connection to the fundamental 'nature' or 'character' of contemporary social life. This is especially important when one is attempting to explain how and why things are changing, or why they differ across different countries. It is probably fair to say that it is generally a turn to social theory that makes criminology 'critical', as opposed to approaches influenced by economics or psychology.

Conversely, a number of social and political theorists place an understanding of the origins of criminal behaviour as well as its management (especially punishment) at the centre of their accounts of modernity, seeing the forms taken by punishment as a kind of index to the whole society. *The New Criminology* was in many respects an extension of these arguments to take crime and punishment from the periphery to the very heart of disciplines such as sociology; a plea for the de-naturalising and de-individualising of crime; for perceiving the mechanisms by which deviance and crime are socially constructed and for a broader sociological analysis of modern and now post- or late-modern society.

Since then, criminology has traversed an enormous expanse of theoretical ground, beginning with the Left Realist reactions against an oversimplified construction of criminal justice as an expression of class domination, through the emergence of feminist approaches to criminology (Smart 1976), the Birmingham Centre for Cultural Studies' analysis of the rise of authoritarian policing (Hall et al

1978), the continuing impact of Foucault's *Discipline and Punish* (1977) and the subsequent analyses of the linkages between changing modes of crime management and contemporary forms of governance 'beyond the state', a linguistic and cultural turn, criminologies of postmodernity as well as postmodern criminologies, just to mention a few of the landmarks.

At the same time there have been ongoing debates about the proper empirical concerns of criminology and arguments about shifting its boundaries, often expanding them to include white-collar and corporate crime and state crimes such as genocide, sometimes in the other direction towards decriminalising victimless crimes such as drug use or forced migration, which have also had theoretical effects in requiring new conceptual tools and modes of analysis.

Many of the other chapters in this book will engage with different aspects of criminology's relationship to a range of orientations and concerns in social theory, and this is not the place to attempt any kind of overview or synthesis. What this chapter will do is select some of the central theoretical themes running through contemporary critical criminology and draw out a number of, hopefully provocative, questions that can be raised about those themes. The selection is entirely idiosyncratic; no claims are being made about their centrality or particular salience. One could make equally valid claims about questions such as the importance of re-thinking the relationship between theory and practice in criminology, the problems associated with conceptualising organised (usually state) violence such as genocide as crime, the importance of analysing crime in terms of masculinity, the theoretical issues raised by the increased use of the terms 'regulation' and 'security' and the 'terrorisation of the world', just to mention a few.

The issues I will address are, first, the conceptualisation of the fundamental shifts which many observers see as having taken place in the criminal justice systems of 'late' or 'post' modern societies. Secondly, the continuing role of a logic of 'social control' in criminological understandings of the state and varying modes of governance, power and authority. Thirdly, how the analysis of contemporary patterns of crime and criminal justice might make more effective use of Norbert Elias' (2000) arguments for analysing what we see, experience, and normatively argue for as 'civilisation' in terms of a long-term historical process including mechanisms of 'decivilisation'.

Theorising 'late modernity'

Critical criminology is marked by a number of on-going arguments about the nature of the changes that have taken place in the dominant perceptions of the incidence and control of crime over the last three decades. On the one hand, there are accounts of how the longer-term tendencies of crime control have significantly changed direction (Garland 2001: 3). The continued rise in recorded crime rates in countries such as the United States and England between the 1970s and 1990s is said to have sparked a 'legitimation crisis' for modernist, welfare-state modes of crime control, and the rejection of their correctional and rehabilitative ideals. These changes are seen as all part and parcel of an overall epochal shift 'from modernity to late modernity' (Garland & Sparks 2000), although different writers may use different terminology: advanced liberalism, postmodernity, risk society, or reflexive modernity. One of the more central and productive theoretical concerns has been to analyse the political rationalities – often described as 'neo-liberal' – underlying the governance of crime within a new overarching 'culture of control' (Garland 2001), producing a variety of important and useful analyses of the inner logic of the various new responses to crime and its control characterising late modern societies.

On the other hand, there are at least as many, perhaps more, critical and sceptical responses to this narrative, pointing out the how inconsistent, diverse, differentiated and contradictory the various changes have been, and indicating the wide range of plausible explanations that do not rely on the idea that we have suddenly moved into a fundamentally different kind of social and criminological ordering.

This conceptual opposition runs through most of the literature on the post-1970s developments, which organises itself around a number of core themes, including the emergence of private security (Shearing & Stenning 1983), 'actuarial justice' (Feeley & Simon 1994, 1996), strategies of 'responsibilisation' (O'Malley & Palmer 1996: 142-144) and the 'enterprising prisoner', the increasing recognition of the victim's perspective and voice, restorative justice, the tendency towards the 'warehousing' (Cohen 1977) of prisoners, and increasing punitiveness in the treatment of criminals. The developments in the field of criminal justice are also analysed within the context of broader changes in the concepts, techniques and practices of liberal government more broadly, towards 'advanced liberalism' (Rose & Miller 1992; Rose 1996: 2000) or neo-liberalism.

Between rupture and process

There are a number of reasons to be cautious about the notion of a radically new configuration of crime control, and here I will only touch on a few of them. One is the binary, 'before and after' logic of the argument. In his critique of the earlier attempts to theorise the transition from tradition to modernity, Bendix (1967) pointed out how that the basic logical problem is that many of the supposed typical characteristics of the 'after' period can also be found in the 'before' period, and vice versa. When you look at Garland and Sparks' (2000: 199) outline of what constitutes 'the coming of late modernity', they are all long-term processes of development with no 'before and after', no 'absence/presence'. Garland's (2001) account of the decline of community and informal social control as characterising the transition to late modernity is also exactly what was said to characterise the earlier transition from tradition to modernity (Tönnies 2001) and the development of law, especially criminal law, itself.

Weber (1949: 101) pointed out that we can be tempted to organise our analysis of what are in fact 'developmental processes' in terms of 'ideal types', which do have important analytic value, but also generate 'the danger that the ideal type and reality will be confused with one another'. Garland (1995) himself argued along these lines by insisting that current changes should be analysed as part of an ongoing long-term process of modernisation, rather than as indicating any kind of significant rupture.

Much of the critical response to the idea of a dramatically different 'late modern' construction of crime and criminal justice is reacting to this problem in one way or another. Brown (2005) observes that the argument only works with a romanticised view of the operation of prisons in the supposedly 'penal-welfare' approach to punishment, which never did have much 'welfare' in it, and was no less punitive. Current developments are contradictory, and sometimes move further along the 'penal welfare' road rather than in the opposite direction. Braithwaite (2005) notes that just about all of the supposedly 'late modern' techniques of crime control have been borrowed from business regulation. The initiatives in the field of restorative justice are often attributed to a recent affective turn in criminal justice and the new responsiveness to victims, especially in relation to the management of victim-offender relations in Indigenous communities. However, Braithwaite (2005: 13) makes it clear that for him the logic of restorative justice has a much earlier origin, in 'business regulatory practices oriented to restitution, victim empowerment (tripartism), community policing, coproduction of security and restoration of trust and relationships'.

In general Braithwaite (2005) thinks most of the features of 'late modern' crime control that are seen as reconfiguring the old penal welfare system are best understood as products of the interplay between markets and the institutions created from the mid-19th century (and earlier) to regulate them (Braithwaite & Drahos 2000). An important problem with the concept 'neo-liberalism' is that the practices referred to by the concept generally have much longer roots, generally paralleling the history of liberal political thought and practice itself, but simply across different fields of state and private economic activity. For Braithwaite (2005), the explanation for shifts in the logic of crime control needs to look as much to changes in the forms of criminal behaviour itself, organised along increasingly complex lines with the relevant criminal 'actors' needing to be understood in the same way as any complex organisation, making the paradigms characteristic of business regulation increasingly relevant to crime management overall.

Secondly, are we really more punitive towards an expanding category of law-breakers being defined as 'criminals'? Yes and no – there are certainly good reasons to search for more specific explanations of the punitiveness that can be observed. Although it is true that there is widespread criticism of the leniency of criminal sentences, it is also the case that the closer the average citizen gets to real crimes committed by real human beings, the more likely they are to support precisely the outcome currently delivered by the criminal justice system (Hough & Roberts 1999; Roberts & Stalans 1997). When asked how crime is best prevented, the respondents to Hough and Roberts' (1999: 22) survey were not indifferent to questions of causation and motivation: 20% believed that crime would be most effectively prevented by making sentences tougher, but the majority felt otherwise: 36% felt that increasing discipline in the family was most important, and 25% rated the reduction of unemployment as most important.

In other words, any increase in prison populations should not be attributed simply to an irresistible tendency in public opinion; it is only very partially true that 'masses of people are now emotionally invested in crime control issues and supportive of tougher legislation' (Garland 2001: 146). Incarceration rates continue to vary enormously across 'late modern' societies (Ruggiero et al 1995), and the majority of people in advanced industrial countries still regard, in an old-fashioned penal-welfare state way, a particular ordering of family life and the work ethic as the primary means of preventing crime. The negative view of judges and sentencing practices thus has more to do with the particular nature of the current relationship between the legal system and the surrounding expectations of it than with the real popular position on crime control.

Thirdly, we should be similarly cautious about assertions concerning how fearful everyone has become about crime, as well as about how central crime is to their fearfulness (Lupton 1999; Lee 2007). Although it is correct to point out that whatever fears and anxieties people have about crime can only partially be addressed by engaging with their degree of rationality and objective 'truth' (Lupton & Tulloch 1999), we also need to recall that fear of crime is only one of a whole complex of fears and anxieties, and by no means the central one (Beckett 2001: 907). In their survey of perceptions of risk in Australia, Lupton and Tulloch (2002: 331) found that people were actually more concerned about social divisiveness along class and race lines, high rates of unemployment and the neo-liberalist avoidance of collective responsibility for social welfare. Even where there was fear of crime, this was accompanied by 'an overwhelming trend ... to politicize risk, emphasising the production of social inequity via deliberate government strategy or neglect'.

There are, in other words, a number of ways of conceptualising the changes taking place that do not rely on a 'coming of late modernity' account. Zedner (2007) frames the shift as a temporal one from a post- to a pre-crime society, from primarily responding to wrongs to giving precedence to assessing risks and forestalling them. This transformation necessarily generates different expectations of the state, individuals and communities: in the first logic, the emphasis is on the state, but in the second, responsibility extends beyond the state. For Braithwaite (2005), many of the key changes are translations from other fields of regulation, particularly that of managing business conduct, and he argues that we should think of it in terms of 'regulatory capitalism' rather than neo-liberalism or late modernity. The conceptual problem remains that of grasping the relationship between continuity and change, and of seeing the ways in which shifts from one decade to another fit within longer-term processes of development and change.

Social control: 'use with caution'

The second issue I would like to address is the concept of social control. In Ross's (1901) original formulation, it was used to refer to forms of regulation directed not just downwards towards the criminal classes, but also upwards, towards the emerging large corporations who appeared, unlike most of the rest of society, to be unconstrained by conventions, public opinion, religious sentiment, or cultural prescriptions in their pursuit of economic gain (Spierenburg 2004).

With the critical turn in the late 1960s and 1970s, social control took on a more restricted meaning as a synonym for domination, by capitalism, the state, the ruling class, welfare, psychotherapeutic and criminal justice professionals, and patriarchy (Cohen 1985). However, even as it was being formulated, this 'social control as domination' approach was subjected to various critiques (Ignatieff 1983; van Krieken 1986, 1991; Rose 1987), and the concept is now used in a more subtle way. In criminology, the concerns have been to 'de-centre the state', to observe the salience of mechanisms of control beyond state agencies (private security, etc), built much more extensively into the fabric of social life itself (the market, organisations, etc), and to acknowledge that a great deal of the social control exercised through the criminal justice system is not simply – sometimes not at all – about class domination, since the types of crime at issue operate *within* working-class communities, and reducing crime is actually rather a good idea, not just a capitalist or state authoritarian plot.

Nonetheless, it still appears difficult to shake off the 'control as domination' paradigm, partly because critical criminologists are particularly interested in paying more attention to questions of power and inequality than 'administrative' criminologists. Often this orientation is useful and productive, but equally often it is not. A remaining theoretical issue is how to tell the difference.

One of the ongoing internal criticisms of contemporary critical criminology thus remains that of its 'chicken little' tendencies, towards a 'criminology of catastrophe' (O'Malley 2000) and dystopian visions (Zedner 2002) of the directions being taken by criminal justice and penal policy. As one of the targets of this critique, Garland (2004: 170) responds by suggesting that these critics:

> might reflect on the nonpunitive modes of managing crime that these deep transformations make possible, the new conceptions of culpability, harm and victimisation that they bring into focus, and the progressive (if problematic) potential that they entail for building security in ways that need not depend upon the increase of state power or the reduction of civil liberties.

These suggestions are interesting, but the broader aims of *The Culture of Control*, as Garland (2004) explains, were to analyse how particular regimes of criminal justice come about by relating changes in penal and criminal justice policy to wider transformations in social and cultural conditions, and the substantive analysis leans heavily towards casting those changes as entailing some kind of loss in relation to penal welfarism.

In contrast, Braithwaite (2003) argues that it is important to keep in view the ways in which corporate entities and state agencies are also being subjected to increased regulation, with a close connection operating between privatisation and new regulatory mechanisms, rather than an opposition between free-for-all marketisation and a regulated welfare state. As well as privatisation of the public, we have also seen publicisation of the private (Freeman 2003), and privatisation is generally accompanied by increased regulation (Scott 2002). Braithwaite (2003: 11) argues that the state gets regulated as much as the private sector, and increasingly so. He gives the example of prisons: their privatisation generates calls for new regulatory mechanisms to ensure their adherence to a range of basic legal and ethical principles, but this then generates a critique of the inadequate regulation of state prisons. The broader picture that Braithwaite (2005: 33) draws is one of a more differentiated separation of powers, with a complex network of different state agencies, non-government organisations (NGOs) and corporate actors bound up in a mutually regulating network.

The question of the extent to which the *absence* of social control may be the object of criminological critique has also tended to be underestimated. Pratt (2002) draws our attention to this with reference to the novel, *The Lord of the Flies*, and suggests that another kind of dystopian vision of the future might be not too much social control, but too little that is too poorly organised, with state power replaced with the tyranny of mob rule. In the history of legal systems, state control has frequently operated precisely to protect people from the justice of their peers. The nurturing aspects of community tend to be constitutive of an over-arching normative consensus that often comes at the expense of individuality and diversity. For Punch (1974: 323), the attempt to create structure- and control-free social institutions (specifically free schools like *Summerhill*) was an inherently unstable contradiction in terms, and only possible because of 'the immense normative power exercised by the group over the individual'. The power exercised over 'deviance', wrote Punch (1974: 323), 'may be exercised as thoroughly as in the most sophisticated police state'.

Civilisation

My third concern is the concept of civilisation. For criminologists, the original attraction of Elias' (2000) theory of processes of civilisation was its contribution to explaining how the techniques of punishment and the sensibilities surrounding it had gradually changed over time, becoming less publicly brutal and cruel, without either adopting a Whig view of history, or seeing this development simply as yet another cunning turn in the exercise of power (Pratt 1999, 2002; Garland 1990). One of Elias' central arguments was that what we experience as 'civilisation' is constituted by a particular *habitus* or psychic structure which has changed over time and which can only be understood as linked to changes in the forms taken by broader social relationships. Elias thought that the restraint imposed by increasingly differentiated and complex networks of social relations became increasingly internalised and less dependent on its maintenance by external social institutions, a shift in the balance between external, social compulsion and internal, psychological compulsion towards the latter. This gradual 'rationalisation' of human conduct, its placement at the service of long-term goals and the increasing internalisation of social constraint was, suggested Elias (2000), closely tied to the processes of state-formation and the development of monopolies of physical force.

This account appeared to make good sense of a variety of features of the history of crime and its control between the 13th and 20th centuries. There is general consensus that the history of criminal violence has seen a long-term trend downwards, that social tolerance of violence, aggression, cruelty and brutality has generally declined (Eisner 2001; Gatrell 1980; Garland 1990: 230; Johnson & Monkkonen 1996; Wood 2006; but for a contrary view, see Macfarlane 1987). This did not mean that such violence and brutality disappeared – in relation to prisons, entirely on the contrary (Pratt 1998; Vaughan 2000; Strange 2001). However, it did mean that increasing proportions of the population of Western European countries lost their stomach for the 'spectacle of suffering', a development in mentality, sensibility and culture which left us with an apparently unresolvable 'conflict between a perceived necessity of punishment and an uneasiness at its practice' (Spierenburg 1984: 207). The more recent developments in crime control and punishment, 'the reappearance in official policy of punitive sentiments and expressive gestures that appear oddly archaic and downright anti-modern', are seen as 'confounding' not only the interpretation based on Elias, but also those of the earlier Foucault, Marx and Durkheim (Garland 2001: 3).

However, it is a misconstruction of the analysis of processes of civilisation to see it as an argument simply for the gradual disappearance of emotive punitiveness. The point is that human emotional life becomes enmeshed in ever more complex webs of interdependence, but this does not mean simply that passion gives way to reason. The conflict between the requirements of punishment and discomfort about its reality remains: despite the continued existence of the death penalty in some states of North America, the search for more 'civilised' way of killing continues, no matter how contradictory that notion actually is. Despite the occasional resurgence, public humiliation of prisoners remains exceptional, and where it does appear, it can be explained in terms of the specific social, political and economic history of the region concerned (Pratt 2002: 146-148).

It is true that a central problem left unaddressed by Elias' original analysis was the continuing persistence of violence and aggression even when processes of civilisation could be seen as relatively advanced. One obvious example was the Holocaust, but one could also include the continuing violence inflicted by the prison system (Garland 1990: 236; Strange 2001). It is also true that although punishment became less visible, this did not mean that its violence simply disappeared; rather, it provided fertile ground for internal instability – the 'incomplete' or only 'partial' civilising of the prison (Pratt 1999; Franke 1995; Vaughan 2000; Strange 2001).

Elias (1996) addressed these kinds of questions in his later work, where he looked at the ways in which civilisation and decivilisation occur simultaneously, with monopolies of force being capable of extreme violence as much as situations where the 'means of violence' is more diffusely controlled (Mennell 1990). Elias (1996: 159-60) argued that the integrative effect of norms tend to be emphasised at the expense of their 'dividing and excluding character', and pointed out that social norms had an 'inherently double-edged character', since in the very process of binding some people together, they turn those people against others. Elias (1996) also placed more emphasis in this later work on the essential precariousness of the forms of *habitus* generated by processes of civilisation, drawing attention to the speed with which established forms of restrained, civilised conduct can crumble when the surrounding social conditions become unstable, threatening and fearful.

If we take the phenomenon of 'emotive and ostentatious' punishment, the trend towards punitiveness can, then, be understood as a marker of decivilisation, indicating increased dis-identification across society (Pratt 2000: 422; 1998, 2005, van Swaaningen 1997: 189). The associated social divisiveness can then also be seen as an outcome of a particular mode of dealing with the increasing length of chains of interdependency (Breuer 1991: 405-406). An important aspect of the increase in crime is an ongoing process of change in our own expectations of each other, in turn related to the changing structure and dynamics of social relations. As Wouters (1999: 420) has argued, 'the development of more egalitarian relationships has exerted pressure towards a rise in the moral standard and a higher level of mutually expected self-restraints', in turn meaning that 'departures and transgressions are met with stricter social sanctions'.

The punitiveness of the response to, say, sex offenders, needs to be seen in this light, as part of a changing understanding of what is or is not acceptable in the realm of sexual activity, especially between adults and children, and a relatively new willingness to sanction particular kinds of sexual conduct. Changes in the legal response to rape and domestic violence are part of the same development, and it is important to recognise the specificity of these dimensions of 'popular punitiveness' rather than simply attributing it to the exclusionary politics of neo-liberalism or neo-conservatism, or some obscure welling-up of populist emotiveness. What Young (2007) calls the 'vertigo of late modernity' can also be understood equally well as the demands of on-going processes of civilisation, in Elias' sense of the increasing complexity and density of social relations, and this theoretical orientation can do a lot to overcome the problems associated with the use of concepts like 'late modernity' and 'social control'.

Conclusion

These are just some of the theoretical challenges with which contemporary critical criminology is grappling. Nelken (1994) has argued for the importance of the question of reflexivity for criminology today, both in the sense of the recursiveness of the relationship between criminology and its 'object' – crime and punishment – and in the sense of self-awareness about the sources and origins of criminological debates, their relationship to broader streams of thought in social theory. To the extent that a 'civilised' social life is a core element of both the analytical and normative concerns of criminology, an important aspect of the development of such reflexivity in criminological thought will be a more vigorous engagement with what it means to be civilised.

Part of such a reflexivity, too, will be the extension of the debates around the ways in which criminal behaviour and criminal justice are changing in association with surrounding social changes. For Brown (2005: 103), an important criminological question is that of the broadening of what constitutes 'crime'. The boundaries between crime and other types of harms is becoming harder to sustain, and 'the criminal' is less and less an individual, and increasingly constituted by organisations, indeed networks of organisations, requiring modes of regulation that go beyond what is normally understood as 'policing'.

Many of these issues converge on the question of how the theorisation of crime and punishment should be linked to that of power and control more broadly. In pursuing his argument for seeing all forms of regulation as interconnected, and pointing to its ongoing expansion and growth, Braithwaite (2005: 2) pauses for a moment to highlight the normative question of 'whether this growth in hybrid governance contracts freedom, or expands positive liberty through an architecture of separated power that check and balance state and corporate dominations'. He leaves the question unanswered, and perhaps it is not the best way of putting it, but one important task for a reflexive criminology will be to continue to develop its theoretical engagement with relations and structures of power in analysing crime, criminal justice and the expanding mechanisms of security and regulation.

References

Beckett, K 2001, 'Crime and Control in the Culture of Late Modernity', 25(4) *Law and Society Review* 899.

Bendix, R 1967, 'Tradition and Modernity Reconsidered', 9(3) *Comparative Studies in Society and History* 292.

Braithwaite, J 2003, 'What's Wrong with the Sociology of Punishment?', 7(1) *Theoretical Criminology* 5.

Braithwaite, J 2005, 'Neoliberalism or Regulatory Capitalism', *RegNet Occasional Paper No 5*, Regulatory Institutions Network, ANU, Canberra.

Braithwaite, J & Drahos, P 2000, *Global Business Regulation*, Cambridge University Press, Cambridge.

Breuer, S 1991, 'The Denouements of Civilisation: Elias and modernity', 128 *International Social Science Journal* 401.

Brown, D 2005, 'Continuity, rupture, or just more of the "volatile and contradictory"? Glimpses of New South Wales penal practice behind and through the discursive', in Pratt, J Brown, D, Brown, M, Hallsworth, S & Morison, W (eds), *The New Punitiveness*, Willan Publishing, Cullompton.

Cohen, S 1977, 'Prisons and the Future of Control Systems', in Fitzgerald, M (ed), *Welfare in Action*, Martin Robertson, Oxford.

Cohen, S 1985, *Visions of Social Control*, Polity Press, Cambridge.

Eisner, M 2001, 'Modernisation, Self-Control and Lethal Violence: the long-term dynamics of European homicide rates in theoretical perspective', 41 *British Journal of Criminology* 618.

Elias, N 1996, *The Germans*, Polity Press, Cambridge.

Elias, N 2000 [1939], *The Civilising Process*, Revised Edition, Blackwell, Oxford.

Feeley, M & Simon, J 1994, 'Actuarial Justice: the emerging new criminal law', in Nelken, D (ed), *The Futures of Criminology*, Sage, London.

Feeley, M & Simon, J 1996, 'The New Penology: notes on the emerging strategies of corrections and its implications', in Muncie, J, McLaughlin, E & Langan, M (eds), *Criminological Perspectives*, Sage, London.

Foucault, M 1977, *Discipline and Punish*, Allen & Unwin, London.

Franke, H 1995, *The Emancipation of Prisoners*, Edinburgh University Press, Edinburgh.

Freeman, J 2003, 'Extending Public Law Norms through Privatisation', 116(5) *Harvard Law Review* 1285.

Garland, D 1990, *Punishment and Modern Society*, University of Chicago Press, Chicago.

Garland, D 1995, 'Penal Modernism and Postmodernism', in Cohen, S & Blomberg, D (eds), *Punishment and Social Control*, Aldine, New York.

Garland, D 2001, *The Culture of Control*, Oxford University Press, Oxford.

Garland, D 2004, 'Beyond the Culture of Control', 7(2) *Critical Review of International Social and Political Philosophy* 160.

Garland, D & Sparks, R 2000, 'Criminology, Social Theory and the Challenge of our Times', 40 *British Journal of Criminology* 189.

Gatrell, VAC 1980, 'The Decline of Theft and Violence in Victorian and Edwardian England', in Gatrell, VAC, Lenman, B & Parker, G (eds), *Crime and the Law*, Europa, London.

Gouldner, AW 1973, 'Foreword', in Taylor, I, Walton, P & Young, J (eds), *The New Criminology*, Routledge & Kegan Paul, London.

Hall, S, Critcher, C, Jefferson, T, Clarke, J & Robert, B 1978, *Policing the Crisis*, Macmillan, London.

Hough, M, & Roberts, JV 1999, 'Sentencing Trends in Britain: public knowledge and public opinion', 1(1) *Punishment and Society* 11.

Ignatieff, M 1983, 'State, Civil Society and Total Institutions: a critique of recent social histories of punishment', in Cohen, S & Scull, A (eds), *Social Control and the State*, Basil Blackwell, Oxford.

Johnson, EA, & Monkkonen, EH (eds), 1996, *The Civilisation of Crime*, University of Illinois Press, Urbana.

Lee, M 2007, *Inventing Fear of Crime*, Willan Publishing, Cullompton.

Lupton, D 1999, 'Crime Control, Citizenship and the State: lay understandings of crime, its cause and solutions', 35(3) *Journal of Sociology* 297.

Lupton, D & Tulloch, J 1999, 'Theorising fear of crime: beyond the rational/irrational opposition', 50(3) *British Journal of Sociology* 507.

Lupton, D & Tulloch, J 2002, 'Risk is part of your life: risk epistemologies among a group of Australians', 36(2) *Sociology* 317.

Macfarlane, A 1987, *The Culture of Capitalism*, Blackwell, Oxford.

Mennell, S 1990, 'Decivilising Processes: theoretical significance and some lines of research', 5(2) *International Sociology* 205.

Nelken, D 1994, 'Reflexive Criminology?', in Nelken, D (ed), *The Futures of Criminology*, Sage, London.

O'Malley, P 2000, 'Criminologies of Catastrophe: understanding criminal justice on the edge of the new millennium', 33(2) *Australian and New Zealand Journal of Criminology* 153.

O'Malley, P & Palmer, D 1996, 'Post Keynesian Policing', 25(2) *Economy and Society* 137.

Pratt, J 1998, 'Toward the "decivilising" of punishment?', 7(4) *Social and Legal Studies* 487.

Pratt, J 1999, 'Norbert Elias and the civilised prison', 50(2) *British Journal of Sociology* 271.

Pratt, J 2000, 'Emotive and Ostentatious Punishment: its decline and resurgence in modern society', 2(4) *Punishment and Society* 417.

Pratt, J 2002, 'Critical Criminology and the Punitive Society: some new "Visions of Social Control"', in Carrington, K & Hogg, R (eds), *Critical Criminology*, Willan Publishing, Cullompton.

Pratt, J 2005, 'Elias, Punishment, and Decivilisation', in Pratt, J, Brown, D, Brown, M, Hallsworth, S & Morison, W (eds), *The New Punitiveness*, Willan Publishing, Cullompton.

Punch, M 1974, 'The Sociology of the Anti-Institution', 25(3) *British Journal of Sociology* 312.

Roberts, J & Stalans, L 1997, *Public Opinion, Crime, and Criminal Justice*, Westview Press, Boulder.

Rose, N 1987, 'Beyond the Public/Private Division: law, power and the family', 14(1) *Journal of Law and Society* 61.

Rose, N 1996, 'Governing "advanced" liberal democracies', in Barry, A, Osborne, T & Rose, N (eds), *Foucault and Political Reason*, UCL Press, London.

Rose, N & Miller, P 1992, 'Political Power beyond the State: problematics of government', 43(2) *British Journal of Sociology* 173.

Ross, E 1901, *Social Control*, Macmillan, New York.

Ruggiero, V, Ryan, M, & Sim, J (eds) 1995, *Western European Penal Systems*, Sage, Thousand Oaks.

Scott, C 2002, 'Private Regulation of the Public Sector: a neglected facet of contemporary governance', 29(1) *Journal of Law and Society* 56.

Shearing, C & Stenning, PC 1983, 'Private Security: implications for social control', 30(5) *Social Problems* 493.

Smart, C 1976, *Women, Crime and Criminology: a feminist critique*, Routledge & Kegan Paul, London.

Spierenburg, P 1984, *The Spectacle of Suffering*, Cambridge University Press, Cambridge.

Spierenburg, P 2004, 'Social Control and History: an introduction', in Emsley, C, Johnson, E & Spierenburg, P (eds), *Social Control in Europe, Vol 2: 1800-2000*, Ohio State University Press, Columbus.

Strange, C 2001, 'The Undercurrents of Penal Culture: punishment of the body in mid-twentieth century Canada', 19 *Law and History Review* 343.

Tönnies, F 2001, *Community and Civil Society (Gemeinschaft und Gesellschaft)*, Cambridge University Press, Cambridge.

van Krieken, R 1986, 'Social Theory and Child Welfare: beyond social control', 15(3) *Theory and Society* 401.

van Krieken, R 1991, 'The Poverty of Social Control: explaining power in the historical sociology of the welfare state', 39(1) *Sociological Review* 1.

van Swaaningen, R 1997, *Critical Criminology*, Sage, London.

Vaughan, B 2000, 'The Civilising Process and the Janus-Face of Modern Punishment', 4(1) *Theoretical Criminology* 71.

Weber, M 1949, *The Methodology of the Social Sciences*, The Free Press, Glencoe.

Wouters, C 1999, 'Changing Patterns of Social Controls and Self-Controls: on the rise of crime since the 1950s and the sociogenesis of a "third nature"', 39(3) *British Journal of Criminology* 416.

Wood, JC 2006, 'Criminal Violence in Modern Britain', 4(1) *History Compass* 77.

Young, J 2007, *The Vertigo of Late Modernity*, Sage, London.

Zedner, L 2002, 'Dangers of Dystopias in Penal Theory', 22(2) *Oxford Journal of Legal Studies* 341.

Zedner, L 2007, 'Pre-Crime and Post-Criminology?', 11(2) *Theoretical Criminology* 261.

PART II

CRITICAL THEORY IN ACTION

7

CRITICAL REFLECTIONS ON FEMINIST CRIMINOLOGIES

Kerry Carrington

Introduction

This chapter provides an overview of the substantial and often neglected contribution of feminist theory and research to critical criminology. There are an array of feminist approaches to studying crime, violence and victimisation (see Naffine 1997: 29; Young 1996: 34). This field of study has bourgeoned and diversified so much over the last decade that it would be a disservice to caricature it as simply 'feminist'. A range of influences and approaches from literary theory, jurisprudence, legal studies, cultural studies, postmodernism, neo-liberalism, post-colonialism and neo-Marxism are apparent across this large disparate body of work.

This chapter does not attempt the mammoth task of taking stock of the impact of feminism on critical criminology. Instead it selects a number of key texts representative of the various approaches, focuses and directions of this body of work. I have loosely bundled feminist research on crime and violence into three main bodies of distinctive scholarship: the woman-centred radical feminism of the 1970s which called for the insertion of the woman question into the discipline of criminology; the outright rejection of criminology as a masculinist knowledge during the 1980s and early 1990s, and the deconstruction of criminology and related fields of social inquiry from the 1990s to the present. These bodies of scholarship did not appear in a strictly linear fashion or time series as might be suggested by this categorisation. These groupings are simply a way of compressing a great deal of complexity and diversity into a coherent conceptual schema for the uninitiated reader and student of critical criminology. Alongside these three distinctive feminist criminologies, feminist critiques of the treatment of victims created the impetus for the emergence of a new discipline specialising in victimology. After reviewing the significant contribution of feminism to this field of study, the chapter concludes by examining more closely some recent feminist/critical work on sexual ethics, youth and the prevention of sexual violence.

First waves – add women and stir

The development of feminist criminologies in Australia as elsewhere loosely resembled the broad developments in feminist theory more generally, with the initial critiques of criminology emerging out of the feminist radicalism of the late 1960s and 1970s. As Garland and Sparks (2000: 13) note, the 1970s was also a watershed decade during which the 'intellectual, institutional and political assumptions of modern criminology were challenged'.

Carol Smart's now classic text *Women, Crime and Criminology* (1976) is frequently noted as the starting point of the feminist challenge to criminology, although Heidensohn (1968), Klein (1973) and Bertrand (1967, 1969) were questioning criminology's neglect of the woman question around the same time. This first wave of feminist scholarship engaged in critique as its main enterprise, taking issue with two main aspects of criminology: firstly its omission of women and secondly its sexist and misogynist analysis of female offenders (Adler 1975; Adler & Simon 1979; Bertrand 1967, 1969; Heidensohn 1968; Klein 1973; Smart 1976). Women, they argued, should not be left out of criminological research just because they comprised a small proportion of the criminal population. To correct this gender blindness they argued for the inclusion of women in studies of crime and punishment (Naffine 1987: 2-5; Rafter 2000: xxv).

Early feminist research in the field of Australian criminology started to appear in print in the early 1980s with the publication of Mukherjee and Scutt's pioneering text on *Women and Crime* (1981) and Linda Hancock's (1980) ground-breaking work on gender and juvenile justice. This was at a time when academic criminology was dominated by men 'not only in the corridors but in the pages of academic journals' (Alder 1996: 19).

While the contribution of initial feminist critiques of criminology is undeniable, this body of scholarship did not adequately challenge the underlying epistemological assumptions of criminology's theories, categories or methods (Cousins 1980: 111). Instead feminists undertook a plethora of empirical studies comparing the treatment of men with women by the court system, the juvenile justice system and the prison system (for an excellent review, see Naffine 1997: 35-37). These studies left unchallenged the core assumptions and methodologies of mainstream criminology (Naffine 1997: 36; Young 1992: 290; Faith 1989). The problem succinctly identified by Alison Young (1992: 291) 15 years ago is that 'much of feminist criminology still exists *as a criticism of something else*' (emphasis in original). To become an intellectually vibrant field of study Young argued that feminist research had to do more than just add women to existing criminological frameworks, concluding that 'Feminist critics in criminology should now be starting to work on what might be distinctively *feminist* about feminist criminology, and developing a paradigm that can encompass more than a series of oppositions' (1992: 291, emphasis in original).

While the project of critique may now seem limited, as Christine Alder (1996: 22),[1] a pioneer and advocate of feminist criminology, has argued, it was a necessary precondition to the development of more sophisticated feminist criminologies. Early feminist criminologies can be proud to have been built on the enterprise of critique, not for the sake of it, but for the purpose of producing knowledge aimed at the exposure of injustice, and the possibility of emancipation, transformation and social change.

---

1   Indeed, I owe a personal debt to Christine Alder, who in 1986 encouraged me to present my first paper at the Annual Conference of the Australian and New Zealand Society of Criminology the following year.

Second waves – transgressive feminist criminologies

A body of feminist scholarship started to emerge in the late 1980s and early 1990s that encouraged the outright rejection of criminology's core disciplinary assumptions and boundaries (Allen 1989; Cain 1990; MacKinnon 1987; Faith 1989; Smart 1990; Young 1992; Naffine 1997). Following broader developments in feminist theory, and in particular the influence of French feminism (see for example, Grosz 1989), this feminist agenda promoted a radical scepticism about phallocentric modes of inquiry engendered in disciplines such as history, science, sociology and criminology. This body of feminist analysis questioned their key concepts, methods of inquiry, and claims to neutrality. This theoretically informed body of feminist scholarship rejected the positivist research methods that had dominated mainstream criminology. Many, but not all, embraced feminist standpoint methodologies that elevated the experiences of women as subjects of knowledge (on this point see Naffine 1997: 45-48; Gelsthorpe 1990: 86; Cain 1986). During this period, criminology and feminism were widely regarded as oxymorons – irreconcilable contradictory enterprises (Britton 2000: 58). Criminology, a discipline dominated by men, had either overlooked or misrepresented half of humanity, and then universalised its theories based on observations of one sex – men (Allen 1989: 20). The discipline failed to question the maleness of criminology and the maleness of crime (Naffine 1997: 36). Criminology was so oblivious to the highly sexualised nature of its empirical referents, it was broadly regarded as beyond redemption (Allen 1989: 20-21; Cain 1990: 11; Gelsthorpe & Morris 1990: 4).

While these transgressive critiques of criminology were powerful they were not without their own conceptual weaknesses. In order to make the argument about the inherent phallocentricism of criminology, this form of feminist scholarship tended to fall into the trap of universalising women as the Other (Rice 1990; Carrington 1994; Naffine 1997). By solely focusing on gender as the primary category of analysis and source of female oppression, feminists inspired by the task of transgression frequently failed to take into account the historical, cultural and material diversity of women's offending and victimisation (Gelsthorpe 1989: 152). They presumed that commonalities shared among the female sex made it possible to analyse women as a singular unitary subject of history (Allen 1990: 88), despite their astonishing historical, cultural, socio-economic, ethnic and racial diversity. The diversity of women's experiences of criminalisation and victimisation could not be adequately represented by merely adopting a singular feminist standpoint. This kind of feminist criminology was accused of being theoretically isolationist, reformist and obsessed with 'middle class concerns' (Green 1993: 193). Essentialist forms of analysis arising from transgressive approaches became the subject of internal feminist critique and renewal (Howe 2000; Rice 1990; Carrington 1994; Naffine 1997; Smart 1990). Following the critique of totalising theories and essentialist forms of analysis, 'Feminism had to abandon its early frame-work and to start to look for other ways to think which did not subjugate other subjectivities' (Smart 1990: 83).

Third waves – deconstructionist feminist agendas

Unlike standpoint feminism, deconstructionsist approaches to feminism reject universal knowledge claims and hence also the notion that there can be a single feminist standpoint (Carrington 1994). This kind of feminism no longer insisted on any singular relation between gender, deviance, law and crime and instead sought to locate its analysis more concretely in the field of power relations. Their aim was not to construct a more correct feminist version of the truth, but to deconstruct and analyse the power relations underpinning truth claims (Smart 1990: 82). Nor does this kind of feminism restrict its focus to the Women Question. Their objects of deconstruction varied widely but concentrated on the images and representations of otherness, femininity, sexuality, masculinity, madness, deviance and other statuses deployed in the criminal justice and legal systems (Young 1996). This approach spawned an array of studies on the discursive effects of the media on legal policy and sexual difference, the role of language in the law's positioning of the Other (Mason 1995; Threadgold 1993); intersections between sex, race and criminalisation (Maher 1997); gender and punishment (Howe 1994) and the representations of crime, deviance and victimisation in popular culture (Alexander 2003). The *Australian Feminist Law Journal*, edited by Judy Grbich[2] since its inception in 1993 – another of Australia's long-standing advocates for feminist scholarship – has been one the main publishing outlets for this highly theorised feminist deconstructionism.

Deconstructionist feminist studies have been especially effective in exposing how the mono-logic reasoning of disciplines like law and criminology exclude sexual difference by privileging masculinity (Naffine 1991: 20-21) and othering women (Kirkby 1995: xviii). One criticism of this approach has been the tendency to elevate 'the symbolic power of the law as an agent of change' and to use individual cases as the basis for reasoning upwards to the predicament of all women (Laster 1996: 196). My own research on the rape and murder of Leigh Leigh can be criticised for taking this approach (Carrington & Johnson 1994; Carrington 1998). Feminist demands for law reform around rape, domestic violence and marriage laws construct a set of priorities for feminist action – a set of priorities that Kathy Laster (1996: 196) argued may be irrelevant to the majority of women. It has also led to what she referred to as 'the feminisation of social control', the entry of women in traditional male domains such as policing, security and the judiciary, losing sight of the critical and radical aspirations of transgressive feminist criminologies. Deconstruction is not, as Stan Cohen (1998: 118) reminds us, an end itself as it does not necessarily undermine the power of dominant discourses, such as law. Hence the inclusion of feminist perspectives on the bench or in legal policy is not necessarily a panacea for the injustices faced by some women, and some women in particular (for example Indigenous women; see also Stubbs this volume).

Feminism and victimology

Critical and feminist critiques of criminology grew out of a similar constellation of concerns that swept the western world from the 1960s (Cohen 1998: 103). This was a time when intellectual critics across a broad spectrum of the academy proposed radical critiques of knowledge, power, patriarchy, capitalism and the state. Nevertheless, feminism and critical criminology have had an uneasy alliance. This is mainly because feminist research on the victims of domestic and sexual violence

---

2   I also owe a personal debt to Judy Grbich who encouraged me at the very beginning of my academic career to publish from my PhD on delinquent girls and later study of the rape and murder of Leigh Leigh.

challenged the romantic assumptions of radical deviancy theory that dismissed concerns about the victim as a preoccupation of conservative thinkers and policy-makers. Over the last three decades there has been an unprecedented interest in the victim by politicians, criminal justice policy-makers and a diverse range of scholars in feminism, criminology, victimology, sociology, law and public policy (Zedner 2003; Garland & Sparks 2000; Young 2002; Rock 2005; Booth & Carrington 2007).

An assemblage of quite distinct feminist intellectual work focusing on women as victims began to emerge in the 1970s with the rise of radical feminism and demands to make violence a public not a private matter (Carmody & Carrington 2000). Significant and influential works include Dobash and Dobash's (1979) study of family violence; Russell's (1975) exposé of rape, including rape in marriage, and Brownmiller's (1975) provocative analysis of rape to name only a few. These were followed by Stanko's (1990) work on everyday violence and Walklate's (1991, 2007) major and ongoing contribution to the field of victimology. This work challenged the hidden and privatised nature of violence against women (Gelsthorpe & Morris 1990: 3). These intellectual feminist challenges were inspired by a great deal of feminist activism around the definition of rape, child abuse and wife battering and the mistreatment of women prisoners and female delinquents (Rafter 2000; Carrington 1993; Daly 1994; Howe 1994; Breckenridge & Carmody 1992).

Feminists working in victim support services in the United Kingdom, United States, Australia, New Zealand and other parts of the world have played a key historical role in elevating the needs of women and children as victims and lobbying for legislative reform to address their needs (Booth & Carrington 2007). Like victim movements in the northern hemisphere, in Australia this movement emerged from an array of interest groups including: the refuge movement, women's support organisations, the women's electoral lobby, Aboriginal and community legal services, and sexual assault centres. The victims championed by these diverse interest groups were mainly women and children survivors of sexual assault and domestic violence who rarely rate a mention in law and order political agendas (Hogg & Brown 1998) and were also absent from both mainstream criminology and radical deviancy theory.

Not surprisingly there has been a close and enduring connection between the intellectual and political projects of feminists working with victims and feminists researching victims, aptly captured in the slogan 'the personal is political'. Reflecting this 'praxis' feminist researchers in Australia set about to expose the experiences of victimisation discredited by a masculinist legal and criminal justice system. They studied sexual assault (Waldby 1985; Brekenridge & Carmody 1992), domestic violence (Scutt 1983; Stubbs 1994; Kaye et al 2003; Egger & Stubbs 1993), violence during pregnancy (Taft 2000); violence against Aboriginal women (Atkinson 1990; Bolger 1991); violence against women in rural settings (Hogg & Carrington 2006); violence against Filipino migrant women (Cunneen & Stubbs 2004) and distinctive Australian cultures of violence (Cook & Bessant 1997). Feminists extended their analyses to the treatment of women as victims of the criminal justice system and the law as well (see for example, Department for Women 1996; Threadgold 1993; Naffine 1991; Carrington 1998). Their research sought to demonstrate how women were doubly victimised by their subsequent treatment by the police, prison, legal and judicial authorities. This led feminist scholars to argue that at best the criminal justice system inadequately addressed the needs of victims, or at worst re-victimised the victim. These were such important insights into the workings of criminal justice that feminism can rightly claim that it has played a leading role in the emergence of a relatively new field of inquiry, victimology. Not all feminist researchers in this disparate field agreed this was a good thing.

Lamenting the growing concern for victims among feminist criminologists, 14 years ago Penny Green (1993: 192) launched a stinging attack on this body of work, arguing that 'Feminist criminology has become, to a large extent, victimology … and accordingly ripe for incorporation by an increasingly punitive state'. Her strident comments are symptomatic of the long and lingering tension between feminist and critical criminologies over the role of the victim. The victim was almost entirely absent from the radical frameworks of much of the early critical criminology (see for example, Taylor et al 1973). At that time victims were the concern of conservatives in criminology and politics, not radicals (Smart 1976: 180). The emergence of radical deviance theory and the new criminology did not initially alter any of this, for its focus was directed at the analysis of victimless crimes, such as drug crimes and participation in working-class youth subcultures, romanticised as resisters to class oppression (see for example, Hall & Jefferson 1976). Feminist research on women and children as victims of crime fitted uneasily alongside the radical insistence that under-played the effects of crime on victims as merely moral panics or law and order nonsense (Young 1998: 298). Feminist research required politicians, policy-makers and criminologists (of critical and traditional orientation) to completely rethink the invisibility of the victim in the system (Sumner in Gelsthorpe & Morris 1990: xii).

The major conceptual problem that has plagued feminist intellectual work around victims has been how to avoid the binary construction of all men as perpetrators, forever poised to pounce, and all women as victims forever in waiting to be raped or bashed (Carmody & Carrington 2000). In what follows I take a critical reflexive look at research on sexual violence to illustrate the complexity involved in applying feminist approaches to critical criminological research.

Young people, sexual violence and ethics

I have had a longstanding research interest in issues relating to the treatment of rape victims (Carrington & Johnson 1994; Carrington 1997, 1998; Carmody & Carrington 2000). Some years ago, with a colleague, Moira Carmody, we attempted to identify what might actually prevent intimate sexual violence. Our joint research grew out of a longstanding frustration we shared with the limits of law reform to bring about positive transformation and social change for rape victims. The erosion of our faith followed some devastatingly negative evaluations of the criminal justice system's treatment of the victims of sexual violence (Department for Women 1996; Bargen & Fishwick 1995; Smart 1989; Threadgold 1993). My own encounter with a masculinist legal system further entrenched our pessimism about the social reform value of the legal system (Byrne-Armstrong et al 1999; Carrington 1998). While we acknowledge that measures such as law reform, apprehended violence orders, post-trauma counselling, provision of victim support were positive developments, none embodied a preventative focus. They were post-assault interventions.

At the time we started this exploration we were acutely aware that most sexual violence remains hidden, unrecognised or unreported and thus outside the scope of regulation (Carmody & Carrington 2000). This is still the case (Lievore 2003). Fear and shame of being stigmatised and further harmed are some of the reasons why so few victims report to the authorities. Those most vulnerable to victimisation tend also to be among those in the community with the least social resources to do much about it anyway. They are disproportionately young women from disadvantaged residential areas. There are perplexing regional differences too with sexual assault rates on the whole higher in rural areas (Hogg & Carrington 2006; Lievore 2003). The special vulnerability of Aboriginal women and children has led to alarming reports of sexual and domestic violence occurring in Indigenous communities (Gordon Report 2002; Northern Territory Government 2007). The majority of sexual assaults occur between acquaintances, with attacks by 'randoms' or strangers being rare (Hogg & Brown 1998: 64). Yet sexual violence between intimates has attracted little attention in crime prevention policy (Egger 1997). Ironically it has been violence between strangers that has attracted by far the greater public policy focus in crime prevention circles (Stanko 1990; Egger 1997).

Once we decided to focus on exploring sexual assault prevention, we had to confront the problem of where to start when the main lesson from 30 years of feminist research was not to bother. Rape was an act of male power – a manifestation of patriarchy as famously expressed by Brownmiller (1975: 15), 'It's nothing more or less than a conscious process of intimidation by which *all* men keep *all* women in a state of fear' (emphasis in original). For at least three decades, rape had been theorised in feminist scholarship as the expression of male power over which individual women were almost completely helpless. Women were seemingly incapable of practising sexual autonomy and men seemingly incapable of practising sexual ethics. Hence, women were universal victims while men were universal perpetrators, leading us to conclude that: 'Prevention is a virtual impossibility within this theoretical framework' (see also Egger: 1997). It leaves women 'in waiting' to experience violence and men forever paused to engage in it (Carmody & Carrington 2000: 346). In rejecting 30 years of feminist wisdom we boldly reversed the conceptual model arguing that the prevention of sexual assault is a real possibility where ethically constituted sexual encounters between same sex or opposite sex partners are regarded as the norm, not the deviation.

Moira Carmody and Karen Willis (2006: 7) from the New South Wales Rape Crisis Centre have since undertaken a major study of young people and sexual ethics. That study has explored the anti-violence educational needs of young men and women aged 16-25. Their sample included young people of diverse sexual orientations from rural and metropolitan New South Wales with a healthy cohort of youth from Indigenous backgrounds. Their findings indicate that the gender double-standard is still a major influence on how young people negotiate sexual intimacy. The real novelty of the study is that it advances our understanding of the complexity of sexual intimacy and the processes of negotiating consent. Communication of verbal and non-verbal cues of consent were vital as whether or not the sexual encounters were ethical and mutually pleasurable. Their study found that the young people engaging in casual sexual encounters were less likely to have the rapport to effectively communicate consent, and hence the 'room for error' was higher in such contexts, especially where alcohol had been consumed (2006: 77). Young women engaging in casual sex in particular reported an inability to speak, increasing the risk of unwanted sexual assaults, feelings of regret and of being used (2006: 77). Herein lies the clue to negotiating mutually pleasurable ethical sexual encounters. The young women in their study who felt they had the capacity to negotiate mutually desirable sexual encounters 'were able to find a voice which was absent in many causal encounters' (2006: 79). Hence Carmody and Willis (2006: 80) argue that sex education which advises girls to simply 'say no' is misled as it places young women in a passive negotiating position and young men in a powerful negotiating position as the sexual aggressor. Their research suggests the emphasis in sex education should be placed, not on how to refuse sex, but how to negotiate sexual intimacy ethically – mindful of the other parties' needs and desires. They conclude, provocatively, that both parents and schools need to offer advice to young people that focuses on the positive aspects of how to successfully negotiate sexual intimacy, something missing from most sex education manuals.

The major lesson I learnt from my own journey from years of advocacy, researching and writing about sexual violence is that sometimes it is necessary to abandon several decades of 'feminist' wisdom if at the end of the day what matters most is transformation and social change and not ideology.

Conclusion

Over a decade ago Kathy Laster (1996: 192) implored feminist criminology in Australia to replace its concern with defeat with an exploration of its relative success. This chapter has tried to do this. On reflection much has been achieved for which feminists working in and around the field of critical criminology can feel proud. Feminist work can rightly claim to have revitalised criminology, contributed substantially to the emergence of victimology as a new field of inquiry and given mainstream criminology reason to rethink several of its key assumptions.

Critical criminology too has had to come to terms with the fact that victims are not just the mirages of moral panics or law and order campaigns (Young 1998: 298). There is a lot more to do though. In the current geo-political climate of neo-liberalism and globalisation the challenge for feminists working in the field of critical criminology is maintaining their critical focus and relevance in the face of what appears as a constant flux, but may be the reinvention of old problems in new guises, as with cyber-stalking and sex crimes using the internet. Feminist criminology has only just begun to research the impact of cybersex crimes, the growing global trade in sex trafficking, cheap labour, the marriage market, violence in new and emerging migrant communities, and the inadequacy of national regulatory approaches to transnational problems such as these. Historically, the greatest gap in feminist research relates to the intersections between post-colonial identities, race, gender and crime, although there are some significant exceptions (see Maher 1997; Pickering this volume). My hope is that the upcoming generation of feminist researchers in the field of critical criminology will take up the unfinished business of addressing these issues.

References

Adler, F 1975, *Sisters in Crime: the rise of the new female criminal*, McGraw-Hill, New York.

Adler, F & Simon, RJ (eds) 1979, *The Criminology of Deviant Women*, Houghton Mifflin, Boston.

Alder, C 1996, 'Feminist Criminology in Australia', in Rafter, N & Heidensohn, F (eds), *International Feminist Perspectives in Criminology: engendering a discipline*, Open University Press, Buckingham.

Alexander, A 2003, 'Sex, Crime and the 'Liberated' Woman in the Virgin Bride and Buffy the Vampire Slayer', 18 *Australian Feminist Law Journal* 77.

Allen, J 1989, 'Men, Crime and Criminology: recasting the questions', 17 *International Journal of the Sociology of Law* 19.

Allen, J 1990, *Sex & Secrets: crimes involving Australian women since 1880,* Oxford University Press, Melbourne.

Atkinson, J 1990, 'Violence in Aboriginal Australia: gender & colonisation part 1', 14(2) *The Aboriginal & Torres Strait Islander Health Worker* 5.

Bargen, J & Fishwick, E 1995, *Sexual Assault Law Reform*, Office of the Status of Women, AGPS, Canberra.

Bertrand, M 1967, 'The Myth of Sexual Equality before the Law', *Proceedings of the Fifth Research Conference on Delinquency and Criminality*, Quebec Society of Criminology, Montreal.

Bertrand, M 1969, 'Self-Image and Delinquency: a contribution to the study of female criminality and women's image', 2 *Acta Criminologica* 71.

Bolger, A 1991, *Aboriginal Women and Violence*, Australian National University.

Booth, T & Carrington, K 2007, 'A Comparative Analysis of the Victim Policies across the Anglo-Speaking World', in Walklate, S (ed), *Handbook on Victims and Victimology,* Willan Publishing, Cullompton.

Breckenridge, J & Carmody, M (eds) 1992, *Crimes of Violence: Australian responses to rape and child sexual assault*, Allen & Unwin, Sydney.

Britton, D 2000, 'Feminism in Criminology: engendering the outlaw', 571 *The ANNALS of the American Academy of Political and Social Science* 57.

Brownmiller, S 1975, *Against Our Will: men, women and rape*, Penguin Books, London.

Byrne-Armstrong, H, Carmody, M, Hodge, B, Hogg, R & Lee, M 1999, 'The Risk of Naming Violence: an unpleasant encounter between legal culture and feminist criminology', 13 *Australian Feminist Law Journal* 13.

Cain, M 1986, 'Realism, Feminism, Methodology, and Law', 14(1) *International Journal of the Sociology of Law* 255.

Cain, M 1990, 'Towards Transgression: new directions in feminist criminology', 18(1) *International Journal of the Sociology of Law* 1.

Carmody, M & Carrington, K 2000, 'Preventing Sexual Violence?', 33(3) *Australian and New Zealand Journal of Criminology* 34.

Carmody, M & Willis, K 2006, *Developing Ethical Sexual Lives: young people, sex and sexual assault prevention*, University of Western Sydney, NSW Rape Crisis Centre, Sydney.

Carrington, K 1993, *Offending Girls: sex, youth & justice*, Allen & Unwin, Sydney.

Carrington, K 1994, 'Postmodernism and Feminist Criminologies: disconnecting discourses', 22(3) *International Journal of the Sociology of Law* 261.

Carrington, K 1997, 'Governing Sexual Violence: criminalisation and citizenship', in Cook, S & Bessant, J (eds), *Women's Encounters with Violence, Australian experiences*, Sage, London.

Carrington, K 1998, *Who killed Leigh Leigh?*, Random House, Sydney & New York.

Carrington, K & Johnson, A 1994, 'Representations of Guilt, Crime & Sexuality in the Leigh Leigh Rape/Murder Case', 4 *Australian Feminist Law Journal* 3.

Cohen, S 1998, 'Intellectual Scepticism and Political Commitment: the case of radical criminology', in Walton, P & Young, J (eds), *The New Criminology Revisited*, Macmillan & St Martins, London & New York.

Cook, S & Bessant, J 1997, *Women's Encounters with Violence: Australian experiences*, Sage, London.

Cousins, M 1980, 'Men's Rea: a note on sexual difference, criminology and law', in Carlen, P & Collison, M (eds), *Radical Issues in Criminology*, Martin Robertson, London.

Cunneen, C & Stubbs, J 2004, 'Cultural Criminology and Engagement with Race, Gender and Post-Colonial Identities', in Ferrell, J, Hayward, K, Morrison, W & Presdee, M (eds), *Cultural Criminology Unleashed*, Glasshouse Press, London.

Daly, K & Maher, L 1998, *Criminology at the Crossroads: feminist readings in crime and justice*, Oxford University Press, New York.

Daly, K 1994, *Gender, Crime and Punishment*, Yale University Press, New Haven.

Department for Women 1996, *Heroines of Fortitude: the experiences of women in court as victims of sexual assault*, NSW Government, Sydney.

Dobash, RE & Dobash, R 1979, *Violence Against Wives*, The Free Press, New York.

Egger, S & Stubbs, J 1993, *The Effectiveness of Protection Orders in Australian Jurisdictions*, AGPS, Sydney.

Egger, S 1997, 'Women & crime prevention', in O'Malley, P & Sutton, A (eds), *Crime Prevention: issues in policy & research*, Federation Press, Sydney.

Faith, K 1989, 'Challenging Privilege: women, knowledge and feminist struggles', 1(1) *Critical Criminology* 1.

Garland, D & Sparks, R 2000, 'Criminology, Social Theory and the Challenges of our Times', in Garland, D & Sparks, R (eds), *Criminology and Social Theory*, Oxford University Press, Oxford.

Gelsthorpe, L 1989, *Sexism & the Female Offender*, Gower, Aldershot.

Gelsthorpe, L 1990, 'Feminist Methodologies in Criminology: a new approach or old wine in new bottles?', in Gelsthorpe, L & Morris, A (eds), *Feminist Perspectives in Criminology*, Open University Press, Buckingham.

Gelsthorpe, L & Morris, A (eds) 1990, *Feminist Perspectives in Criminology*, Open University Press, Buckingham.

Gordon Report 2002, *Interim Report, Inquiry into Response by Government Agencies to Complaints of Family Violence & Child Abuse in Aboriginal Communities*, Western Australian Government, Perth.

Green, P 1993, 'Review of Feminist Perspectives in Criminology', 33(1) *British Journal of Criminology* 112.

Grosz, L 1989, 'The In(ter)vention of Feminist Knowledges, Crossing Boundaries: feminisms and the critique of knowledges', Allen & Unwin, Sydney.

Hall, S & Jefferson, T (eds) 1976, *Resistance Through Rituals*, Hutchinson.

Hancock, L 1980 'The myth that females are treated more leniently than males in the juvenile justice system', 16(3) *Australian and New Zealand Journal of Sociology* 4.

Heidensohn, F 1968, 'The Deviance of Women: a critique and an enquiry', XIX(2) *British Journal of Sociology* 160.

Hogg, R & Brown, D 1998, *Rethinking Law & Order*, Pluto Press, Sydney.

Hogg, R & Carrington, K 2006, *Policing the Rural Crisis*, Federation Press, Sydney.

Howe, A 1994, *Punish and Critique: towards a feminist analysis of penality*, Routledge, London.

Howe, A 2000, 'Postmodern Criminology and Feminist Discontents', 33(2) *Australian and New Zealand Journal of Criminology* 221.

Kaye, M, Stubbs, J & Tolmie, J 2003, 'Domestic Violence, Separation and Parenting', 15(2) *Current Issues in Criminal Justice* 73-94.

Kirkby, D (ed) 1995, *Sex, Power and Justice*, Oxford University Press, Melbourne.

Klein, D 1973, 'The Etiology of Female Crime: a review of the literature', 8(2) *Issues in Criminology* 3.

Laster, K 1996, 'Feminist Criminology: coping with success', 8(2) *Current Issues in Criminal Justice* 192.

Lievore, D 2003, *Non-Reporting and Hidden Recording of Sexual Assault: an international literature review*, Commonwealth Office of the Status of Women, Canberra.

MacKinnon, C 1987, *Feminism Unmodified: discourses on life and law*, Harvard University Press, London.

Maher, L 1997, *Sexed Work: gender, race and resistance in a Brooklyn drug market*, Clarendon Press, Oxford.

Mason, G 1995, 'Reforming the Law of Rape: incisions into a masculinist sanctum', in Kirkby, D (ed), *Sex, Power and Justice*, Oxford University Press, Melbourne.

Mukherjee, A & Scutt, J (eds) 1981, *Women and Crime*, Australian Institute of Criminology, Canberra.

Naffine, N 1987, *Female Crime*, Allen & Unwin, Sydney.

Naffine, N 1991, *Law and the Sexes*, Allen & Unwin, Sydney.

Naffine, N 1997, *Feminism & Criminology*, Allen & Unwin, Sydney.

Northern Territory Government 2007, *Report of the Northern Territory Board of Inquiry into the Protection of Aboriginal Children from Sexual Abuse 2007 (Little Children are Scared)*, Government Printers.

Rafter, N 2000, 'Preface' in Rafter, NH (ed), *Encyclopaedia of Women and Crime*, Oryx Press, Arizona.

Rice, M 1990, 'Challenging Orthodoxies in Feminist Theory: a black feminist critique', in Gelsthorpe, L & Morris, A (eds), *Feminist Perspectives in Criminology*, Open University Press, Buckingham.

Rock, P 2005, Victims Rights in the United Kingdom, Paper presented to the Australian Institute of Criminology Occasional Seminar Series, 24 August, <www.aic.gov.au/conferences/occasional/2005-08-rock.html>.

Russell, D 1975, *The Politics of Rape: the victim's perspective*, Stein & Day, New York.

Scutt, J 1983, *Even in the Best of Homes: violence in the family*, Penguin, Australia.

Smart, C 1976, *Women, Crime and Criminology*, Routledge & Kegan Paul, London.

Smart, C 1989, *Feminism and the Power of Law*, Routledge, London.

Smart, C 1990, 'Feminist Approaches to Criminology – or Postmodern Woman meets Atavistic Man', in Gelsthorpe, L & Morris, A (eds), *Feminist Perspectives in Criminology*, Open University Press, Buckingham.

Stanko, E 1990, *Everyday Violence*, Pandora, London.

Stubbs, J 1994, *Women, Male Violence and the Law*, Institute of Criminology, University of Sydney, NSW.

Taft, A 2000, *Violence against Women in Pregnancy and after Childbirth*, Australian Domestic and Family Violence Clearinghouse: Issues Paper 6, Sydney.

Taylor, I, Walton, P & Young, J 1973, *The New Criminology*, Routledge, London.

Threadgold, T 1993, 'Critical theory, feminisms, the judiciary & rape', 1 *Australian Feminist Law Journal* 7.

Waldby, C 1985, 'Breaking the Silence: a report based upon the findings of the Women Against Incest Phone-in Survey', Dympna House, Sydney.

Walklate, S 1991, 'Victims, crime prevention and social control', in Reiner, R & Cross, M (eds), *Beyond Law and Order: criminal justice policy and politics into the 90s*, Macmillan, London.

Walklate, S (ed) 2007, *Handbook on Victims and Victimology*, Willan Publishing, Cullompton.

Young, A 1996, *Imagining Crime*, Sage, London.

Young, A 1992, 'Review of Feminist Perspectives in Criminology', 19(2) *Journal of Law and Society* 289.

Young, J 1998, 'Breaking Windows: situating the new criminology', in Walton, P & Young, J (eds), *The New Criminology Revisited*, Macmillan & St Martins, London & New York.

Young, J 2002, 'Critical Criminology in the 21st Century', in Carrington, K & Hogg, R (eds) *Critical Criminology: Issues, debates, challenges*, Willan Publishing, Cullompton.

Zedner, L 2003, 'Victims', in *Oxford Handbook on Criminology*, Second edition, Oxford Press, London.

8

MASCULINITIES, CRIME AND CRIMINALISATION

Stephen Tomsen

Introduction

This chapter provides an overview of some key features of the recent theoretical literature regarding masculinity and crime, as well as some of the more significant empirical studies in this new field. It describes the evident strengths of the emerging 'masculinities' paradigm in criminology. But it also notes the pitfalls of any gender-centric analysis of criminality that could overlook a skewed criminalisation process that frequently targets, criminalises and punishes men and boys from disadvantaged and marginal social settings.

Male offenders carry out the great majority of crimes. The reasons for this have been a puzzle for researchers, officials and commentators. Although criminal justice agencies focus heavily on detecting, prosecuting and punishing the offending of working class, poor and minority males, it is apparent that high levels of recorded and reported offending reflect a real and pervasive social phenomenon of disproportionate male criminality. Since its origins at the end of the 1800s, criminology had ongoing difficulty with explaining the link between masculinity and crime, and research often disregarded the link between criminal offending and maleness.

Much traditional criminological discourse had a close concern with the study and control of 'dangerous' forms of masculinity, particularly working-class male delinquency, but did not tackle the relation between criminality and the socially varied attainment of male status and power. It studied crime by a male norm and never developed a sufficiently critical view of the link to gender, especially to non-pathological and widespread forms of masculine identity that are tied to offending. The result of this has been a tendency to naturalise male offending and reversion to gender essentialism by explaining male wrongdoing as an inherent and pre-social phenomenon that men are drawn to.

The positivist stress on biology often viewed crime as a reflection of defective male and female identities (Gould 1981). A range of subsequent accounts also disregarded the social link between crime and masculinity. These have included Marxist and left accounts that focused on class differences to explain crime, and then either relied on biological sex differences to explain the gendered pattern of most criminal offending or else said nothing about it (Bonger 2003; Taylor et al 1973).

This legacy has been challenged by contemporary research on the social construction of masculinities and the 'everyday' qualities of their aggressive and destructive forms.

Masculinity theory

There has been a shift since the 1980s in response to wider reflection on gender and identity from social movements including feminism, gay and lesbian activism and sections of 'the men's movement'. In particular, research on violence against women stressed the relationship between offending and everyday, often legitimated, constructions of manhood. In the academy, there has been a growth in research on male violence and a general expansion of research on masculinity or 'men's studies' (see Kimmel 1987; Segal 1990; Connell et al 2005).

This new field also owes much of its inspiration to the theoretical contribution from Australian left-feminism, which developed a key explanatory model of different forms of masculinity. 'Hegemonic masculinity' has been defined not as a particular character type, but a whole complex of historically evolving and varied social practice in societies which either legitimate, or attempt to guarantee, the shoring up of patriarchy and male domination of women (Connell 1995). Any attainment or approximation of this empowered hegemonic form by individual men is highly contingent on the uneven levels of real social power in different men's lives. A key marginalised form is 'protest masculinity' (1995: 109). This is a term that has been used before by criminologists and it appropriates the psychoanalytic description of 'masculine protest'. It describes a gender identity that is characteristic of men in a marginal social location with the masculine claim on power contradicted by economic and social weakness (1995: 116). Protest masculinity may be reflected in hypermasculine aggressive display, anti-social, violent and criminal behaviour. Frequently, it exhibits a juxtaposition of overt misogyny, compulsory heterosexuality and homophobia.

This model of hegemonic and marginalised masculinities has been very influential but also much contested in social sciences including criminology.[1] For some liberal critics, this model could seem too closely tied to Marxist ideas about an overarching dominant ideology as a ruling set of oppressive masculine beliefs. Yet much of the critique has come from the left and postmodern camps. Critics have suggested this model downplays social class and reflects a degrading view of working-class men as inherently violent and destructive (Hall 2002). Jefferson suggests that this model results in a narrow view of true masculinity as a wholly negative set of personal attributes (Jefferson 2002). And Collier (1998) argues that the model offers an imprecise notion that 'masculinity' comprises whatever men do. He rejects the gender/masculinities approach for a particular focus on the male body that may overstate gender differences and struggle to explain the diversity, contradictions and subtleties of social forms of masculinities.[2] Nevertheless, the notion of hegemonic and marginalised masculinities has been deployed in a rich and widening range of criminological studies that study the spectrum of masculine offending.

---

1   For replies to specific critiques in criminology and to a very wide-related social science literature see Connell (2002), Connell & Messerschmidt (2005).
2   Few participants in these debates have engaged with the threat from the wider scientific status of evolutionary psychology and its explanation of male violence as a reflection of early patterns of instinctive competition for sexual reproduction (see Polk 1998).

New studies

Recent critical work has emphasised that masculinity is linked to more than just violent crime by less powerful men, and relates widely to such matters as motor vehicle offences, theft, drug use and dealing, white collar offending or even official corruption. In the 'new masculinities' approach there is an emphasis on the relations between different masculinities, the causes and patterns of most criminal offending and victimisation, and the broader workings of the wider criminal justice system of public and private policing, criminal courts, corrections and prisons (Newburn & Stanko 1994).

These scholars share the view that masculinities are plural, socially constructed, reproduced in the collective social practices of different men and embedded in institutional and occupational settings. Furthermore, masculinities are intricately linked with struggles for social power that occur between men and women and among different men. They vary and importantly intersect with other dimensions of inequality. Messerschmidt's (1993, 1997) influential account of crimes as 'doing masculinity' and to be understood within a structured action framework incorporates differences of class, race/ethnicity, age, sexuality and the common concern with power. As there are different forms of masculinity that are differently linked to the attainment of social power, crime itself is a means or social resource to achieve masculinity and analyses must balance consideration of structural forces and human agency (Messerschmidt 1993, 1997).

The differences in masculinity that shape violence against women are a frequent topic of interest. For example, Kersten (1996) maps out cross-cultural evidence to illustrate an underlying link between male domination and a wide range of reported and unreported rapes, forms of sexual harassment and coercion from both male strangers and acquaintances. Additionally, he stresses the national differences in gender relations and evolving masculinities in order to argue that although these assaults are related to a range of social and historical factors, they are higher in Australia (rather than Germany or Japan) with its overtly aggressive public masculine culture. Such violence is viewed as a means of asserting or seeking a male identity that is increasingly under threat of change from new social forces.

The most important local analyses that explore masculine offending and make an important contribution to this new literature have been various studies of homicide. A key analysis from the 1990s concluded that the typical 'masculine scenarios' of most killings are disputes between men regarding insults and slights to personal honour or assaults directed at controlling female spouses and domestic partners (Polk 1994). Detailed discussion of many incidents reflects the masculine and everyday forms of most fatal interpersonal violence. Furthermore, the criminal defences (particularly provocation) that are invoked by many accused and defence counsel have been generally unavailable to women who kill, and the status of these suggests a link with notions of masculine violence that have a degree of respect in the criminal justice system and wider culture.

Australian research on anti-homosexual killings has also suggested a masculine pattern in much of this violence and the official criminal justice system response to it (Tomsen 2002). Anti-homosexual killings occur within two general masculine scenarios. These typically comprise fatal attacks in public space that are perpetrated by groups of young males concerned with establishing a manly self-image, and more private disputes with allegations of an unwanted homosexual advance by a perpetrator protecting a masculine sense of honour and bodily integrity with retaliatory violence. Thus many hate crimes (racist attacks as well as violence directed at gay men, lesbians and transsexuals) are not a form of offending that is wholly distinct from other masculine violence (Tomsen 2001).

Until quite recently, the wide level of male violence against other men has not been well researched or examined as a form of gendered violence. Similarly, there has been little analysis of masculine attitudes towards subjection to violence beyond the general finding that men as a group tend to be less fearful in relation to crime. Australian and overseas research within the new masculinities approach has studied the experience of confrontational violence by tracing the role of victimisation in establishing power relations between men, and the mixed effects on victims that both undermine and reinforce conventional ideas of manhood (Stanko & Hobdell 1993; Tomsen 2005).

The narrow view that masculine crime just comprises acts of physical violence has been balanced by accounts of the gendered patterns of theft, economic and corporate offending. An important early local example of this was an analysis of the particular attractions that motor vehicle offending and thefts hold for many working-class boys (Cunneen 1985; see also Cunneen & White 1996). The broad potential of this explanation of non-violent offending has been realised in international studies. For example, an important interview study, which gives further understanding of the motivations and processes involved in the male attraction to a range of non-violent offending by exploring the group interactions and exchanges that precede collective offending, including robbery, burglary and vehicle theft by groups of young risk-taking males (Copes & Hochstetler 2003).

The masculine seductions of criminal risk at higher levels of social class and privilege are apparent in a classic account of the 1985 Challenger disaster that seriously undermined confidence in the United States Space Shuttle program. The fatal decision to launch against strong evidence of equipment failure and the resulting crew deaths reflected the dominance of a particular managerial masculinity that valued risk and decisiveness and discounted human consequences (Messerschmidt 1995). Institutional crime by collective decision-making or oversight does not fit the classic liberal notion of a single reasoning (presumptive male) criminal actor. These insights into the masculinity of corporate crime might well inform the recent criminological interest in state crime. There is a range of major public institutional offending of concern to critical criminology including internal and external official violence, paramilitary activity and warfare, that is also deeply masculine and it remains a fertile but mostly untouched field for researchers with this approach. Destructive military masculinities have been a particular concern in recent discussion about the potential success of international peace-keeping efforts in a range of post-war settings (Breines et al 2000).

Culture, ethnography and life histories

A particular highlight of the new crime and masculinities research has been the discursive analysis of cultural representations and a variety of ethnographic studies that seek out the viewpoints that inform masculine social action in relation to crime and criminal justice. The significance of a general vicarious masculine interest in vio-

lence, crime and wrongdoing are evident from the contributions of researchers exploring the status of cultural meanings in a range of societies. Sparks (1996) has explained how popular Hollywood depictions of male heroism as a critical aspect of policing and law enforcement in such films as *Dirty Harry, Lethal Weapon* and *Total
Recall* shape and skew public understanding of crime and the law. The strident asser-
tion of masculinity in recent movies about crime reflects the instability of current
gender identities. Core tensions and attractions of both hegemonic masculinity that is
official, pro-state and respecting authority and the protest masculinity that more
usually animates the identity of criminal offenders, are inscribed within these heroic
characters and triumphant narratives. It is noteworthy that by contrast, Australasian
films including *The Boys, Idiot Box, Once Were Warriors* and *Chopper* depict a
range of criminal masculinities that are less heroic and even more disturbing for
elements of their apparent ordinariness.

The cultural studies emphasis on the establishment of social identities in
patterns of leisure and consumption rather than by the traditional means of the
workplace and occupation, is evident in research on young British males who
establish a respected masculine street identity through a range of public criminal
activities and poly-drug use. These patterns are formed against a social backdrop
that strictly limits the possible mechanisms for establishing male status (Collison
1996). The tension between individual agency and objective factors in masculine
criminal activity and the value of an insider understanding of that tension are evident
in the fully ethnographic picture drawn by Bourgois's (1996) study of New York
crack dealers from a deprived Puerto Rican neighbourhood.

These are men who also struggle for respect in their wrongdoing. Drug-
dealing, violence and sexual assaults provide a distorted mirror of the limited
empowerment that was won by male forebears in a traditional rural patriarchy where
protection and provision for women and families were vital aspects of gender dominance. Graphic snapshots of brutality, gang rapes and other crimes and cultural
detail gathered by painstaking and dangerous fieldwork fleshes out the racialised,
criminal masculinities assumed by these young gang members.

The theme of masculine crime in de-industrialised settings has been pursued
by Australian and British ethnographic researchers studying night-time leisure and
related offending and it's policing (Hobbs et al 2003; Tomsen 1997; Winlow 2001).
There are sensual attractions in the liminal 'night-time' economy for its many young
participants, and an allied official ambivalence towards the male aggression and disorder that characterise it. In Monaghan's (2002) insider account of 'bouncing' in a
study of private security officers working in nightclubs and pubs in city centres in
Wales and South West England, physicality and violent potential are transformed
into a workplace skill, built on the importance of forceful bodies. The mixed official
response to the economic benefits and social costs of the expanding night economy
that foster drunkenness, male conflicts and disorder problems, is also evident in the
discomfort with, and reliance on, the aggressive masculinity of security officers
instructed to maintain a semblance of public order.

The danger of this work generates hierarchies of male physical ability within
private policing, particularly the contrasts between 'hardmen', 'shopboys' coming
from security work in retail stores and 'glass collector types' that are less physically
imposing and are unable to deal with the risks of violent encounters. The same masculine hierarchy inflects the positioning of the minority of women working in this

occupation; these are either denigrated as unmasculine and physically incapable or in fewer cases given a marginal position in a masculine hierarchy.[3]

This is a specific form of masculinity that has global manifestations and corresponds with images from a general culture. It also seems to involve a form of private policing that is laxly regulated and reproducing forms of masculine identity that are close to the original aggressive physicality of traditional unreformed public policing. With the fine line between legitimate force and actual assault, bouncing itself encapsulates a gendered identity at the edge of the protest and official masculinities that criminal justice systems so often express the tensions and convergence between.

The importance of life histories research to studies of crime and masculinity that seek out insider perspectives on offending has been seen in a range of recent accounts. Jefferson (1997) argues that researchers in this field should not ignore the unconscious and contradictory personal aspects of any criminal masculine identity. Obviously, he had in mind the lessons of his own life history account of Mike Tyson that traces the evolution of a vulnerable boy into a champion athlete and convicted rapist and draws out the links between racial marginality and hypermasculine violence. Similarly, in one of Messerschmidt's (1999) recent studies, a dynamic interplay of hegemonic and other masculinities is demonstrated by discussion of the lives of two juvenile offenders from a working-class American neighbourhood. This interplay occurs against the backdrop of different relations to the body and achievable masculinities, as social understandings of the body shape offending in two different criminal pathways (Messerschmidt 1999).

The life histories approach has also been deployed to offer clues about questions raised by non-offending. As crime is a ready resource for attaining masculinity and this is particularly the case among socially marginal or highly competitive groups of men, researchers wonder what this means for the masculinity of non-offenders. Thus, British researchers have explored the subjective significance of 'desistance' for male working-class offenders (Gadd & Farrell 2004). Ending criminal offending and criminal careers is a puzzle for conventional criminology that the masculinities approach could help to unravel.

By following the signposts in Jefferson's analysis of violence and the masculine unconscious and balancing individual agency with structural determination (of the sort stressed in research on risk factors and life course stages) these researchers conclude that desistance is a complex gendered process (Gadd & Farrell 2004). A detailed discussion of life circumstances draws out the contradictory nature of this desistance. An apparent ending of criminality is shaped around heroic male discourses of redemption and protectiveness and the uncertain possibilities of male renunciation of actual or phantasised violence, with the latter being more widespread and commonly shared by offenders and other males alike.

The further value of insider understanding in accounts of masculine offending and non-offending is signalled by a study of young Australian men and security offi-

---

3　There is growing research evidence and debate about masculine performance and appropriation of fluid elements of masculinity by women in criminal justice occupations or criminal activities (see Miller's (2002) critique of 'gender dualism' in this field and her discussion of female street crime and girls 'doing masculinity'). For most researchers, masculinity still refers to social identities and practices that are substantially monopolised by men and they are given their fullest social meaning in these contexts.

cers involved in regular episodes of drinking violence and disorder (Tomsen 2005). This points out that although the link between masculinity and criminality has been newly emphasised, researchers have little understanding of the means by which a withdrawal from violence can sit with a socially respected masculine identity. 'Disengagement' is understood here as a process of situational decision-making and withdrawal from conflicts and offending that may characterise a broad population of 'non-criminal' men rather than as any full 'desistance' from a set criminal pathway and identity. Involvements in drinking-related public violence are tied to matters of male group status, the protection of honour in episodes involving insults and slights that must be responded to, and the collective pleasure of carnival-like rule breaking in public disorder. Yet an awareness of danger and a disengagement from occasions of conflict can sit with rational and restrained models of a masculine self. This may even be cultivated by public safety campaigns that give an exaggerated belief that individual agency always prevails in avoiding violence.

The masculinity and criminalisation conundrum

Most importantly, a growing number of studies in this new field explore the ties between masculinity and elements of the whole justice system of policing, courts, prisons and probation. A consideration of these suggests the contradictory relations that exist between criminal 'protest' masculinities and 'official' state masculinities in this sphere. Any full understanding of this evidence must consider the ways in which criminalised masculinities are produced in tension with the official forms of masculinity inscribed in policing and criminal justice systems. As Connell (1995: 76) has suggested, dynamic relationships exist between the hegemonic and other subordinated or marginalised forms of masculinity producing different masculinities and a gender politics within masculinity. The criminological implication is that social forms of masculinity linked to violence and offending are both policed and produced by aspects of the criminal justice process and state formations.

In this sense, the mostly rhetorical critique of 'hegemonic masculinity' by Hall (2002) does usefully draw attention to the interrelation of different masculinities, and how problematic conceiving the differences between hegemonic and potentially criminal protest masculinities has become for criminologists with an elastic use of these terms in some discussions of male criminality. Furthermore, the commentator hypocrisy in this field that he refers to, suggests that there is still an insufficient understanding of the condoning and cultivating of violent forms of manhood by capitalist, imperial and contemporary post-colonial states. Male violence is deployed internally and externally in a range of state forms, and both legitimated and denounced in different historical and social circumstances.

The paradox of regulating criminalised masculinities with the formally lawabiding though sexist and aggressive official masculinities of criminal justice systems is reflected in research on policing (Prokos & Padavic 2002). Responses to criminal justice intervention that foster and reproduce masculinities with a direct or indirect relation to criminality are uncovered in other contemporary studies. Most notably, the general failure of prisons to deter crime or to rehabilitate inmates with any certainty is now informed by accounts of masculinity in these studies. These illustrate the sharp struggles over male power and status and the masculine hierarchies that characterise prison subcultures and the lives of incarcerated men.

An interview study with British prisoners, suggests that a sp
'manliness' that is hard, aggressive, bullying and conformist is a usua
prison (Jewkes 2005). There is a dehumanising impact of prisons as to\
that threaten personal identity with a climate of 'mortification and br   . This
engenders a hard, public, masculine social performance among inmates. Related
work on prison masculinities cogently suggests that it is aspects of the intervention
process itself that affirm destructive forms of male identity that criminal justice systems are ostensibly opposed to (Sabo et al 2001).

This contradiction leads to a major conceptual problem for the new crime and
masculinities paradigm, as a critical analysis of masculine offending necessitates an
understanding of the historically shifting and fluid way that destructive masculinities
have been either condoned or denounced by policing and criminal justice processes.
Moreover, this problem results in dilemmas for programs of punishment, correction
and crime prevention that may appear to both treat and foster male criminality (Holland & Scourfield 2000).

Feminists have been critical of the way in which male violence against women
has been simultaneously denounced yet condoned or ignored in the wider culture and
in traditional 'hands off' police responses. Further examples of the mixed official
reaction to male violence from the new literature on masculinity and crime concern
the shifting historical responses to public violence and various forms of hate crime
(Tomsen 2001). In many of these cases, discouraged reporting, lax policing and
lenient sentences signal support for the generation of an aggressive masculinity in
relation to public leisure and spaces. Male on male violence that results from this
may be regarded as a minor public nuisance or inevitable aspect of the social reproduction of appropriate masculinities.

Furthermore, violence and criminal offending by groups of men can even
signal resistance against social hierarchy. Historical and cross-cultural scholarship
has demonstrated that much male violence is an ambiguous form of protest or rebellion against social hierarchies based on social class, caste and racial/ethnic
differences. This research includes studies of disorder, unruly leisure, festivals, carnivals, and more direct acts of insubordination including rallies and riots, as means
of symbolic protest and collective cultural resistance against the moral values of
ruling groups (Scott 1985; Rude 1995; Tilly 2003). In fact, official and police concerns about collective male disorder that refer to a compelling need to protect the
broader public are also driven by anxiety about the symbolic challenge to state, class
and racial authority that this disorder can comprise.

These different examples draw out the complexities of official reactions and the
criminalisation process in relation to different crimes and masculinities. Male crime
is gendered crime, yet when commentators on the masculinity-crime nexus cannot
acknowledge the link between the bulk of male offending and other factors such as
social class and race, they risk inadvertently naturalising male offending. This
reinforces a widespread public belief in a commonsense view about masculinity as a
force inevitably leading millions of men to involvement in crime and violence.

The danger of any gender-centric approach is a view of the criminalisation process as little more than a straightforward official response to problematic male
offending. This forgets the lessons about criminality stressed by a previous generation of critical criminologists arguing that a key aspect of the criminal justice reaction
to violence and crime in liberal capitalist and racially and ethnically divided societies

is the targeting of the deviant acts of members of particular poor, marginal and minority groups. A sobering reminder of the ongoing importance of these lessons concerns a classic criminological account of the 1989 'Central Park jogger' case. This gave an apparently plausible interpretation of the masculine motives of the five black and Latino youths imprisoned for the alleged gang bashing and rape of a middle-class white woman in New York (Messerschmidt 1993). Yet a later re-examination of the evidence suggests that the investigation and trial process were an apparent case of police targeting and criminal justice processing of socially marginal males who fitted ready stereotypes of sexually predatory offenders (Schanberg 2002).

The dilemmas of problematic gendered male offending and an overlapping criminalisation process have also been very evident in the debate raised by some key local examples of contentious crimes and their policing. These include the controversies surrounding acts of public disorder perpetrated by young 'Middle Eastern' men in south-western Sydney, and the trials and imprisonment of key offenders with heavy sentences in a series of group rape cases (Poynting et al 2003; Warner 2004). More recently, the ongoing concern about how to deal progressively with the issue of domestic and sexual assaults in Indigenous communities has become more public (Human Rights and Equal Opportunity Commission 2006). In these cases, different forms of violence are related to particular racialised protest masculinities that reflect distinct histories of marginality due to the effects of migration and racial dispossession in a white Anglo-dominated culture.

Conclusion

Research findings do affirm the overall value of acknowledging the link between crime and masculinities for criminological understanding. It is now incumbent upon critical criminology to move beyond the impasse generated between explanations of crime that either downplay male offending or focus on it to the exclusion of evidence about criminalisation and other social factors. Criminalisation is a common strategy in a contemporary era of post-left new social movement activism around crime that may dovetail with punitive law and order politics (Snider 1998). This can encourage the major expansion of police and prisons, and the imposition of longer and often mandatory sentences with an erosion of commitment to alternative punishments. Any such harsh penality will have the pernicious effects of net-widening, mass incarceration and punishment for vengeance rather than reform or rehabilitation. It particularly targets and brutalises poor, black and Indigenous men with further divisive and negative impacts on their own fragile communities.

Masculine crime may appear to be inevitable or even abhorrent. Yet there is little progressive gain in simple essentialist understandings of male offending, a denial of human agency or a cynical dismissal of substantial efforts to educate and promote diverse and non-violent masculinities among marginalised boys and men. To be critically aware of the extent and effects of the criminalisation process and its secondary effects in racist and class-divided societies means a constant reflexivity in analysing the masculinity-crime nexus.

References

Bonger, W 2003, 'Criminality and economic conditions', in McLaughlin, E, Muncie, J & Hughes, G (eds), *Criminological Perspectives: essential readings,* Sage, London & Thousand Oaks.

Bourgois, P 1996, 'In Search of Masculinity: violence, respect and sexuality among Puerto Rican crack dealers in East Harlem', 36(3) *The British Journal of Criminology* 412.

Breines, I, Connell, RW & Eide, I (eds) 2000, 'Male Roles, Masculinities and Violence: a culture of peace perspective', UNESCO Publishing, Paris.

Collier, R 1998, *Masculinities, Crime and Criminology: men, heterosexuality and the criminal(ised) other,* Sage, London.

Collison, M 1996, 'In Search of the High Life: drugs, crime, masculinities and consumption', 36(3) *The British Journal of Criminology* 428.

Connell, RW 1995, *Masculinities,* Allen & Unwin, Sydney.

Connell, RW 2002, 'On Hegemonic Masculinity and Violence: response to Jefferson and Hall', 6(1) *Theoretical Criminology* 89.

Connell, RW & Messerschmidt, J 2005, 'Hegemonic Masculinity: rethinking the concept', 19(6) *Gender and Society* 829.

Connell, RW, Kimmel, M & Hearn, J (eds) 2005, *Handbook of Studies on Men and Masculinities,* Sage, Thousand Oaks.

Copes, H & Hochstetler, A 2003, 'Situational Construction of Masculinity among Male Street Thieves', 32(2) *Journal of Contemporary Ethnography* 279.

Cunneen, C 1985, 'Working Class Boys and Crime: theorising the class/gender mix', in Patton, P & Poole, R (eds), *War/Masculinity,* Intervention Publications, Sydney.

Cunneen, C & White, R 1996, 'Masculinity and Juvenile Justice', 29(1) *Australian and New Zealand Journal of Criminology* 69.

Gadd, D & Farrall, S 2004, 'Criminal Careers, Desistance and Subjectivity: interpreting men's narratives of change', 8(2) *Theoretical Criminology* 123.

Gould, S 1981, 'The Ape in Some of Us: criminal anthropology', *The Mismeasure of Man,* WW Norton & Co, New York.

Hall, S 2002, 'Daubing the Drudges of Fury: men, violence and the piety of the 'hegemonic masculinity' thesis', 6(1) *Theoretical Criminology* 35.

Hobbs, D, Hadfield, P, Lister, S & Winlow, S 2003, *Bouncers: violence and governance in the night-time economy,* Oxford University Press, Oxford.

Holland, S & Scourfield, JB 2000, 'Managing Marginalised Masculinities: men and probation', 9(2) *Journal of Gender Studies* 199.

Human Rights and Equal Opportunity Commission (HREOC), 2006, *Ending Family Violence and Abuse in Aboriginal and Torres Strait Islander Communities: key issues,* HREOC, Sydney, June.

Jefferson, T 1997, 'Masculinities and Crime', in Maguire, M, Morgan, R & Reiner, R (eds), *The Oxford Handbook of Criminology,* Clarendon Press, Oxford.

Jefferson, T 2002, 'Subordinating Hegemonic Masculinity', 6(1) *Theoretical Criminology* 63.

Jewkes, Y 2005, 'Men Behind Bars: "doing" masculinity as an adaptation to imprisonment', 8(1) *Men and Masculinities* 44.

Kersten, J 1996, 'Culture, Masculinities and Violence against Women', 36(3) *The British Journal of Criminology* 381.

Kimmel, MS (ed) 1987, *Changing Men: new directions in research on men and masculinity,* Sage, Thousand Oaks.

Messerschmidt, J 1993, *Masculinities and Crime: critique and reconceptualisation of theory,* Rowman & Littlefield, Lanham.

Messerschmidt, J 1995, 'Managing to Kill: masculinities and the space shuttle Challenger explosion', 3(4) *Masculinities* 1.

Messerschmidt, J 1997, *Crime as Structured Action: gender, race, class, and crime in the Making*, Sage, Thousand Oaks.

Messerschmidt, J 1999, 'Making Bodies Matter: adolescent masculinities, the body, and varieties of violence', 3(2) *Theoretical Criminology* 197.

Miller, J 2002, 'The Strengths and Limits of "Doing Gender" for Understanding Street Crime', 6(4) *Theoretical Criminology* 433.

Monaghan, LF 2002, 'Hard Men, Shop Boys and Others: embodying competence in a masculinist occupation', 50(3) *The Sociological Review* 334.

Newburn, T & Stanko, E (eds) 1994, *Just Boys Doing Business? Men, Masculinities and Crime*, Routledge, London.

Polk, K 1994, *When Men Kill: scenarios of masculine violence*, Cambridge University Press, Melbourne.

Polk, K 1998, 'Violence, Masculinity and Evolution: a comment on Wilson and Daly', 2(4) *Theoretical Criminology* 461.

Poynting, S, Noble, G & Tabar, P 2003, 'Protest Masculinity and Lebanese Youth in Western Sydney: an ethnographic study' in Tomsen, S & Donaldson, M (eds), *Male Trouble: looking at Australian masculinities*, Pluto Press, Melbourne.

Prokos, A & Padavic, I 2002, '"There Oughtta Be a Law Against Bitches": masculinity lessons in police academy training', 9(4) *Gender, Work and Organizations* 439.

Rude, G 1995, *The Crowd in History*, Serif, London.

Sabo, D, Kupers, T & London, W (eds) 2001, *Prison Masculinities*, Temple University Press, Philadelphia.

Schanberg, S 2002, 'When justice is a game', *The Village Voice*, 20-26 November.

Scott, J 1985, *Weapons of the Weak: everyday forms of peasant resistance*, Yale University Press, New Haven.

Segal, L 1990, *Slow Motion: changing masculinities, changing men*, Virago, London.

Snider, L 1998, 'Towards Safer Societies: punishment, masculinities and violence against women', 38(1) *The British Journal of Criminology* 1.

Sparks, R 1996, 'Masculinity and Heroism in the Hollywood "Blockbuster": the culture industry and contemporary images of crime and law enforcement', 36(3) *The British Journal of Criminology* 348.

Stanko, E & Hobdell, K 1993, 'Assault on Men: masculinity and male victimization', 33(3) *The British Journal of Criminology* 400.

Taylor, I, Walton, P & Young, J 1973, *The New Criminology: for a social theory of deviance*, Routledge & Kegan Paul, London.

Tilly, C 2003, *The Politics of Collective Violence*, Cambridge University Press, Cambridge.

Tomsen, S 1997, 'A Top Night: social protest, masculinity and the culture of drinking violence', 37(1) *The British Journal of Criminology* 90.

Tomsen, S 2001, 'Hate Crimes and Masculine Offending', 10 *Gay and Lesbian Law Journal* 26.

Tomsen, S 2002, *Hatred, Murder and Male Honour: anti-homosexual killings in New South Wales 1980-2000* (Research and Public Policy Series No. 43), Australian Institute of Criminology, Canberra.

Tomsen, S 2005, '"Boozers and Bouncers": masculine conflict, disengagement and the contemporary governance of drinking-related violence and disorder', 38(3) *The Australian and New Zealand Journal of Criminology* 283.

Warner, K 2004, 'Gang Rape in Sydney: crime, the media, politics and sentencing', 37(3) *The Australian and New Zealand Journal of Criminology* 344.

Winlow, S 2001, *Badfellas: crime, tradition and new masculinities*, Berg, Oxford.

9

NARRATING THE CHASE: EDGEWORK AND YOUNG PEOPLES' EXPERIENCES OF CRIME

Mark Halsey

Introduction

In this chapter I examine the relationship between young people and crime and do so by drawing on the narratives of young men who have been involved in successive high-speed pursuits.[1] Beyond their reputedly addictive elements (Kellett & Gross 2006), or their association with personality types (Homant et al 1993, 1994), I hope to show that being pursued by police is an event marked by complex social and interactional aspects and that identifying these is essential to developing a better understanding of this type of crime. The chapter proceeds in three directions. In the first, high-speed pursuits are placed in the context of car crime and youth offending generally. Secondly, the dimensions of high-speed pursuits are explicated using the concept of edgework (placing oneself in situations which, if unsuccessfully negotiated, will most likely result in serious injury or death). Here, I look specifically to the visceral and cultural aspects of being pursued by police in order to ground debate in the lived experience of key actors. Finally, I focus on the subjective conceptions of risk and safety evinced by young men in such circumstances in order to discuss the critical implications of offender narratives for policy and practice in this area.

Car crime and youth offending

It should come as little surprise that car-related crime constitutes a sizeable proportion of offences committed annually by young people; 'The car shapes the built

---

1   Primary data for this chapter has been drawn from initial and follow-up interviews conducted by the author with young men aged 15 to 21 in juvenile and adult custodial institutions in South Australia since September 2003. Participants were (and continue to be) interviewed under the auspices of an Australian Research Council-funded study of young mens' experiences of repeat incarceration. Participants have spoken to a wide array of issues concerning the three main themes of pathways into offending, experiences of custody, and transitions to release. It was in this context that conversations about high-speed pursuits came often to the fore. The ARC research is due to be completed in December 2008.

environment, cuts through the landscape, dominates the soundscape, [and] is a key commodity in production and consumption' (Dant 2004: 61). Critically, 'cars have been deeply integrated into the affective networks of familial life and domestic spaces, as well as friendship networks and public sociability' (Sheller 2004: 230). Cars, in short, mark peoples' lives in indelible and complex ways. They are objects of desire and demand, even if the precise meanings and values of the automobile are highly contested. In 2004, there were around 90,000 vehicles recorded by police as stolen across Australia, constituting around 10% of all recorded property crime, and was the fourth most common offence committed by juveniles (Australian Institute of Criminology 2005: 9, 64). This chapter focuses on South Australia – it is the State where I have spoken extensively with young men about motor vehicle theft generally and high-speed pursuits more particularly. It can be noted, however, that offence type and rates share a broad similarity with other Australian states and territories.

In 2004, car-related juvenile crime in South Australia constituted just over 18% of all police apprehensions (Office of Crime Statistics and Research 2005: 58). Of the juveniles apprehended for driving offences, 57% were alleged to have engaged in 'dangerous or reckless driving' (2005: 77). A further 21% were alleged to have been driving whilst their license was suspended or cancelled. Of those apprehended for larceny and receiving, 20% were alleged to have engaged in 'illegal use of a motor vehicle' (2005: 73). Further indicative of the prominence of car crime is that of the 85 secure detention orders given to juveniles in 2004, 27 of these were for 'larceny/ illegal use of vehicle' and three for 'driving while license suspended or cancelled'. Put another way, over 1 in 3 detention orders were for motor vehicle related offences. Of the 157 finalised cases where the major offence proved was 'larceny/illegal use of vehicle', 94% (147) involved males, predominantly aged 14 to 17 years, and almost one third (44) identified as Indigenous Australians (2005: 132-133, 135).

Beyond the spectacle

High-speed chases are particularly newsworthy due to the vision (most often provided by news teams in helicopters) of 'good cops' tracking down 'bad criminals'. The paraphernalia of the chase – road spikes (tyre deflation devices), excessive speeds, running of red lights, convergence of many police vehicles in pursuit of a lone offender, the fact that the offender may be declared or assumed to be armed and dangerous, the potential for things to go wrong – takes the viewer beyond the mundane activities of everyday life. At the time of writing, high-speed pursuits were being given sustained media and political attention in South Australia. Headlines such as 'Terror Reign: gang launches high-speed rampage', 'Crash Car's Trail of Crime', 'Serial Car Thief Free to Steal', 'Speeder Spiked: four car chases in five hours', 'The Chilling Trap of Gang Anarchy', confronted readers of the state's main newspaper (*The Advertiser*) from January to March 2007. In response to public 'outrage', the Premier of South Australia even went so far as to direct the Social Inclusion Unit to report on ways of curtailing the activities of what had colloquially become known as the 'Gang of 49' (essentially a list of names generated by the police of those believed to be at the core of pursuit (and other related crime) problems in the state). Needless to say, there was a good deal of sensationalism and misinformation in these stories – and as to be expected, the perspectives of suspects were nowhere canvassed. The result of this is that the lived experience of those pursued by police – their emotions, rationalisations, reflections, circumstances and justifications – continue to be effaced in favour of more sinister and simplistic portraits of young criminals. In Garland's (1996) terms, a criminology of the Other has emerged wedding conversations about car crime and high-speed pursuits to intrinsically mad, bad or just plain dangerous and disrespectful individuals. Without wishing to glorify high-speed pursuits, nor those young men involved in such activity, I believe it necessary to reach past the stereotype toward a more nuanced conversation about how and why these events occur. Doing this means paying something more than lip service to the narratives of those arrested and convicted of such crimes.

Beyond the pursuit as public spectacle lies the fact that some of these events end with devastating consequences. Between 1990 and 2005, 136 persons were killed in such scenarios (Joudo 2006: 77). This is higher than the 132 shooting deaths occurring in police custody over the same period (six of which related to motor vehicle pursuits). High-speed pursuit fatalities account for almost one third (28.5%) of all deaths in police custody (476 for period 1990 to 2005). Of these deaths, 90% occurred in the context of a pursuit that was initiated as a result of a theft-related or traffic incident. Death, admittedly, and fortunately, is the exception to the rule, but the potential for fatalities seems constantly to underpin debate about pursuits in two ways. First, there is the notion that *not* pursuing an offender is counteractive to saving lives and/or avoiding future injury. The logic here is that it is safer and better to have police in pursuit of a dangerous driver than to allow this driver to escape custody (Palmer 2003: 34).[2] Secondly, there is the notion that high-speed pursuits are inherently unpredictable events and that the risk of death or injury increases according to the speeds attained during the chase and the time elapsed from the onset of the pursuit (Alpert & Dunham 1990). As Dunham et al (1998: 31) put it, two key critical questions in this context are: '(a) When [is] a pursuit reasonable to fulfil a law enforcement function, and (b) When should a pursuit be terminated?'. In order to help build a cogent response to such questions it is important to first draw a clear distinction between events which are too often conflated: theft of a motor vehicle as against vehicles becoming the object of pursuit.

Although nearly half of all vehicles pursued in urgent duty driving scenarios prove to be stolen, it is essential to recognise that car theft is a distinct event to high-speed pursuits, and only a small proportion of offenders who steal cars get caught up in pursuit activity. Copes (2003: 327-328) argues that the motivation behind car theft, at least in the United States, centres on six things: *money* (selling the whole or parts of the car, doing ram raids for alcohol, cigarettes or clothing); *style* (car as an extension and display of personal and sub-cultural distinction and belonging); *mobility* (to get home, to get to a friend's house, to transport oneself from one side of town to another); *action* (to kill time, to elicit a thrill through burn outs, joyriding); *settling a score* (stealing cars as targeted retribution); and *staying low* (getting into and out of the scenes of crime without betraying one's identity). This typology neatly captures the range of reasons given by offenders for stealing cars. However, it is also important to think about why some car-related offences evolve into high-speed pur-

---

2   In his Chicago study, Falcone (1994: 146) found that the policy associated with the least pursuits and – against the predictions of police – with *no further rise in criminal activity*, was that which specifically discouraged pursuits 'except under exceptional circumstances clearly outlined by formally promulgated department policy'.

suits – very few offenders tell of stealing cars specifically to become the subject of a pursuit (Light et al 1993: 59; Cherbonneau & Copes 2006):

Interviewer: So when you … stole some of these cars, … would you drive fast in them?

Participant: No, I'd … treat 'em like … my own cars. I'd drive it normal until the police come and when the police come I'd start acting like a maniac (B, 9: 29).

Pursuits overwhelmingly emerge from the confluence of events arising in the wake of, rather than at the point of, motivations for stealing a car, or committing a traffic violation. In fact, and in the tradition of Jack Katz (1988), if one asks: What are people trying to do when they steal a car or violate traffic rules?, and then pose the question: What are (these sometimes same) people trying to do when they become the subject of a pursuit?, two quite different analytical paths need to be countenanced. Very simply, pursuits are not about settling scores, staying low, or generating an income (although, as will emerge, action and style retain somewhat greater salience as key pursuit variables).

In their study of the United Kingdom, Light et al (1993: 59) frame offenders' experiences very much as an ambivalent event – one which instils a mixture of 'fear and excitement' in suspects, and which very rarely, if ever, induces the 'decision' to voluntarily surrender to the pursuing vehicle. I use the term vehicle as opposed to police officer quite deliberately, as pursuits are as much about the performance of each car as they are about the decisions or safety considerations evoked by each driver. The sights and sounds of the street, the attention from passers-by, the smell of the interior, the comfort of the seats, the quality of the stereo, the responsiveness of the engine, the demands of the occupants of the vehicle, the feeling of independence, the feeling of being mobile, the thought of what one is going to do with the cash likely to be received for the whole car or for certain of its parts, the feeling of being a step closer to carrying out the next ram raid, the feeling of having done something 'grown up' – these are the kinds of thoughts typically occupying suspects' minds in the time before a joyride or cruise switching into a pursuit. In fact, I think it is useful to think in terms of *two distinct yet similar bodies straddling two distinct if contiguous moments* – one very much attuned to staying low (to not attracting attention, to playing it cool, to getting a job done) as against one suddenly threatened with capture (having to see 'what this vehicle can do', and having to push things to the edge). This is something I'm concerned to draw out below – the inescapable contradiction surrounding the body police imagine they are pursuing (one whose willingness and ability to surrender increases as the pursuit progresses) as opposed to the body they inadvertently help to produce (one whose willingness and ability to surrender reduces exponentially as the pursuit progresses). The concept of edgework is integral to executing this task as it facilitates the explication of the meanings attributed to the chase by those fleeing from police, and, I will go on to suggest, by those in pursuit of suspects.

Edgework: on being pursued (at high speed)

Lyng (1990) posits the two defining characteristics of edgework as having to do with a particular kind of risk and particular mode of (losing and regaining) control. One defining element is high risk. Engaging in edgework means creating 'a clearly observable threat to one's physical or mental wellbeing or one's sense of an ordered existence' (1990: 857):

> Interviewer: What went through your mind when the cops were first chasing you?
>
> Participant: You'd do anything to get away, you know, like we'd come to an intersection, all the cars are stopped, we'll just bang, straight through the middle of them all, you know, where they're parked. Just smashed all their mirrors off. Come through the middle ... [T]hat's what we did [when we] come to the red light. [We] went through the red light and we T-boned a 4-wheel drive and rolled it. We spun out. Another car veered off ... just ploughed into the traffic lights ... [We] got fucked up ... (C, 13: 51).

In terms of the second defining characteristic, Lyng (1990: 859) writes, 'Th[e] unique skill, which applies to all types of edgework, is the ability to maintain control over a situation that verges on complete chaos, a situation most people would regard as entirely uncontrollable':

> The first chase where I got away ... I was with a couple of other boys .... [T]hey were younger than me but they'd been in a few other chases. [A]nd ... I'm in a slow car, but I'm still doing, you know, 140 to 150 [kms] and I've gone through Adelaide and they said, 'This car can't lose it man. You have to scare the cop off'. And I've gone 150 ks and then just gone onto the wrong side of the road and the cops have just gone, 'Whoops, stuff him', you know, 'He's going to kill himself'. And they just let me go, man (D, 17: 27).

In laying out the more specific dimensions of edgework, Lyng (1990) articulates the *skills* and *sensations* accompanying this practice. Skills centre primarily on the desire to 'discover the performance limits of a piece of technology or other form' (1990: 859). This seems particularly apt in the context of high-speed pursuits as suspects frequently talk about what their car could or could not do during the course of the chase:

> Participant: We don't back off. Like I don't back off at all. [I'll] just like turn the lights off going on the wrong side of the road and drive ...
>
> Interviewer: And you'll drive, even if it is on the rims or whatever?
>
> Participant: Yeah, yeah. Until the car's dead. I won't stop (A, 10:46).

The sensational axis of edgework involves a number of complex elements. First, there is the production of 'a purified and magnified sense of self' (Lyng 1990: 860):

> Interviewer: [D]escribe the feeling [...] you look in the mirror and there's whatever – half-a-dozen ... cops [behind] you. How do you feel?
>
> Participant: I feel like a tin god, you know ... The adrenalin just takes over, you know ... And suddenly you're not that [regular] person any more, do you know what I mean? ... Like, you're invincible (E, 23: 36; 4: 13).

Secondly, Lyng (1990: 860) contends that 'the individual typically feels a significant degree of fear during the initial, anticipatory phases of the experience', but that ultimately, 'as one moves to the final phases of the experience, fear gives way to a sense of exhilaration and omnipotence':

At first I was scared, man, at first. [Then] [i]t started turning into a good rush …
Like now … I'd hide from cops and I don't freak out. I just turn my music up –
it's a normal thing to me now, you know, turn there, turn there … go on the
wrong side of the roadway. You [get to] know how to call a chase off. But that
first one … [I] got one in the back [from the police] … [But] then you pull that
off and you think, 'Oh, I'm still alive, man, I'm still alive', and it gets to a normal
thing and then you get to the point where you're used to it (D, 16: 15).

A third dimension of the sensational aspect of edgework concerns actors
'report[ing] that, at the height of the experience (as they approach the edge), their
perceptual field becomes highly focused'. Here, 'background factors recede from
view, and … perception narrows to only those factors that immediately determine
success or failure in negotiating the edge' (Lyng 1990: 861):

Interviewer: And how fast would you be going sometimes in these chases?

Participant: Oh, I'd be hittin' 200 to 220 kilometres, yeah …

Interviewer: Did you worry about what the police would do to you when they
               eventually caught you? … Did that cross your mind?

Participant: Nah, nothing's ever crossed my mind when I'm driving 'cause it's
               just the road. You just got to watch the road and handle – try to
               handle the car as good as you can 'cause nothing comes to your
               mind when you're [driving] … (B, 10: 33).

An adjunct of this streamlining of vision and attention to the smallest detail is
the loss of time – the inability to say just how long one was at or near the edge. This
is indisputably true of those engaged in pursuits insofar as the young men I have
interviewed can recall the specifics of the chase (down to which wheel was on its
rim) but not the length of time they were pursued for (beyond saying a few minutes
or a long time).

A fourth sensation depicted by Lyng (1990) relates to the notion that '[e]dge-
workers sometimes speak of a feeling of "oneness" with the object or environment'
(1990: 861). For young men involved in high-speed pursuits, the oneness with the
vehicle has more to do with imposing propriety over the car than with any fundamental dissolution of the line between subject and object:

[W]hen you start it and you're actually driving away and you're driving around,
there's that freedom there, you know. It's not your car but you don't have to think
like that when you're in the car. You think [while] you steal it and after you leave
it, 'That's not your car'. But when you're in a car, you don't think this is not
yours. You think, 'This is mine', you know … (D 9: 26).

The hyper-reality of edgework is another important dimension given by Lyng.
Here, the attraction of the edge involves elevating oneself above the mundane
dimensions of regular life:

Participant: I was going flat out, you know. Like this is brilliant, you know, and
               looking behind me … One copper's turned into two, two's turned
               into four, you know, there was so many. In the end I had … 18 po-
               lice cars and a helicopter chasing me … Yeah, it was unreal … I
               was loving it (E, 19: 26).

The final sensational dimension canvassed by Lyng is the idea that edgework
is not amenable to narration – that the intensity of the experience is beyond description. I would argue that all experience is always singular but that out of habit, or

for the sake of social convenience, we perceive much of experience to be identical to those of others in our immediate and sometimes distant worlds. Having said this, it is worth noting that several young men, when asked to describe the feeling of being pursued at speeds in excess of 200 kilometres per hour, responded by inviting the interviewer to experience the rush of the chase for himself. Words, in this context, appear to be inadequate to the task of fully explicating the intensity of events.

There is more to edgework than risk and control. It is also about the confluence of social-structural factors and micro-political events. It is a means for thinking about the body, and peoples' motivations for action, in a grounded manner. Lyng's original formulation of the concept paid specific attention to the work of Marx (1846) and Mead (1934) as a way of situating particular ways of *bodying forth,* of reclaiming the visceral and vital aspects of life, in a materialist and phenomeno-logical framework (2004: 360). Here, social, economic and political forces – all demanding a certain amount of routinisation and predictability of conduct – produce a wide variety of (fleeing and morphing) subject positions which have as their goal the temporary suspension of the three great stratifying forces of late-capitalism: alienation, clock time, and commodification (see O'Malley & Mugford 1994: 201-206). Lyng (1990: 878) sums up this situation by remarking:

> The experience of self in edgework, then, is the direct antithesis of that under con-ditions of alienation and reification. If life under such circumstances leads to an oversocialized self in which numerous institutional 'me's' are present but ego is absent, edgework calls out an anarchic self in which ego is manifest but the per-sonal, institutional self is completely suppressed. It is the suppression of reflective consciousness that ultimately produces the sensations [of edgework].

Mead's distinction between subjects' awareness of themselves as a socially produced organism (Me), as against (some) subjects' desire to become other than the series of selves imagined or imposed on them by the world (I), is central to under-standing what is occurring in events given the name edgework. Indeed, Lyng (1990: 877) goes so far as to say that edgework is the 'I' made manifest and that the two terms 'could be used interchangeably'. Let me ground this in terms of high-speed pursuits by making the key point that all such events are inflected through structural (background/predominately impersonal) factors and active (foreground/predominately personal) dimensions. The 'I' which manifests itself in pursuits is not epiphenomenal to the world but is, in as concrete a fashion as possible, *of* the world. It is an 'I' produced by one and the same forces which produce and try to render predictable the conventional citizen (the 'Me'). But here, rather than edgework being enacted by, and functioning as, an elixir to law abiding oversocialised selves, it instead presents as an antidote to *under*socialised selves, or more accurately, to lives interrupted by intrusions of a very different kind (cautions, charges, arrests, court hearings, bail procedures, hearings, convictions, community service, license suspen-sion, periods of imprisonment and so forth). Working full time, paying the rent or a mortgage, enduring the rigors of marriage or coupledom, submitting to the routines of domestic life, raising children, playing the career game, should not be seen as the main route to edgeworking. Indeed, and for good reason, persons who hold little or no chance of being the subject of such constraints are just as likely to look for ways of suspending their own kinds of institutional difficulties and to find a solution (as fleeting as it may be) in edgework. It is worth recognising, therefore, that a large proportion of those pursued at high speed by police are caught in entrenched cycles of crime and social marginalisation where the means to engage in (licit forms of) pleasure are severely limited:

Participant: Just in one car we had … about fuckin' 30 high speed chases in it but I got caught in the long run.

Interviewer: Did you keep that car because it was a good chase machine?

Participant: Yeah, yeah. We had it for three days and fuckin' we'd hit and run coppers and drag coppers and shit. They all tried to stop it.

Interviewer: [T]here would be people out there in the community who would say, 'Well, […], you know, I understand people want to get a thrill and all that sort of thing. Why not go skydiving or why not do this or that?'

Participant: You need the money to do it though, don't you?

Interviewer: Right, right and [it's] as simple as that, really?

Participant: Yeah, nothing's free these days, is it?

Interviewer: Yeah, sure.

Participant: They say there's heaps of things to do but fuckin' where are you meant to get the money for it? Centrelink? Two hundred bucks a fuckin' fortnight? Where does that go? Fuck all (C, 20: 52).

On balance, young men pursued at high speed can be characterised as opportunistic (even reluctant) edgeworkers as opposed to edgeworkers of a more orthodox (or willing) variety. Mountain climbers, base jumpers, and so forth, approach the edge but have a fair degree of control over their equipment, and indeed the conditions they choose to perform in. Suspects in high-speed pursuits, I would argue, do not have these same 'luxuries'. This is not to say that young men – confronted with the 'choice' to pull over or chance their luck – do not in some sense take a calculated risk. But it is a risk most often calibrated against personal biographies and a background of events where, in many senses, the prospect of getting away from the police is an extension rather than an aberration of lives 'already lived'.

Interviewer: And where mainly have you lived […]?

Participant: In Taperoo and Mansfield Park.

Interviewer: [A]nd what did you think of living there? … Was it okay, [was it] a good neighbourhood?

Participant: No, very – it's a pretty bad neighbourhood with all the drugs and the violence.

Interviewer: Did you find that … problems came looking for you in that sense, like it was hard to sort of just be yourself or get away from things? …

Participant: Yeah, because they carry weapons, like either a gun or some shit like that … I've been done for dealing before, possession of firearms … I started carrying a firearm at 13 …

Interviewer: Yeah? And what was the specific reason you started carrying a firearm […] ?

Participant: Because of protection …

Interviewer: Protection in terms of … the drug scene, is that what you mean?

Participant: Yeah … Bad neighbourhood and that (F, 1: 48).

These passages speak to the importance of the social – in particular, neighbourhood – context within which people develop ideas about conventional as opposed to extra-ordinary events. Here, in the tradition of the Chicago School, 'crime is an environmentally structured choice for those seeking to survive in socially disorganized neighborhoods' (Einstadter & Henry 1995: 133). Such crime can range from small-scale drug dealing (and the networks and sense of identity this brings) to armed robbery, to car theft, and, on occasion, fleeing from police at high speed.

Young men involved in high-speed pursuits live a good portion of their lives as edgeworkers – drifting into and out of scenarios which place them in physical danger. There is always a greater or smaller risk of getting caught, of being ratted on by one's mates, of suffering injury to one's body, or to one's reputation as a 'straight up' operator. Under these conditions, being chased by police is not so much *the* means for edgeworking but merely the most visible way of bodying forth in a personal milieu replete with such performances (breaking and entering, shooting up, sticking up, stabbing and being stabbed, assaulting and being assaulted, avoiding arrest, escaping from custody).

Discussion and concluding remarks

A key issue emerging from the above involves the subjective experience and construction of risk harboured by those engaged in pursuit activity. If one again poses the question: What are young men trying to do when they become the subject of a pursuit?, the answer, I believe, is that they are trying to escape capture without death or serious injury being incurred to themselves or passengers of the pursued vehicle. The critical and confronting point here is that young men pursued at high speed overwhelmingly privilege their *own* life over those of police, other motorists, or bystanders. This in itself bursts the terrain of probable outcomes during the pursuit event wide open. Once the chase is in motion, from the point of view of those pursued, all bets are off:

> Participant: Like, when the cops come up and chase us, we don't think about, 'Oh, if we go through this red light who's going to die?', or something … That don't come on board. We just think about getting away from them … We don't think about who we're going to hurt. Some person walking across the road, clean them up … We don't, like, really think about that … I've had a car crash before, a stolen car … High speed chase … We hit three cars … (I, 19: 21).

The following excerpt, from a young man commenting on the Victim Awareness program offered to him whilst in detention, illustrates that the sociology of risk has no set path or logic:

> Participant: We're still doing [Victim Awareness] at the moment … The ambulance [people] do come in … Some of the pictures and shit he showed us are pretty terrible. Ah, he showed us a video. It was five dead people in a car after a high-speed chase and you could see, like, the faces all messed up and shit, his heart hanging out of his chest. It looked pretty funky but it didn't get me thinking. I liked it.
>
> Interviewer: Right, so it didn't scare you or worry you or anything? …
>
> Participant: Nah … But if I get in a high-speed I take my seatbelt off straight away because I'd rather fly through the window and die rather than get all fucked up (J, 34: 22).

Admittedly, this may be a little bit of bravado. But the prospect of building resilience to engaging in pursuits through punitive sanctions, driver education campaigns, or shock tactics appears unlikely to serve much more than a symbolic function (especially since the threat of sanction tends only to be reflected on *after* the chase):

> I've actually had heaps bad car accidents, man, and, you know, been arrested or whatever and you think – you're sitting in the cell at the cop shop and you think, 'Far out, I could've died, man'. You know, I could've killed someone else. But then when you get out six months later, you go back and do the same thing … (D, 8: 52).

Perhaps of greatest concern, is that the most direct attempt at halting high-speed pursuits – police giving chase – seems mainly to intensify the visceral dimensions of the pursuit and to remind suspects that there are indeed high stakes worth playing for. Light et al (1993) note that 14% (100) of their interviewees said that getting away from police surpassed all other experiences associated with car theft. This trend is reflected in interviews undertaken in the South Australian context:

> Interviewer: [H]ow were you feeling when you [had] the cops behind you and [you were] trying to get away from them?
>
> Participant: It blows you away, because the adrenalin rush just takes over … Just seeing the sirens on normally scares the shit out of me.
>
> Interviewer: Does it? … So, it doesn't make you, sort of think, 'I should stop and pull over … '.
>
> Participant: Just makes you go, go, go (K, 11:35 I2).
>
> Participant: I've been in a high-speed chase doing 180 and they're [ie the police] right behind me … So, they're the problem why people are getting killed on roads, or causing crashes, because they're suppose to be backed off …
>
> Interviewer: So if they backed off, would you back off as well then in that case? Like, once you'd lost them, like, you would slow down? …
>
> Participant: Yeah, I will slow down, yeah. If they backed off. I would've been getting rid of the car like I usually do. I go down a quick street, jump, you know, leave the car there (N, 54:44 I2).

The role of police in amplifying and intensifying high-speed pursuits has support from a number of studies (Dunham et al 1998; Light et al 1993). And when couched in terms of law enforcement and public safety, this is, quite plainly, an incredibly difficult issue to address. But when placed in the context of edgeworking, the policy path ahead seems much clearer – namely, remove the key catalyst responsible for switching a traffic violation or suspected stolen vehicle into a high-speed pursuit, and reserve pursuits for only those circumstances where the driver is known, beyond all reasonable doubt, to have perpetrated offences of a serious violent kind and/or is projected to do so unless apprehended. This would eliminate in excess of 90% of reported pursuit activity each year (Brewer & McGrath 1990: iii; Hoffmann & Mazerolle 2005: 534-535). Obviously, such a strategy is far more easily mooted than put into practice – especially if one takes the view, as seems reasonable, that police too in a sense constitute themselves as edgeworkers (as persons placed in scenarios where the prospect of serious injury or death is real and ongoing for the duration of the event in question). But my argument is that high-speed pursuits unfold along particular lines because the stakes of each chase are in fact similar in kind for *both* the pursuer (ie police) *and* the pursued (ie young offender). No one wants to relinquish the pursuit or cede it to the opposing party. The key difference, though, as shown graphically above, is the lengths to which those pursued are willing to go in order to successfully negotiate their way out of the controlled chaos of the chase.

If one accepts that police and suspects are both, in effect, engaged in edge-work, then it follows that both parties risk damage to their reputations depending on how the chase unfolds. More particularly, and with reference to a key concept in the lexicon of Katz (1988), both stand to be *humiliated*.[3] Katz argues that where humiliation threatens to break loose, there are only two courses of action to be followed: one either finds the antidote to humiliation (humour, recalibration of the event as trivial), or one risks humiliation morphing into rage, from which there is no regress. Police, it is important to realise, run the real risk of being humiliated by those they pursue. This is especially the case where trained officers, in specialised vehicles, find themselves repeatedly outwitted by someone who can barely see over the steering wheel, is likely to be under 16 years of age, and will probably be driving a vehicle of questionable mechanical status.

> [The police officer] was pissed off, [and] he punched me in the back of the head ... Gave me a mouthful of crap, so I looked back at him ... All dirt over my face ... A nice big bruise. I looked real bad. I said, 'Are you just pissed off because I blew you off in a shit car?' ... And he just looked at me and he said, 'You're funny', and smacked me again ... And then I walked out and the copper comes out and he goes, 'YOU!' ... I just smiled at him, and he come up with a torch and smacked me with it in my guts ... And they chucked me in the cop car and took me down to Port Adelaide (O, 43: 32).

Such scenarios, when matched with evidence suggesting there are many occasions when pursuits are not called off despite relevant speed thresholds having been exceeded, show that police do indeed have something to lose in pursuits. And this potential for loss is not solely to do with the risk to one's life or physical wellbeing, or with the loss (or short-term escape) of the suspect. Police, just like those they pursue, trade in the currency of honour, respect and fame (or infamy). And this trade, I would venture, is fertile ground for humiliation to find its footing – especially where there are few or no tangible means for backing down with one's reputation (the 'Me') in tact. In terms of public policy on high-speed pursuits, the essential question therefore is: Under what conditions might the parties involved in pursuits be prepared to pull back from the edge? Dunham et al (1998: 38) show very clearly that in order for suspects pursued at speed by police to slow down they need to *feel safe* about doing so. Specifically they need to feel safe from police getting heavy handed with them should they surrender, and they need to feel safe in terms of the harm dealt to their reputation as hardened, street wise, 'real deal', 'never say die' people should they cease fleeing. As Katz (1988: 24) remarks, 'Image or reputation is social'. However, creating the (social) space for backing down goes beyond the issue of safety. Indeed, 'From the driver's perspective, social identity or social competence and tact perhaps are *more* important than safe driving. Operating a vehicle includes not only perceptual and motor skills, but also *the need for a smooth social performance*' (COMSIS Corporation and The Johns Hopkins University 1995: 81 emphasis added).

---

3   A concept extended by O'Malley and Mugford (1994) and by Lyng (2005).

If edgework is about the 'I' – the temporary suspension of what Lyng (2004: 362) has termed the 'social self' – then pulling back from the edge, emerging unscathed from controlled chaos, would seem to a very large extent to be about the opportunity to re-engage (with) the social in as smooth a fashion as possible. Young men pursued at speed seem only to have two paths toward a smooth social performance (one that guarantees respect) – escape custody, or be apprehended in a manner that accrues fame and respect in proportion to the carnage wrought throughout the chase (where the latter goes some way toward compensating for being caught and makes the consequences 'worth it'). Police, on the other hand, have, or should have, a far wider array of means for assisting their transition to a competent social performance in situations where a chase might otherwise have ensued (or have continued to unfold). Presently, police policy in South Australia stipulates, 'Urgent duty driving may only be undertaken: in response to an emergency involving obvious danger to human life; or when the seriousness of the crime warrants it. In all cases the known reasons for the urgent duty driving must justify the risk involved'. And, as an overarching rule, 'Safety must be the primary concern ahead of capture' (see SAPOL General Order 210/01 as quoted in Coroner, South Australia, Inquest Number 5/2005 (2704/2002)).

To an extent, therefore, there are unambiguous rules in place, which police can invoke to assist them to save face or maintain respect in the context of neutralising the humiliation accompanying voluntarily terminated pursuits. But if the testimonies of the young men cited in this chapter reflect reasonably accurately the lived reality of pursuits, then it is clear that safety is on occasion being subverted by the desire to capture suspects. Moreover, the perceived seriousness of offences is being incorrectly determined by police at the outset of many pursuits. This again points to the idea that, even, or perhaps especially, for police, high-speed pursuits offer a seductive mix of risks and rewards – a visceral and reasonably rare moment in which an officers' social (vocational) competence can be directly put to the penultimate test.[4]

To be clear, the behaviour of suspects is undeniably a critical aspect of high-speed pursuits. But such behaviour cannot be divorced from the decisions and actions of officers in pursuit. Here, in terms of public policy, police discretion emerges as particularly germane since there are, quite literally, countless moments where the decision to cease pursuing a vehicle could be enacted by police with minimal danger to life or property. To this extent, and by definition, it is important to consider police as concomitant with edgeworkers – with those who have the capacity and opportunity to avert or pull back from extreme danger but often and for varying periods of time refrain from doing so. Edgework, in short, means that the traditional binaries of good cops versus bad offenders, skilled police versus dangerous suspects, and responsible citizens versus irresponsible young people, need to be supplanted by a more nuanced analysis of pursuits as primarily corporeal events brought to life by specific socio-economic, gendered, peer-oriented and ecological factors.

References

Alpert, G & Dunham, R 1990, *Police Pursuit Driving: controlling responses to emergency situations*, Greenwood Press, New York.

---

4   SAPOL annual reports give the number of urgent duty driving instances as 353 in 2000-2001, 422 in 2001-2002, and 449 in 2002-2003.

Australian Institute of Criminology 2005, *Australian Crime Facts Figures*, Australian Institute of Criminology, Canberra.

Brewer, N & McGrath, G 1990, *Progress Report on Urgent Duty Driving: high speed pursuits: offender and pursuit characteristics*, Australasian Centre for Policing Research (formerly National Police Research Unit), Report Series 89, Payneham.

Cherbonneau, M & Copes, H 2006, '"Drive it Like You Stole It": auto theft and the illusion of normalcy', 46(2) *British Journal of Criminology* 193.

COMSIS Corporation & The Johns Hopkins University 1995, *Understanding Youthful Risk Taking and Driving, Interim Report*, US Department of Transportation, National Highway Traffic Safety Administration

Copes, H 2003, 'Street Life and the Rewards of Auto Theft', 24 *Deviant Behaviour* 309.

Dant, T 2004, 'The Driver-car', 21(4/5) *Theory, Culture, Society* 61.

Dunham, R, Alpert, G, Kenny, D & Cromwell, P 1998, 'High Speed Pursuit: the offenders' perspective', 25(1) *Criminal Justice and Behaviour* 30.

Einstadter, W & Henry, S 1995, *Criminological Theory*, Harcourt Brace, New York.

Falcone, D 1994, 'Police Pursuits and Officer Attitudes: myths and realities', 13(1) *American Journal of Police* 143.

Garland, D 1996, 'The Limits of the Sovereign State: strategies of crime control in contemporary society', 36(4) *British Journal of Criminology* 445.

Hoffman, G & Mazerolle, P 2005, 'Police Pursuits in Queensland: research, review and reform', 28(3) *Policing: an international journal of police strategies and management* 530.

Homant, R, Kennedy, D & Howton, J 1993, 'Sensation Seeking as a Factor in Police Pursuit', 20(3) *Criminal Justice and Behavior* 293.

Homant, R, Kennedy, D & Howton, J 1994, 'Risk Taking and Police Pursuit', 134(2) *The Journal of Social Psychology* 213.

Joudo, J 2006, *Deaths in Custody in Australia: national deaths in custody program annual report 2005*, Technical and Background Paper Series, 21, Australian Institute of Criminology, Canberra.

Katz, J 1988, *Seductions of Crime: moral and sensual attractions in doing evil*, Basic Books, New York.

Kellet, S & Gross, H 2006, 'Addicted to Joyriding? An exploration of young offenders' accounts of their car crime', 12(1) *Psychology, Crime and the Law* 39.

Light, R, Nee, C & Ingham, H 1993, *Car Theft: the offender's perspective*, Home Office Research Study 130, London.

Lyng, S 1990, 'Edgework: a social psychological analysis of voluntary risk taking', 95(4) *The American Journal of Sociology* 851.

Lyng, S 2004, 'Crime, Edgework and Corporeal Transaction', 8(3) *Theoretical Criminology* 359.

Lyng, S (ed) 2005, *Edgework: the sociology of voluntary risk taking*, Routledge, New York.

Marx, K & Engles, F 1846, *The German Ideology*, reproduced in McLellan, D 2002, *Karl Marx: selected writings*, Second Edition, Oxford University Press, Oxford.

Mead, GH 1934, in Morris, CW (ed), *Mind Self and Society from the Standpoint of a Social Behaviorist*, republished in 2004, University of Chicago Press, Illinois.

Office of Crime Statistics and Research 2005, *Crime and Justice in South Australia: Juvenile Justice 2004*, South Australian Justice Department.

O'Malley, P & Mugford, S 1994, 'Crime, Excitement and Modernity' in Barak, G (ed), *Varieties of Criminology*, Praeger, Westport.

Palmer, D 2003, '"Hot Pursuit": law enforcement practice and the public interest', 28(1) *Alternative Law Journal* 32.

Sheller, M 2004, 'Automotive Emotions: feeling the car', 21(4/5) *Theory, Culture, Society* 221.

10

ETHNIC MINORITY IMMIGRANTS, CRIME AND THE STATE

Scott Poynting

Introduction: critical criminology and ethnicity-crime links

Crime is often linked with ethnic minorities in popular ideology, political debate and media reporting. Criminologists have accordingly concerned themselves with these linkages, most often from an empiricist perspective. Critical criminologists need to ask, not only about empirically identifiable connections between ethnic minorities and crime, but why the questions are raised in the first place. Why are they raised in this way? Whose interests does this serve? What are the organising categories (and their related interests) which define 'ethnicity', 'minority' and 'majority' or 'mainstream', and how are they connected to those which define crime, wrongdoing, degree of harm, need for intervention and punishment, justice of intervention and punishment, and so on?

These questions will necessarily lead us to probe underlying causal relations, to uncover the structural reality, which produces the surface patterns that can be empirically observed (given the predominant ways of looking at and organising the data). That is, a criminology which is genuinely critical will entail searching for explanations deeply rooted in social reality, rather than remarking on superficial constant conjunctions of facts. These arguments are influenced by *critical realism* (Bhaskar 1978, 1989; Sayer 2000; Hartwig 2007).[1] Such critical criminological explanations, in short, will comprehend the causes of observed connections between, say, ethnicity and crime, as well as the predominance and popularity of the prevailing empiricist accounts. That is a tall order. For the purposes of this chapter, we will confine our discussion to *immigrant* ethnic minorities, and many of our examples will deal with those in Australia. The same conceptual principles will generally apply elsewhere, though the histories, cultures and particularities will differ.

---

1   Also see White this volume for a class analysis of criminology consistent with critical realism; for some criminological comments about applying critical realism to 'risk' theory, see Mythen & Walklate 2006: 236-238.

An instance of uncritical linking of ethnicity and crime, and a critique

Given these politics of ethnic crime, what are we to make of it when both Opposition Leader and Premier in the State of New South Wales agree, as they did during the 2007 election campaign, that there is a serious problem with 'ethnic crime', and each competes with the other in identifying the purported problem as an ethnic one and in promising tough law and order measures against 'Middle Eastern thugs' (Clennell 2006) or 'grubs' of 'Middle Eastern appearance' (Davies 2006)? Apart from the short-lived spontaneous violence in reprisal to the racist mob attack in the 'Cronulla riots' of 2005 by young men of communities targeted in those attacks (Poynting 2007), this supposed ethnic crime wave covers a multitude of sins, not all properly classified as 'crime', not all correctly identified as 'ethnic', and not all indicated by empirical evidence.

The wide range of misrepresentations and deficiencies in the reporting of the 'ethnic crime wave' included the following:

First, much of the fear of 'crime' in relation to 'gangs' of ethnic minority youth, for example, is rather about boisterous, space-claiming or uncivil behaviour by friendship groups of young men, perceived to be threatening because of unfamiliarity to, or prejudice on the part of, dominant ethnic groups, engendered by media and popular representations (White et al 1999; Collins et al 2000).

Secondly, those identified by a minority ethnicity in such cases (and in instances of actual crime) include people born, raised and schooled in Australia: the 'ethnic' label is dubious, or certainly not straightforward.

Thirdly, there is rarely a causal link credibly demonstrated between the ethnicity or culture in question and the crime.[2]

Fourthly, evidence for or against a statistical connection between ethnicity and crime is scant in Australia, patchy in quality everywhere (because of haphazard data collection and aggregation, lack of comparability, and problematic categories of ethnicity), and where it does exist, it sometimes suggests disproportionately low representation of immigrants in crime (Francis 1981 and Hazlehurst 1987, cited in Mukherjee 1999: 23, 24; Easteal 1989, cited in Cunneen 1995: 388-389).

Fifthly, as Mukherjee (1999) also argues, where there is an empirical conjunction of minority ethnicity and crime, the real causal link could be with, for example, poverty, unemployment and lack of educational qualifications, or age, or other factors which coincide demographically in some instances with certain immigrant groups. These links, of course, have been well established and explained in criminology, though sometimes with a measure of 'culture of poverty' argument, as White (1996: 303-304) points out.

Then, of course, sixthly there is the over-policing of ethnic minority youth pointed to by Cunneen (1995), and the evidence in a number of countries of discrimination in the criminal justice system against immigrant minorities, both of which could in part explain any over-representation of these minorities in crime statistics and also in media reports and popular perceptions.

---

2   See for example the discussion in Poynting et al (2004), on the widely reported 'ethnic' gang rapes in Sydney in 2000 and 2002.

History of immigrant-crime linking in Australia

With the landing of the First Fleet in 1788, the British and Irish comprised a tiny minority of the population on the Australian landmass; all were immigrants of sorts – mostly involuntary – and the majority were convicted 'criminals'. This continued to be the case for some time, though with tickets of leave and increasing migration of free settlers, by the mid-19th century, convicts in Sydney, for example, accounted for only about 3% of the (white) population. By the 1880s, the propertied and res- pectable classes had come –ironically given earlier crime fears about 'foreigners' – to fear the Australian-born generation of (male) working-class youth, known as white 'natives', who had never known the civilising influences in the mother coun- try, for their supposed unruliness and proneness to crime (Gleeson 2004).

From the 1860s there were widespread popular campaigns of anti-Asian racism in Australia, notably directed at Chinese immigrants, but the small minority of Afghans and those from neighbouring parts labelled as such who came to Australia as camel drivers were also denigrated as 'Asiatics'. In this racialisation, both groups were othered as bringing immorality (including the corruption of white womanhood) and indeed crime (Kabir 2004: 43, 54, 60). These and other anti-immigrant cam- paigns (such as against Pacific Islanders) led to the White Australia policy, which was instituted legislatively upon Federation at the beginning of the 20th century, and which remained in place formally until the 1960s, with its cultural and political legacy lasting even longer (Tavan 2005). The *Immigration Restriction Act* 1901 (Cth) prohibited the entry to Australia of (a) anyone who failed a dictation test in any European language (used in practice to exclude non-White immigrants); (b) those deemed likely to depend on the public purse or charity; (c) 'idiots' and the insane; (d) those bearing infectious diseases; (e) those convicted of unpardoned crimes within the past three years and sentenced to over a year's imprisonment; (f) prostitutes and pimps; (g) indentured labourers. There they were: non-white immigrants classified, as in folklore about the 'Chinaman' and to some extent the 'saddle-coloured Asiatic', the 'Afghan', in the same list as the mendicant, the mad, the diseased, the criminal and the enslaved.

As a result of these policies, by 1947, the Australian population was 90% Australian-born, with a further 8% born in the British Isles or other English- speaking countries, and only 2% born in non-English speaking countries. Over the post-war decades, Australia embarked on an immigration program which was to see the population double in 40 years, with more than half of the increase from immigrants and their children (Castles et al 1988: 24-25). While most of the overseas-born have always come from the United Kingdom and Ireland, the immi- gration program, needing greater numbers, looked next to northern and eastern Europe, then for larger numbers to southern Europe and eventually further afield. This has within a lifetime produced an Australia that is one of the most culturally and linguistically diverse nations in the world.

It was not long into this immigration program before the Australian state moved to investigate possible connections between immigrants and crime, commis- sioning three reports in the 1950s on the question by the Commonwealth Immigration Advisory Council: the 'Dovey Reports' of 1952, 1955 and 1957. These reports showed that immigrants were actually under-represented in crime, with the convictions for 'aliens' at 3.9 per 1000 being less than that for adult Australians at 5.7 per 1000. Indeed, the convictions of southern European immigrants were a quarter of that of the population at large. Moreover, the recidivism rate of immigrants was half that of the Australian-born (cited in Borowski & Thomas 1994).

Nevertheless, popular prejudices and misconceptions persisted, and the media and police were no exception. With the influx of migrants from Italy and Greece predominating in the 1950s and 1960s, the attention of the state and the 'fourth estate' (media) were directed towards them. In 1961, for instance, the Sydney *Observer* newspaper reported that southern European immigrants were involved in organised prostitution in Melbourne (Bureau of Immigration Research 1990: 2). In the 1970s, the notorious 'Greek conspiracy case' alleged social security benefit fraud by Greek immigrant doctors in collusion with patients of the same ethnicity, in what Alex Kondos (1992) analyses as an instance of institutional racism. Approximately $100 million – far more than was alleged to have been defrauded – was spent on prosecutions which were eventually quashed; police were found to have used inappropriate methods, public servants found to have acted improperly, and a magistrate found to have denied natural justice (Grabowsky 1989; Bureau of Immigration Research 1990: 10).

In the 1970s, the whole community of Italian immigrants around Griffith in southwest New South Wales was criminalised following widespread allegations and indeed some convictions in relation to the cultivation and sale of cannabis. In 1977 the disappearance and presumed killing of Griffith Liberal Party Branch President Donald McKay, an anti-marijuana campaigner and former state Liberal candidate in the region, amplified fears of 'Italian organised crime' to a moral panic about the 'Mafia' in Australia (Collins et al 2000: 13).

In the 1980s, the burgeoning immigration from Indo-China following the Vietnam War led to a familiar 'debate' about 'Asian immigration' leading to 'ethnic ghettos', and, of course, crime. Long-term residents of Cabramatta in southwest Sydney began in the early 1980s to complain about the selling of drugs on the local streets (NSW Ombudsman 2005: 191). When controversial historian Geoffrey Blainey (1984) in the 1980s promoted an attack on multiculturalism as leading to social disintegration, it was South-East Asians, mainly Vietnamese – and to a smaller extent Arabs, mainly Lebanese – who represented the epitome of otherness and refusal to integrate. Both of these backgrounds were associated in such attacks with crime. As Andrew Jakubowicz (2004: 2) puts it, the Vietnamese 'were implicated in the rising paranoia about unsafe cities in the late 1980s, where [the presence of] Vietnamese became a popular indicator for the presence of violent and drug-related crime'. This clamour reached a crescendo in the middle to late 1990s, when Cabramatta was dubbed 'the heroin capital of Australia', and its Indo-Chinese immigrant communities were under a constant media barrage (Dreher 2007). Maher et al (1997) have detailed some of the harsh, arbitrary and at times reportedly unlawful police responses to the calls for 'zero tolerance' to 'clean up the streets'.

Since the mid-1990s, there has been a series of moral panics in Australia, and particularly in the two most populous and ethnically diverse cities of Sydney and Melbourne, about 'ethnic gangs' and crime, especially involving young people. At first 'Asian gangs' were the object of popular fear and state surveillance and intervention, then from the late 1990s more attention has been given to 'Lebanese' gangs (White et al 1999; Collins et al 2000; Poynting et al 2004). Following the fatal stabbing in 1998 of a Korean-background schoolboy in a fight between groups of young men outside a party in Punchbowl in Western Sydney, whole suburbs were ethnically targeted by police in a protracted campaign of discriminatory 'stop-and-search' and other high-profile 'zero tolerance' tactics against 'Lebanese gangs', including the intimidatory use of police dogs and mounted police (Collins et al 2000). In Melbourne, 'Turkish gangs' have attracted some media notoriety, and more recently in Sydney, Pacific Islanders have been focused upon. Both in Melbourne and Sydney and in regional cities most recently, there has been media and youth worker worry about 'youth gangs' from the Horn of Africa. In a classic working of moral panic, youth crime became, in Jakubowicz's (2004: 8) words, 'the trope through which the fears about social cohesion were voiced'.

This brings us back to our original question: why are connections between ethnicity and crime raised in this way? Why the concern with, say, 'Southern European' prostitution rings in Melbourne when there were doubtless plenty such enterprises run by Anglo-Saxon and Celtic background criminals that were never labelled as such? Why 'Greek' social security fraud? Why 'Asian crime' and 'Middle Eastern crime' squads, with the attendant publicity? To look for answers to such questions (too rarely asked), we need to consider the history and nature of the state in relation to structured racism.

The state, ethnicity and crime

Critical criminologists have long recognised that it is the state that defines crime (see also Grewcock this volume) and which is uniquely responsible for controlling and punishing crime. The state is usually defined as all of the institutions of government of a particular society within a determinate geographic space: the state includes the bodies which make laws and which police them within those boundaries. The state has a formal monopoly over the legitimate means of violence; only the state can declare and prosecute war. The state alone can impose taxes. The state is responsible for providing those goods and regulating those areas of social life where civil society or the private sector cannot or will not do so. The state might not simply be the 'executive committee of the capitalist class', a concept much pilloried by anti-Marxists, but it certainly, in capitalist social formations (which are just about everywhere), mediates between the (often short-term) and competing interests of individual capitals to secure the (long-term) interest (in the last instance, survival) of capital as a whole. The capitalist state also intervenes against the working class in the interests of capital as a whole, and even sometimes individual capitalists. Despite the much-discussed process of globalisation, the state is almost everywhere practically coterminous with the nation-state.

This latter point, connected with the geographic boundedness of states, has vital and sometimes deadly implications for ethnicity. The modern nation state came into being during the long transition from feudalism to capitalism. Regions and peoples which previously had only porous and indeterminate liminal zones between them, became amalgamated or separated but always divided off by formal borders, represented as lines on maps and guarded to various extents by state forces on either side. Nationalism accompanied the formation of the modern state, and sustains it to this day. The peoples which defined each space as their own had their own foundational stories, their own cultures, their own languages, their distinctive values and often their own religions, which were always contrasted to the 'other' who did not belong in 'their' space.

The protection of the law in many cases did not apply, certainly not equally, to the 'other'. The Jews in Nazi Germany and the territories it occupied may be an extreme case, but the same principle applies to the Rom ('Gypsy') people there and elsewhere, Armenians at the end of the Ottoman Empire (however much holocaust denial the Turkish nation state indulges in), the Kurds in all the nations now ruling the lands where they have lived for much longer than those nation-states, the Palestinians, and Indigenous peoples everywhere.

Moreover, in the processes of colonialism that marked the primitive accumulation of capital in the original transition to capitalism and lingered on to shape global capitalism even today, the culture of the other can be made unlawful or at best deviant and marginal to the dominant or 'mainstream' ethnic definers of the nation. Thus colonised peoples have been often forbidden from speaking their own languages, practising their own religions, educating their young in their own ways. The Aboriginal peoples of Australia were no exception.

It is important to recall that the 'White Australia' policy, discussed above, while indeed a local product of specific historical and geographical circumstances, was also very much a legacy of the British Empire, equating whiteness with British-ness in its southern outpost. Thus the 'aliens' designated in crime statistics, even in the 1950s a half-century after Federation and two decades after the Statute of West-minster, did not include immigrants who were British subjects. In fact, Australians were British subjects until 1984.

The 'Mediterranean appearance' of police media releases is really a marker of perceived non-British phenotype. Italians are 'of Mediterranean appearance'; Greeks are 'of Mediterranean appearance'; Lebanese are 'of Mediterranean appearance' and 'Middle Eastern appearance', too. A Lebanese-background journalist, an expatriate Australian born and reared in Bankstown, phoned me from Boston to talk about the Cronulla riots. She reflected that, over there, she was simply 'white'. Very often, non-whiteness in the Australian sense means what Ghassan Hage (1998) calls 'Third World looking'. It does not simply mean skin colour. It is a symbolic indicator of place in the hierarchy of national belonging, which is also a measure of differential entitlements to citizen rights. There are similarities, still, in Britain. The innocent young Brazilian tradesman, Jean Charles de Menezes, shot dead with seven rounds to the head by special police on the London Underground in 2005, was said in original media accounts (and who knows what briefings?) to have been of 'Asian [meaning South Asian] appearance'. The colonialist colour chart pays little heed to geography.

As Collins et al (2000) detail, particular forms of street crime and disorder in Sydney associated in the late 1990s with youth 'of Middle Eastern appearance' were labelled as 'unAustralian'. They follow the argument of Pearson (1983), who showed how particular types of street crime in 19th-century Britain were deemed (in complete denial of the historical record) to be 'unBritish' and seen as a foreign phenomenon. Here Pearson (1983) was at pains to bring a historical perspective to the apparently new and by definition unBritish crime of 'mugging', which was the subject of moral panic in the United Kingdom in the 1970s, entering the vocabulary of police and judiciary after its importation and popularisation by the media (Hall et al 1978). Coming from the United States, the term had built-in connotations of Black perpetrators, and its very use criminalised, or at best rendered suspect, racialised members of the population.

This form of classification then becomes a mechanism of institutional racism, from 'ethnic' profiling, to discriminatory 'zero tolerance' targeting, to unequal outcomes in the courts, in Australia as in Britain. Now since 9/11, we have seen a transmutation of the most recent epitome of otherness, from Arab Other to Muslim Other in Australia – or, in Britain, from 'Asian' Other to Muslim Other. Muslim communities indeed in all 'Western' countries have become subject to intensified surveillance, regulation, and perhaps what is justified as preventative harassment by the state in the name of the 'War on Terror'. Muslims have been subjected to menacing and sometimes violent raids by state security services. New laws make it a criminal offence to publish details of these. Organisations have been proscribed as terrorist organisations, without any evidence of their purported terrorist activities having to be made public, let alone proven with some accountability (Hocking 2004; McCulloch 2006; Lynch & Williams 2006). All organisations proscribed under the Australian anti-terror laws to date are Muslim ones (AMCRAN 2005).

Laws safeguarding civil liberties have been relaxed, rewritten, or just ignored by the state. Freedom of expression no longer incorporates freedom for Muslims to express or especially to exhort support for those whom some of them regard as freedom fighters, and the state defines as terrorists (as Nelson Mandela, Gerry Adams and Xanana Gusmao once were). Freedom of religion no longer guarantees freedom to preach sermons defined by state authorities as 'radical': at least not without harassment and vilification, threats of cutting off funding to community organisations, threats of prosecution or detention for inciting support for terrorism, and plans for state intervention in the training and in the licensing of imams.

Ethnicity, the state and victims of crime

For all the state attention to minority ethnic groups as supposedly disproportionate *perpetrators* of crime, there is comparatively little notice of them as *victims* of crime. The crime statistics in Australia, moreover, have all the flaws in tracking victimisation of ethnic minorities that are discussed above in relation to those arrested or charged or convicted of a crime. It is probable that, given the socio-economic factors related to immigration and settlement, and on various forms of qualitative evidence, that non-English-speaking immigrant minorities are in fact over-represented among victims of crime. Certainly this is so, almost by definition, for hate crime (see Mason this volume).

There is evidence that crimes which victimise such minorities are under-reported, and where reported under-recorded and often not acted upon (See Poynting & Noble 2004, for these factors in relation to violence, vilification and discrimination against Arab and Muslim Australians). For an example of a lack of response to reports from NSW immigrant community members, a young police constable (male, early 20s) whom I interviewed in 1999 in a south-western Sydney suburban Local Area Command with a large immigrant minority of Arabic-speaking background, told me that many members of this community, especially women, came into the station very often to make complaints of various sorts. He regarded these complaints as 'rubbish', and encouraged them to go away, believing that otherwise he would not be able to do his (real) job.

The consequences of such a work culture for the policing of, say, domestic violence, should be obvious. As I write, the story reaches the British press of a young immigrant woman who reported to the Metropolitan Police no less than four times, including with physically obvious wounds, that her family were trying to murder her. She was disbelieved and ignored. Her father and uncle were convicted of her eventual murder, after her corpse was found buried in a suitcase in a backyard. The press, of course, reported this case of familial homicide as an 'honour killing' (McVeigh 2007). There is no concept of 'honour killing' among white families in which there is a murder by a family member over amorous or sexual relations or domestic affairs.

These couple of examples must serve here to point to the salience of 'intersections' of gender relations with the social relations of ethnicity (and indeed, of class). An exemplary analysis of such 'intersection' is given by Cunneen and Stubbs (2002) in the case of domestic violence and even homicide against Filipina immigrant women in Australia. Not only does the state underplay the threat of such violence against racially 'othered' immigrant woman, it also tends to work with egregious, offensive, fallacious and dangerous assumptions about 'Filipina brides' or perhaps Asian sex workers, as the Vivian Alvarez Solon case notoriously demonstrated about an unwell Australian citizen who was falsely identified as an illegal immigrant and unlawfully deported (Grewcock 2005).

It would be remiss to leave off this chapter without mention of what have been called 'safety crimes', which also victimise ethnic minorities disproportionately. Safety crimes have been usefully defined as 'infractions of a legal duty placed upon an employer or corporate entity, this legal duty defined within the framework of the criminal law … which result in traumatic injury or death' (Tombs 2007; see also Hocking & Guy this volume). The fact that most of these are not treated as crimes by the criminal justice system, because of the need to prove intentionality and the strong foundation of individualism, does not mean that critical criminologists should follow this logic – indeed they should do the contrary, and challenge it (Tombs 2007). Tombs and Whyte (2006), in arguing against the propositions of the 'Risk Society' thesis (see O'Malley this volume) that risk is ubiquitous and shared by all in contemporary societies, demonstrate that health and safety risks of capitalist production impinge far more on the less powerful and especially the marginal – in production relations, in labour markets and indeed in the global inequalities inherited from colonialism. They argue that:

> the greater part of the burden of health and safety risks generated by work continues to fall upon workers. … Moreover, these burdens are by no means distributed along new social divisions of risk, but intensify traditional racialized and gendered social inequalities (Tombs & Whyte 2006: 179).

As the Department of Immigration and Multicultural and Indigenous Affairs (DIMIA) (2006: 26) observed:

> Safety and health at work is a major issue for all workers, but it specially affects migrants from NESC [non-English-speaking countries] because they disproportionately work in manufacturing, construction and other heavy industries where the majority of workplace accidents and injuries occur.

The DIMIA submission cites a 1994 WorkSafe Australia report showing that overseas-born workers from NESCs have a much higher rate of work-related fatality than Australian-born, with 40% of deaths in manufacturing and construction compared to 22% for Australian-born. It further cites the 1995 Industry Commission's

Inquiry into Occupational Health and Safety finding that immigrant workers had nearly four times the risk of fatal injury than the Australian-born (DIMIA 2006: 26). These examples must suffice to indicate that immigrant ethnic minorities bear the brunt disproportionately of crimes against human safety committed in the pursuit of maximum profit by employers and corporations.

Conclusion

This chapter has argued that a critical criminology worthy of the name must go beyond empiricist 'putting the facts straight' in popular accounts of ethnicity and crime, and probe the underlying relations which both produce those constant conjunctions of facts, and which make certain of them (for example, minority ethnicity and criminality) appear salient. Historical and contemporary examples have been discussed in which ethnic minorities were represented as (more) deviant, to advance a range of interests: because their cultural difference was perceived as a threat to the majority or mainstream, because they provided convenient scapegoats for a raft of social ills, because it was a was an effective way to recruit the state in combating (lawful or illicit) economic competition, and much else besides. Underlying all of these instances is the reality that it is the state which defines (and controls and punishes) crime, and the history that everywhere the nation-state is the arbiter and guardian of ethnicity, and deploys a battery of legislative and bureaucratic nationalism against the ethnic 'other'. This nature of the state, in a class society riven by gender as well as ethnic inequalities, comes clearly into play in cases where ethnic minorities are victims. Hate crime and safety crime, for instance, are disproportionately suffered by immigrant minorities, but human rights and citizen rights are circumscribed by ethnicity.

Thus we have seen that the criminalisation of minority immigrant communities, with which we began our discussion in this chapter, is causally related not only to the obsession with taken-for-granted statistics and anecdotes of 'ethnic crime', but also to their victimisation in hate crimes. Moreover, the sort of systematic 'invisibility' of hate crime and lack of state duty of care for its victims, applies similarly to 'safety crime' and its victims. These sorts of causal relations cannot be adequately explained at the level of individual racism; the phenomenon of racism needs to be comprehended in its institutional context. More than that, however, even 'institutional racism' needs to be seen as produced by structural racism deeply constitutive of our social formation, built into the state, and formed out of the history of the nation state.

References

AMCRAN (Australian Muslim Civil Rights Advocacy Network) 2005, *ASIO, the Police and You*, Second Edition, AMCRAN, Sydney, <www.law.uts.edu.au/clc/publications/Anti TerrorLaws2ndEd_8_12_05.pdf>.

Bhaskar, R 1978, *A Realist Theory of Science*, Second Edition, Harvester Press, Hassocks.

Bhaskar, R 1989, *The Possibility of Naturalism: a philosophical critique of the contemporary human sciences*, Second Edition, Harvester Wheatsheaf, Hemel Hempstead.

Blainey, G 1984, *All for Australia,* Methuen, Sydney.

Borowksi, A & Thomas, D 1994, 'Immigrants and Crime', in Adelman, H, Borowski, A, Burstein, M & Foster, L (eds), *Immigration and Refugee Policy: Australia and Canada compared,* Vol II, Melbourne University Press, Melbourne.

Bureau of Immigration Research 1990, *Immigrants and Crime in Australia,* Library Bibliography Series, AGPS, Canberra.

Castles, S, Kalantzis, M, Cope, B & Morrissey, M 1988, *Mistaken Identity: multiculturalism and the demise of nationalism in Australia,* Pluto Press, Sydney.

Clennell, A 2006, 'Police Tough on Both Sides of Cronulla Riots', *Sydney Morning Herald* 19 July, p 2.

Collins, J, Noble, G, Poynting, S & Tabar, P 2000, *Kebabs, Kids and Cops: youth, ethnicity and crime,* Pluto Press, Sydney.

Cunneen, C 1995, 'Ethnic Minority Youth and Juvenile Justice: beyond the stereotype of ethnic gangs', 6(3) *Current Issues in Criminal Justice* 387.

Cunneen, C & Stubbs, J 2002, 'Migration, Political Economy and Violence Against Women: the post immigration experiences of Filipino women in Australia', in Freilich, JD, Newman, G, Shoham, SG & Addad, M (eds), *Migration, Culture Conflict and Crime* Ashgate, Dartmouth.

Davies, A 2006, 'Iemma Plays the Race Card on Crime', *Sydney Morning Herald,* 23 January, 9.

DIMIA (Department of Immigration and Multicultural and Indigenous Affairs) 2006, *Submission to the Australian Government Productivity Commission Study of the Economic Impacts of Migration and Population Growth,* <www.pc.gov.au/study/migrationandpopulation/subs/sub022.pdf>.

Dreher, T 2007, 'Contesting Cabramatta: moral panic and media interventions in "Australia's heroin capital"', in Poynting, S & Morgan, G (eds), *Outrageous! Moral panics in Australia,* ACYS Publishing, Hobart.

Gleeson, K 2004, 'From Centenary to the Olympics: gang rape in Sydney', 16(2) *Current Issues in Criminal Justice* 183.

Grabowsky, PN 1989, 'The Great Social Security Conspiracy Case', in *Wayward Governance: illegality and its control in the public sector,* Australian Institute of Criminology, Canberra, <www.aic.gov.au/publications/lcj/wayward/ch6t.html>.

Grewcock, M 2005, 'Slipping Through the Net? Some thoughts on the Cornelia Rau and Vivian Alvarez Inquiry', 17(2) *Current Issues in Criminal Justice* 284.

Hage, G 1998, *White Nation: fantasies of white supremacy in a multicultural society,* Pluto Press, Sydney.

Hall, S, Critcher, C, Jefferson, T, Clarke, J & Roberts, B 1978, *Policing the Crisis: mugging, the state, and law and order,* Macmillan, London.

Hartwig, M (ed) 2007, *Dictionary of Critical Realism,* Routledge, London.

Hocking, J 2004, *Terror Laws, ASIO, Counter-Terrorism and the Threat to Democracy,* UNSW Press, Sydney.

Human Rights and Equal Opportunity Commission (HREOC) 2004, *Isma − Listen: National Consultations on Eliminating Prejudice Against Arab and Muslim Australians,* <www.hreoc.gov.au/racial_discrimination/isma/report/index.html>.

Jakubowicz, A 2004, Vietnamese in Australia: a generation of settlement and adaptation, University of Technology Sydney, <www.multiculturalaustralia.edu.au/doc/viet_aust.doc>.

Kabir, N 2004, *Muslims in Australia: immigration, race relations and cultural history,* Kegan Paul, London.

Kondos, A 1992, 'The Politics of Identity: "conspirators" against the state, or institutional racism?', 28(1) *Australian and New Zealand Journal of Sociology* 5.

Lynch, A & Williams, G 2006, *What Price Security? Taking stock of Australia's anti-terror laws,* UNSW Press, Sydney.

Maher, L, Dixon, D, Swift, W & Nguyen, T 1997, *Anh Hai: young Asian background people's perceptions and experiences of policing,* University of New South Wales Faculty of Law Monograph Series, Sydney.

McCulloch, J 2006, 'Australia's Anti-Terrorism Legislation and the Jack Thomas Case', 18(2) *Current Issues in Criminal Justice* 357.

McVeigh, K 2007, 'Murder Victim Told Police Four Times she Feared her Family: each time in vain', *Guardian,* 12 June, 1-2.

Mukherjee, S 1999, *Ethnicity and Crime: an Australian research study,* Report prepared for the Department of Immigration and Multicultural Affairs, Australian Institute of Criminology, Canberra.

Mythen, G & Walklate, S 2006, 'Conclusion: towards a holistic approach to risk and human society', in Mythen, G & Walklate, S (eds), *Beyond the Risk Society: critical reflections on risk and human security,* Open University Press, Maidenhead.

NSW Ombudsman 2005, *Review of the Police Powers (Drug Premises) Act 2001,* NSW Ombudsman, Sydney.

Pearson, G 1983 *Hooligan: a history of respectable fears,* Macmillan, London.

Poynting, S, Noble, G, Tabar, P & Collins, J 2004, *Bin Laden in the Suburbs: criminalising the Arab other,* Institute of Criminology, Sydney.

Poynting, S & Noble, G 2004, *Living with Racism: the experience and reporting by Arab and Muslim Australians of discrimination, abuse and violence since 11 September 2001.* HREOC, <www.humanrights.gov.au/racial_discrimination/isma/research/index.html>.

Poynting, S 2007, '"Thugs" and "Grubs" at Cronulla: from media beat-ups to beating up migrants', in Poynting, S & Morgan, G (eds), *Outrageous! Moral Panics in Australia,* ACYS Press, Hobart.

Sayer, A 2000, *Realism and Social Science,* Sage, London.

Tavan, G 2005, *The Long, Slow Death of White Australia,* Scribe, Carlton North.

Tombs, S 2007, '"Violence", Safety Crimes and Criminology', 47(3) *British Journal of Criminology* 531.

Tombs, S & Whyte, D 2006, 'Work and Risk', in Mythen, G & Walklate, S (eds), *Beyond the Risk Society,* Open University Press, Maidenhead.

White, R 1996, 'Racism, Policing and Ethnic Youth Gangs', 7(3) *Current Issues in Criminal Justice* 302.

White, R, Perrone, S, Guerra, C & Lampugnani, R 1999, *Ethnic Youth Gangs: do they exist? Overview Report,* Australian Multicultural Foundation, Melbourne.

11

COLONIAL CRITIQUE AND CRITICAL CRIMINOLOGY: ISSUES IN ABORIGINAL LAW AND ABORIGINAL VIOLENCE

Harry Blagg[1]

> *Stanley Brown (was) ... an Aboriginal man heavily involved in matters affecting traditional Aboriginal law and active in the revival of its ceremonies ... his role as Law man provided him with respect and status in his own community ... In contrast (this) is how a police sergeant describes him and the manner of his death in custody: 'I was really surprised that he had hung himself because he was such a wimp. I never thought he would have enough guts to do something like that. His only attempts at violence were at Mary ... basically he was gutless'.*
>
> *... The essentially contradictory perceptions of this one person stem, at least in part, from the way in which non-Aboriginal law, and the enforcers of that law, refused to recognise what the law meant for Aboriginal men* (Dodson 1991).

Patrick Dodson produced his two-volume study of the issues underlying Aboriginal deaths in custody in Western Australia in a highly charged atmosphere. The killing of John Patt in Roebourne police lock-up in the remote north of Western Australia in 1986 had sparked the deaths in custody inquiry: Western Australia had the highest rate of custodial deaths in police lock-ups over the period reviewed by the Royal Commission into Aboriginal Deaths in Custody (RCIADIC). In highlighting the case of Stanley Brown, however, Dodson touches on a rarely discussed aspect of the deaths in custody issue. Protagonists in the carceral drama were governed by two different systems of law, one of which – the dominant one that built the prisons, empowered the police, robed the judiciary – refused to acknowledge the existence of the other. Dodson also illuminates another distressing consequence of colonial his-

---

1   Some of the themes in this paper were developed in a paper presented to the Queensland Centre for Domestic and Family Violence Research's 2007 *Breaking the Chains: Indigenous Family Violence Prevention Forum,* in Mackay, 'Zero Tolerance or Community Justice? The Role of the Aboriginal Domain in Reducing Family Violence'. I am grateful to the conference organisers and participants for their generous feedback. Other themes in the paper are developed further in a forthcoming book. See also Blagg, H, *Restorative Visions: Crime, Aboriginality and the De-colonisation of Justice,* Federation Press, forthcoming.

tory; denial of Aboriginal law had stripped away the dignity and status of Aboriginal men, with catastrophic consequences for Aboriginal society.

A carceral gulag

Nationally, rates of Aboriginal over-representation in the prison system have changed little since the RCIADIC. Aboriginal people constitute roughly 2% of the population yet constitute around 20% of all prisoners nationally. In Western Australia over 42% of the adult prison population is Aboriginal – Aborigines constitute less than 4% of the relevant population. On one day in early 2007 a staggering 90% of youth in detention was Aboriginal (Aboriginal youth represent roughly 4% of the youth population): the figure generally hovers around 80% and it is widely assumed in youth law circles that most of the other 10 or 20% are there because they hang out with Aboriginal kids. The increase in the arrest and incarceration of Indigenous women causes increasing concern. In Western Australia Aboriginal women are 29 times more likely to be incarcerated than non-Aboriginal women, on some days 50% of women in the state's main women's prison are Aboriginal; the majority being there for fine default and good order offences (Ferrante et al 2005).

Moreover, during the 1990s statistical inquiries began to confirm what Aboriginal women and respected leaders had been telling government for a long time: violence – particularly alcohol fuelled violence – was a serious problem and was tearing Indigenous communities apart. Research revealed that Aboriginal women were upwards of 45 times more likely to be victims of violence than non-Aboriginal women (Ferrante et al 1996).

Criminology and cognate disciplines have played a largely positive role in identifying these high rates of Aboriginal over-representation and measuring the suite of risk factors that make Aboriginal people vulnerable to enmeshment in the criminal justice system. The question I would like to pose in this chapter is a simple one, is this enough? Is there another dimension to the issue of Aboriginal over-representation that criminology, and other disciplines formed within the canons of western scholarship, simply does not get? I want to suggest that, as a product of western scholarship, critical criminology must constantly question its own presuppositions, its methodologies and its relevance to aspirations of Indigenous peoples. This requires doing more than simply ensuring that research is conducted in a 'culturally appropriate' fashion, if the research itself is essentially geared towards increasing the already substantial horde of information the system holds on Aboriginal people, as opposed to giving Aboriginal people themselves some leverage when they deal with government. Criminologists tend to focus on isolated criminal justice institutions, such as the police, courts, prisons, lock-ups, and sometimes this focus obscures the fact that these institutions have functioned as nodal points in a broader system of controls designed to formalise white power and privilege. Unlike much mainstream criminology, critical criminology does recognise that criminal justice policy and practice is powerfully influenced by structural forces but has – perhaps understandably in view of its European origins – tended to privilege categories such as class, age, gender and ethnic difference as the essential driving forces of social conflict. In the context of Aboriginal over-representation in the criminal justice system, however, these conceptual categories have only limited explanatory force. They need to analyse the role justice has played in the construction and maintenance of colonial relationships.

Epistemic violence

The temptation for researchers schooled in western criminology is to simply extend existing conceptual categories to accommodate Aboriginal issues – albeit lightly adorned with a few cultural embellishments. As criminologists we can draw on a rich and diverse storehouse of theories and perspectives – as other contributions to this volume amply demonstrate. The question is, to what extent do these categories unwittingly harm the unique realities of late-colonial Australia, given that so many have been formed within environments utterly different from the colonial frontier? The violence of colonial conquest included what Spivak (1986) called 'epistemic violence', a form of violence concerned with ripping open the symbolic and cultural world of the colonised and imposing new forms of knowledge. Among the new forms of western knowledge Aboriginal people had to absorb was the fact of their own imminent demise as a 'doomed race'. Police officers, magistrates, jailers did not, and do not, simply impose *the law*, they imposed the law of an alien culture; and the instruments of the law have been employed both as tools of dispossession and as mechanisms for transforming the space of the colony into a colonised space. Spivak (1985) captures this admirably in her notion of 'worlding', which describes the ways even the lowest of low-level functionaries (police, soldiers, clerks) consolidated the colonial space as a European space, forcing the native to 'experience his home ground as an imperial space' (cited in Ashcroft et al 1995: 241-242).

As part of their long resistance to this process, Aboriginal people have found ways to keep their own subjugated knowledge alive. They do this through the practise of law and ceremony, through the maintenance of kinship obligations, through story telling and through respect for the traditional wisdom and knowledge of elders. Many of these cultural rituals take place in urban as well as rural and remote parts of Australia. Together they contribute to the production and reproduction of *Aboriginal domain*, by which is meant those spaces where the dominant languages, cultures, structures of sentiment and feeling are Aboriginal (Von Sturmer 1984; Nicholas 2000; Rowse 2002).

Domain should not be conceived of in strictly geographic terms, synonymous, for example, with the remote 'outback'. There are Aboriginal domains dotted around urban and sub-urban space where Aboriginal people have traditionally congregated; they include particular parks and open spaces, Aboriginal cultural and social organisations and parts of the 'Aboriginal sector' (Rowse 2002). Aboriginal people even successfully build enclaves of domain within prison.

Resistance also takes place in the contested spaces between Aboriginal and non-Aboriginal domains through a number of cultural and linguistic turns that allow Aboriginal people to retain a degree of control over the meanings attached to certain forms of language; as a means of preventing significant arenas of experience from being wholly colonised, consumed and represented in the narrative structures of the dominant culture. A current example of this is the general Aboriginal preference for the term 'family' rather than 'domestic' violence in discussions around Aboriginal violence. As I shall discuss in more detail later, the family violence construct also provides a space for the articulation of subjugated knowledge. This subjugated knowledge is directly concerned with the injuries inflicted by the founding violence of colonisation and the ways these injuries are reproduced within contemporary Aboriginal society (Atkinson 2002).

Marginalised or colonised?

Instead of looking at Aboriginal issues as though Aboriginal people were simply an extremely disadvantaged, marginalised – even 'hyper-marginalised' – sub-section of Australian society, we should view Aboriginal Australia as constituting, in a number of crucial respects, a separate society, or domain, with its own distinctive laws.[2] We should begin any inquiry into Aboriginal crime and justice from this starting point. Aboriginal laws create their own specific sphere of obligations, rights and responsibilities; they set limits to behaviour and govern many aspects of daily life. Seen through this lens Aboriginal justice issues take on a *radical alterity*, setting them apart from other disadvantaged minorities. While there are many intricate crossing points, hybrid zones and liminal spaces between Aboriginal and non-Aboriginal domains, there are aspects of Aboriginal cultural, cosmological and social reality that remain profoundly incommensurate, which have to be accepted, and respected, *in difference*. We may have to accept that we cannot, and should not, have access to some Aboriginal knowledge. This creates problems for us as researchers because we can cope with just about anything but not knowing: 'knowing', after all, is what research is about.

Problems emerge when we employ the discursive apparatus of western scholarship to make sense of issues in the Aboriginal domain without first engaging in dialogue with Aboriginal people to determine the relevance of these constructs. Michel Foucault (1976: 92-102) demonstrated how knowledge becomes power when it is inscribed into various forms of professional discourse. Knowledge confers authority and gives the keeper of this knowledge considerable status as an accredited source or expert. White researchers and scholars frequently impose contextually inappropriate structures of meaning onto Aboriginal communities, interpreting and processing what they see (which is usually only a surface snapshot) on the basis of ideas brought with them from the non-Aboriginal domain. Our status as white researchers then grants us significant power to establish and frame the discursive structures through which the 'problems' of the Aboriginal domain will be received and understood by a non-Aboriginal audience. This raises important issues regarding the way 'knowledge' of the Aboriginal domain is generated by white researchers and then how this knowledge is freighted to other locations and unpacked for consumption. Criminological theory provides us with a ready made template for understanding new phenomenon. We need to be vigilant when uncritically imposing this template on the Indigenous domain. A brief illustration from the criminology of youth culture may help to illustrate this.

---

2   This is the approach adopted by the Western Australian Law Reform Commission throughout its five-year inquiry into Aboriginal law. See <www.lrc.justice.wa.gov.au> and follow links for Aboriginal Customary Law.

Diaspora or difference?

Criminology is a discipline born of modernity. Its origins lay in the 19th century philosophies of Europe, but it came of age in the great cities of the United States. It shares its life story with the immigrants who made this same journey; the immigrant experience is deeply embedded in the criminological unconscious. The Diasporic community of the immigrant was the birthplace of street-level criminological inquiry. The birth of the modern cities of the United States like Chicago provided a social laboratory where the consequences of cultural conflict and social dislocation could be studied: alongside various strategies and techniques of adaptation, co-exis- tence and integration (Shaw & McKay 1942).

The overall message contained in this emergent criminology is one of *adap- tation,* as new languages, cultures, values, political process have to be learned, or at least negotiated: some aspects of the old culture are left behind, others modified, some displayed as emblems of ethic pride and difference. Immigrants learned, and modified, the rules of the new society. One of the richest streams of inquiry flowing out of the work of the Chicago School is the study of the delinquent gang and deviant sub-cultures. The study of delinquent sub-culture provided the engine room for critical criminological inquiry from the 1930s onwards.

Aboriginal experiences of dispossession were not Diasporic. They were never new arrivals to a new country. Their country was taken from them. A complete set of foreign laws, institutions, peoples, economies, beliefs, rituals, diseases, flora and fauna simply dropped on them uninvited. Despite attempts by the state to smash Aboriginal society, Aboriginal people have retained strong links with country, law and language. Culture for Aboriginal people is not a set of nostalgic reminiscences of a foreign place kept alive through cultural rituals, but a compelling and immediate force in their lives; animate in the landscape around them and renewed on a daily basis though connection with kin, ceremony and ritual. Aboriginal youths tend not to form street sub-cultures and gangs in the western sense of the term, but kin-based groups with a high degree of age and spatial differentiation. They tend not to pin down territory; instead they roam traditional places and sites. Nyoongars, the traditional owners of the south west of Western Australia, call these connecting paths that once traversed sacred sites their 'runs'. Much of the rivalry with other groups does not take place on the basis of ethnic rivalry or different youth styles but represents the continuation of traditional clan and family rivalries and feuds as well as ongoing resistance to the demands of the dominant culture (Beresford & Omaji 1996; Cunneen & White 2007). A good deal of the conflict between the police and Aboriginal youths takes place in urban spaces – streets, parks, etc – over which Aboriginal people claim ownership. Aboriginal sense of 'ownership' of these places is quite unlike the 'magical' or 'symbolic' appropriation of the neighbourhood or 'mean street' discussed by sub-cultural theorists such Phil Cohen (1972) and collea- gues from the Birmingham Centre for Cultural Studies (Hall & Jefferson 1975).

While some of the core perspectives of western criminology – such as labelling, strain/anomie, conflict theories – have general applicability, they lack explanatory force without a theory of racism and colonialism. Rather than viewing Aboriginal society through the lens provided by western criminological scholarship, and imposing concepts such as class/community, inclusion/exclusion, culture/sub-cul- ture, state/civil society, public/private, law/lore etc, it is necessary to engage with the Aboriginal domain on the basis of its *radical alterity* – as a space where these conceptual couplets may not fit – and approach this domain as a separate entity, albeit interwoven with our own in a complex and dynamic way. Aboriginal men, Aboriginal women, Aboriginal children tend to view themselves as Aboriginal first – the core of their identities adheres around their Aboriginality with its demands, obligations and unique collective experiences. While acknowledging the impact other forms of disadvantage (sexism, unemployment, poor housing, low levels of educational attainment) have on their life paths and life chances, they tend to see the core issues revolving around their status as Aboriginal people and attempts by the state to (variously) eliminate, restructure and re-constitute this Aboriginal identity. Criminological theory in the Indigenous context is partial and incomplete without this insight.

Periodisations

In the face of some new anthropological writing questioning the relevance of over-arching structural explanations for the position(s) of contemporary Indigenous people (see Lea et al 2006), Dipesh Chakrabarty (2006: iv) recently made an appeal to scholars not to abandon 'the colonial model' as a way of making sense of the position of Aboriginal people: arguing that such levels of '*systemic* and *systematic* discrimination*' require an over-arching category; jettisoning the colonial paradigm is premature (emphasis in original). The colonial paradigm provides a space within which Aboriginal difference can be explored and its unique experiences reflected upon. Australian scholars have been aware of the radical bifurcation of policy along racial lines based upon colonial discourse. The work of Finnane and McGuire (2001), Cunneen (2001b) and Broadhurst (2002) have shown that the content and trajectory of punishment for Aboriginal people has always been – and remains – different; reflecting specifically colonial anxieties and preoccupations.

It is therefore necessary to treat with caution periodisations of correctional discipline and penalty produced on the basis of European and American carceral history. Feeley and Simon's (1992) 'new penology' thesis, for example lacks relevance, on the grounds that there was never an 'old penology' primarily concerned with the rehabilitation of Indigenous people. Similarly, Garland's (2001) 'cultures of control' thesis, in which he maintains that the rise of punitive sanctions and expressive justice signified a radical departure from liberal strategies of social engineering in favour of punitive segregation and control of offenders, may have little relevance to the world of the colonial frontier, where control has consistently required punitive sanctions against the colonised Other. The colonial paradigm stresses *the pervasive continuities over time* in the ways the control system handles Indigenous people, rather than stressing breaks, ruptures and discursive shifts. It focuses our gaze on the pervasiveness of 'frontiers', and the ways the control system reproduces the frontier in the modern era through forms of discriminatory and segregatory policing and linked social policies (Cunneen 2001a, 2001b; Havemann 1999; Broadhurst 2002).

Inclusion and exclusion

Critical criminology played a crucial role in broadening the framework of criminological debate by introducing two important layers of inquiry; first that the genesis of crime has to be located within the social, economic and political structures of society, and; secondly, that the criminal justice system itself is complicit in manufacturing the very deviance it seeks to eliminate, and actively reproduces rather than reduces social inequalities (Taylor et al 1971). What remains exciting about the project of critical criminology is the overt commitment to human emancipation and social justice. However, there are pitfalls as well as strengths in this approach where Indigenous cultures are concerned. The politics of liberation, underpinning the works of critical criminologists like Jock Young (1999) for example, places the melting of tradition and the construction of new forms of individualism at the centre of progressive and 'transformative change'.

Indigenous peoples have been engaged in a protracted struggle since colonisation to prevent the meltdown of their traditions and fear precisely those forms of transformative change that further deracinate and individualise. Critical criminology needs, therefore, to acknowledge the importance of self-determination for Indigenous peoples who may place the revival of traditional culture ahead of the politics of personal identity. It must critically interrogate the implications of some of its own most cherished constructs: if 'social exclusion' is the problem, is 'assimilation' the solution? Should Australian critical criminology be supporting initiatives designed to melt Indigenous tradition and transform Indigenous people into empowered individuals? Many Aboriginal people see the revival of traditional Aboriginal law as a necessary component of any progressive strategy designed to raise Indigenous people out of poverty and reduce levels of over-representation in the criminal justice system.

Where should critical criminologists turn then for ideas about reform if our most cherished texts provide only a partial answer? We have to turn to forms of inquiry less focused on individual 'issues' and categories (youth, women, offenders, drug takers) and look at the problems from within an Aboriginal 'terms of reference'. Between 2001 and 2006 the Western Australian Law Reform Commission conducted an intensive inquiry into *Aboriginal Customary Law*, which set out to build a consensus with Aboriginal communities about the scope and nature of the inquiry, creating an Aboriginal Reference Group, employing Special Aboriginal Commissioners (Professor Mick Dodson, a Yawuru man, and Beth Woods, a Wongi woman), working with key Aboriginal law bodies (for example, the Aboriginal Legal Service because of its role in the white-fella legal system and Kimberley Aboriginal Law and Culture). The inquiry involved a lengthy process of community meetings, feedback processes and writing to build a picture of law as it is lived and practised by Aboriginal people in a diversity of settings. The focus on Aboriginal law and culture constructed a dialogic space within which a host of issues could be discussed, ranging from governance, family, inheritance, policing, young people, alcohol, the courts and family violence. Some of the discussion about these issues took place in separate men's and women's forums.

These processes represented a radical departure from the way issues in the Aboriginal domain are often captured and represented within mainstream discourse. The issue of violence in Indigenous communities is an example. There are key differences between Indigenous and non-Indigenous narratives about the causes of violence and this has, for example, led to a number of prominent Aboriginal women questioning the right of non-Indigenous feminists to provide an over-arching explanation of its cause: particularly where they describe the violence as patriarchal violence in the context of a traditional culture (Cripps 2005). A number of Abori-

135

ginal women have rejected the authority of non-Aboriginal feminists to speak for them on the basis of the 'universal female subject' and manufacture a false equivalence between middle-class white women's experiences and those of black women subjected to layers of oppression rooted in colonial violence and dispossession (Moreton-Robertson 2000). I will return to the issue of violence later, first I will sketch out in more detail some of the issues in Aboriginal law.

What is Aboriginal law?

The issue of Aboriginal Customary Law has been pushed onto the political agenda in Australia in connection with the issue of violence in Indigenous communities. But what is Aboriginal law? Is it really about violence and a charter for abusers? There have been a number of landmark inquiries into Aboriginal law, the most comprehensive national inquiry was undertaken by the Australian Law Reform Commission (1986) and there have been recent inquiries in the Northern Territory (2003) and Western Australia (discussed earlier), as well as a number of important studies which have examined the continued relevance of Aboriginal law in sentencing offenders (see for example, Law Reform Commission of New South Wales 2000) and in building community justice mechanism (see for example, Fitzgerald 2001).

Customary law is difficult to define in non-Indigenous terms, as it encompasses far more than the infliction of physical punishment: 'law' represents a grammar for living and an intricate set of religious principles, which make the world meaningful and intelligible. Aboriginal customary law cuts across the divisions we impose in western thinking between law, culture and religion. Anxieties about the recognition of Aboriginal customary law are interwoven with colonial history and Britain's claim to sovereignty over Australia and the definition of Aboriginal people as British subjects. Recognising Aboriginal forms of law means acknowledging the existence of a separate Aboriginal society with a pre-existing claim to this continent.

Anthropologists have tended to see Aboriginal law as a mechanism for establishing and reproducing balanced relationships between social/kinship systems, the natural environment and religious deities. It is hazardous to attempt a legal definition or attempt to squeeze the construct into already existing legal categories: customary principles are not like statutes and codes (Toohey 2006). Aboriginal law does resemble other forms of law in the sense that it constitutes a body of rules, even if these rules are not written down, which are widely accepted as legitimate by those who uphold them and which are enforced by sanction and penalty.

The Law Reform Commission of Western Australia (2005) found widespread support for the recognition of Aboriginal customary law amongst Aboriginal people and evidence that continued non-recognition, and constant attempts to dismantle traditional practices, profoundly disadvantaged Aboriginal people by undermining social structures and systems of authority. The Commission heard evidence to the effect that the western system of justice and allied agencies alone were ineffective in dealing with issues within Aboriginal communities. The Northern Territory Law Reform Committee (2003: 13) also found that:

> Aboriginal customary law is a fact of life for most Aboriginal people in the Northern Territory, not just those in Aboriginal communities. This is because it defines a person's rights and responsibilities, it defines who a person is, and it defines that person's relationships to everybody else in the world.

The overall aim of the Law Reform Commission of Western Australia's (2005) review of Aboriginal Customary Law was to reconcile Aboriginal and non-Aboriginal systems of law. Underpinning the inquiry was the recognition that Aboriginal people are frequently disadvantaged in their dealings with the non-Aboriginal system of justice. Moreover, this disadvantage appears to be the product of systemic factors rather than a reflection of individual racist attitudes and beliefs. Consultations revealed that:

- Aboriginal law still governs many aspects of daily life for many Aboriginal people, providing the maps of meaning that make communal life possible and predictable.

- Law provides an overarching framework of rules and obligations, forms of penalty and censure, codes of conduct, etiquette and address.

- It informs people about with whom they can associate and under what conditions, as well as their obligations and relationships to those around them.

- There was widespread support for greater recognition of Aboriginal law.

At a meeting with senior law men and women at Wuggubun in the East Kimberley the view was:

Traditional law says that justice should be administered by the community. Traditional law is potentially stronger than European law, in terms of addressing the underlying concerns in offending. Our law has been practised for some time. But it needs reinforcement, and greater respect (Law Reform Commission of Western Australia 2005).[3]

In consultations, Aboriginal people would describe non-Aboriginal law as a 'Johnny come lately law' resembling a kind of table cloth, a thin veneer, beneath which a solid table of Aboriginal laws still functioned (Blagg & Morgan 2004). The consultations also found that law was still respected and practised in prison – for both men and women.

One clear message received through the consultations was that violence against women and children is not culturally sanctioned. Practices such as 'promised marriages' (girls being married off to much older men against their will) are virtually unknown in Western Australia – and are rare in the Northern Territory. Moreover, Aboriginal women did not want to be saved from their law and culture – they wanted help dealing with alcohol-induced violence on their communities and with negotiating the bewildering complexities and ambiguities, the capriciousness and arbitrariness of *the white justice system*. When Catherine Wohlan (2006) consulted Aboriginal women in the remote Kimberley region of Western Australia on Aboriginal law they demanded that discussions of family violence be decoupled from discussions of Aboriginal law; as maintaining the conflation was disrespectful and misrepresentative of the real situation. Family violence, they claimed, was the consequence of community dysfunction caused by alcohol, the decline of traditional law and culture and unemployment. These accounts of communal violence are at odds with dominant images of Aboriginal violence as 'traditional violence' and Aboriginal women as victims of traditional violence.

---

3   Taken from the Wuggubun (East Kimberley) consultations, see <www.lrc.justice.wa.gov.au>.

Ideal victims?

It is an accepted tenant of critical victimology that becoming a 'socially sanctioned victim' (Walklate 1989) requires the fulfilment of a number of criteria. Traditionally, Aboriginal women have found it hard to achieve the status of victim because of degrading, racist stereotypes about them and because of a lack of empathy by enforcement authorities and courts. They are not considered to be what Nils Christie (1986) called 'ideal victims'. In fact Aboriginal women are routinely viewed as 'offenders' by the criminal justice system – they are, as I mentioned earlier, massively over-represented in the criminal justice system. It is noteworthy, however, that some Aboriginal women are now being accorded victim status, provided they are positioned within victim discourse as *helpless, hopeless victims of traditional Aboriginal male violence, sanctioned – even encouraged – by Aboriginal law.*

It is difficult to see, however, how a justice system that already tends to penalise victims of sexual violence can work in the interests of a group of women routinely incarcerated as offenders (Taylor 2004; Cripps & Taylor 2007; McGlade 2006; Kilroy 2007). For example, Western Australian Indigenous women have been arrested as perpetrators of violence (usually when fighting back) and have been arrested under the State's new domestic violence laws for aiding and abetting breaches of restraining orders, an offence under the new legislation. Aboriginal women do not tolerate violence, and the want to see perpetrators of violence made accountable. The question becomes: accountable to whom and under what conditions? A family violence approach would see a greater role for *traditional justice mechanisms* to balance out the tendency of the white justice system to doubly victimise.

Family violence

Unlike the notion of domestic violence, Aboriginal family violence is difficult to define. Its usage within Aboriginal communities remains diverse and localised, indicating, perhaps, that we are not dealing with a single construct but with a series of intersecting narrative strands requiring multiple and situated readings. There is good reason to retain a degree of distance between the two constructs. Aboriginal women may see violence as being connected with a web of issues in their communities that the present pre-occupation with domestic violence minimises or ignores.

Let us then dispense with the notion that there is, or can be, a unitary definition of family violence and explore the construct in its diversity. The family violence category generally relates to violence against women and children, but the category is capacious enough to contain:

- clan and family feuds: one consequence of colonisation has been the breakdown of traditional dispute resolution mechanisms, clan conflicts are not amenable to resolution through white-fella justice, left unresolved they erupt with devastating consequences between (and within) families;
- jealous fights and *jealousing up* behaviour: *jealousing* is a major concern to Aboriginal people, it reflects insecurity about relationships, is immensely destructive and kept active by the involvement of kin. Pretty girls have been 'bashed ugly' so they are not pursued by others, partners in relation-

ships often maintain high levels of mutual surveillance, and imprisonment can intensify these tendencies;

- rape and the sexual abuse of children; a number of inquiries note the widespread nature of this problem (see Aboriginal Women's Task Force on Violence (Queensland) 2000; and the Report of the Northern Territory Board of Inquiry into the Protection of Aboriginal Children from Sexual Abuse (Northern Territory Board of Inquiry 2007));

- neglect of children: leaving aside cultural differences and expectations over what constitutes good child-rearing practice, there are major concerns within the Aboriginal community about the neglect of children, problems such as violence, alcohol and drug use, imprisonment and unemployment;

- the bitterness and uncertainties left in the wake of 'wrong way' marriages (people marrying outside of 'skin' relationships, that is, culturally appropriate relationships). A little studied issue, but there is a hiatus in some communities where old skin related marriage practices are in decline but no one is entirely sure what the new rules are;

- alcohol and drug fuelled violence: alcohol has ceased being simply a symptom but a substantial problem in its own right – Aboriginal communities see closing down or restricting access to grog as a fundamental prerequisite for reducing violence;

- neglect of obligations around kin and country: connection with country forms the basis for Aboriginal law, loss of connection deracinates and fractures social connections, while structures of mutual obligation maintain social harmony and make life predictable and certain;

- men on women violence: Aboriginal women are the most routinely victimised section of society, Aboriginal women are less convinced that feminist patriarchal theories, centred on male power, adequately explain the incidence of male violence. While not condoning the violence, many Aboriginal women point to the impact of colonisation on male status, they tend not to see 'their' men as powerful;

- men on men violence: an under-researched area, drink-related violence between men has ripple effects across communities;

- less frequent women on men violence: Aboriginal women as well as men talk about this as a real issue in some families, although less common than man on woman violence;

- losing money on gambling: this is a highly destructive process, children and dependent kin go hungry, money is taken out of the community – the winners spend the money on grog in town;

- the 'humbugging' of elderly relatives for food and money: a practice that elderly Aboriginal people find particularly distressing, it transgresses deeply held cultural beliefs on reciprocal obligations and respect for elders;

- providing petrol to sniffers in return for sexual favours on some remote communities;

- white on black institutional violence: Aboriginal people see white violence, particularly when systemically institutionalised in state violence as part of the cycle of communal violence: white institutions (prisons, lock-ups, detention centres, missions, children's homes, orphanages, boarding facilities) have been sites of violence and exploitation of Aboriginal people since colonisation; and

- colonial violence: the 'founding violence' of colonisation devastated Indigenous Australia. For example, Atkinson (2002) traces distinct 'trauma lines' in families dating from the moment of first contact between Indigenous people and colonists.

Working at the community level with Aboriginal people to end family violence may require being flexible enough to deal with a host of issues underpinning violence, and work with, rather than against, Aboriginal law and culture. This may challenge the current orthodoxy around domestic violence with its exclusive focus of male power and criminalisation. Reducing family violence has to be set in the context of holistic and integrated reforms; as Cunneen (2001a: 9) observes in relation to family violence prevention:

> The common themes in evaluations of family violence programs include the need for holistic approaches, the utilisation of community development models which emphasise self-determination and community ownership, the provision of culturally sensitive treatment which respects traditional law and customs and involves existing structures of authority such as elders, including women.

Overcoming family violence requires a focus on empowerment and a broad governmental commitment to working in partnership with communities to transform the structural causes of violence. A key part of the process requires we respect Indigenous women as cultural beings rather than as docile victims who require rescuing from their culture.

Signs of change

In recent years there have been a number of promising developments in Australia that offer, if not exactly a road map, then potential pathways to work in the liminal spaces between Aboriginal and non-Aboriginal domains.

These include developments such as local Community Justice Groups, Negotiating Tables and other developments under the Queensland Aboriginal and Torres Strait Islander Justice Agreement, new courts such as Circle Sentencing Courts (New South Wales) and the Koori Courts (Victoria), law and justice strategies in the Northern Territory particularly driven by senior Aboriginal women who have established their own safe houses and night patrols, and the development of local justice plans under the *Aboriginal Justice Agreement* in Western Australia and the creation of family violence 'healing centres'.

One of the crucial dimensions of these processes is that they are Aboriginal community *owned* initiatives, where communities themselves drive and manage the processes, as opposed to being simply community *based* initiatives where they are simply annexes for government delivered services (Blagg 2005). They combine a number of key ingredients, including: a strong focus on achieving sustainability, a willingness to take into account Aboriginal law and culture, a commitment to nurturing the necessary governance structures and a process of capacity building (see also the Aboriginal and Torres Strait Islander Social Justice Commissioner 2003: 2-3).

In July/August 2007 the Federal Government chose to take the entirely opposite tack and, in the name of protecting Aboriginal children from abuse enacted the *Northern Territory National Emergency Response Bill* giving the Federal Government wide control over Aboriginal lands and the Federal Families, Community Services and Indigenous Affairs Minister total control over Indigenous community governance. There is a real danger that many of the community-based reforms of the past decade will unravel in the face of a new coercive paternalism designed to break down what remains of the Aboriginal domain.

In the face of such an attack, what should be the role of critical criminology? In my opinion, we need to retain commitment to dialogue with Indigenous communities and resist calls for the wholesale remaking of Indigenous society in the name of victim protection. We have yet to find a way of making Indigenous women and children safe, as well as addressing the broad raft of family violence issues discussed. Experience suggests that Aboriginal communities have alternative scenarios that are based on local justice mechanisms, and include Aboriginal courts, self-policing initiatives, healing centres, strong problem-solving partnerships with the police and other agencies that take a long-term approach, reductions in supply of alcohol and – importantly – building on traditional law and culture and the authority of elders. As criminologists we have to acknowledge that Aboriginal people are subject not to one, but two laws. The politics of liberation needs to be reconstructed to include the politics of tradition.

References

Aboriginal and Torres Strait Islander Social Justice Commissioner 2003, *Social Justice Report 2002,* Human Rights and Equal Opportunity Commission, Sydney.

Aboriginal and Torres Strait Islander Women's Task Force on Violence 2000, *Full Report,* Department of Aboriginal and Torres Strait Islander Policy and Development, Queensland, <www.women.qld.gov.au/_Documents/OFW+resources/ATSI_Violence+Report.pdf>.

Ashcroft, B, Griffiths, D & Tiffen, H 1995, *The Post-Colonial Studies Reader*, Routledge, London.

Atkinson J 2002, *Trauma Trails, Recreating Song Lines: the transgenerational effects of trauma in Indigenous Australia,* Spinifex Press, North Melbourne.

Australian Law Reform Commission 1986, *Recognition of Aboriginal Customary laws,* ALRC 31, Sydney.

Beresford, Q & Omaji, P 1996, *Rites of Passage: Aboriginal Youth, Crime and Justice*, Fremantle Art Centre Press, South Fremantle.

Blagg, H 2005, *A New Way of Doing Justice Business? Community Justice Mechanisms and Sustainable Governance in Western Australia,* Background Paper No 15, Law Reform Commission of Western Australia, <www.lrc.justice.wa.gov.au>.

Blagg, H & Morgan, N 2004, 'Aboriginal Law in Western Australia', *Indigenous Law Bulletin* 74.

Board of Inquiry into the Protection of Aboriginal Children from Sexual Abuse 2007, *Ampe Akelyernemane Meke Mekarle 'Little Children are Sacred': Report,* Northern Territory Government, Darwin, <www.nt.gov.au/dcm/inquirysaac/report_summary.html>.

Broadhurst, RG 2002, 'Crime and Indigenous People', in Graycar, A & Grabosky, P (eds), *Handbook of Australian Criminology*, Cambridge University Press, Melbourne.

Chakrabarty, D 2006, 'Foreword', in Lea, T, Kowal, E & Cowlishaw, G (eds), *Moving Anthropology: critical Indigenous studies,* Charles Darwin University Press, Darwin.

Christie, N 1986, 'The ideal victim', in Fattah, EA (ed), *From Crime Policy to Victim Policy: reorienting the justice system,* St Martin's, New York.

Cohen, P 1972, *Sub-cultural Conflict and Working Class Community,* Working Papers in Cultural Studies, No 2, University of Birmingham, Birmingham.

Cripps, K 2005, 'Review of J Kimm, "A Fatal Conjunction: two laws, two cultures"', 5(1) *QUT Law and Justice Journal,* <www.law.qut.edu.au/about/ljj/editions/v5n1>.

Cripps, K & Taylor, C 2007, 'White Man's Law, Traditional Law, Bullshit Law: customary marriage revisited', 12 *Balayi: Culture, Law and Colonialism* (forthcoming).

Cunneen, C 2001a, 'The Impact of Crime Prevention on Indigenous Communities', Institute of Criminology, Sydney, <www.lawlink.nsw.gov.au/lawlink/ajac/ll_ajac.nsf/vwFiles/impact_of_crime_prevention_on_aboriginal_communities_chris_cunneen_sep2001.pdf/$file/impact_of_crime_prevention_on_aboriginal_communities_chris_cunneen_sep2001.pdf>.

Cunnen, C 2001b, *Conflict, Politics and Crime: Aboriginal Communities and the Police,* Allen & Unwin, Sydney.

Cunneen, C & White, R 2007, *Juvenile Justice: youth and crime in Australia,* Oxford University Press, Sydney.

Dodson, P 1991, *Regional Report of Inquiry into Underlying Issues in Western Australia,* 2 vols, Royal Commission into Aboriginal Deaths in Custody, AGPS, Canberra.

Feeley, M & Simon, J 1992, 'The New Penology: notes on the emerging strategy of corrections and its implications', 30 *Criminology* 449.

Ferrante, A, Morgan, F, Indermaur, D & Harding, R 1996, *Measuring the Extent of Domestic Violence,* Hawkins Press, Sydney.

Ferrante, A, Fernandez, J, & Loh, N 2005, *Crime and Justice Statistics for Western Australia 2004,* Crime Research Centre, UWA, Perth.

Finnane, M & McGuire, J 2001, 'The Uses of Punishment and Exile', 3(2) *Punishment & Society* 279.

Fitzgerald, T 2001, *The Cape York Justice Study,* Department of the Premier, Brisbane, <www.datsip.qld.gov.au>.

Foucault, M 1976, 'Power as Knowledge', in *The History of Sexuality, Vol 1: An Introduction,* translated by Borchardt, G 1990, Vintage Books, New York.

Garland, D 2001, *The Culture of Control: crime and social order in contemporary society,* Oxford University Press, Oxford.

Hall, S & Jefferson, T (eds) 1975, *Resistance Through Rituals: youth subcultures in post-war Britain,* Hutchinson, London.

Havemann, P (ed) 1999, *Indigenous People's Rights in Australia, Canada and New Zealand.* Oxford University Press, Oxford.

Kilroy, D 2007, 'Key Note Address', *Breaking the Chains: Indigenous family violence prevention forum,* Queensland Centre for Domestic and Family Violence Research, Mackay.

Kurduju Committee 2001, *Reports,* The Combined Communities of Ali-Currung, Lajamanu and Yuendumu Law and Justice Committees, <www.dcdsca.nt.gov.au/dcdsca/intranet.nsf/Files/RDPublications/$file/Kurduju.pdf>.

Law Reform Commission of New South Wales 2000, *Sentencing Aboriginal Offenders,* Report 96, NSWLRC, Sydney.

Law Reform Commission of Western Australia 2005, *Aboriginal Customary Law in Western Australia: Thematic Summaries of Community Consultations,* WALRC, Perth, <www.lrc.justice.wa.gov.au>.

Law Reform Commission of Western Australia 2006a, *Aboriginal Customary Laws,* Discussion Paper No 94, WALRC, Perth.

Law Reform Commission of Western Australia 2006b, *Aboriginal Customary Laws: Final Report: The Interaction of Western Australian Law and Culture,* WALRC, Perth.

Lea, T, Kowal, E & Cowlishaw, G (eds) 2006, *Moving Anthropology: Critical Indigenous Studies,* Charles Darwin University Press, Darwin.

McGlade, H 2006, 'Aboriginal Women, Girls and Sexual Assault: the long road to equality within the criminal justice system', *Aware,* ACSSA Newsletter, 12, Institute of Family Studies.

Moreton-Robertson, A 2000, *Talkin' Up to the White Woman: Indigenous Women and Feminism,* University of Queensland Press, Brisbane.

Nicholas, P 2000, 'An Expanding Aboriginal Domain: mobility and the initiation journey', 70(3) *Oceania* 205.

Northern Territory Law Reform Committee 2003, *Report of the Committee of Inquiry into Aboriginal Customary Law: Report on Aboriginal Customary Law,* NTLRC, Darwin.

Northern Territory Board of Inquiry 2007, *Report of the Northern Territory Board of Inquiry into the Protection of Aboriginal Children from Sexual Abuse.*

Rowse, T 2002, *White Flour, White Power: from rations to citizenship in Central Australia* Cambridge University Press, Melbourne.

Shaw, C & McKay, H 1942, *Juvenile Delinquency in Urban Areas,* Chicago University Press, Chicago.

Spivak, GC 1985, cited in Ashcroft, B, Griffiths, G & Tiffin, H (eds) 1998, *Key Concepts in Post-Colonial Studies,* Routledge, London.

Spivak, GC 1996, reproduced in Landry, D & Maclean, G (eds), *The Spivak Reader: selected works of Gayatri Chakravorty Spivak,* Routledge and Kegan Paul, London.

Taylor, I, Walton, P, & Young, J 1971, *The New Criminology,* Routledge & Kegan Paul, London.

Taylor, SC 2004, *Court Licensed Abuse,* Peter Lang, New York.

Toohey, J 2006, *WALRC Background Paper,* <www.lrc.justice.wa.gov.au>.

Von Sturmer, J 1984, 'The Different Domains', in *Aborigines and Uranium: Consolidated Report on the Social Impact of Uranium Mining on the Aborigines of the Northern Territory,* AIAS, Canberra.

Walklate, S 1989, *Victimology: the victim and the criminal justice process,* Unwin Hyman, London.

Wohlan, C 2005, 'Aboriginal Women's Interest in Customary Law Recognition', *Background Paper No 13,* WALRC, Perth.

Young, J 1999, *The Exclusive Society: social exclusion, crime and difference in late modernity,* Sage, London.

PART III

BROADENING DEFINITIONS
OF CRIME AND CRIMINOLOGY

12

STATE CRIME:
SOME CONCEPTUAL ISSUES

Mike Grewcock

Introduction

This chapter discusses the concept of state crime. With a few notable exceptions,[1] criminologists have neglected this theme, but if criminology is to develop as a discipline that studies and analyses criminal, violent, abusive and deviant behaviour, then subjects such as mass killing, genocide, ethnic cleansing, arbitrary detention, torture and rendition ought to be a primary focus for us.

The fact that such activities are typically carried out by police forces, armies and other agencies representing the authority of the state poses the question: how do we police the institutions that make and enforce the law? Answering this presents two significant and enduring challenges for criminologists: first, departing from the notion that criminology is principally concerned with the study of individual or group criminal behaviour that is codified and policed by the state; and second, developing a framework for analysing the criminal dimensions of state behaviour.

Since the 1970s, criminologists have made sporadic attempts to address these issues, but there is a lack of continuity in the concepts employed. At one end of the spectrum, is Chambliss (1989: 184), whose legalistic approach limits conceptions of 'state organised crime' to 'acts defined by law as criminal and committed by state officials in the pursuit of their job as representatives of the state'. At the other end, are the Schwendingers (1975: 131-138), whose human rights-based approach suggests crime should be re-defined according to 'some traditional notions of crime as well as notions organised around the concept of egalitarianism'.

This polarity between conceptions of state crime based on breaches of the law and conceptions based on breaches of human rights reflects long-standing debates within criminology about the scope and subject matter of the discipline. This chapter cannot resolve such debates but argues for the further development of a paradigm of state crime based on the concepts of human rights and deviance. Using Green and Ward's (2004: 2) definition of state crime as 'state organisational deviance involving the violation of human rights', it suggests that a focus on the state's use of force and the systemic quality of state crime provides a basis for examining how state criminality might become a central focus of critical criminology.

---

1 For example, Barak (1991); Green & Ward (2004); Kauzlarich & Kramer (1998); Pickering (2005); Ross (1995); and Rothe & Friedrichs (2006).

State crime as a legal concept

State crime is not a clearly defined concept in either domestic or international law. This presents immediate challenges when trying to base a criminological theory of state crime on legal definitions.

Within the realms of domestic law, state crime is almost a contradiction in terms. The state does not police itself in any collective sense; rather it can target individuals who have broken the laws the state enforces. Thus, while in most domestic jurisdictions, it might be possible to charge particular individuals with criminal offences such as murder or assault; the criminal justice process is concerned with the behaviour of the allegedly deviant few within its control. As the recent trials of United States army personnel engaged in torture at Abu Ghraib illustrates, this leaves open the question of how to locate responsibility for the offending acts within the wider culture, policies and practices of the state (Human Rights Watch 2005). Within a domestic legal framework, there is little room for the concept of political accountability.

State crime is perhaps a more coherent concept within international law, where the prospect of international tribunals might remove some of the problems associated with states policing themselves. However, attempts to devise a body of enforceable international law have met with mixed success. From its inception in 1948, the International Law Commission engaged in extensive deliberations on state responsibility for breaches of international law, including international crimes and delicts arising from state acts. Conceptually, such breaches would amount to state crime but no agreement could be reached on how they should be defined. Instead the *Draft Articles on the Responsibility of States for Internationally Wrongful Acts* provide for 'particular consequences of a serious breach of an obligation arising from a peremptory norm of general international law' (See Draft Articles 19, 40 and 41). No list is provided of what might constitute such a breach, although the commentary includes as examples aggression, slavery, genocide, racial discrimination, torture, and the suppression of the right to self-determination. The Articles now await future adoption by way of a convention or declaration, but this does not appear likely to happen in the foreseeable future (Crawford 1998: paras 76-100. See also Crawford 2002; Jørgensen 2003).

The draft formulations of the International Law Commission reflected the growing body of international human rights law in areas such as genocide and racial discrimination, and the emerging concept of crimes against humanity, established as a principle by the 1945 Nuremberg Tribunal. Under the Tribunal's Principles these crimes included 'murder, extermination, enslavement, deportation and other inhuman acts done against any civilian population; or persecutions on political, racial or religious grounds, when such acts are done or such persecutions are carried on in execution of or connection with any crime against peace or any war crime' (Principle VI (c)).

The 'logic of the crime against humanity', notes Robertson (2006: xxii), 'was that future state agents who authorised torture or genocide against their own populations were criminally responsible, in international law, and might be punished by any court capable of catching them'. However, while the Nuremberg Trials might have succeeded in bringing justice to a handful of prominent Nazis, they did not trigger an extensive system of international criminal justice. This not only reflected the paralysing influence of the Cold War, when commitments to the international enforcement of human rights were very much subordinated to geopolitical interests (Douzinas 2000; Evans 2005; Robertson 2006), but also the systemic difficulties in establishing an international legal regime in a world political system comprised of competing nation states and shifting geopolitical alliances. As if to highlight this, the United States, China, Israel and India refused to sign up to the International Criminal Court, established in 2002 to prosecute cases of genocide, crimes against humanity, war crimes and the crime of aggression, on the grounds that it represented an unacceptable risk of politically motivated prosecutions (Robertson 2006: 419-467).

While the linkage of a criminological paradigm of state crime with codified and enforceable law is therefore seriously constrained, Rothe and Friedrichs (2006: 156) suggest nevertheless that international law and its principles provide a 'foundational basis' for understanding state criminality because they incorporate concepts such as human rights and social harm. However, criminologists have reached no clear agreement on how to draw on such themes.

State crime as a criminological concept

In a landmark article first published in 1970, Herman and Julia Schwendinger (1975: 137) threw down a challenge to mainstream criminology. They argued that 'imperialism, racism, sexism and poverty can be called crimes'; and that criminology should focus on the 'social relationships or social systems which cause the systematic abrogation of basic rights'. The Schwendingers based their call for this radical reorientation of criminology, away from the technical enforcement priorities of the state and towards the role of the state in promulgating human rights abuses, on a critique of a long-running controversy between criminologists in the United States.

This dispute, which initially involved Thorstein Sellin (1938), Edwin Sutherland (1949) and Paul Tappan (1947), centred on whether criminologists should rely on definitions of crime prescribed by the criminal law to set the boundaries of criminology. As part of his case for including white collar or corporate crime[2] as a focus for criminology, Sutherland (1949) suggested that definitions of crime could incorporate 'social injury'. Drawing on this, the Schwendingers (1975: 134) argued that developing a paradigm that utilised moral definitions of crime would enable criminologists to focus on subjects such as the socially injurious activities of the state. This could be achieved by making human rights the central conceptual tool of criminology and the mechanism by which to judge socially injurious behaviour. Empirically, this would require criminologists undertaking concrete assessments of particular human rights abuses and developing methodologies for determining which systemic violations should be challenged in a specific state or political economy.

The Schwendingers did not explicitly formulate a paradigm for understanding state crime; rather, their work formed part of an emerging body of critical criminology that aimed to develop a broader understanding of how deviance is socially produced (Taylor et al 1973, 1975). Nevertheless, the association of human rights abuses with criminal or deviant behaviour provides a valuable starting point for examining whether the state can be understood as a criminal entity.

---

2   Much white collar crime was not covered by the criminal law at the time.

Here, the Schwendingers' legacy is not entirely helpful. They create a significant problem by seeking to include a broad spectrum of rights within the realm of criminology. 'Food, shelter, clothing, medical services, challenging work and recreational experiences' were joined with 'security from predatory individuals or repressive and imperialistic social elites' as rights to be distinguished from 'rewards or privileges'; while genocide and economic exploitation were offered as examples of socially injurious action (Schwendinger & Schwendinger 1975: 133-134). Such a sweeping approach, criticised by Cohen (1993: 98) as 'a moral crusade', risks blurring significant distinctions between social harm and serious human rights abuses (Green & Ward 2000a: 104) and invites the criticism that the notion of state crime provides no basis for coherent criminological perspectives because it is indistinguishable from the state 'doing nasty things' (Sharkansky 1995).

Cohen (1993: 98), while also not offering an explicit definition of state crime, suggests human rights and criminological concerns can be brought together in a meaningful way through a 'more restricted and literal use of the concept of state crime' limited principally to so-called first generation rights, that is, 'gross violations of human rights – genocide, mass political killings, state terrorism, torture, disappearances'. He further argues that the growing recourse to human rights concepts, though problematic (see below), provides a basis on which criminologists can draw together the increasing awareness of state-organised human rights abuses and the experience of victims of criminal acts:

> There is no logical reason why the identity of the offender should be assumed to be fixed as citizen against citizen, rather state agent against citizen when talking about, say, murder, assault or rape. In fact there are good *moral* reasons why any grading of seriousness should take this into account in particular, the fact that the very agent responsible for upholding law, is actually responsible for the crime. And there is a good *empirical* reason: that for large parts of the world's population, state agents (or paramilitary groups, vigilantes or terrorists) are the normal violators of your "legally protected rights" (Cohen 1993: 101-102, emphases in original).

Cohen's approach might add some certainty to the concept of state crime by limiting it to activities that are unambiguously in breach of international law and incorporate the most serious criminal offences such as murder, rape, espionage, kidnapping and assault. However, limiting state criminality in this way risks excluding from its orbit practices such as the Australian state's highly abusive and damaging mandatory detention policy for 'unauthorised non-citizens', which is legal in domestic law but in breach of a range of Australia's international legal obligations (Grewcock 2007; Pickering 2005 also this volume).

Cohen's criticism of the 'American focus' of state crime literature[3] also implies criminologists should reorient towards non-Western states, where crimes such as torture might not be so 'anomalous'. This downplays the ways in which state crime in Western democracies 'shades imperceptibly into the routine, "legitimate" activities of the state' (Green & Ward 2000a: 103); or, in the case of torture, is exported by Western states elsewhere (Grey 2007; Thompson & Paglen 2006).

---

3   At the time, this was reasonable criticism but more recent state crime literature, especially Green and Ward (2004), goes some way to redressing this.

Rather than seeking arbitrarily to limit the types of human rights violations than can qualify as state crime, or to assume that certain types of state are less likely to be implicated in it, it might be more useful to focus on the systemic quality of human rights violations; their centrality to the state's enforcement policies as a whole; and the impact these violations have on the affected groups or individuals. In other words, as in the case of the mandatory detention policy, state crime can be understood as the product of a continuum of violations, often starting with actions by the state that are not grossly in breach of international law or human rights norms, but culminating in the systemic and often violent denial of the victims' legitimate expectations of state protection and support. Such an approach is consistent with Cohen's (1993: 100-101) emphasis on victimisation as a criminological theme that can illuminate concepts of state crime, and the approach of Green and Ward (2000a, 2000b, 2004), who define state crime as 'state organisational deviance involving the violation of human rights'.

In developing this definition, Green and Ward (2004: 4-5) draw on important criminological studies of deviance as an institutional, rather than individual criminal phenomenon,[4] and locate state crime as a category of organisational deviance, in which 'the relevant actors are state agencies' and:

> the relevant rules are rules of international law, domestic law and social morality, as interpreted by audiences that include domestic and transnational civil society … international organisations, other states and other agencies within the offending state itself.

Green and Ward's focus on a social audience that can determine and challenge state acts as deviant is the most dynamic aspect of this definition. It removes from the state its monopoly over understandings of criminality and suggests that criminality can be a feature of all states, including liberal democracies, rather than a deviant few engaging in activities such as genocide. How, then, can we further our understanding of the deviant state?

The deviant state

With the partial exception of Green and Ward (2004), there is a lack of attention within state crime literature to what constitutes a deviant state, or whether such an entity as opposed to 'rogue' agents or agencies, can be deemed even to exist. However, isolating the potentially criminogenic features of the state is important to understanding the subsequent development of criminal practices.

This is not a straightforward task. The nature of the state is a subject of considerable controversy amongst social theorists and there are substantial differences between states. Green and Ward (2004: 185), for example, distinguish for explanatory purposes three types of states:

1. capitalist states, divided into advanced industrialised democracies and transitional states;
2. state capitalist states, a description reflecting more accurately the political economy and class relationships within the officially socialist states; and,

---

4   For example, Braithwaite (1985, 1989); Kauzlarich & Kramer (1998); and Passas (1990).

3.   predatory states, 'where the state elite rules essentially for its own benefit'.

Nevertheless, all states have certain common features: they exercise power through a combination of administrative and coercive institutions; they seek to control a specified territory from which they can extract revenue and command loyalty; they seek to maintain the social and economic relations within that territory; they can be distinguished from the communal whole, although the extent of the state's autonomy and the class nature of the interests it represents vary enormously; and all conduct activities which can be declared criminal if carried out by private individuals.

The most potentially criminogenic feature of the state is its monopoly of the means of force. This takes a range of forms, spanning from full-scale military mobilisations through to various forms of detention and restraint. It also operates in a routine and 'peaceful' way as the ultimate sanction that can sustain the state's authority. Ideologically, acceptance of the state's monopoly of force is important in three general senses.

First, organised violence or warfare played a crucial role in the consolidation of virtually all contemporary states. Nationalist narratives therefore explicitly justify or at least acknowledge a degree of state violence as a necessary or inevitable precursor to securing the viability of the state.

Secondly, the state's military and policing apparatus is the most potent symbol of its existence and the primary mechanism by which it asserts its capacity to protect its subject population, and thus its legitimacy.

Thirdly, force can be diffused through a variety of state institutions. Modern liberal democracies, for example, operate through complex hierarchies of control. In particular, the transition from feudalism to capitalism gave rise to separate but reinforcing judicial and penal systems that shifted the locus of state power in relation to individuals away from private ecclesiastical and absolutist sources to a central, public sphere where the rule of law is buttressed not only by 'armed men' but also 'material adjuncts, prisons and institutions of coercion of all kinds' (Engels 1973: 327-328). While the boundaries between the various types of state institution are to some degree inscribed by the separation of powers; the sources of legal authority, chains of command, routine operation and social networks underpinning state institutions often overlap.

However, the state's use of violence, typically in the name of national security or defence, is neither the sole nor principal mechanism for maintaining its integrity. For the state to maintain its legitimacy and its right and capacity to exercise force, a degree of 'willing compliance', 'passive acquiescence' or 'ingrained dependence' (Draper 1977: 251) is required. The state, and its use of force, needs to be accepted as legitimate by its social audience.

Legitimacy and the state

The relationship between the state's potentially deviant acts and its social audience is addressed in part by Cohen (1993: 107-109), who applies Sykes and Matza's

(1970) formulations of 'techniques of neutralisation'[5] – denial of injury; denial of victim; denial of responsibility; condemnation of the condemners; and appeals to higher loyalty – to analyse how state actors might morally justify acts they know will be perceived as abusive. Cohen (2001) builds on similar themes in his subsequent work on the complex mechanisms of denial employed collectively by state and by individual participants in gross human rights violations. This demonstrates a need to analyse the relationship(s) between the state and what can broadly be described as civil society; the impact this has on the ways in which ideas and values are generated and shared; and how this conditions responses to activities that can be defined as state crime.

Green and Ward (2000b: 80; 2004: 3-6) develop these themes by adapting interpretations of Italian Marxist Antonio Gramsci's (1971, 2000) writings on hegemony to explain the relationship between the state and civil society and how this 'involves the internalisation, by the ruled and rulers alike, of a complex set of shared beliefs'. Gramsci sought to use the concept of hegemony to explain how ideological control could be maintained within a capitalist state. His writings emphasised the 'interweaving of coercion and consent' (McLennan 1984: 95) – the many subtle and complex forms by which non-violent, internal controls enable the state to operate with popular consent or legitimacy – and were formulated around the twin themes of civil society and hegemony.[6]

For Gramsci, civil society incorporated a 'range of structures and activities like trade unions, schools, the churches, and the family' that formulate, filter and consolidate 'an entire system of values, attitudes, beliefs, morality, etc. that is in one way or another supportive of the established order and the class interests that dominate it' (Boggs 1978: 39). However, this process of hegemony, while capable of creating a 'common social-moral language' (Femia: 1981: 24) by operating as an 'organising principle' for the diffusion of ideas which help 'ruling elites perpetuate their power, wealth and status ... [as] part of the natural order of things' (Boggs 1978: 39), is not a one-sided, formal or closed system. While the state's claimed role in, for example, protecting the nation's law and order, borders or national identity might for periods be relatively uncontested or indeed positively embraced, the ideological underpinnings for such beliefs are not fixed or stable.

Rather, the state, partly because of the overlap between state and civil institutions, can be subject to challenge from below, or in some circumstances from within. In this sense, civil society comprises sites of contradiction in which various classes with conflicting interests and social formations contest prevailing ideologies. While it can help legitimise the state's activities, civil society (or counter-hegemonic formations operating independently of the state) 'can also play a crucial role in defining state actions as illegitimate where they violate legal rules or shared moral beliefs' and 'label state actions as deviant' (Green & Ward 2004: 4). In this context, human

---

5   This study, first published in 1957, challenged the notion of 'juvenile delinquency as a form of behaviour based on the values and norms of a deviant sub-culture', and sought to explain why 'the juvenile delinquent would appear to be at least partially committed to the dominant social order in that he frequently exhibits guilt or shame when he violates its proscriptions, accords approval to certain conforming figures, and distinguishes between appropriate and inappropriate targets for his deviance' (Sykes & Matza 1970: 294).

6   Gramsci's writings on hegemony, mainly drafted in prison in the 1920s, have been the subject of extensive debate. Written in an opaque style to avoid difficulties with the censor, they might best be described as a series of insights rather than a rounded theory.

rights provide the conceptual basis for identifying and challenging state crime, especially when human rights violations are committed by states that proclaim to uphold those rights.

Human rights and state crime

While Cohen was concerned to limit the potential elasticity of human rights norms as a measure of state deviance, Green and Ward pay more attention to the contradictory nature of human rights discourse and how this penetrates perceptions of state activity within civil society.

The basic contradiction at the heart of rights discourse is the disjuncture between the rights that states proclaim to uphold and promote, and the often very limited protection or application of those rights. It is this disjuncture that provides the basis for challenging state acts as criminal.

The contemporary human rights discourse dates back to the revolutionary upheavals in Europe and North America that laid the foundations for modern liberal democracy. The American *Declaration of Independence* 1776 and the French *Declaration of the Rights of Man and of the Citizen* 1789 spoke of a new world in which natural and universal rights replaced a divine order. In Jefferson's (1939: 13) famous words, 'We hold these truths to be self-evident: that all men are created equal; that they are endowed by their Creator with inherent and unalienable rights; that among these are life, liberty and the pursuit of happiness'.

However, this was a very qualified form of equality that challenged the static order of European feudalism and entrenched the political authority of a new class largely comprised of white, property owning men (Callinicos 2000). The declarations of universal rights did not result, for example, in the abolition of slavery; Jefferson was himself a slave owner, while the French Government sent troops to what is now Haiti, when its slave population rebelled to demand 'liberty, fraternity and equality' (James 1980). Even minimal measures of formal political equality, such as the universal right to vote and hold public office, were denied within liberal democracies until well into the 20th century (Foot 2005).

The revolutionary origins of contemporary human rights and their limited realisation pose the question: is there an emancipatory kernel within rights ideals that can provide a means of confronting state crime? Critical analyses of human rights suggest a pessimistic response to such propositions. Reflecting on the fate of refugees and stateless people in the 1930s, Hannah Arendt (1976: 299-300) concluded:

> The conception of human rights, based upon the assumed existence of a human being as such, broke down at the very moment when those who professed to believe in it were for the first time confronted with people who had indeed lost all other qualities and specific relationships – except that they were still human. The world found nothing sacred in the abstract nakedness of being human ... If a human being loses his political status, he should, according to the implications of the inborn and inalienable rights of man, come under exactly the situation for which the declarations of such general rights provided. Actually the opposite is the case.

For Arendt, the failure of non-totalitarian Western states to protect the stateless highlighted the profound contradiction between universal rights and the political organisation of society around the nation state.[7] Those excluded from the protection of a national polity found their rights were rendered brutally meaningless in any practical sense.

Viewed against the experiences of the 1930s, this was a compelling critique that loses little of its sharpness when applied to contemporary responses to forced migration. Nevertheless, there was a substantial growth in international human rights law during the latter part of the 20th century, when human rights ideals resonated within many of the most compelling challenges to state power. The rights discourse gained enormous momentum from the popular political movements that developed during the Cold War in both the West and the East. Campaigns for civil rights in the United States and Northern Ireland, the struggle against apartheid and the emergence of independent unions in Poland challenged dominant state structures and reverberated internationally. Inchoate concepts of racial and sexual equality, free speech, freedom of association and freedom of movement became powerful mobilising ideals that continue to confront the political realities of contemporary liberal democracy.

Viewed in this light, Green and Ward's framework enables us to focus on the ways in which concepts of rights enliven the contradictions between the state and civil society and within civil society itself. Notwithstanding attempts by the dominant states to tie concepts of human rights to neoliberalism;[8] the 'enormous gap between the normative ideal of human rights ... and the selective and hypocritical promotion of such rights by powerful states and transnational institutions such as the World Bank and International Monetary Fund' (Green & Ward 2004: 9); and the ambiguous role of many NGOs (Petras 1999; Ungpakorn 2004), the fact that most states claim to support the *Universal Declaration of Human Rights* and the *International Covenants on Civil and Political Rights and on Economic, Social and Cultural Rights* illustrates how the idea that all humans share an entitlement to basic human rights is now deeply ingrained. While Cohen (1993: 99) might be overstating his case by describing human rights as '*the* normative language of the future' (emphasis in original), conceptions of human rights are afforded a unique and contested ideological space.

By claiming this space and embracing the 'common moral language' of rights, Green and Ward have provided a framework within which deviance can be determined from below, rather than at state level. Put simply, the systematic denial of rights becomes a basis for declaring the state's acts as criminal. Redefining deviance in this way also enables rights to operate as a source of empowerment for victims that is not reliant primarily on demands for the state to acquire further policing powers.

Ongoing challenges

While Green and Ward provide the most coherent and considered criminological framework for understanding state crime, there are a number of dimensions to their work that could be further developed.

- *The role of force in state crime.* Ultimately, it is the capacity of the state to physically impose its will over individuals that gives it both its legitimacy

---

7   This was part of Arendt's extensive thesis on 'totalitarianism', in which she traced the development of the Nazi and Stalinist states.

8   For example, Articles 1-3 of the proposed Constitution for the European Union enshrines the free market within an 'Area of Freedom, Security and Justice'. See also Grewcock (2003).

and its capacity to commit organised abuse. Therefore, rather than debate which categories of rights might provide benchmarks for judging state crime, we could use a sharper focus on the sociology of state force.

- *The systemic nature of state crime.* While the criminal justice system can process individual state actors, it cannot play a direct role in sanctioning those more broadly responsible for the underpinning policies and practices, many of which might be legal. By contrast, a criminological assessment of state crime should endeavour to analyse the institutional dynamics of the acts in question.

- *The transnational nature of state crime.* State crime rarely occurs within a complete national vacuum. It is often the by-product of complex political and socio-economic relationships and might be supported directly by other states, for example, through the export of arms or the provision of safe havens for high profile offenders.

- *The relationship between state crime and transnational policing.* The internationalisation of Western policing, on the back of various 'wars' against drugs, people smuggling/trafficking and terrorism, is often justified as necessary to protect human rights. Yet the policing measures, such as arbitrary detention, that these wars adopt, often involve the systemic abuse of human rights.

- *The role of history and tradition in legitimising state crime.* State crime is often legitimised as necessary to protect long-established social and cultural norms or 'ways of life'. In particular, the experience of colonialism embedded deeply mainstream ideologies such as nationalism. The role of such 'acceptable' ideologies in shaping, for example, racist ideas, is important to our broader understanding of how deviant state practices develop.

- *The universality of human rights.* The human rights discourse is essentially a modern Western construction. Norms in relation to racial equality, for example, have changed enormously over the past 50 years. Can such norms be used as a measure of deviance in all times and places? Does the concept of universality allow such norms to be used as an interpretative tool to analyse the forcible dispossession of Indigenous land; or the exclusionary practices of the White Australia Policy?

This is not an exhaustive list and none of these themes is absent in Green and Ward's work. It is an attempt to emphasise substantial areas of interdisciplinary research that would consolidate a specifically criminological body of literature on state crime.

Conclusion

Recent attention to state crime has coincided with an increasingly disordered international polity in which the authority of a growing number of states has been undermined and challenged from within and without. Military and policing operations against 'rogue' and 'failed' states; policing 'wars' against transnational crime and terrorism; and the seemingly indeterminate refinement of the means of mass killing and torture present any intellectual discipline devoted to examining deviant and abusive behaviour with tremendous challenges.

The sheer scale of the violence committed by states ought in itself to be sufficient to merit the attention of criminologists given the centrality of violent crime to mainstream policing practice and discourse. Yet criminologists have struggled to define state crime; break from the notion that ultimately it is states that determine what criminal behaviour is; or reorient away from the acts of citizens towards institutional sources of violence and abuse.

Having said that, the focus on human rights the Schwendingers introduced into critical criminology is not without its problems. Rights are often contested and contradictory and expectations and perceptions of them evolve. The enforcement of rights does not lend itself to any easy state or institutional structure at either a national or international level. Nevertheless, Green and Ward's use of rights as a mechanism for understanding state deviance suggests rights provide criminologists with a powerful interpretative tool. How well that tool works will depend on the extent of the critical analyses of state actions that are undertaken in the immediate future.

References

Arendt, H 1976, *The Origins of Totalitarianism*, Harvest, Harcourt Inc, New York.

Barak, G (ed) 1991, *Crimes by the Capitalist State: an introduction to state criminality*, State University of New York Press, New York.

Boggs, C 1978, *Gramsci's Marxism*, Pluto Press, London.

Braithwaite, J 1985, 'White Collar Crime', (11) *Annual Review of Sociology* 1-25.

Braithwaite, J 1989, 'Criminological theory and organizational crime', 6(3) *Justice Quarterly* 338-358.

Callinicos, A 2000, *Equality,* Polity Press, Cambridge.

Chambliss, W 1989, 'State-Organized Crime', 27(2) *Criminology* 183-208.

Cohen, S 1993, 'Human Rights and Crimes of the State: the culture of denial', 26(97) *Australian and New Zealand Journal of Criminology* 97-115.

Cohen, S 2001, *States of Denial: knowing about atrocities and suffering,* Polity Press, Cambridge.

Crawford, J 1998, Special Rapporteur, *First Report on State Responsibility*, International Law Commission, UN General Assembly, A/CN.4/490/Add.3

Crawford, J 2002, *The International Law Commission's Articles on State Responsibility: Introduction, Text and Commentaries*, Cambridge University Press, Cambridge.

Douzinas, C 2000, *The End of Human Rights: critical legal thought at the end of the century*, Hart Publishing, Oxford.

Draper, H 1977, *Karl Marx's Theory of Revolution, Volume 1: state and bureaucracy,* Monthly Review Press, New York.

Engels, F 1973, 'Origins of the Family, Private Property and the State', in Marx, K & Engels, F, *Selected Works* Vol III Lawrence and Wishart, London.

Evans, T 2005, *The Politics of Human Rights: a Global Perspective*, Pluto Press, London.

Femia, J 1981, *Gramsci's Political Thought*, Clarendon, Oxford.

Foot, P 2005, *The Vote: how it was won and how it was undermined*, Viking, London.

Gramsci, A 1971, in Hoare, Q & Nowell-Smith, G (eds), *Selections from the Prison Notebooks*, Lawrence & Wishart, London.

Gramsci, A 2000, in Forgacs, D (ed), *The Gramsci Reader: selected writings 1916-1935*, New York University Press, New York.

Green, P & Ward, T 2000a, 'Legitimacy, Civil Society and State Crime', 27(1) *Social Justice* 76-93.

Green, P & Ward, T 2000b, 'State Crime, Human Rights and the Limits of Criminology', 27(4) *Social Justice* 101-115.

Green, P & Ward, T 2004, *State Crime: governments, violence and corruption*, Pluto Press, London.

Grewcock, M 2003, 'Irregular Migration, Identity and the State: the challenge for criminology', 15(2) *Current Issues in Criminal Justice* 114-135.

Grewcock, M 2007, 'Shooting the Passenger: Australia's war on illicit migrants', in Lee, M (ed), *Human Trafficking*, Willan Publishing, Cullompton.

Grey, S 2007, *Ghost Plane: the untold story of the CIA's torture program*, Scribe, Melbourne.

Human Rights Watch 2005, *Getting Away with Torture? Command Responsibility for the US Abuse of Detainees*, Author, New York.

James, CLR 1980, *The Black Jacobins*, Revised edn, Allison and Busby, London.

Jefferson, T 1939, in Padover, S (ed), *Thomas Jefferson on Democracy*, The New American Library, New York.

Jørgenson, N 2003, *The Responsibility of States for International Crimes*, Oxford University Press, Oxford.

Kauzlarich, D & Kramer, R 1998, *Crimes of the American Nuclear State at Home and Abroad*, Northeastern University Press, Boston.

McLennan, G 1984, 'Capitalist state or democratic polity? Recent developments in Marxist and pluralist theory', in McLennan, G, Held, D & Hall, S (eds), *The Idea of the Modern State*, Open University Press, Milton Keynes.

Merton, R 1968, *Social Theory and Social Structure*, Free Press, New York.

Passas, N 1990, 'Anomie and Corporate Deviance', 14(3) *Contemporary Crises* 157-178.

Petras, J 1999, 'NGOs: in the service of imperialism', 29(4) *Journal of Contemporary Asia* 429-440.

Pickering, S 2005, *Refugees and State Crime*, The Federation Press, Sydney.

Robertson, G 2006, *Crimes Against Humanity: the struggle for global justice*, Third Edition, Penguin Books, Camberwell.

Ross, J (ed) 1995, *Controlling State Crime: an introduction*, Garland Publishing, New York & London.

Rothe, D & Friedrichs, D 2006, 'The State of the Criminology of Crimes of the State', 33(1) *Social Justice* 147-161.

Schwendinger, H & Schwendinger, J 1975, 'Defenders of order or guardians of human rights?' in Taylor, I, Walton, P, & Young, J (eds), *Critical Criminology*, Routledge & Kegan Paul, London.

Sellin, T 1938, *Culture, Conflict and Crime*, Social Science Research Council, New York.

Sharkansky, I 1995, 'A State Action May Be Nasty But Is Not Likely To Be A Crime', in Ross, J (ed), *Controlling State Crime: an introduction*, Garland Publishing, New York.

Sutherland, E 1949, *White Collar Crime*, Holt, Rhinehart & Winston, New York.

Sykes, G & Matza, D 1970, 'Techniques of Delinquency', in Wolfgang, M, Savitz, L & Johnston, N (eds), *The Sociology of Crime and Delinquency*, John Wiley & Sons, New York.

Tappan, P 1947, *Juvenile Delinquency*, McGraw-Hill Book Co, New York.

Taylor, I, Walton, P & Young, J 1973, *The New Criminology – for a social theory of deviance*, Routledge & Kegan Paul, London.

Taylor, I, Walton, P & Young, J (eds) 1975, *Critical Criminology*, Routledge & Kegan Paul, London.

Thompson, AC & Paglen, T 2006, *Torture Taxi: On the trail of the CI's rendition flights*, Hardie Grant Books, Melbourne.

Ungpakorn, J 2004, 'NGOs: enemies or allies?', (104) *International Socialism* 49-64.

13

TORTURE AND TERROR

Elizabeth Stanley

Introduction

According to the United Nations *Convention Against Torture and Other Cruel, Inhuman or Degrading Treatment or Punishment* 1984, Article 1.1, torture is severe pain or suffering (mental or physical) that is inflicted by or with the acquiescence of a public (state) official.[1] It is also conducted for a particular purpose such as to punish or obtain information from a victim. To reach the legal threshold of torture, rather than inhuman or degrading treatment, the victim has to experience an intense degree of suffering. In reality, as campaigners like Amnesty International argue, these different harms often overlap; and, none are permissible.

For victims, torture represents shocking forms of violence, including: beatings; kickings; stretchings; whippings; burnings; electro-shocks; genital mutilation, rape and other forms of sexual assault; cuttings; suspension, including hangings and cruci-fixions; breaking bones; amputation; teeth or fingernail extraction; *falanga*, the blunt trauma to the soles of the feet; attacks by animals; *submarino*, forced submersion into water, urine, vomit, blood, faeces or other matter; injections or the use of chemicals to cause, for example, blindness; *teléfono*, boxed ears; asphyxiation; deprivation of food, water, sleep or sanitary conditions; sensory deprivation or overload; and, psychological pressures[2] (Arcel 2002; Rasmussen et al 2005; Rejali 2003). Many victims die from torture and those who survive regularly endure chronic long-term pain and psychological disturbances. Given these realities, torture is one of the few legal rights that is applied universally and cannot be derogated from.

Nonetheless, the late 20th century marked a resurgence in the use of torture. Between 1997 and 2000, torture was inflicted in 70 countries by three quarters of the world's governments (Amnesty International 2000). In more recent times, this

---

1   The *Rome Statute of the International Criminal Court* 1998 presents a wider definition of torture as a crime against humanity (Art 7.2.e). Here, the International Criminal Court (ICC) foregoes the public status of the torturer. In doing so, it allows a consideration of torture by other actors such as militia members, paramilitaries, private contractors or resistance groups. Of course, as a crime against humanity, this torture would need to be part of a widespread or systematic attack directed against a civilian population.

2   These can include: techniques of humiliation (for example, forced nakedness); brain-washing; infected surroundings (for example, by lice or rats); confined isolation; mock executions; death threats or forced witnessing of others being tortured (Arcel 2002).

ascendancy has been illustrated boldly in the treatment of prisoners held within United States-governed detention centres in Iraq, Afghanistan, Cuba, and elsewhere. The initial graphic depictions of detainees being subject to violations brought international attention and a military tribunal, which was an unusual response to torture events. In return, a vigorous legitimising discourse in support of torture has emerged within political, academic, legal and social spheres.

Torture has remained on the periphery of criminology when, arguably, it should – for reasons of its violence, criminality and popularity – be an essential part of the criminological endeavour (Grewcock this volume). Human rights violations like torture present a vital opportunity for criminologists to provide a fuller recognition of what constitutes crime. Examining torture can develop our analyses on how states build or retain power through violence, and how this violence can be made acceptable to wider populations. It may allow us to make connections between the structural, institutional, social and personal frames through which violence is undertaken and experienced. It can also deepen our understanding of, and responses to, violations in terms of victimisation and accountability debates. To progress these debates, this chapter begins with an examination of torture's historical basis.

Torture's use value: historical aspects

Torture is commonly linked to the rise of Western civilisations. In ancient Greece and Rome, the infliction of pain was seen by the judiciary to be the quickest way to gather proof of offences.[3] Accordingly, torture developed systematically with clear rules and safeguards for its application (Lea 1878). These early legal codes were reflected in the 're-emergence' of torture across most European states from the 12th century. From this time, torture became an integral part of policing and legal procedure as accused individuals were presumed guilty from the outset and the role of the judge was to prove this by obtaining a confession (Evans & Morgan 1998). The safeguards held within the ancient societies were disregarded and torture was often recklessly applied (Peters 1985).

The early modern period of torture was, therefore, linked to pre-emptive actions against threatening others however it is also associated with overt spectacles of state power. The torture so graphically illustrated in the first sections of Foucault's (1977) *Discipline and Punish* presents an exhibition of violent excess. Torture took place in the public streets or squares and the punishment of the criminal act, on the body, was symbolically and quantitatively applied (Foucault 1977; Rejali 1994). The public was encouraged to meditate on the crime, punishment and the judicial system by witnessing the event. Thus, 'The victim was an integral part of the ritual performance of [state] power through their confession, bodily destruction and public agony' (Humphrey 2002: 30).

These forms of torture gradually faced opposition, notably as the spectators that were positioned to learn their lessons from the ceremonies also found a place to express their revolt (Foucault 1977). Towards the end of the 18th century, public displays often became regarded as the pinnacle of unjust violent state power. The

---

3   The proposition that torture is capable of extracting the truth or proof has always been debateable. The Romans, for instance, accepted that any retrieved evidence was weak and acknowledged that those who were subject to torture would remain silent or lie rather than endure pain (Lea 1878).

subsequent growing disdain felt towards torture can be linked to a shift to humanitarian practices, bolstered by the writings of Beccaria, Voltaire and others (Evans & Morgan 1998). Alongside this, there were legal and political changes that provided pragmatic reasons for the decline in torture: in particular, the formation of a professional judiciary, changes in the law of evidence (to a system where circumstantial evidence was accepted), the introduction of new criminal sanctions and the development of state institutions (Evans & Morgan 1998).

Modern states began to find new ways to control their populations and other forms of power and subjugation developed – the administration of bodies could now be undertaken through education, health and work systems that might more securely guarantee domination in line with the growth of capitalism (Foucault 1977). And, for those who did not conform as they should, punishment was re-directed in the 'birth of the prison'. The contemporary systems of punishment represented a move away from the public spectacle of brutality. Accordingly, the 19th and early 20th centuries are often regarded as a period in which torture significantly declined.

However, the moral claims put forward during this 'humanitarian period' may be viewed with scepticism (Evans & Morgan 1998). Sentence punishments continued to be harsh for those brought before the courts (who were, invariably, those most economically disadvantaged) and while some states took the moral high ground regarding the use of torture at home, they continued to vigorously engage in torture (as well as genocide and other crimes) abroad. The violence sustained in colonies across Africa, South-East Asia, the South Pacific, India, Latin America, and elsewhere, had the purpose of killing populations but it also sought to retain a compliant, albeit dehumanised, population to provide labour and act as a potential market of goods (Fanon 1963; Taussig 2002). In colonial settings, torture was used to 'encourage' productive bodies for labour; it presented a means by which economic and ideological control could be established through the colonies. Torture is linked, therefore, to wider programs of violence, not just to criminal justice processes.

But what of the contemporary situation in the so-called 'post-colonial world'? The global dispersal of modern forms of control (such as those related to the advanced global economy, migration, surveillance or policing) might lead us to presume that torture would have little contemporary use-value – and, the widescale acceptance of international instruments and bodies[4] against torture would similarly seem to indicate that states have come to this conclusion on pragmatic as well as moral grounds. However, as Peters (1985: 7) opines, 'in an age of vast state strength, ability to mobilise resources, and possession of virtually infinite means of coercion', official policy has paradoxically focused on the idea that the state remains insecure and vulnerable to attack. In recent times, the use of torture has been 'regarded by many practitioners to be a practical necessity' to ensure state control of 'crime', 'terrorism' and 'disorder' (Morgan 2000: 182).[5]

---

4   Including the *United Nations Convention against Torture and Other Cruel, Inhuman or Degrading Treatment or Punishment* 1984, the *Universal Declaration of Human Rights* 1948, the *International Covenant on Civil and Political Rights* 1966, a Special Rapporteur and a focused United Nations Committee.

5   This is not to argue that torture is exercised by all States, to the same degree, at all times. Torture is differentially applied. While we might be able to identify current, persistent violators, other States take active steps to ensure that torture does not occur.

In this context of the strengthened state, torture has never been abandoned, but has progressed in new and varied ways. Torture continues to be made officially acceptable for those who threaten state control. When state power is in question, torture presents a 'wholly convincing spectacle' (Scarry 1985: 27); it can terrify and disband perceived opponents, and demonstrate to the general populace the risks of acting against powerful interests (Stanley 2004). Torture remains, therefore, a product of measured decision-making to facilitate state domination (Crelinsten 2003).

Managing and legitimising torture

This section explores how torture is managed. It shows how torture is sometimes hidden or denied while, in other circumstances, it is carefully exposed by violators. This dual nature operates to make it more difficult for victims to gather proof; it isolates victims and embeds confusion and fear among the wider population. Overall, it can incapacitate victims and their communities to challenge torturers. These limits on resistance are intensified by the academic discursive support for torture as well as the ways in which torture gathers legitimacy through global, institutional frameworks.

While states engage in techniques of denial to minimise their involvement in torture (Cohen 2001), torturers also employ 'stealth' techniques – such as forced standing; electric shocks; torture by water, ice, heat or cold; and psychological pressures – to hide evidence (Rejali 2003). Stealth techniques are not necessarily innovative, for example the use of sleep deprivation was viewed as one of the most refined and effective forms of judicial torture in 17th century Europe (Peters 1985). However their popularity rests on the fact that they 'leave no obvious physical marks other than the looks of vacant exhaustion' (Evans & Morgan 1998: 19). These methods are useful additions for states that wish to counter monitor, or want to appear as being compliant to human rights norms and laws.

Yet, the invisibility of torture is not meant to be total as regimes often seek to control what is said and not said, and they want to ensure that individuals and groups remember fear (Stanley 2004). At a societal level, the fact of torture will emerge through local gossip, by strange sounds behind walls, in unusual arrests on the street and through the blank faces that emerge from detention centres (Humphrey 2002). In some situations, knowledge about torture will also surface through photographs and film, pictorial evidence that is crafted by the torturers and distributed between officers, local communities and occasionally the global media. These representations tend to be carefully managed; their powerful, symbolic evidence of victim's denigration sends a deterrent message to the wider population however it also encourages isolationism by distancing the viewer from the debased tortured subject (Kappeler 1986).

The control of messages is apparent, too, within modern torture methods that reflect the historical spectacles of state power that involved whole communities (Green & Ward 2004). For example, during the recent 36-year long conflict in Guatemala that killed over 200,000 people, villagers would be forced to watch the torture, rape and execution of their neighbours or family members by military officials and their militias; they would also be continually reminded of violations by the victims' mutilated bodies which would be subsequently displayed in prominent sites – along roads or at the entrances to schools, churches or other public institutions (Rothenberg 2003). This overt presentation of power was 'designed to inspire generalised fear, mistrust and uncertainty', the torture had a performative role to magnify militaristic threats and create an atmosphere of constant terror (2003: 476).

As a result of fear, confusion, isolation, shame or lack of evidence, victims find it very difficult to be recognised *as* victims. Consequently, they struggle to access assistance, seek redress or take their case through criminal justice systems. Their plight is further hampered by the legitimisation of torture within official and academic discourse. For example, in the current 'war on terror', torture has been cast as an 'appropriate' and 'civilised' response given the circumstances. Dershowitz (2002), for instance, calls for the introduction of torture warrants so that torture can be subject to judicial review and accountability. Ignatieff (2004) argues that we need to make a distinction between torture and, to him, the more acceptable 'torture lite' involving psychological or stress-induced violence. And, Bagaric and Clarke (2005) propose that torture is morally justifiable as an act to collect information, even if it results in the victim's annihilation. Such writings reiterate others, such as the political philosopher Cicero of 45 BC or the 17th century jurisprudist Sebastian Guazzini, who attempted to instil support and enforce regulations for torture when the ruling powers were threatened or experiencing crisis (Peters 1985). These neutralising texts authorise torture, constructing the violation as a possibility within certain 'civilised' limits. Against this backdrop, victims enjoy less opportunity to make claims against the state. It appears that academic discourses have, then, legitimised torture.

Legitimacy is also invoked through torture's use in sustaining employment and trade for individuals, groups and states. Torturers tend to operate within policing or military bodies that promote a hierarchical culture marked by male domination and the persistent use of force (Green & Ward 2004; Huggins et al 2002). These institutions benefit from an insular culture that depicts who belongs on the basis of 'bonds of solidarity, the sense of common purpose and mutual understanding' (Chan et al 2003: 256). This culture may assist officers to shield themselves from feelings of alienation or criticism from the public but it can also encourage officers to perceive that 'outsiders' have a degraded status. The institutional context can therefore create situations in which violence is more likely to be operationalised and accepted.[6] Consequently, individual torturers are often held as legitimate and rational professionals who are deserving of national awards, good pay, career enhancements and standing privileges (Haritos-Fatouros 2002; Huggins et al 2002).

Added to this, torture often incorporates many state officials. Torture is impossible to sustain without a network of officials working towards a common aim.[7] Army personnel, police officers, doctors, nurses, judges and magistrates, psychologists, amongst others, all contribute to the implementation and maintenance of state torture (Cohen 2001). For instance, Lawrence Weschler (1998) notes how, in 1985, at the height of repression in Uruguay, more than one-fifth of all medical personnel were involved in torture activities. This sustained involvement was based on 'professional ambition and financial reward' (1998: 127). However, as Elaine Scarry (1985: 42) highlights, those doctors who refused to cooperate with the regime

---

6   Angela Davis (2005: 64-65) details that these institutional 'ideologies of male dominance' mobilise 'ordinary' people, including women, to torture. To challenge violations like torture, therefore, one has to critique and challenge the institution.

7   For this reason, Rejali (1999: 9) argues that 'there is no such thing as "THE torturer" ... To speak of the torturer abstracts the fact that the torturers are all situated in an institution known as the State. It disguises a complex institutional and social relationship as a relationship between two individuals'.

'disappeared at such a rate that ... medical and health care programs entered a state of crisis'. Medical personnel had to give themselves over as 'servants of the state' or suffer the consequences.

Finally, the legitimisation of torture is also apparent in the way that many states and corporations pursue brisk trades in torture technologies such as stun guns, leg shackles, trauma-inducing drugs, electroshock weapons and chemical gases. Torture equipment is directed along trade lines, regularly being designed and made in European or North American states (notably from companies in France, Germany, the United Kingdom and the United States) and shipped to other perpetrating states around the globe (Amnesty International 2001a). The research for and training of personnel is undertaken along similar tracks, as torturers learn and adapt their techniques through training manuals, courses and practical instruction, acquired from 'Global North' professionals (Weschler 1998). Consequently, while we might want to talk about conflicts and gross human rights violations as being localised, in reality they are connected to international structures of dominance (Galtung 1994). For this reason, torture has to be viewed within a global economic context – 'not merely as a problem of infraction of human rights in the country where torture shows up, but as one of the strategies of capitalist and social imperialism' (1994: 133).

Torture victims

Torture is commonly directed towards marginalised and vulnerable groups within society. Structural relations of power determine who is tortured and the kind of violence they endure. Those placed at the edge of markets and those who are at the bottom of the socio-economic hierarchies are more likely to face violations than those who hold economic capital. As Rusche and Kirchheimer (1968) detailed in 1939, torture gains justification as the poorer individuals become, the more poisonous or threatening they are deemed to be. Moreover, those individuals that hold economically marginalised positions – having non-productive bodies – fall below the 'threshold of outrage', their pain cannot be subject to the same level of indignation as that of another who is economically valuable. In these instances, the essential feature of torture practices is that 'one class of society claims absolute power' over those with lesser class status (Vidal-Naquet 1963: 167).

These perspectives on marginalisation and economic disparity resonate with the manner in which torture gained popular support within colonising conditions. The circumstances of colonial rule were guided by desires of economic expansionism and settler beliefs that colonised populations were racially inferior. Cast as 'other', the colonised person was an abject body, presumed guilty from the outset (Fanon 1963). This stance was further strengthened by beliefs that the colonisers and the colonised country could be more economically stable or affluent as a result of colonising activities, and that violence was a worthy cost given the prize (MacMaster 2004).

These racist underpinnings form the backdrop for contemporary forms of torture. It is perhaps of no surprise that Indigenous populations, travelling people and ethnic minority groups are regular torture targets. For instance, consider the torture of Australian Muslim Mamdouh Habib. Habib was detained for over three years in Pakistan, Egypt and Guantanamo Bay. During this period, he suffered a barrage of physical and psychological violence that focused on denigrating his religion. Easily identified as 'different', his marginalisation and victimisation were made acceptable and his return home was met with continued suspicion from Australian politicians and commentators (McLean et al 2005).

Such racist ideologies have dovetailed with other notions of identity that operate across geographical, political and economic boundaries. It is clear that torture operates not just across black and white divides, 'but at the newer categories of ... displaced and dispossessed' or 'outsider' people (Sivanandan 2001: 2). This xeno-racism, as Sivanandan calls it, is more about status than skin colour. For example, new torture technologies – such as taser anti-personnel mines, high-powered micro-waves or chemical incapacitants – are being developed to respond to the mass movement of vulnerable people across borders due to political or environmental disasters (Wright 2007).

Alongside these structural relations of class and 'race', gender relations are also central to torture practices. The gendered basis of torture has been recently exemplified with the photographs emanating from Abu Ghraib prison in Iraq. Some of these photographs detailed male prisoners stripped naked with electric wires attached to their genitalia, others depicted naked men held on a leash by a petite, smiling woman. At the centre of these techniques lay the idea that male Muslim prisoners would endure psychological harm through both the measured attack on their sexuality and by their enforced subjugation to a white, female officer. Using a woman during the torture was viewed, by officers, to be the quickest way to induce prisoner degradation and powerlessness (Hersh 2004). The technique struck at the heart of patriarchal societal ordering.

Patriarchal divisions are also identified in the ways in which female victims of torture frequently endure specific violations (Kois 1998). Over the past decade, the rape and sexual assault of women during torture has gained greater recognition in political, academic and legal circles. Nonetheless, while significant progress has been made in highlighting the need for gender-sensitivity in legal or societal responses to torture, most female victims continue to be sidelined as victims and suffer unsatisfactory outcomes on their cases (Harris Rimmer 2004).

Torture's use is also connected to other power relations. For instance, torture has been linked to: age – for example, children are subject to torture and may be violated in front of parents to make adults comply with officials (Suarez-Orozco 2004); ability – for example, through enforced medical experimentation on individuals with mental or physical disabilities (Hornblum 1998); sexuality – for instance, in relation to the torture of gay men, lesbians, bisexuals and trans-gendered people (Amnesty International 2001b); and, social status – for example, groups that are cast as politically or culturally dangerous, such as 'common' offenders, are more likely to face torture (Stanley 2004). In their 'outsider' status, these groups are also seen as 'torturable'.

Overall, torture tends to be directed towards those groups who are most marginalised within societies. Structural relations contextualise which individuals become targets for torture and, then, how they are violated. They also have an effect on how victims are able to move forward following torture.

Torture's aftermath

The aftermath of torture can be a period in which the status disparities between the torturer and the tortured are sustained and even widened. The repercussions of torture for victims are wide-ranging and encompass medical, psychological, social, economic, legal and political arenas.

Torture victims can emerge from their experiences with an array of medical complaints that require treatment. Alongside this, many victims suffer numerous psychological effects. These bring significant challenges to the individual's very sense of identity and impact on how victims are able to function (Arcel 2002). Among other effects, victims may: report feelings of depression, anxiety, anger or irritability; have disturbed or violent behaviour; lack energy, cannot sleep or sleep all the time; suffer nightmares and flashbacks; become utterly dependent on others and fear being alone; avoid situations, locations or things[8] that remind them of their violation; have feelings of shame, self-blame, dirtiness, humiliation or embarrassment; be unable to eat; feel suicidal or want to harm themselves; no longer desire sexual relations; constantly fear another attack; have a diminished ability to concentrate; and, fear that they are going crazy (Arcel 2002; Becker et al 1990; Hardy 2002; Stanley 2004; Turner & Gorst-Unsworth 1990). These conditions impact severely on the abilities of individuals to move forward from the status of 'victim' to 'survivor'.

The psychological repercussions are, therefore, long-lived. Victims can experience such sequelae in ways that resonate with the debates on structural relations detailed above. For example, women who have experienced sexual assault may transfer their fears and begin to see their partners as potential 'attackers' (Arcel 2002: 13). They can also experience intense shame because of the humiliating sexual practices inflicted against them (Becker et al 1990). These feelings are also shared by male victims of sexual torture, who may also experience crises of sexual identity. Following sexual violation, heterosexual men can perceive that they have lost their 'manhood', they may feel feminised and sense that their sexual orientation has been compromised or changed (Hardy 2002). These reactions are explicitly tied to dominant notions of masculinity, manhood and sexuality that underpin mainstream gender relations. Thus, torture practices impact differently on different groups as a result of structural relations and social norms.

Family members of torture victims may also experience a range of trauma. This 'secondary traumatisation' is common and it shows how trauma has 'systematic and ripple effects that go through space and time, beyond the initial impact' (Kira 2004: 39). As a result, 'children of tortured parents reveal more psychosomatic symptoms, headaches, depression, learning difficulties and aggressive behaviour' (2004: 40). More broadly, victims' families can endure a devalued social status. For instance, families can be deeply affected by the fact that the victim is no longer able to work, is incapacitated or has had to move to another area or country.

Given these experiences, it is important to identify that torture victims are not a homogenous group and each (along with their family and community) will face unique medical and psychological consequences. These effects will link with other social, cultural and political repercussions, including: family breakdown; the collapse of trust between community groups; dislocation and exile; the loss of schooling; and problems in accessing work or appropriate health care (Arcel 2002; Hardy 2002; Kira 2004; Stanley 2004). The lived realities of these issues cannot be

---

8   Feitlowitz (1998) shows how torturers incorporate everyday items (such as forks, irons, kettles) into their methods so that, on release, victims find it difficult to function normally. In this way, torture's pain is remembered well after the physical attacks have stopped.

underestimated. Torture rips apart social and personal relations, it creates short and long-term problems not just for those directly affected but also for their families, friends and communities. Moreover, these after-effects illustrate how torture, as a civil and political violation, connects with 'second generation' violations related to work, health, housing, education, and so on.

The official and societal responses to torture victims often underpin and reinforce these consequences. Victims are seldom acknowledged *as* victims, they rarely experience legal or social sanctioning of their perpetrators, or reparational support to assist them (Stanley 2004). In addition, the demonisation of those subject to torture permeates most aspects of political, social and cultural life, and victims are often imagined to be complicit in their own violations (Crelinsten 2003). As a result, many audiences distance themselves, disbelieve and do not engage with stories of torture (West 2003). Perhaps, the denigrated and abject status of victims can be perceived as being contagious. To demonstrate allegiance with a torture victim is to potentially present as a member of the maligned group. In these circumstances, torture invokes solitude as it envelops its victims in silence and disrupts 'normal' relations (Weschler 1998). This silencing is a perpetuation of violence as it 'becomes a second form of negation and rejection' for the victim (Scarry 1985: 56).

Conclusion

Despite the fact that torture is prohibited under international law, it continues to be used with some vigour. Its persistence may be understood in terms of how it operates as a tool to build or consolidate state power and control over populations. Thus, torture is applied to incapacitate opponents and to terrorise communities that are perceived to be 'criminal' or 'threatening'. While it may be overtly undertaken, its exposure is often tempered by techniques of distancing and denial; it is also made palatable through legitimising discourses and institutional practices that emphasise torture's acceptability within certain circumstances.

In this context, torture tends to be experienced by those most marginalised or criminalised within society. Structural relations are pertinent with regard to which individuals become the targets for torture, how they are violated, how they cope with their treatment and whether they will ever enjoy redress. Yet, torture is not solely an individualised violation as it produces a range of medical, psychological and social consequences for victims, their families, communities and countries. Torture wipes out 'normal' social relations and, in this way, it destroys human security, creates conflict and provides a platform for further violations.

All too often, torture is ignored. Critical criminological attention – to analyse, for example, the nature of state institutional power, the legitimisation of violence, differential victimisations, and the limits on truth and justice – could play a vital part in exposing and challenging such violent criminality by states.

References

Amnesty International 2000, *Take a Step to Stamp out Torture,* Amnesty, London.

Amnesty International 2001a, *Stopping the Torture Trade*, Amnesty, London.

Amnesty International 2001b, 'Crimes of Hate: conspiracy of silence', July-Aug, *Amnesty Members Magazine* 4.

Arcel, LT 2002, 'Torture, Cruel, Inhuman, and Degrading Treatment of Women: psychological consequences', 12 *Torture* 5.

Bagaric, M & Clarke, J 2005, 'Not Enough (Official) Torture in the World? The circumstances in which torture is morally justifiable', 39 *University of San Francisco Law Review* 581.

Becker, D, Lira, E, Castillo, M, Gómez, E & Kovalskys, J 1990, 'Therapy with Victims of Political Repression in Chile: the challenge of social reparation', 46 *Journal of Social Issues* 133.

Chan, J with Devery, C & Doran, S 2003, *Fair Cop: learning the art of policing*, University of Toronto Press, Toronto.

Cohen, S 2001, *States of Denial: knowing about atrocities and suffering,* Polity, Cambridge.

Crelinsten, RD 2003, 'The World of Torture: a constructed reality', 7 *Theoretical Criminology* 293.

Davis, A 2005, *Abolition Democracy: beyond prisons, torture and empire,* Seven Stories Press, San Francisco.

Dershowitz, A 2002, *Why Terrorism Works: understanding the threat, responding to the challenge,* Yale University Press, New Haven.

Evans, M & Morgan, R 1998, *Preventing Torture: a study of the European convention for the prevention of torture and inhuman or degrading treatment or punishment*, Clarendon Press, Oxford.

Fanon, F 1963, *The Wretched of the Earth*, translated by Farrington, C, Penguin Books, London.

Feitlowitz, M 1998, *A Lexicon of Terror: Argentina and the legacies of torture*, Oxford University Press, Oxford.

Foucault, M 1977, *Discipline and Punish: the birth of the prison,* translated by Sheridan, A, Penguin Books, London.

Galtung, J 1994, *Human Rights in Another Key*, Polity Press, Cambridge.

Green, P & Ward, T 2004, *State Crime: governments, violence and corruption*, Pluto Press, London.

Hardy, C 2002, 'An Act of Force: male rape victims', 12 *Torture* 19.

Haritos-Fatouros, M 2002, *The Psychological Origins of Institutionalized Torture*, Routledge, London.

Harris Rimmer, S 2004, 'Untold Numbers: East Timorese women and transitional justice', in Pickering, S & Lambert, C (eds), *Global Issues, Women and Justice*, Institute of Criminology, Sydney.

Hersh, S 2004, *Chain of Command: the road from 9/11 to Abu Ghraib,* Allen Lane, Camberwell.

Hornblum, A 1998, *Acres of Skin: human experiments at Holmesburg Prison,* Routledge, New York.

Huggins, MK, Haritos-Fatouros, M & Zimbardo, PG 2002, *Violence Workers: police torturers and murderers reconstruct Brazilian atrocities*, University of California Press, Berkeley.

Humphrey, M 2002, *The Politics of Atrocity and Reconciliation: from terror to trauma*, Routledge, London.

Ignatieff, M 2004, *The Lesser Evil: political ethics in an age of terror*, Princeton University Press, Princeton.

Kappeler, S 1986, *The Pornography of Representation*, Polity Press, Cambridge.

Kira, I 2004, 'Assessing and Responding to Secondary Traumatisation in the Survivors' Families', 14 *Torture* 38.

Kois, LM 1998, 'Dance, Sister, Dance!', in Dunér, B (ed), *An End to Torture,* Zed Books, London.

Lea, HC 1878, *Superstition and Force*, Third Edition, HC Lea, Philadelphia.

MacMaster, N 2004, 'Torture: from Algiers to Abu Ghraib', 46 *Race and Class* 1.

McLean, T, Hutchings, C & Schubert, M 2005, '"Terrorist" Habib free to go home', *The Age*, 12 January 2005.

Morgan, R 2000, 'The Utilitarian Justification of Torture: denial, desert and disinformation', 2 *Punishment and Society* 181.

Peters, E 1985, *Torture*, Expanded Edition, University of Pennsylvania Press, Philadelphia.

Rasmussen, OV, Amris, S, Blaauw, M & Danielsen, L 2005, 'Medical Physical Examination in Connection with Torture', 15 *Torture* 37.

Rejali, D 1994, *Torture and Modernity: self, society and state in modern Iran*, Westview, Boulder.

Rejali, D 1999, 'Ordinary Betrayals: conceptualizing refugees who have been tortured in the global village', July-Sep *Human Rights Review* 8.

Rejali, D 2003, 'Modern Torture as a Civic Marker: solving a global anxiety with a new political technology', 2 *Journal of Human Rights* 153.

Rothenberg, D 2003, '"What we have seen had been terrible". Public presentational torture and the communicative logic of state terror', 67 *Albany Law Review* 465.

Rusche, G & Kirchheimer, O 1968, *Punishment and Social Structure,* Russell & Russell, New York (first published 1939).

Scarry, E 1985, *The Body in Pain: the making and unmaking of the world*, Oxford University Press, Oxford.

Sivanandan, A 2001, 'Poverty is the New Black', 43 *Race and Class* 1.

Stanley, E 2004, 'Torture, Silence and Recognition', 16 *Current Issues in Criminal Justice* 5.

Suarez-Orozco, M 2004, 'The Treatment of Children in the "Dirty War": ideology, state terrorism, and the abuse of children in Argentina' in Scheper-Hughes, N & Bourgois, P (eds), *Violence in War and Peace: an anthology,* Blackwood Publishing, Oxford.

Taussig, M 2002, 'Culture of Terror – Space of Death: Roger Casement's Putumayo Report and the Explanation of Torture', in Hinton, AL (ed), *Genocide: an anthropological reader*, Blackwell, Oxford.

Turner, S & Gorst-Unsworth, C 1990, 'Psychological Sequelae of Torture: a descriptive model', 157 *British Journal of Psychiatry* 475.

Vidal-Naquet, P 1963, *Torture: cancer of democracy, France and Algeria 1954-62*, Penguin, Harmondsworth.

Weschler, L 1998, *A Miracle, A Universe: settling accounts with torturers*, University of Chicago Press, Chicago.

West, HG 2003, 'Voices Twice Silenced: betrayal and mourning at colonialism's end in Mozambique', 3 *Anthropological Theory* 343.

Wright, S 2007, 'Preparing for Mass Refugee Flows: the corporate military sector', in Cromwell, D & Levene, M (eds), *Clearing the Pathways to Survival: the state, ourselves and climate change*, Pluto Press, London.

14

THE NEW CRIMINALS: REFUGEES AND ASYLUM SEEKERS

Sharon Pickering

Introduction

This chapter overviews the criminalisation of refugees. It considers the criminological description and categorisation of state responses to refugees, and outlines future directions for developing a criminological account of the changing nature of borders and mobility.

Forced migration presents the international community with an enormous challenge. The most recent available figures indicate that in 2005 the global population of concern to the United Nations High Commission for Refugees (UNHCR) was 21 million persons. Pakistan and Iran host the largest number of refugees, 1.1 million and 1 million respectively, with most refugees flowing into developing nations. Developed nations collectively received 15% of all asylum claims in 2005, a total of 310,000 claims, and adjudicated that a total of 85,100 qualified for Convention refugee status in 2005 (UNHCR 2005).

Overwhelmingly, however, the most repressive approaches to refugees have come from developed nations taking in much smaller refugee populations. Moreover, developed nations have increasingly sought to identify refugee populations as suspect, often criminally suspect, even though half of the population of concern to UNHCR are females and 44% in 2005 were children.

Who is a refugee?

Refugees are generally considered to be those people who because of persecution have been forced to flee their country of origin to seek protection in another country. Refugee protection has historically been organised around the United Nations *Convention Relating to the Status of Refugees* (1951), developed in the aftermath of the Second World War to address those people made stateless by persecution. The Convention defines refugees as a person who:

> Owing to a well-founded fear of being persecuted for reasons of race, religion, nationality, membership of a particular social group or political opinion, is outside his country of origin and is unable or, owing to such fear, is unwilling to

avail himself of the protection of that country, or who, not having nationality and being outside the country of his former habitual residence as a result of such events, is unable or, owing to such fear is unwilling to return to it.

For the decades following the Second World War this definition was broadly accepted by the international community, adopted into domestic law and utilised to determine claims for refugee status. The Convention definition is important because it legally recognises who should not be *refouled* [1] to face persecution and should be granted entry to the country of protection.

In the wake of the Second World War the Convention and its definition of the refugee were considered a sensible and humanitarian compromise of the absolute right of sovereign nations to determine who could and could not enter a country (Hathaway 1991). In large part this was because during the Cold War refugees from the East aligned with the geopolitical interests of the West and were often regarded as 'evidence' of the cruelty and incivility of those regimes.

Since the end of the Cold War, and under conditions of globalisation, the exercise of sovereign power and authority over national borders has changed and arguably diminished. There is no longer a clear geopolitical need, or desire, to represent the refugee in a positive political light. Under conditions of globalisation mobility has been considered primary both in terms of goods and people. However the literature indicates that while there has been a discernible global shift to relax borders for the flow of goods, services and some people, there has been a fortification of borders for 'suspect' people crossing irregularly, including refugees. In fact there is now a compelling argument that borders have become increased sites of state control that restrict rights (such as refugee rights) and entry for some people, and facilitate the entry of others (Wonders 2006). Crossing borders unauthorised and entering a country in an irregular fashion has been increasingly regarded as deviant activity by governments in the global north. While this is a position not supported at international law, it has proved pivotal in the adoption of law and order style politics in relation to refugee policies and the development of what can be considered the systematic criminalisation of refugees.

How do refugees relate to the study of crime?

Refugees and refugee protection directly relate to the critical study of crime and social control in three key ways. First, the refugee definition identifies the role of the state in acts of persecution and arguably state crime. Secondly, persecution is now considered a crime by the International Criminal Court (ICC). Third, criminologists have now documented how criminalisation practices are increasingly targeting refugees as a vulnerable population.

Persecution is the central plank in the Convention definition of refugee status. It has generally been interpreted as being a sustained or systematic risk of harm and that this harm is perpetrated at odds with state responsibility for protecting citizens. In simple terms, persecution = serious harms + failure of state protection (Crawley 2001; Hathaway 1991). In the first instance, such a definition relates to crime because it is based on the issue of state responsibility for not harming citizens (potentially state crime) and/or protecting citizens from serious harm that may

---

1   'Refoulement', set down in art 33(1) of the United Nations *Convention Relating to the Status of Refugees* (1951), is the expulsion of persons who have the right to be recognised as refugees.

amount to persecution (the failure of a legal or other state system to redress harm perpetrated by state or non state actors) (Pickering 2005b). The refugee definition is interesting for criminologists for often its application has related to whether the harm suffered could be understood as being the result of random crime carried out by individuals rather than systematic or sustained harm carried out by the state or by non-state actors with state complicity.

More recently and in a traditionally legalistic sense, the ICC has come to define the production of refugee flows and acts of persecution as crime. This includes the deportation or forcible transfer of population, the persecution of any identifiable group or collectivity on political, racial, national, ethnic, cultural, religious or gender grounds. The classification of persecution as a crime by the ICC opens up the study of persecutory practices that produce refugee flows to the methods and analysis of criminology.

Typically criminologists have been interested in charting the processes of criminalisation to which refugee populations have been subject, and which is the focus of the next section.

The demonisation of refugees

Since the end of the Cold War refugees have been considered a problem for the global north. It has been argued that when refugees have arrived in countries in an irregular fashion, the refugee problem has come to be talked about in terms of deviancy or criminality (Pickering 2001).

Protecting the border, as a marker of sovereign control and territory, has been at the heart of the criminalisation of refugees. The expression of the border in discourses surrounding refugees has taken a number of forms. Overall, media coverage of refugee-related issues, particularly regarding what has been termed in Australia 'unauthorised entry', has become part of the politics of fear and the generation of a new crop of vulnerable populations subject to a nationalised law and order rhetoric of exclusion. Specifically research indicates that we can discern key themes (invasion, race, disease, untrustworthy legal system) in public discourse that have served to demonise and criminalise refugees (Pickering 2001; Pickering 2005a).

There is now a considerable international literature documenting the ways that media discourse and public debate around refugees has primarily utilised discourse of invasion to denote the deviancy of refugees. In an analysis of the *Sydney Morning Herald* and the *Brisbane Courier Mail*, such deviancy has been described in the following ways:

> [*W*]e are soon to be *awash, swamped, weathering the influx, of waves, latest waves, more waves, tides, floods, migratory flood, mass exodus* of *aliens, queue jumpers, illegal immigrants, people smugglers, boat people, jumbo people, jet-loads of illegals, illegal foreigners, bogus* and *phoney* applicants, and *hungry Asians* upon *our shores, isolated coastlines*, and *deserted beaches* that make up the *promised land*, the *land of hope*, the *lucky country, heaven, the good life, dream destination* and they continue to *slip through, sneak in, gathering to our north, invade* with *false papers* or *no papers, exotic diseases, sicknesses* as part of *gangs, criminal gangs, triads, organised crime*, and *Asian crime*. In response, *we* should have *closed doors* only sometimes having *open doors*, we should respond *nationally* with the *navy and armed services at the ready, we* should *send*

messages, deter, lock up and *detain, we* should not be *exploited played for a fool*, be seen as *gullible* or be a *forelock-tugging serf* (Pickering 2001: 172).

Invasion anxiety has been regarded by commentators as rooted in the cultural and historical context of nations, such as Australia, where it has colonial and racial resonance (Burke 2001). More recently such anxiety has played out in relation to concerns for national security post-9/11 and the integrity of the nation state in terms of its territorial sovereignty. This manifests in discourses of war being mobilised against asylum seekers that not only resonate with the need to militarily repel unwanted foreign invasion, but also raises the spectre of the asylum seeker as a potential terrorist threat in relation to the war on terror.

Australian studies of the media and refugees have highlighted the related theme of race in the demonisation process. Criminologists working in the field have identified how the media has utilised notions of racial otherness in the depiction of the threat the nation faces from refugees (Pickering 2001; Poynting et al 2004). This work draws on broader criminological and media research highlighting the ways race is ideologically used in the media to develop forms of racial inclusion and exclusion, and often relying on both implicit and explicit racial messages (see for example, Ferguson 1998). It has been argued that the racialisation of media discourses has relied on intertwining race with crime. Examples of such reporting have included a focus on the relationship between asylum seeking and transnational crime (often by alleging that an ability to pay a people smuggler undermines the veracity of claims of persecution), and the usually ill defined 'threat' to social (read racial) harmony that increased numbers of asylum seekers pose.

The third theme discernible in studies of the media and refugees is that of disease. Researchers have argued that the metaphor of disease has underpinned discourses of refugee deviancy (Pickering 2001). For example, representations of asylum seekers have reported on the absence of medical and health checks and the avoidance of 'quarantine measures' on refugees in ways that have often utilised vocabulary which depicts refugees as health hazards (Pickering 2001). These inform representations that asylum seekers not only represent an 'invasion' but a sickness.

A final theme in the demonisation of refuges in the press is the refugee aided and abetted by the courts and international law. Media discourses on refugees have included vocabulary which has rendered suspect the use of Australian courts to pursue claims of refugee status and to challenge conditions of treatment during the refugee determination process. Extending the protection of Australian law, and the application of international law in Australia, to non citizens has been considered further evidence of the deviancy of refugees – by considering such legal action as a fiscal drain on the nation, by undermining legal attempts to deter and to deport asylum seekers, and by exploiting 'activist' judges in the interpretation and application of statute (Pickering 2005a). The utilisation of international law in this process has often been reported as a challenge to Australian sovereignty and the integrity of an orderly immigration system.

These four themes are not exhaustive of all media coverage of refugees. Rather they trace the ways that the media has participated in the demonisation of refugees from the late 1990s in Australia. Not all media coverage has been negative, not all has been blatant or explicit. However, studied as a whole and over extended periods of time, indications suggest that the above themes are discernible in the media in an everyday sense. The overall outcome of this has been to render the deviancy of refugees a matter of common sense.

Case study in criminalisation: Australia

Criminalisation, however, is only partially achieved through the demonisation of refugees in the media and public discourse. Criminalisation is more complete when it is underpinned by the realignment of the coercive force of the state generally and the law specifically. In the case of Australia, refugees are criminalised through policies and practices which taken collectively prove how the refugee has been criminalised without the protections that a 'criminal' ordinarily attracts in the criminal justice system.

Policies of deterrence

The Australian government has shaped its response to refugees as one of deterrence. Deterrence rests on familiar law and order rhetoric and draws on the populism of law and order approaches to 'social problems' (see Hogg this volume) despite the failure of such campaigns to produce effective results. Specifically deterrence raises familiar elements of the criminal justice system as a *rationale for punishment*: guilt, incarceration and exclusion. It rests on a logic that the action targeted is to be discouraged, and can be discouraged. Deterrence also facilitates the response to refugees shifting from a 'difficult to understand international legal obligation' to a 'domestically controlled and knowable criminal problem'. Problematically for this logic, however, is that those seeking asylum have committed no criminal offence but rather have sought Australia's protection. There have been three key elements in the deterrence strategy of Australia: mandatory detention; extra-territorial processing and detention; and policies of social exclusion.

Mandatory detention has been the key feature of the deterrence suite. Since 1992 Australia has detained all asylum seekers who arrived 'unauthorised' even though the *Convention Relating to the Status of Refugees* (1951) has specific provision for the need for many refugees to utilise unauthorised methods to seek asylum in order to escape persecution. Immigration Detention Centres (IDCs) were set up around the country, often in isolated regions, vast distances from major cities or regional centres. IDCs were equipped with provision for solitary confinement and punishment but often poorly resourced for education or work provision or for the housing of families or children. In 1997 the operation of IDCs was privatised. Successive governments maintained that mandatory detention was required in order to stop refugees from choosing or targeting Australia and arriving 'illegally'. A range of legislation was introduced that rendered criminal a range of activities within IDCs and authorised the use of various control methods including strip searches. Refugees were being indefinitely detained for the duration of the refugee determination process (including appeals). The length of detention was indeterminate as it was related to the process of administrative determination rather than a set period of confinement. A range of issues have plagued the operation of IDCs, particularly since the late 1990s, including the high rates of self-harm and suicide, the long term impacts of indefinite and isolated detention (Silove et al 2000) and the specific impact of indefinite detention on children and unaccompanied minors

(Human Rights and Equal Opportunity Commission 2004). The mandatory detention policy is legal under Australian domestic law but in breach of international legal obligations.

Deterrence has also underpinned the development of the extra-territorial processing of refugee claims and offshore detention of asylum seekers. In the wake of the *Tampa* incident in September 2001 (see Marr & Wilkinson 2003), the Australian Federal Government sought to extend the policy of mandatory detention offshore in an effort to avoid refugees making a claim on Australia's protection obligation. In essence this meant that by not setting foot on the Australian mainland a refugee could not invoke domestic legislation to support their claims. It was underpinned by the excision of parts of Australia for the purposes of migration legislation (under which refugee protection is located). The use of extra-territorial sites, that is other countries, for the purposes of administering refugee claims, came to be known as the 'Pacific Solution', and involved the taking of refugees to declared countries (Papua New Guinea and Nauru) for refugee determination. Those that were found to be refugees were then either resettled in Australia, or preferably in other countries.

The Pacific Solution has been widely condemned for its compromise of international law, as well as the domestic and constitutional laws of both Australia and the host countries. In particular it located refugee determination in countries which were either not signatories to the *Convention Relating to the Status of Refugees* (1951) or had placed reservations against key articles of the Convention. The hastily put together solution was considered to compromise attempts at instituting processes of good governance in a region that was increasingly considered unstable. The realisation of the solution required the erection of poorly equipped detention facilities operated by private contractors and non-government organisations.

The Pacific Solution facilitated the location of refugees in sites that were even more remote than IDCs on mainland Australia, where lawyers, advocates, and the media struggled to gain access. It enabled Australia, in the course of allegedly protecting its sovereignty from unwanted arrivals, to abdicate its sovereign responsibilities under international and national law to other nations who in turn were legally compromised (ceding of their territory to the requirements of Australia, through privatised companies) but financially rewarded. Refugee determination was not conducted under Australian law, and the repatriation of those found not to be refugees was facilitated through Australia via the drafting of specific laws that meant individuals could transit Australia but in the process of doing so were not able to make a claim under Australian law for protection. This legislation also enabled the use of coercive force in the repatriation of unsuccessful refugee applicants with little or no independent legal oversight.

The Pacific Solution, as an extension of deterrence policies instituted a system of coercive sovereign control enacted beyond the boundaries of the nation state, largely away from public scrutiny and oversight. It imposed the domestic priorities of Australia on its much poorer regional neighbours. The Pacific Solution was considered an act of escalated deterrence: if refugees managed to physically arrive on the Australian mainland, then that land was considered as unable to reject them (largely due to requirements to submit to international law). Therefore the mainland must be protected from its own inability to wash its hands of the unwanted, even if this meant the reconfiguration of sovereign control of its borders through a third country. The rhetoric of such deterrence logic is about protecting sovereignty at the same time that sovereignty is moved offshore and largely unseen.

Deterrence was not only realised through detention and processing mechanisms but also via the conditions by which those refugees granted protection status were allowed to stay in Australia. Most significant in the development of policies of social exclusion were the punitive conditions attached to the introduction of the temporary protection visa (TPV) system instituted in 1999. This policy sought to ensure that even if refugees were granted protection, their visa and concomitant stay in Australia would only be temporary. Moreover, that visa would restrict their access to basic services in the community particularly in relation to health, education and employment and thus compromise their ability to successfully integrate into Australian society. Numerous studies have now documented the ways the TPV system instituted uncertainty in the lives of refugees and the deleterious effects on their social inclusion both in Australia and elsewhere (Esmaelli & Wells 2000; Fitzpatrick 1999, 2000; Gibney 2000). It rendered them in many ways suspect to other refugees and migrants and ensured an uncertain future in Australia.

Policies of non-entrée

The criminalisation of refugees has also been realised through the escalation in border policing efforts designed to stop refugees from making the journey to Australia. The focus of this effort has been on the role of the people smuggler in transporting refugees from countries in the region to Australia. The criminalisation of people smuggling under Australian law has been central to this, although not all neighbouring countries have criminalised these and associated activities. Regardless, people smuggling has become a key focus of Australian law enforcement efforts to better police the border and police out potential refugees (Pickering 2004). Increasingly those efforts require Australian law enforcement to work beyond the nation state, within other countries, and often within a conflated concern for national security and transnational criminal activity.

Weber (2006) has argued that border policing efforts are not simply a response to people being 'on the move' in unregulated ways, but that national borders, and their policing are also increasingly mobile. As a result, border policing for the purposes of migration control is increasingly multifaceted involving a range of pre-emptive measures not just at the physical border. The border policing effort therefore realises its exclusionary aims through a range of sites involving 'increasingly sophisticated and extensive networks of public and private agencies' (Weber 2006: 24-25). In Australia this has involved an array of inter-governmental and inter-agency taskforces, often spearheaded by the Australian Federal Police (Pickering 2004). The criminalisation of border crossing for those with refugee protection claims to be made compromises the capacity of nations to genuinely consider those claims for protection – for if the border crossing is made impossible, then so to many claims for refugee protection go unheard. Increasingly, border policing has been tied to security narratives, often in relation to organised crime and terrorist threats without demonstrable evidence of a connection between refugee claims of persecution and the need (or what many consider to be the human right) to seek refugee protection.

From the criminalisation of the new criminals to state crime

The processes of criminalisation have the potential to tell critical criminologists much more about the nature of the state than any inherent properties of the individual or the actions/omissions being criminalised, and this is particularly true with refugees. In short, practices of criminalisation make it possible for the criminologist to question the approach of the state to the construction of new criminals and the ways that state activity itself may be considered suspect or even criminal.

As Grewcock (this volume) notes, state crime is not a clearly defined legal concept. As a criminological concept however, it has required greater precision over the past few decades moving from a concept that incorporates all forms of human rights abuses (Schwendinger & Schwendinger 1975), into a subset of human rights violations involving organisational (rather than individual) deviancy that attracts the censure of a social audience (Green & Ward 2004).

In the first instance, criminologists could turn their attention to the criminality of the state that produces refugees by engaging in practices of persecution from which people are forced to flee. In particular, the practices of the state that are recognised as persecutory, or the omissions of the state that fail to redress systematic serious harm perpetrated by others. The failure of the legal systems of persecutory states to effectively check deviant state activity, or other censure mechanisms internal to the state, is another way by which state criminality may come to be better analysed. The concomitant role of external organisations and agencies, as well as international and regional legal systems, in responding to acts of state crime that have involved persecution and forced migration has the potential to not only increase the effectiveness of such systems but to further the efforts of a more genuinely international criminology.

There are further opportunities available for critical criminologists to consider how the criminalisation of refugees by refugee receiving states presents reason to consider state acts and omissions criminal. It is an example of how criminologists can understand liberal democracies as potentially deviant states and in particular how the apparent legitimate functions of those states may be inherently criminal or may come to be regarded as such. The simplest way to consider this in relation to refugees is in regard to actual or potential breaches of human rights and state monopoly on the legitimate use of force.

It has been argued that in the case of refugee receiving countries there is a need to focus on the coercive use of force against refugees in conjunction with the ideological force of civil society. In the case of Australia there are various elements of the demonisation of refugees in the media coupled with policies and practices of coercion that taken together with a failure to meet human rights norms can amount to criminality, particularly when a range of internal and external audiences level censure at the practices in question.

I have argued previously that naming state practices as crimes serves important ideological and discursive functions (Pickering 2005a), particularly at a time when we are witnessing the increasing selectivity of liberal democracies in relation to respecting human rights norms, particularly those relating to unauthorised border crossing. Moreover, I have argued that various refugee policies and practices place great physical and other barriers in the path of various social audiences recognising, documenting and censuring potentially deviant state acts. This includes erecting various legislative barriers (often in the form of privative clauses) before the judiciary in checking executive power in relation to areas now subsumed under a general concern with 'border control' and the fortification of sovereignty.

The sovereign right to 'territorial integrity' has been regarded as a trump right in relation to the human rights of individuals who have sought to cross borders unauthorised. This has been coupled with the sovereign right of nations to handle their own affairs, namely that of migration, without external 'interference' from other states or state-like entities, let alone to be labelled criminal by various social audiences. Specifically in relation to the refugee, the Refugee Convention has been at the fore of neutralising the absolute expressions of such sovereignty against refugees and even to some extent checking deviant state activity by requiring particular legal processes and practices and the respect of various international legal customary norms. However we are now witnessing the relocation of unauthorised border crossings by refugees from the *Convention Relating to the Status of Refugees* (1951) to the *Convention against Transnational Organized Crime* (2000) whereby the need to cross borders in order to gain protection from persecution is lost amid transnational law and order rhetoric in relation to the eradication of cross border crime.

Crime, borders and beyond the new criminals

Increasingly critical criminologists will be confronted by the radically changing nature of borders, and their unregulated crossing by refugees and others. This will require not only a greater criminological deconstruction of state responses to refugees but also the reconsideration of border spaces for the study of crime and social control as well as protection from persecution. There are some immediately apparent challenges for criminologists to consider in developing such studies:

- *The changing nature of the border*: Borders are no longer physical or territorial lines on a map, but are opening into inter- and extra-territorial frontiers where processes of exclusion are multi-layered and often criminalising. Borders are not fixed and determinate but rather frequently changing and renegotiated. Criminological boundaries have often corresponded to national borders and this needs to alter if the border is going to be better understood as an ongoing process, mobile in both time and space in relation to its capacity to include and exclude. Moreover, the border, wherever and however it may manifest, is increasingly a site for the expansion and reconfiguration of various policing-type entities and functions, often unshackled by territorial (domestic) constraints.

- *The reconfigurations of sovereignty:* Sovereignty as a rationale for exclusion as well as a way to free the state from territorial accountability in the face of the unwanted mobile collides many of the traditional functions of the criminal justice system with concerns for national security, international relations and human rights. Refugee law is now avoided as a way to reconcile sovereign control of the border with individual rights claims. Sovereignty needs to be at the centre of criminological understandings of state legitimacy, particularly in terms of the monopoly over the use of force as well as the ideological force it can coopt. Such an approach needs to reconceptualise sovereignty as a process rather than as an effect. This requires the deconstruction of attempts to disconnect an inside from an out-side, a citizen from another.

- *The discursive force of state crime:* State crime is an important criminolo-gical concept however its use as a powerful discursive tool must be consi-dered against other approaches such as denoting acts as 'serious harms' rather than 'state crime'. This is an important consideration in an era where human rights are selectively utilised not only by governments but also by populations where rights culture has not taken root – discursively or other-wise.

- *The accommodation of persecution:* To be vigilant in the deconstruction of persecution and its role in forced migration, criminology is presented with challenges of knowing and responding to individual and widespread tragedy and the further development of analytical tools in documenting and understanding it in relation to an increasingly more interdependent world where the practices of states, and between states, are often intertwined and even indeterminate.

- *The neutralising effect of transnational crime:* Criminology could easily reject the complex challenges presented by issues such as forced migration, persecution and state crime and instead of sorting through the difficulties of refining and applying various concepts of human rights, censure and organisational state deviance could instead turn to the law and order char-ged approach to transnational crime now preoccupying international com-mentators concerned with mobility. Critical criminology needs to map the ways forward in responding to this challenge that to date has failed in responding to the key conceptual and lived challenges that borders and mobility present to the way we include and exclude in a globalised world.

Conclusion

The criminalisation of refugees and the potential for state responses to be considered criminal can be primarily understood in relation to the increasing complexity of both the border and the theoretical and lived experiences of state sovereignty. They pre-sent the critical criminologist with sophisticated questions to be resolved. They involve both the basic elements of the standard criminological enterprise (from poli-cing to punishment), while also requiring criminology to go well beyond traditional disciplinary boundaries and into the international legal realm.

The enormity of forced migration, the persecution involved, and the impact of state responses to refugee protection has a profound effect on individual lives as well as on the health of the body politic. How critical criminology adapts to the enormity of this challenge will greatly depend on how adequately it can grapple with the rapidly changing nature of borders, sovereignty, criminalisation and deviant state activity in an age of hyper-mobility, forced or otherwise.

References

Burke, A 2001, *In Fear of Security: Australia's invasion anxiety*, Pluto Press, Annandale.

Crawley, H 2001, *Refugees and Gender: law and processes*, Jordan Publishing, London.

Esmaelli, H & Wells, B 2000, 'The 'Temporary' Refugees: Australia's legal response to the arrival of Iraqi and Afghan boat-people', 23(3) *UNSW Law Journal* 224.

Ferguson, R 1998, *Representing Race: ideology, identity and the media*, Arnold, London.

Fitzpatrick, J 1999, 'The End of Protection: legal standards for cessation of refugee status withdrawal of temporary protection', 13 *Georgetown Immigration Law Journal* 382.

Fitzpatrick, J 2000, 'Temporary Protection of Refugees: elements of a formalized regime', 94 *American Journal of International Law* 278.

Gibney, M 2000, 'Between Control and Humanitarianism: temporary protection in contemporary Europe', 14 *Georgetown Immigration Law Journal* 689.

Green, P & Ward, T 2004, *State Crime: governments, violence and corruption*, Pluto Press, London.

Hathaway, J 1991, *The Law of Refugee Status*, Butterworths, Toronto.

Human Rights and Equal Opportunity Commission (HREOC), 2004, *A Last Resort? National Inquiry into Children in Immigration Detention*, HREOC, Sydney.

Marr, D & Wilkinson, M 2003, *Dark Victory*, Allen & Unwin, Sydney.

Pickering, S 2001, 'Original Deviance and Normality: representations of asylum seekers and refugees in the Australian press', 14(2) *Journal of Refugee Studies* 169.

Pickering, S 2004, 'The Production of Sovereignty and the Rise of Transversal Policing: people smuggling and federal policing', 37(3) *Australian and New Zealand Journal of Criminology* 340.

Pickering, S 2005a, *Refugees and State Crime*, Federation Press, Sydney.

Pickering, S 2005b, 'Crimes of the State: the persecution and protection of refugees', 13 *Journal of Critical Criminology* 141.

Poynting, S, Noble, G, Tabar, P & Collins, J 2004, *Bin Laden in the Suburbs: criminalizing the Arab other*, Sydney Institute of Criminology Series, Sydney.

Schwendinger, H & Schwendinger, J 1975, 'Defenders of Order or Guardians of Human Rights?', in Taylor, I, Walton, P & Young, J (eds), *Critical Criminology,* Routledge & Kegan Paul, London.

Silove, D, Steel, Z & Watters, C 2000, 'Policies of deterrence and the mental health of asylum seekers', 284 *Journal of the American Medical Association* 604.

United Nations High Commissioner for Refugees (UNHCR), 2005, *Statistical Yearbook 2005: trends in displacement, protection and solutions*, UNHCR, Geneva.

Weber, L 2006, 'The Shifting Frontiers of Migration Control', in Pickering, S & Weber, L (eds), *Borders, Mobility and Technologies of Control*, Springer, Dordrecht.

Wonders, N 2006, 'Global Flows, Semi-Permeable Borders and New Channels of Inequality', in Pickering, S & Weber, L (eds), *Borders, Mobility and Technologies of Control*, Springer, Dordrecht.

15

HATE CRIME

Gail Mason

Introduction

The term 'hate crime' has the potential to be misleading. It may lull us into thinking that feelings of hatred alone can adequately explain racist, homophobic or ethno-religious crime. In the Sydney suburb of Cronulla in December 2005, people assumed to be of Lebanese and/or Muslim heritage were viciously attacked by an intoxicated and aggressive crowd who apparently saw themselves as ethnically and/or religiously distinct from their victims. If we construct an event of this nature as a hate crime do we risk reducing it to an expression of hatred alone and thereby downplay the role of other factors, such as international politics, nationalism, pride or moral panic? Does the concept of hate crime assist us to understand this riot and the hateful sentiments that were expressed that day or does it obfuscate the issues? The answers to these questions depend on how we engage with the concept of hate crime.

Hate crime is not an objective classification that simply describes a type of criminal behaviour. It is a highly politicised criminological construction that, certainly, is designed to draw attention to very real problems but, in addition, functions to make a wider moral claim that group hatred and prejudice are wrong. Whilst there are advantages to labelling a given incident as a hate crime, there are difficulties associated with the category itself and the legal responses designed to address it. This chapter will attempt to engage with the topic of hate crime by recognising some of the controversies that surround it. It will consider how the concept of hate crime has come into being, the kinds of problems it seeks to represent, the close relationship between its 'causes' and 'effects' and the nature of the legal response. Hence, the chapter examines various forms of hate crime as problems in themselves whilst undertaking a critique of hate crime as a socio-legal concept used to categorise and construct such behaviour.

Defining and constructing Hate Crime

Hate crime is a recent socio-legal construct which is neither 'familiar nor self-defining' (Jacobs & Potter 1998: 27). Commentators such as Jacobs and Potter suggest that hate crime is not really about hate but, rather, is about bias or prejudice.

Many definitions of hate crime support this position. Thus Lawrence (1999: 9) defines hate crime as a 'crime committed as an act of prejudice'. Not dissimilarly, the federal United States *Hate Crime Statistics Act 1990* defines it as '[c]rime that manifests evidence of prejudice based on race, religion, sexual orientation or ethnicity'. Taking a slightly more expansive approach, the London Metropolitan Police define it as 'any crime where the perpetrator's prejudice against an identifiable group of people is a factor in determining who is victimised' (Association of Chief Police Officers 2002: 10). Coined in the US in the 1980s, the term 'hate crime' initially competed with the term 'bias crime' as a means of collectively describing crimes motivated, at least in part, by racism, homophobia, and ethno-religious sentiment. Although the term bias crime is still used in the US, it is the more emotive and highly charged terminology of hate crime that has been successfully imported into the social and/or legal lexicon in Australia and the UK. Whilst hate might not be the most accurate language through which to categorise crimes motivated by racism, homophobia, anti-Semitism and so on, it is overstating the case to say that such behaviour is not about hate at all. The 'hate' in hate crime signifies a form of *collective* hate or animosity towards particular racial, sexual, ethnic and religious groups. Given that the concept of prejudice has a history of individualising and pathologising these problems, there is no reason to assume that it offers a better means of conceptualising this kind of crime. We can use the term 'hate crime' and remain attuned to the collective nature of the sentiment it seeks to describe.

The proliferation of social and legal definitions that have emerged over the past 25 years or so make it difficult to pin down the key components of hate crime. However, two relatively neutral, albeit far from exhaustive, components are implicit to most definitions. First, is a perpetrator whose conduct is motivated, at least in part, by bias, prejudice, hatred or animosity towards the group affiliation of the victim. Secondly, is a victim who belongs, or is presumed to belong, to a group that is recognised as the object of prejudice or group hatred. It has been argued that the term hate crime is most useful if it is not tied to a strictly legal definition:

> Hate crime, then, involves acts of violence and intimidation, usually directed towards already stigmatized and marginalized groups. As such, it is a mechanism of power and oppression, intended to reaffirm the precarious hierarchies that characterise a given social order (Perry 2001: 10).

Perry's definition is significant not just because it refuses to limit hate crime to violations of the criminal law alone but also because it ties its meaning to the question of effects and not just causes, in particular its capacity to reinforce unequal power relations of race, sexuality, gender and so on. In emphasising the fact that it is usually subjugated groups who are targeted for hate crime, Perry reminds us that such power relations are intrinsic to the commission of hate crime (discussed further below).

Like all criminological categories, the manner in which hate crime is defined is the product of its specific cultural, political and legal origins. Some have suggested that the concept of hate crime emerged in 'direct response to the recognition in the 1980s of the return of visceral racism in the public sphere' (Goldberg 1995: 268). Others, however, disagree: 'the current anti-hate crime movement is generated not by an epidemic of unprecedented bigotry but by heightened sensitivity to prejudice, and more important, by our society's emphasis on identity politics' (Jacobs & Potter

1998: 6). In the US in the early 1980s, an informal alliance of various social justice and victims right's movements came together to demand legislative intervention in particular response to perceived problems of racist, anti-Semitic and homophobic violence (Jenness & Broad 1997). By arguing that such violence is unique – because it goes to the core of both the victim's identity and all other members of his or her racial, ethno-religious or sexual group – these pressure groups were successful in placing hate crime on the public agenda and compelling legislatures across the country to introduce sentence enhancement provisions for hate crime or substantive new offences.

Critics of punitive approaches to hate crime have argued that, rather than dealing with the problems of discriminatory violence in a measured and extra-legal manner, a moral panic has been created and then used to justify the introduction of retributivist legal measures (McLaughlin 2002). Moreover, it has been suggested that:

> [H]ate crime laws encourage citizens to think of themselves as members of identity groups and encourage identity groups to think of themselves as victimized and besieged, thereby hardening each group's sense of resentment (Jacobs & Potter 1998: 31).

Whilst there is some validity to this claim, the difficulty with it, of course, is that in this era of late modernity most citizens already experience the world through a profusion of identity categories and some groups have very good reasons for feeling 'under siege' in the face of racial, ethno-religious or sexual animosity.

Intense controversy exists over which groups should be recognised as the bona fide victims of hate crime and, especially, which groups should be given 'protected status' under the law. There are two main angles to this debate. First, can hate crime be committed against members of dominant groups as well as subjugated groups (for example, can whites or heterosexuals be the victims of hate crime)? In most cases, this question has been answered in the affirmative. Although the concept of hate crime was initially intended as a mechanism for addressing disproportionate levels of abuse and violence directed towards members of minority groups by members of majority groups, it very quickly emerged that protection must be extended to both groups in order to avoid accusations of inequality (for example, hate crime laws usually apply generally to people on the basis of their race and not just to those citizens who are Aboriginal or Asian). Secondly, which categories of identity deserve to be included in the definition of hate crime: race, ethnicity, religion, colour, sexuality, nationality, disability, age or gender? The simple answer here is that policy and legislative definitions of hate crime tend to follow well established 'social fissure lines' (Lawrence 1999: 13) by including those groups who are the historical objects of prejudice (categories which are often already recognised in discrimination law). Yet, some disadvantaged groups have had greater success than others in achieving protection under the law. Race, for example, is the most recognised category under the law in Australia, the UK and the US.

The most intense debates in relation to criminalising hate crime have been over the inclusion of sexuality and gender. Despite a very active anti-violence movement, the gay and lesbian community in the US struggled for many years, in the face of religious conservatism, to be given protected status under hate crime laws (Jenness & Grattet 2001). Recognition has now been granted in many jurisdictions; however, violence by men towards women continues to remain outside many legal definitions of hate crime. Some argue that excluding gender from the category of hate crime performs a normalising function, in that it makes rape, sexual assault, sexual harassment and the like a normal and acceptable part of life for adult women and girls (Gelber 2000). Defining rape as a hate crime would assist us to acknowledge that it is an ideological act of prejudice that debases both the individual victim and women as a group (Brown 2004). An opposing position, however, asserts that many gender-specific offences are already defined as aggravated offences and attract higher penalties (for example, sexual assault is an aggravated form of common assault). Moreover, given the progress that feminism has made in our under-standings of, and responses to, gendered violence, it is important to ask whether there is much political or explanatory mileage to be gained by bringing such vio-lence under the hate crime umbrella.

The problem

Accurate data on the character, prevalence and trends of hate crime is very difficult to collate. Whilst the concept of hate crime itself may be new, one thing we do know is that (individual and institutional) hostility and violence towards people on the basis of their race, ethnicity, religion or sexuality is not. Brutality towards the Indigenous population in Australia was intrinsic to the process of colonisation that began in the late 1700s. Accounts of violence against the Chinese community on the goldfields of early Australia are equally notorious. One might even argue that the death penalty that was metered out to men who were convicted of engaging in sex with other men in the early colony of New South Wales was a form of homophobic violence.

More recently, those communities who appear to be most vulnerable to verbal abuse, vandalism or physical violence that matches the above definitions of hate crime include the Aboriginal, Asian, Jewish, Muslim, gay, lesbian, disabled and elderly communities, as well as women of course. For example, a recent survey of over 600 gay men and lesbians in New South Wales found more than half reported having experienced one or more forms of homophobic abuse, harassment or vio-lence in the previous 12 months, with 85% reporting such abuse at some point throughout their lives (Attorney General's Department of NSW 2003). Whilst some forms of prejudice, such as anti-Semitism, have a long and violent history, the levels of victimisation against particular groups do appear to change according to socio-political and economic shifts. For instance, at least two major world events appear to have generated spikes in abuse and violence against Muslim and/or Arab Aus-tralians: the 1991 Gulf War and the events of 11 September 2001 (Human Rights and Equal Opportunity Commission (HREOC) 1991; Dreher 2005; Poynting & Noble 2004).

In terms of the perpetrators of hate crime, perhaps the most that can be said is that they tend to be young and male (HREOC 1991; Tomsen 2002). Whilst there is some reason to believe that those who commit one type of hate crime are also likely to commit other types (for example, those who commit racist violence are likely to commit homophobic violence and so on), this assumes that perpetrators are also largely white/Anglo and heterosexual. On the contrary, there is no reason to assume, for example, that young Aboriginal, Muslim or Asian men do not perpetrate homo-phobic violence or that white/Anglo gay men are never involved in racist abuse.

Women do not appear to be heavily involved in serious or physical violence but do appear to engage in minor acts of verbal abuse and harassment. Whilst international research points to some connection between organised groups (such as the National Front or the Ku Klux Klan) and hate crime, such groups are not generally considered to be the primary perpetrators (Levin & McDevitt 2002). This does not mean, of course, that potential perpetrators are not influenced by the rhetoric of these groups, especially as it is now highly accessible on the internet and has taken on a new tone of respectability (Mason 2007). It is a mistake to characterise those who hold or act upon prejudiced views as evil people. Racism (and other forms of group hate) may be felt by 'normal' people who 'feel morally righteous and justified in having the attitude towards certain others that they have' (Hage 2006: 13). As Hage (2006: 13) puts it, in the context of the Cronulla riot, 'there may be nice people' among a racist crowd but 'this does not make the crowd any less racist'. Failing to acknowledge that the road to racism may be paved with good intentions simply makes it easier to deny prejudice when it erupts in the most ordinary of places or spills from the mouths of nice, normal, caring people. We need to come to terms with this in order to construct effective anti-hate crime campaigns that do not over-simplify the problem or misread their target audience.

The cultural context of Hate Crime

It is not sufficient to think of hate crime as the extreme behaviour of a few prejudiced individuals in an otherwise accepting and tolerant socio-political environment. Hate crime emerges out of an intricate network of broad-spectrum and specific discourses which are refracted through a shifting body of global and local structures, institutions and processes. Broad discourses of otherness and difference underpin the perspectives and emotions that are implicit to all hate crime and more specific variables produce an environment conducive to the commission of particular forms of hate crime, such as anti-Semitic, anti-Muslim or homophobic violence. To understand these contextual or 'causal' factors we also need to consider the implications or 'effects' of hate crime.

All hate crime is enacted within a cultural climate characterised by power relations of otherness and difference. We live our lives through a spectrum of socially constructed identities that craft (but do not determine) our sense of who we are, how we should behave, with whom we should socialise, how we should dress, who we should love, who we should hate and so on. These identity categories – white, gay, Aboriginal, Vietnamese Australian, heterosexual, immigrant, Muslim, masculine, Jewish, disabled, Aussie and so on – are normative rather than neutral. They contain within them value judgements and stereotypes about the merits of each identity relative to others: for instance, heterosexual is to homosexual as normal is to abnormal, good to bad, moral to immoral, clean to dirty, safe to dangerous, pleasant to disgusting etc. It is through these values that hierarchies of 'in groups' and 'out groups' are created: for instance, heterosexuality is accorded a natural, superior, insider status in most societies whilst homosexuality is, by comparison, accorded an unnatural, inferior, outsider status. It is only through the subjugation of so-called 'minority' groups that dominant groups are able to maintain the illusion of superiority and the material benefits that attach to this (in order for one group to be 'on top', another group must be on 'the bottom').

Hate crime only makes sense in the context of these hierarchies of difference. Hate crime is a means of affirming established relations of power between different groups. Whilst this need for affirmation has been variously traced to an individual's fear of their own inadequacies or vulnerabilities (Mason 2001a) or love of their own privilege (Allport 1954), at the collective level an act of verbal abuse or physical violence against 'the other' performs a dual-sided function that tells us which groups 'occupy positions of dominance' and which groups occupy positions of 'subjugation' (Mason 2002: 128). In marking 'those it targets with signs of vulnerability and victimhood' (Mason 2002: 97) hate crime tells its victims, and all who identify with them, that they are outsiders, do not belong, are not wanted and, ultimately, are inferior. In so doing, hate crime simultaneously bolsters the dominance of the perpetrator's group by telling us 'who it is that occupies the position of power' (Goldberg 1995: 270). In short, as Perry (2001: 56) suggests, hate crime is a means of 'doing difference' that 'provides a context in which the perpetrator can reassert his/her hegemonic identity and, at the same time, punish the victim(s) for their individual or collective performance of identity'. In this way, the underlying 'causes' of hate crime are closely tied to its potential 'effects': it emerges from hierarchies of difference (its 'causes') in order to bolster these same hierarchies (its 'effects').

Whilst it may be the case that hate crime is more likely to erupt when subordinated groups are more visible, demanding or assertive, it is probably more accurate to conceptualise hate crime, not simply as a strategy for members of dominant groups to respond to a perceived crisis or acute threat to their status but, more broadly, as a constant and regular mechanism for policing the norms and boundaries that keep 'the other' in place. This is not to suggest, however, that hate crime is necessarily successful in performing this border-policing function. It is crucial to distinguish between the capacity of hate crime 'to partially or momentarily *constitute* an identity category and its inability to *determine* how that category will be lived and reinvented everyday' (Mason 2002: 117). In other words, hate crime may bolster relations of superiority/inferiority between identity categories (it may make members of the Aboriginal community hesitant to move into certain neighbourhoods or gay men hesitant to openly express their sexuality) but the limits of these restrictions and expectations are constantly being tested and resisted (Aboriginal families *do* live in the leafy suburbs and gay men *do* hold hands in public). Moreover, at the same time that hate crime functions to maintain rigid and hierarchical distinctions between social groups it also 'betrays the permeability of the very boundaries and categories' that it seeks to bolster by revealing the need to continually monitor and manage them (Mason 2002: 57).

Racist, homophobic or anti-Semitic acts of violence and abuse are distinct behaviours. Whilst the conditions that make them possible (the broad-spectrum factors described above) have much in common, each form of hate crime emerges out of factors peculiar to the power relation in question. For instance, to understand hate crime towards members of the Arab and/or Muslim communities in New South Wales, we need to consider a range of global, national and local factors: the international environment since 9/11 and the so-called 'war on terror'; nationalist debates around 'illegal boat people' and the desire of many Australians to feel 'at home' amongst people who are 'like us' (Hage 1998); and localised moral panics over 'ethnic rape gangs' or assaults to lifesavers. These more specific variables are never static, leading to shifts in the patterns of hate crime across time and between places. For example, the 1991 National Inquiry into Racist Violence by HREOC (1991) reported that the primary victims of racist violence in Australia appeared to be the Jewish, Aboriginal, Asian and Arabic/Muslim communities. In relation to the latter, the Inquiry noted that incidents such as the Gulf War or he 'Rushdie affair' produced escalated levels of violence. In 2003, HREOC was sufficiently concerned about abuse against the Arab and/or Muslim population to commission specific research solely on this form of hate crime: research which found that Australian Arabs and Muslims report experiencing higher levels of racism, abuse and violence following 11 September 2001 (Poynting & Noble 2004). These kinds of shifts signal, not just the changing face of racism and ethnocentrism but, more particularly, the fact that hate crime by dominant groups towards minority groups may have less to do with the characteristics and behaviour of the victims themselves and more to do with the insecurities and desires of the perpetrators and the groups to which they belong. In the 1980s and early 1990s, moral panics around a so-called 'flood' of Asian migration, unemployment and socio-economic disadvantage came together to produce a cultural climate that, given Australia's colonial history as a white Christian society, was conducive to the commission of racist abuse and violence against Asian Australians (White 1997). In the 2000s, discourses around these variables have been reconfigured, with some becoming less important (unemployment) and new ones entering the picture (the threat of terrorism). The result is an apparent increase in the level of abuse and violence towards Arab and/or Muslim Australians. Whether this is accompanied by a decline in anti-Asian or other forms of racist violence is not clear. Nonetheless, this trend reminds us that the target of hate crime is often a 'relatively powerless innocent who is made to take the blame for something that is not his or her fault': a scapegoat (Aronson 1999: 132). As Sartre (1946: 178) put it in the wake of the attempted genocide of the Jewish people by the Third Reich:

> The Jew is only a pretext: elsewhere it will be the Negro, the yellow race. The Jew's existence simply allows the anti-semite to nip his anxieties in the bud by persuading himself that his place has always been cut out in the world, that it was waiting for him and that by virtue of tradition he has the right to occupy it.

This is not to suggest that victim groups are simply interchangeable with each other but, rather, that in certain socio-political environments some victim groups will fulfil defensive border-policing functions better than others.

The implications of Hate Crime

Hate crime adversely affects both individuals and communities. Although there is considerable variation in how an individual victim will react to being targeted for hate crime, research shows that the most common emotional responses include anger, fear, anxiety, sadness and depression. This in turn produces a heightened sense of vulnerability that often leads victims to alter their behaviour to varying degrees, such as moving from their neighbourhood, avoiding certain places or types of people (Garnets et al 1990; Herek et al 1999; Leets 2002; Barnes & Ephross 1994). This heightened sense of vulnerability is not restricted to those who have actually experienced hate crime. Like some other forms of crime, such as sexual assault, hate crime also has the capacity to create a 'climate of unsafety' amongst those who identify with the victims and thereby see themselves as potential victims as well (Stanko & Curry 1997). Even minor incidents of harassment or verbal abuse operate as a reminder to subjugated groups that they may be targeted for more serious violence.

This knowledge of hate crime can engender a plethora of daily routines or regular habits designed to maximise one's safety. For instance, members of targeted groups may avoid going to places they perceive to be dangerous, steer clear of people they identify as prejudiced, modify how they dress, restrict their behaviour in public and so on. In effect, to know that one may be the target of hate crime is frequently to feel an imperative to 'map' one's safety by monitoring and managing situations and signs that render one visible and thereby vulnerable to abuse or attack (Mason 2001b). Whilst this form of self-regulation is sometimes so ingrained as to be taken for granted, it is rarely all-encompassing. For example, many gay men and lesbians choose to 'flaunt' their sexuality and many Muslim Australian women continue to wear the hijab irrespective of the fact that such choices render them visible. Self-regulation does not necessarily amount to self-denial.

Legal responses to Hate Crime

Internationally, the law is one of the major avenues for responding to hate crime. The US, UK, Australia, New Zealand, Canada and many European countries have all enacted hate crime laws of some type. Whilst there is much variation between these laws, generally, they fall into three categories: those that provide for some kind of substantive hate crime offence (for example, Western Australia); those that impose a structured system of increased penalties for hate crimes (this is probably the most common model and has been enacted in Western Australia, the UK and many states in the US); and those that specify group hatred or prejudice as an aggravating factor at sentencing (for example, New South Wales).

Since 2004, Western Australia has had the most extensive hate crime laws in the country, including substantive offences and sentence enhancement provisions. However, unlike the NSW sentencing provisions, which apply to religion, race, ethnicity, language, sexual orientation, age and disability, these laws apply only to race. Most Australian states, including New South Wales, Victoria, Queensland, South Australia and the Australian Capital Territory have also created a criminal offence of 'serious vilification' under anti-discrimination law (in addition to the civil wrong of vilification). In New South Wales, serious vilification will be made out if an offender incites hatred towards, serious contempt for, or severe ridicule of a person or group of persons on the grounds of race, homosexuality, transgender or HIV/AIDS status, and they do so by means which include threatening physical harm or property damage or inciting others to threaten such harm (*Anti-Discrimination Act* 1977 (NSW), s 20D). Critics of this approach – situating the offence of serious vilification within anti-discrimination legislation – argue that it has prevented 'the new offence from taking root in the existing criminal law framework' (Meagher 2006: 9). This is supported by the fact that, to date, there have been no prosecutions for serious vilification. As Meagher (2006: 9) argues, this sends a 'mixed and diluted message regarding the seriousness of criminal racial vilification to the community and those public officers responsible for its administration and enforcement'.

There is much controversy over whether the law provides an effective or desirable means of responding to the problem of hate crime (as opposed to, say, education). In addition to technical legal difficulties, such as providing evidence of motive, a number of broader jurisprudential questions arise. Is the harm of hate crime, or the culpability of its perpetrators, so much more serious than other crimes as to warrant higher penalties? What about crimes where prejudice is not the driving force but is expressed during the commission of the offence? Can the inclusion of some categories, such as race, be justified when other categories, such as sexuality or disability are less likely to be accorded protected status under legislation? Is it appropriate to introduce motive into the definition of an offence when it is not normally an element? Do hate crime laws actually penalise expression and speech more than criminal conduct itself?

Despite these concerns, some advocates justify hate crime laws on the grounds that they perform an important 'expressive' function by publicly condemning violence that is motivated by racism, homophobia, religious intolerance and so on (Lawrence 1999: 67). In making a broad 'moral claim' that 'prejudice is wrong', hate crime laws are said to operate as a 'symbolic statement' (Jacobs & Potter 1998: 65) to 'reinforce pro social values of tolerance and respect' for subjugated groups (Jenness & Grattet 2001: 179). Yet, this is a point recognised by critics of hate crime legislation who argue that such laws are effectively a form of 'affirmative action' (McLaughlin 2002) that seek to 'extend the civil rights paradigm into the world of crime and criminal law' (Jacobs & Potter 1998: 27). As Jenness and Broad (1997: 173) demonstrate, this means that the process by which some groups are recognised over other groups as the bona fide victims of hate crime is 'not a mere reflection of an objective state of affairs' but, rather, is the product of contestation between advocacy groups, politicians and institutions, to shape 'public and legal definitions of who is and who is not harmed unjustly'. Problematically, this has uneven effects. For instance, as noted above, race is the most protected category in Australia, the UK and the US. Whether a given group will be granted victim status is also affected by the impact that this will have on the moral claims of other victim groups. For example, Jacobs and Potter argue that resistance to including crimes motivated by gender prejudice in US hate crime laws is partly the product of concern by other advocacy groups. Violence against women is so common that there are concerns that if it were included in the definition of hate crime it would divert attention away from other forms of hate crime, thereby diminishing 'the significance of their victimisation and the force of their moral claim' (Jacobs & Potter 1998: 78).

Conclusion

There is little doubt that some communities in Australia are targeted for harassment, vandalism and violence that is prompted by intolerance, disrespect, animosity or hatred. In theory, hate crime can be committed by members of any group against members of any other group. Whilst Australian data is thin, there is ample international evidence to suggest that, in reality, most hate crime is committed by members of dominant groups against those 'minority' groups who are the historical or traditional objects of prejudice. Hate crime reflects and reinforces these established hierarchies of difference. Whilst young men may be the primary perpetrators of hate crime, it is important to recognise that there is no single profile of a hate crime perpetrator and, certainly, no fixed profile of its victims. Hate crime is a dynamic phenomenon that shifts according to global and local socio-political variables. Whilst the power imbalances that underlie hate crime may fluctuate little, the likelihood that these will be expressed in violence towards a particular group at a given time in a given location is changeable, yet predictable. Tragically, the patterns of hate crime appear to follow, to a certain extent, 'fashions' in chauvinism and bigotry.

Hate crime is not a neutral concept. It is a highly politicised by-product of the identity politics movements that gathered force in the 1980s to promote the interests of disadvantaged groups. To some observers, the creation of the concept of hate crime and the development of hate crime laws represent much-needed tools in the fight against prejudice-related discrimination and violence. To others, they are an over-reaction to a series of moral panics that have encouraged disadvantaged groups to see themselves as victims. Such criticisms cannot be dismissed as right-wing rhetoric. Some of the strongest critiques of the hate crime movement come from dedicated anti-racist or anti-homophobic campaigners who are concerned that advocates of hate crime laws tend to over-state the extent of the problem, over-simplify its complexities, promote inter-group resentment and assume that legal punitivism is a helpful response. These tensions are not unique to hate crime. They reflect, and make an important contribution to, broader debates within criminology about the construction of crime categories and the utility of criminal law as a preventative tool. There is no doubt that effective remedies to hostility and violence that is fuelled by racism, ethnocentrism, anti-Semitism, homophobia and misogyny are needed. We continue to grapple with how to achieve this.

References

Allport, G 1954, *The Nature of Prejudice*, Addison-Wesley Publishing, Boston.

Aronson, E 1999, 'Causes of Prejudice' in Baird, M & Rosenbaum, S (eds) *Hatred, Bigotry, and Prejudice: definitions, causes and solutions*, Prometheus Books.

Association of Chief Police Officers 2002, *ACPO Guide to Identifying and Combating Hate Crime*, <www.acpo.police.uk>.

Attorney General's Department of NSW 2003, 'You shouldn't have to hide to be safe': *Report on Homophobic Hostilities and Violence Against Gay Men and Lesbians in New South Wales*, Attorney General's Department of NSW.

Barnes, A & Ephross, P 1994, 'The Impact of Hate Violence on Victims: emotional and behavioral responses to attacks', 39(3) *Social Work* 247.

Brown, C 2004, 'Legislating Against Hate Crime in New Zealand: the need to recognise gender-based violence', 35 *Victoria University of Wellington Law Review* 591.

Dreher, T 2005, *'Targeted': experiences of racism in New South Wales after September 11, 2001*, UTS Shopfront, Sydney.

Garnets, L, Herek, G & Levy, B 1990, 'Violence and Victimization of Lesbians and Gay Men: mental health consequences', 5(3) *Journal of Interpersonal Violence* 366.

Gelber, K 2000, 'Hate Crimes: public policy implications of the inclusion of gender', 35(2) *Australian Journal of Political Science* 275.

Goldberg, D 1995, 'Afterword: hate, power?' in Kirk Whillock, R & Slayden, D (eds), *Hate Speech*, Sage, California.

Hage, G 1998, *White Nation: fantasies of white supremacy in a multicultural society*, Pluto Press, NSW.

Hage, G 2006, 'Racism is not simply black and white', *Sydney Morning Herald*, 12 June, p 13.

Herek, G, Gillis, J & Cogan, J 1999, 'Psychological Sequelae of Hate-Crime Victimization Among Lesbian, Gay, and Bisexual Adults', 67(6) *Journal of Consulting and Clinical Psychology* 945.

Human Rights and Equal Opportunity Commission (HREOC), 1991, *Racist Violence: Report of the National Inquiry into Racist Violence in Australia*, HREOC, Canberra.

Jacobs, J & Potter, K 1998, *Hate Crimes: criminal law and identity politics*, Oxford University Press, New York.

Jenness, V & Broad, K 1997, *Hate Crimes: new social movements and the politics of violence*, Aldine de Gruyter, New York.

Jenness, V & Grattet, R 2001, *Making Hate a Crime: from social movement to law enforcement*, Russell Sage Foundation, New York.

Lawrence, F 1999, *Punishing Hate: bias crimes under American law*, Harvard University Press, Cambridge, MA.

Leets, L 2002, 'Experiencing Hate Speech: perceptions and responses to anti-semitism and antigay speech', 58(2) *Journal of Social Issues* 341.

Levin, J & McDevitt, J 2002, *Hate Crimes Revisited: America's war on those who are different*, Westview Press, Colorado.

Mason, G 2001a, 'Not Our Kind of Hate Crime', 12 *Law and Critique* 253.

Mason, G 2001b, 'Body Maps: envisaging homophobia, violence and safety', 10(1) *Social and Legal Studies* 23.

Mason, G 2002, *The Spectacle of Violence: homophobia, gender and knowledge*, Routledge, London.

Mason, G 2007, 'The Reconstruction of Hate Language' in Gelber, K & Stone, A (eds), *Hate Speech and Freedom of Speech in Australia*, Federation Press, Sydney.

McLaughlin, E 2002, 'Between Rocks and Hard Places: the politics of hate crime', 6(4) *Theoretical Criminology* 445.

Meagher, D 2006, 'So Far No Good: the regulatory failure of criminal racial vilification laws in Australia', 17 *Public Law Review* 209.

Perry, B 2001, *In the Name of Hate: understanding hate crime*, Routledge, New York.

Poynting, S & Noble, G 2004, *Living with Racism: The Experience and Reporting by Arab and Muslim Australians of Discrimination, Abuse and Violence since 11 September 2001*, Report to the Human Rights and Equal Opportunity Commission, Centre for Cultural Research, University of Western Sydney.

Sartre, JP 1946, 'Portrait of an Anti-Semite', 13(2) *Partisan Review* 163.

Stanko, E & Curry, P 1997, 'Homophobic Violence and the Self "At Risk": interrogating the boundaries', 6(4) *Social and Legal Studies* 513.

Tomsen, S 2002, *Hatred, Murder and Male Honour: anti-homosexual killings in New South Wales 1980-2000* (Research and Public Policy Series No 43), Australian Institute of Criminology, Canberra.

White, R 1997, 'Immigration, Nationalism and Anti-Asian Racism' in Cunneen, C, Fraser, D & Tomsen, S (eds), *Faces of Hate: hate crime in Australia*, Hawkins Press, Sydney.

16

DEAD MAN WORKING? CRITICAL CRIMINOLOGY, HUMAN RIGHTS AND THE WORKPLACE

Barbara Ann Hocking and Scott Guy

In 1944 in the USA, singer Johnny Cash's then 14-year-old brother was virtually cut in two when he was pulled into a whirling table saw in the mill where he worked, dying a week later after considerable suffering. In 2004 in Australia, 18-year-old apprentice toolmaker, Daniel Madeley, was seriously injured while operating a horizontal borer – working alone, he was pulled into the borer by his coat and unable to stop the machine, dying the next day.[1]

Introduction

Violence and criminal victimisation both feature prominently in the Australian criminological academic literature. Together with many contributors to this volume, we argue in this chapter that our area of study – the workplace – has until recently been largely neglected as a site for criminological analysis in the mainstream Australian criminological literature. This neglect mirrors the inadequacy of the criminal law to deal with this harmful conduct. It flies in the face of the extensive deaths and injuries that occur in workplaces. As Elizabeth Stanley (this volume) says of torture, so with workplace violence: it provides a 'vital opportunity for criminologists to provide a fuller recognition of what constitutes crime'.

Criminology is largely concerned with violence and criminality, and the most widely known and traditional acts of violence (homicide, rape, robbery) are rightfully the subject of its disciplinary inquiry. Violence in the workplace crosses traditionally distinct boundaries in criminology: concern with individual behaviour as the subject of study (the sociology of deviance), and concern with matters that become the subject of criminal law (crime as defined by the criminal law). Workplace violence is an extremely elusive subject of criminal law, and violence in the workplace ranges across both direct, as well as more subtle and insidious, acts such

---

1   See *Oaten v Engineering Employers' Association SA Group Training Scheme Inc* [2006] SAIRC 70.

as threats of violence, sexual harassment and workplace bullying. It extends as well to indirect acts, which have quite serious and dramatic consequences, such as industrial manslaughter. We argue that in order to bring this extensively harmful conduct within the rubric of critical criminology, there is an increasing need for empirical analyses to document the pervasive and entrenched nature of workplace violence and how incidences of workplace violence are closely associated with organisational and management practices, as well as wider government economic and social policy.

To demonstrate the prevalence of workplace violence we set out a case study of nursing, including several facts and figures concerning the broader 'caring' profession, together with estimates of apprentice deaths and injuries across Australia. We include details only recently made known as to bullying and victimisation in the defence forces. Many of these incidents concern young people and many have only become publicly known when their parents decided to go to the media. It is precisely this invisibility and secrecy that make it difficult to realistically estimate and define what constitutes workplace violence – let alone to address its legacy through the criminal law, and to articulate the human rights of those most at risk of harm. Much of the harm is perpetrated by multinational corporations who are frequently able to avoid responsibility through the mechanism of the corporate veil and through the extensive use of 'commercial in confidence' clauses (see Freiberg 1997: 125).

Our central argument is that workplace violence and harms are under-criminalised, and under-policed relative to other harms that are over-policed and over-criminalised relative to risk (such as terrorism and refugee matters). The bottom line is that critical criminology can contribute to an understanding as to why we appear benign to this harm.

The extent of workplace violence

Workplace violence has traditionally been considered under the more general rubric of occupational health and safety and not as a distinct concern or focus in itself. Prosecutions for corporate manslaughter, for example, have been considered to be matters that involve the enforcement of occupational health and safety legislation. Academic debate, however, has focused on the issue of whether occupational health and safety statutes *should* be vehicles for more serious workplace offences, such as manslaughter and related offences, or whether recourse should be made to general criminal law (Gray & Scholz 1991, 1993). Carson and Johnstone (1990) have argued that recourse to the general criminal law for very serious cases, such as manslaughter, may reinforce the view that occupational health and safety offences are 'quasi-criminal' in nature. They emphasise the need for the incorporation of serious workplace offences within general occupational health and safety statutes (1990: 126). There have also been powerful arguments made for the need for occupational health and safety legislation to develop a greater armoury of compliance measures – rather than being exclusively reliant on monetary fines – in order to deter acts of workplace violence (Clayton 2003). In this context of workplace health and safety, there have been further calls for incorporating a more community-oriented role in preventing workplace violence (Carson 2003).

The popular perception of workplace violence is one mainly concerned with high profile incidents where staff is traumatised by external robberies or assaults.

However, as will be seen below, a different picture is emerging where staff from a range of occupations, including nurses, social workers, teachers and human service workers, are being subjected to physical attacks. It is difficult to establish precisely whether workplace violence is increasing given that there are also increases in awareness and reporting rates. Nevertheless, there does seem to be a growing consensus about what factors may be leading to increases in workplace violence, such as the political and economic factors of increasing rationalisation of the workforce, the greater insecurity of the workforce and the constant push to make workplaces more productive and efficient (Bowie 2000: 7).

Irrespective of whether the actual incidence of workplace violence is increasing, there would seem to be an increasing number of high profile corporate cases appearing in the news which have involved the violation of workers' human rights. For example, in recent times, litigation arising out of the treatment of employees has implicated major corporations as James Hardie, Rio Tinto, Thor Chemicals, the World Bank and the Inter-American Development Bank. Workplace violence, then, has become a highly visible issue that needs to be addressed.

Explanations for workplace harms

Much has been written of the contemporary organisational restructuring processes that, coupled with associated job insecurity and pressures, can produce more confrontational styles of management and contribute to friction amongst employees (Australian Institute of Criminology 2003: 58). Increases in organisational violence have been traced to government policies which have impacted adversely on social and economic welfare indicators such as levels of employment opportunities and income equality (for example, incidences of workplace bullying have been perceived to be partly a consequence of increasing government emphasis on, and commitment to, the ideals of competition, productivity and efficiency). The undermining of employment security and the notion of lifelong employment has been perceived as contributing to an environment in which workplace bullying can take place (Kleiner & Whitmore 1998: 287). Similarly, the globalisation of the economy and the associated shift to downsizing companies and ensuring that they are more flexible and responsive to economic trends has fostered insecurity, stress and (as Margaret Thornton (2004) argues) a more 'corrosive' style of management, which has facilitated workplace bullying. Across a broad spectrum of working environments, workplace change and restructure has resulted in downsizing and increased workloads so that everyone is expected to do more with less. Not only has the global transformation of corporate workplaces led to insecurity, frustration and stress, but a new style of 'managerial' leadership has proven to be a correlative hazard. A common source of workplace stress is bullying (Thornton 2004: 9).

This focus on underlying structural and organisational causes of workplace violence is important since it does, indeed, emphasise the essentially 'structural' and recurrent – as opposed to 'random' – character of workplace violence. It therefore promotes a heightened awareness and appreciation of surrounding political and socio-economic factors that contribute to situations of workplace violence. In this respect, it deflects attention *away* from the individual perpetrators and victims of workplace violence and seeks to address the underlying conditions or circumstances that give rise to these actions of violence. Hence, it moves attention from a focus on individual pathology/personality factors and a potentially destructive 'blaming the victim' paradigm (Nelsen & Tanks 2004: 115).

Inequalities of power in the workplace have resulted in *systemic* forms of workplace bullying and workplace violence against groups such as workplace apprentices. For example, systemic workplace violence includes the common process of apprentice initiation or 'bastardisation' in which apprentices have to experience 'initiation rites' as part of their occupational training and professional development. There have been well-publicised cases in the past of this form of apprentice 'bastardisation' – in particular, it was the subject of a defence force inquiry in 1998 (Defence Equity Organisation 1998).

The example of violence against apprentices emphasises the point – and one that will recur in this chapter – that the causes of workplace violence can be traced to underlying structural and systemic factors. While prevention strategies that focus on individual perpetrators of workplace violence and that predict which individuals may become violent are useful because they seek to identify 'at risk' personality types, they do not seek to address the structural or socio-economic causes of workplace violence. As the Employment Rights Watchdog (1998: 4) recently declared in its Discussion Paper:

> These strategies could be seen as a 'piecemeal' approach because they concentrate on the individual psychological or physical elements that may contribute to violence, but fail to address the structural factors which may contribute to internal manifestations of workplace violence.

In terms of understanding, teaching and (most importantly) developing preventative strategies for workplace violence, it is important then to move *beyond* a focus on personality, criminality and the pathology of the individual employee/employer as the main contributor of violence to a wider examination of organisational practices, management styles and underlying socio-economic factors. What may superficially appear as an organisation being subject to a 'crime wave' from external sources may in actual fact be 'the result of devalued staff being less safety conscious or even staff colluding with outsiders to commit crimes if they feel no longer valued by their organisations' (Bowie 2002: 6). Government 'law and order' campaigns that draw attention to escalating crime statistics or 'crime waves', and seek to impose even more punitive penalties on offenders, are clearly inadequate as a means of addressing workplace violence. Workplace violence may, for example, be the product of organisational demands or management pressure on employees to work harder and more efficiently. More broadly it may be the result of a wider government economic rationalist agenda, which is placing increasing emphasis on workplace productivity and efficiency at the expense of equally important factors such as occupational security and employee welfare. Accordingly, to focus on the criminality of workplace violence and the individual pathology of perpetrators – as the mass media has done – is to miss the root causes and facilitators of workplace violence.

The impact of workplace violence

There are highly persuasive reasons to undertake criminological research into the causes and the incidence of workplace violence – the primary one being its significant impact on workers, as well as workplace productivity. Violence in the workplace is an emerging problem affecting increasing numbers of workers and employers, and studies into workplace violence have reported high incidences of victimisation in the workplace. In particular, there are growing reports of low-level violence, such as abuse and threats, being reported in a range of jobs (Mayhew & Chappell 2005: 346; 2003: 3). A Morgan Poll (1998) found that 46% of Australians have been verbally or physically abused by someone with whom they work, and the Australian Institute of Criminology (2003: 41) cited data which indicated that one in two Australian employees had been verbally abused by a member of the public during the course of their occupational duties and one in ten had been physically abused by an employee.

The Australian Institute of Criminology (2003) also cited various other surveys highlighting the prevalence of violence in the workplace. In particular, it cited surveys to indicate that, on average, 10% of all acts of victimisation reported by women were experienced whilst they were at work. The comparable figure for men was 13%. In addition, sexual incidents constituted the highest proportion of all workplace victimisations (2003: 32). In terms of violent physical attacks in the professions, the Australian Institute of Criminology cited surveys to demonstrate that, in the preceding 12 months, one-third of all nurses had been violently attacked or abused at work by patients (2003: 36).

Workplace violence also involves fatal assaults. The Australian Institute of Criminology (2003: 28) reported that occupational homicide represented 2% of all traumatic workplace deaths in Australia and that 62% of the victims were employees compared with 36% who were either self-employed or business owners. Those occupational status categories most affected were 'managers and administrators' (24%) followed by 'sales and professional service workers' (20%).

Workplace bullying and violence has also had a prejudicial impact on the productivity and performance of the workforce and the social and the psychological condition of workers. As Keashly and Neumann (2004: 336) argue, workplace bullying, intimidation and physical violence produces an essentially 'toxic' workplace – one engendering feelings of suspicion, resentment and distrust, all of which undermine a productive work setting.

In this respect, workplace violence results in significant financial costs associated with absenteeism, lost productivity, higher workers' compensation premiums, medical expenses and the less easily quantifiable personal costs of emotional trauma suffered by victims and their families (Wakefield 1993: 130). It also has consequential impacts on (third party) family members of the victims (Hockley 2003: 2). More fundamentally than this, there is growing evidence to suggest that workplace violence has a significant effect on peoples' occupations and their future career prospects (Quinlan & Mayhew 1999: 491). Essentially, studies have demonstrated that the infliction of workplace violence leaves workers vulnerable and (more) insecure, thereby putting their employment at greater risk (Campbell 1997: 4). There are correlations between precarious forms of employment and exposure to harassment from superiors (Dale et al 1997: 3).

The incidence of workplace violence: case study – the nursing profession

It appears that certain industries and occupations are more predisposed to incidences of workplace violence than other industries and these include occupations which involve significant client/patient contact; the handling of cash; isolated work environments; or occupations that entail reduced occupational security. Specifically, these occupations include the nursing, health care, medical, education, and security professions.

To illustrate the growing problem which workplace violence is having, attention can be particularly drawn to the increasing incidence of workplace violence in the health care profession. Workplace violence is becoming a growing concern for health care workers (Mayhew & Chappell 2003: 3). It has been estimated that between six and 13 billion dollars is lost each year in productivity due to workplace violence in the health care industry (Chappell 2003).

In this context, Mayhew and Chappell (2003: 5) were involved in the New South Wales Health 'Taskforce on Prevention and Management of Violence in the Health Workforce' which conducted one of the most extensive studies of violence in the health industry and, in particular, the nursing sector to date. It found that of the 200 nurses surveyed, 147 had experienced a total of 311 separate violent events in the 12-month period which preceded the survey. Of those surveyed, two-thirds said that they had been verbally abused in the previous 12-month period. Further, 10.5% said that they had been bullied and 12% indicated that they had been assaulted. The authors also found, that an Australian health worker had been murdered at work within the previous 12 months of their study and that (on average) more than 50% of health workers would experience one or other form of workplace violence in the following years.

To reinforce the Mayhew and Chappell study, a Tasmanian study was undertaken which recorded that 64% of all nurses that had been surveyed had experienced some form of verbal or physical abuse (Cubit & Farrell 2005: 1). A survey of workplace violence among nurses was also undertaken in Queensland and this involved a random sampling of 3000 nurses from the Queensland nurses union in both public and private aged care (Hegney et al 2006: 220). The survey indicated increases in violence among both the public and private sectors. It noted, in particular, a significant increase in the incidence of workplace violence in the public (47%), as opposed to the private sector (23%). It also found that acts of violence were perpetrated against nurses from a variety of sources – including patients, relatives, management and other nurses.

Another study of similar extent was undertaken in Western Australia and this indicated that of workplace assaults, 74% of them occurred in the community services industry and this included nurses, social workers, guards, security officers and prison officers (WorkSafe Western Australia 1999).

What this brief review of the incidence of workplace violence in the nursing profession indicates is that workplace violence is quite pervasive – particularly in the form of lower levels of violence, such as insults and threats. It also highlights the fact that workplace violence frequently involves issues of inequality of power in the workplace and is often inflicted on those employees with less workplace status. In this respect, issues of gender, power and violence arise. For example, because the majority of nurses are women, a gender analysis of workplace violence is useful. It may be that women in the nursing profession are caught in an organisational framework that keeps them in subordinate and powerless positions and which effects acts of violence, bullying and aggression against them (Barron 2006: 24).

Strategies to respond to workplace violence

The widespread and pervasive nature of workplace violence raises the issue as to how it can be appropriately addressed and countered. Until more recently the criminal law has been viewed as the principal safeguard against traditional forms of violence (such as homicide, rape and robbery) irrespective of whether they occurred in or out of the working environment. Yet, the difficulty with the criminal law is that it is oriented to essentially *individual* and *overt* (or traditional) unlawful acts of violence, whereas (as has been outlined) workplace violence can assume more subtle, institutionalised and insidious forms, such as verbal threats and (sexual) harassment. As the Australian Institute of Criminology (2003: 70) declares:

> [T]he individual basis of the criminal law means that it is not very adept at dealing with many forms of non-traditional violence ... Essentially these forms of violence may be unlawful, though not strictly criminal.

Another mechanism for countering workplace violence is sourced in the common law. The common law has long recognised that employers owe a duty of care to their employees and where employers fail to discharge those duties, the victims of workplace violence may claim redress under the civil law. In the United States, an employer may be prosecuted for negligence relating to deficient hiring, training, supervision and retention of employees (Laibig 1995). Whilst in Australia there is no such (common law) legal concept as the negligent hiring doctrine, the importance of background checks has been acknowledged by many industries (several businesses, such as *The PRM Group*, now provide employment screening services in various industry sectors).

A final legal mechanism used for countering workplace violence can be found in workers' compensation and occupational health and safety legislation. Occupational health and safety legislation, in particular, has served as a principal counter against employee harms (Johnstone 2004). While the various Australian State and Territory health and safety Acts do not expressly address workplace violence, their respective general duties provisions are broadly based and (under these provisions) employers are generally required to bear the primary responsibility for providing their employees a working environment free from recognised risks, hazards, and potentially dangerous situations and processes (Johnstone & Wilson 2006: 59). As Dale, Tobin and Wilson (1997: 3) point out; Victoria has been at the forefront of efforts to address directly the problem of bullying in the workplace by launching a workplace health and safety prosecution against an employer in relation to the 'bastardisation of apprentices'.

Non-legislative violence prevention measures have also emerged in the form of practical guidance documentation. They seek to counter the incidence of workplace violence. In this respect, there would seem to have been an acknowledgement in Australia that the prevention of violence cannot be achieved through law enforcement alone. However, as Russell (1999: 9) concedes, the vast bulk of this material is essentially general in nature and, therefore, potentially inadequate since 'violence is not the sort of hazard that is amenable to sharing solutions at this level'.

The shortcomings of present legislative and policy responses to workplace violence highlight the need for a better underlying *theoretical* understanding of the causes of this problem and how to go about developing strategies that address the more insidious and systemic (non-traditional) forms of violence, such as those forms of violence relating to workplace bullying and sexual harassment. Accordingly, attention is now turned to the contribution which critical criminology can make to an understanding of the causes of workplace violence and developing a more contextual and rights-based theory of workplace violence.

Critical criminology and violence in the workplace

Critical criminology seeks to locate and understand the reasons for crime within wider structural and institutional contexts (McLean 1998: 566). The value of this approach for ameliorating workplace violence is that it offers a holistic approach to this issue – individuals not only shape the world, but are also shaped by it. Accordingly, critical criminology stresses the co-production of crime and workplace violence and draws attention to the fact that issues pertaining to workplace violence cannot be divorced from the wider social and economic contexts within which they are situated (Simons 2004: 599; Bowie 2002: 10).

According to Pavlich (2000: 331), the overriding aim of critical criminology is to deconstruct the privileged meanings and discourses which frame the reality of crime and social control and to draw attention to the possibility for more inclusive and liberating interpretations. Constitutive criminology, a strand of critical criminology, also draws attention to the fact that conceptions of crime and criminality are inevitably political and socially constructed. Truth, in this respect, is impossible to attain and knowledge can only be comprehended within the wider context of the existing power relations which are in existence in society (Stuart & Milovanovich 1996; Scheingold 1998: 857).

The importance of critical criminology, then, for understanding workplace violence and criminality is that it draws attention to the essentially situated or contextual nature of the criminal law. In other words, the concept of criminality is a socially constructed one that cannot be divorced from its wider historical, as well as social, context. In this respect, alternative and more liberating concepts of criminality and social control in the workplace can be developed (Hogeveen & Woolford 2006: 681).

The difficulty has been, however, that critical criminology has in more recent times tended to lose its critical and liberating emphasis and to become more mechanistic, more technical and 'administrative' in orientation. In this respect, Pavlich (2000: 327) argues that critical criminologists have 'allowed critical discourse to drift even closer to administrative discourses focused on solving the crime problems' (see also Hogg 1996: 43). Nonetheless, the emphasis on the part of critical criminology on the contingent and situated nature of criminality and social control leaves the way open to develop potentially liberating perspectives of, and theories on, workplace violence.

An understanding of the wider contextual circumstances and structures that give rise to workplace violence may assist in attempts in decreasing its numbers or incidence. For example, a focus on the broader problems of job insecurity, economic uncertainty, productivity and management or organisational practices may assist in ameliorating the problem of workplace violence. Critical criminology, then, can assist us to articulate the problems with 'dysfunctional management' and the anger that it generates (Nelson & Tanks 2004: 115). There is always the danger, however, that in contextualising workplace violence in this broader manner the problem becomes *too* difficult to address and one that is never confronted (Perrone 1999: 3).

Nevertheless, in spite of this argument, there is significant value in drawing attention to the wider social and economic causes of workplace violence and how, without wider institutional reform, the problem will never be effectively addressed. We would argue that critical criminology needs to engage with the very non-criminalisation of the extensive workplace violence experienced in contemporary workplaces. Just as Pickering argues that critical criminology should engage with the criminalisation of non-criminals (refugees), so in the workplace context, the reverse applies: it is the very non-criminalisation of harmful conduct that is of relevance here.

New and more liberating approaches to workplace violence would need to embrace a *rights-oriented* perspective (Chappell & Di Martino 2003: 10). Safety from physical attack, harassment or other forms of aggression or abuse is central to an employee's sense of wellbeing and this, in turn, is closely associated with fundamental notions of human rights (Australian Institute of Criminology 2003: 8). The issue of workplace violence, in this regard, is inextricably connected to individual rights and, in particular, rights of employees to be safe in their own work environment. The United Nations has explicitly acknowledged in Article 11 that violence in the workplace challenges feelings of safety and security in its adoption of the *Convention on the Elimination of all forms of Discrimination against Women* (see also Di Martino 2006: 1).

Any contemporary criminological approach to workplace violence, then, needs to confront issues regarding infringements of human rights in the workplace. Extending beyond this, it needs to confront issues of social justice and how social and economic inequality contributes to workplace violence and the trenching of human rights. It has been shown that more 'peripheral' members of the workforce (and those who are usually less skilled), such as casual and part-time employees, are more subject to workplace bullying than 'core' or permanent full-time employees (Johnstone et al 2005: 93). Generally, then, critical criminology needs to be concerned with the interrelationship between crime, human rights and social justice (Hill & Robertson 2003: 102).

Workplace violence and *Work Choices*

The principal Commonwealth Act that imposes duties regarding workplace safety is the *Occupational Safety and Health Act* 1991 (Cth). This federal legislation imposes duties requiring employers and managers in control of workplaces to provide safe and healthy workplaces so employees and others at the workplace are not exposed to hazards. It also provides that employers must consult and cooperate with safety and health representatives and employees about safety and health in the workplace. This legislation means that employers must take all practicable measures to reduce the risks of violence at work and any other hazard (see ss 16-22).

There has been some suggestion that the recent *Workplace Relations Amendment (Work Choices) Act* 2005 (Cth) has promoted increased incidences of workplace violence and a greater number of contraventions of the *Occupational Health and Safety Act* 1991 (Cth) (Kelly 2006: 10). According to Kelly (2006: 56), *Work Choices* has introduced (or facilitated) greater competitive pressures, accentuated business values and has, indeed, ascribed lesser importance to the principles of fairness and social justice. In this respect, the *Work Choices* legislation has not reduced, but has had the effect of *promoting*, the incidence of workplace violence.[2] It has been argued that the legislation will impact disproportionately on women in terms of workplace bullying and violence. This is consistent with the analysis above which emphasises that workplace violence needs to be understood in a wider social and economic context. In addition, organisational pressures to increase productivity and general government attempts to deregulate the labour market, reduce employment security and promote more flexible work practices may have contributed to workplace bullying, intimidation and violence. Kelly (2006: 56) indicates that this general economic situation may have led to a greater incidence of workplace violence against women:

> Considerable evidence points to increases in workplace bullying as a consequence of competitive pressures; the predominance of business values; and the declining legitimacy ascribed to principles of fairness and social justice. The legislation will enhance and extend women's labour market disadvantage by shifting the employment relationship to the private sphere, together with informalisation of workplace relations, reduced access to formal procedures and reduced accountability and transparency.

Furthermore, it may be that the introduction of Australian Workplace Agreements are engendering a climate of fear whereby workers are reluctant to report deteriorating occupational health and safety situations for fear of retaliation and retribution. This would seem to have been the case recently in Western Australia where miners, under threats of intimidation, have been reluctant to disclose safety risks in relation to the mines (see Norington 2007).

Conclusion

Violence and criminal victimisation has been a recurrent theme in the Australian academic literature. However, the focus has generally been confined to more traditional acts of violence, such as homicide, rape and robbery. Workplace violence cannot be accommodated in this traditional paradigm of violence since it involves more subtle and insidious acts, such as threats of violence, sexual harassment, and workplace bullying. In this respect, a more inclusive and embracing conception of violence is needed if workplace violence is to be properly understood and addressed.

The chapter sought to contextualise workplace violence within a broader social and criminological framework. We argued that workplace violence is closely asso-

---

2   As a postscript, a new workplace relations system is foreshadowed under the new Rudd Labor Federal Government, which will reform significantly the existing 'Work Choices' industrial relations regime and promote greater equity and social justice in the workplace. The Australian Labor Party has already sought to implement a new workplace relations system by January 2010. In the meantime the Rudd Labor Government is formulating a 'Transitional Bill' which is expected to be introduced to Federal Parliament early next year and which will require employment contracts to incorporate a minimum of 10 guaranteed standards in relation to hours of work; parental leave; flexible work for parents; annual leave; personal carers and compassionate leave; community services leave; public holidays; information in the workplace; termination of employment and redundancy; and long service leave. According to the analysis that has been presented in this chapter, the implementation of these changes and the consequent promotion of a more fair, equitable and socially just workplace should lead to a reduction of incidence of workplace violence. Whether this, in fact, occurs remains to be seen ...

ciated with organisational/management practices, as well as wider government economic and social policy and this emphasises the important point that workplace violence can only be ameliorated by focusing on wider institutional and structural factors which interact with circumstances in the workplace to produce workplace violence.

We have suggested that the importance of critical criminology for an understanding of workplace violence is that it situates mechanisms of social and criminal control within their historical context and draws attention to the possibilities for developing alternative (and potentially more progressive) processes. An understanding of the wider contextual circumstances and structures that give rise to workplace violence may assist in attempts to reduce the incidence of workplace violence. For example – as has been suggested – a focus on the broader problems of job insecurity, economic uncertainty, productivity and management or organisational practices may assist in ameliorating the problem of workplace violence. Critical criminology, then, can assist in contextualising workplace violence and drawing attention to the wider institutional or socio-economic factors that contribute to its onset and continuance.

In the Australian context, with the now constitutionally valid introduction of the *Workplace Relations Act* and the recent *Work Choices* amendments, which have been widely criticised as rolling back workers' rights in the name of freedom of choice, vigilance as to employment rights must cease to be invisible. Critical criminology can perform a key role in enhancing labour rights and in promoting a safer working environment through embracing a more explicitly political and rights-oriented perspective – one, for example, that challenges the neo-liberal paradigm underpinning recent industrial relations legislation.

References

Australian Institute of Criminology 2003, *Violence in the Workplace: personal and political issues,* paper presented at the Secretary in Government Conference, Canberra.

Bowie, V 2000, 'Current Trends and Emerging Issues in Workplace Violence', 13(3) *Security Journal* 7.

Bowie, V 2002, *Workplace Violence: a second look,* paper presented at the Crime Prevention Conference convened by the Australian Institute of Criminology and Crime Prevention Branch, Commonwealth Attorney-General's Department, Sydney.

Campbell, I 1997, 'Beyond Unemployment: the challenge of increased precarious unemployment', 11 *Just Policy* 4.

Carson, WG 2003, *Engaging the Community,* paper presented at the Agenda for Change Conference, Department of Justice, Canberra.

Carson, WG & Johnstone, R 1990, 'The Dupes of Hazard: occupational health and safety and the Victorian sanctions debate in historical perspective', 26 *Australian and New Zealand Journal of Sociology* 126.

Chappell, D 2003, *Towards Violence Free Workplaces: international trends and prospects,* paper presented to the Transnational Crime Prevention Centre, University of Wollongong, NSW.

Chappell, D & Di Martino, V 2003, *Violence in the Workplace: personal and political issues,* paper presented at the Secretary in Government Conference, Canberra.

Clayton, A 2003, 'Regulating Occupational Health and Safety: the need for a new paradigm', 7(1) *Safety Science Monitor* 8.

Cubit, K & Farrell, G 2005 'Aggression in Nursing: a time to look closely at aged care', 25 *Contemporary Nurse* 1.

Dale, R, Tobin, W & Wilson, B 1997, 'Workplace Violence', 10 *Just Policy* 3.

Defence Equity Organisation 1998, *Report of the Review into Policies and Practices to Deal with Sexual Harassment and Sexual Offences at the Australian Defence Force Academy,* Department of Defence, Canberra.

Di Martino, V 2006, *Terrorism in the Workplace,* International Labour Organisation.

Employment Rights Watchdog (Job Watch), 1998, *Violence in the Workplace: protecting the rights of employees,* Discussion Paper.

Freiberg, A 1997, 'Commercial Confidentiality, Criminal Justice and the Public Interest', 9 *Current Issues in Criminal Justice* 125.

Gray, WB & Scholz, J 1991, 'Analysing the Equity and Efficiency of OSHA Enforcement', 3 *Law and Policy* 185.

Gray, WB & Scholz, J 1993, 'Does Regulatory Enforcement Work? A panel analysis of OSHA enforcement', 27 *Law Society Review* 177.

Hegney, D, Eley, R, Plant, A, Buikstra, E & Parker, V 2006, 'Workplace Violence in Queensland, Australia: the results of a comparative study', 12 *International Journal of Nursing Practice* 220.

Hill, R & Robertson, R 2003, 'What Sort of Future for Critical Criminology?', 39 *Crime, Law and Social Change* 91.

Hockley, C 2003, 'The Impact of Workplace Violence on Third Party Victims', *Australian E' Journal for the Advancement of Mental Health* 2.

Hogeveen, B & Woolford, A 2006, 'Critical Criminology and Possibility in the Neo-Liberal Ethos', 48 *Canadian Journal of Criminology and Criminal Justice* 681.

Hogg, R 1996, 'Criminological Failure and Governmental Effect', 1 *Current Issues in Criminal Justice* 43.

Johnstone, R 2004, *Occupational Health and Safety Law and Policy,* LawBook Co, Sydney.

Johnstone, R, Quinlan, M & and Walters, D 2005, 'Statutory Occupational Health and Safety Workplace Arrangements for the Modern Labour Market', 47 *Journal of Industrial Relations* 93.

Johnstone, R & Wilson, T 2006, 'Take Me to Your Employer', 19 *Australian Journal of Labour Law* 59.

Keashly, L & Neumann, JH 2004, 'Bullying in the Workplace: its impact and management', 8 *Employee Rights and Employment Policy Journal* 335.

Kelly, DJ 2006, 'Work Choices and Workplace Bullying', 6(2) *Journal of the Australian Society for the Study of Labour History* 32.

Kleiner, B & Whitmore, L 1998, 'Workplace Violence', 50 *Australian Company Secretary* 287.

Laibig, CE 1995, *Preventing Violence in the Workplace,* AMACOM, New York.

Mayhew, C & Chappell, D 2003, 'The Occupational Violence Experiences of Some Australian Health Workers: an exploratory study', 19 *Journal of Occupational Health and Safety* 3.

Mayhew, C & Chappell, D 2005, 'Violence in the Workplace', 183 *Medical Journal of Australia* 346.

McCallum, R 2000, 'A Robust National Industrial Relations System for Australia', *Business Council of Australia Forum,* 17 November.

McLean, B 1998, 'The Political Economy of Crime', 79 *Journal of Criminal Law and Criminology* 566.

Morgan Poll 1998, 9 June, Finding No 3091.

Nelson, L & Tanks, G 2004, 'Contextual Factors in Workplace Violence', 20 *Journal of Occupational Health and Safety: Australia and New Zealand* 115.

Norington, B 2007, 'Miners Attack BHP on AWAs', *The Australian*, 12 June.

Pavlich, G 2000, 'Just Promises: Tracing the Possible in Criminology', 11 *Current Issues in Criminal Justice* 327.

Quinlan, M & Mayhew, C 1999, 'Precarious Employment and Workers' Compensation', 22(5) *International Journal of Law and Psychiatry* 491.

Russell, B 1999, *Violence in the Workplace*, briefing document prepared by the Strategic Operation Group, WorkCover (NSW), Sydney.

Scheingold, SA 1998, 'Constructing the New Political Criminology: power, authority and the post-liberal state', 23 *Law and Social Inquiry* 857.

Simons, G 2004, 'Critical Criminology at the Edge: postmodern perspectives, integration and applications', 23 *Contemporary Sociology* 599.

Stuart, H & Milovanovich, D 1996 *Critical Criminology: beyond postmodernism,* Sage, London.

Thornton, M 2004, 'Corrosive Leadership: a corollary of the corporatised academy?', 17 *Australian Journal of Labour Law* 9.

Wakefield, H 2003, 'The Impact of Workplace Violence on Third Party Victims', *Australian E' Journal for the Advancement of Mental Health* 2.

WorkCover New South Wales 1999, *Workplace Violence: intervention strategies for your business,* WorkCover Corporation of NSW, Sydney.

WorkSafe Western Australia 1999, *Annual Report for 1998-1999*, Department for Consumer and Employment Protection, Perth.

PART IV

RESPONSES TO CRIME

17

KEY ISSUES IN A CRITICAL APPROACH TO POLICING

Jude McCulloch

Introduction

States and powerful actors like corporations commit far more serious and extensive crimes and harms than individuals or low status groups. Nevertheless criminology largely analyses crime and violence committed by individuals and low status groups with the result that crimes and harms committed by the state and the powerful are too frequently ignored (Green & Ward 2004; Tombs & Whyte 2003). In western countries, where the military has been largely confined to dealing with external enemies, the police are the primary agents of state harms and crimes domestically. A focus on police violence and abuse of power is consistent with critical criminology's interest in state crime and crimes of the powerful (Grewcock this volume). Analysing and understanding the genesis and impacts of police violence and abuse of power is also consistent with a broader critical focus on the way criminal justice systems work to mirror, maintain and reinforce social divisions and hierarchies based on race, ethnicity, class and gender.

Police are the primary interface between citizens and the law. Essentially they represent the law on the streets and have enormous potential to impact on the lives of those they encounter. As criminal justice 'gatekeepers', police profoundly define the activities, individuals and groups that are brought within the remit of the formal criminal justice system. Liberal and conservative approaches to studies of policing understand the police as neutral enforcers of the criminal law. Critical approaches acknowledge that the systematic exercise of police discretion works to shape the contours of what and who are understood and treated as crime and criminals. Police discretion is officially designed to ensure that the criminal law is applied with a degree of flexibility to avoid injustice. In reality, however, a large body of evidence demonstrates that discretion is regularly used in highly discriminatory ways, allowing groups low on the social hierarchy to be treated essentially as 'police property' (Reiner 1992: 118; Skolnick & Fyfe 1993).

Selective law enforcement leads to the overpolicing of low status groups who are targeted for surveillance and intervention. These groups experience close police attention as provocative – a situation that frequently leads to a negative spiral of mutual aggression and hostility. 'Street offences', crimes that result almost exclusively from encounters between police and those charged, provide police with the tools to engage in a form of social sorting that 'cleans up the streets' in favour of 'respectable' citizens and sanctioned commercial activities (see for example, Blagg & Wilke 1995; Fitzgerald 1989). Ultimately the assumption of high crime areas and crime prone groups that underlie overpolicing 'prove' themselves through criminalisation of socially and economically disadvantaged groups.

Selective law enforcement also encompasses underpolicing. The same groups that are overpoliced as potential offenders are overrepresented as victims of crime but frequently receive inadequate police service or protection. Additionally, the crimes that most typically include women and children as their primary victims, family violence and sexual assault, have traditionally not been seen as 'real' police work and, at least until recently, have been policed in ways that failed to respect and respond to the experience and needs of victims. The police response to these crimes worked to reinforce the status of women and children as male property, effectively placing many women and children outside the protection of the criminal law (Scutt 1990: 444-484).

Beyond selective and discriminatory law enforcement, police abuse of powers takes a number of forms, all of which are well documented in Australian scholarly literature, various Royal Commissions and official inquiries. These include verbal abuse, especially racist taunts, offensive remarks to women, physical and sexual intimidation, and the fabrication of evidence and charges (Human Rights and Equal Opportunity Commission (HREOC) 1991). Allegations of gratuitous brutality, excessive force, and the use of physical violence to coerce 'confessions', obtain information and silence complainants are among the most ubiquitous and serious of complaints made against police (Fitzgerald 1989; Wood 1997).

Police abuse of powers extends beyond the actions of a few 'bad apples'. Broader institutional, occupational, social, political, historical and economic factors influence the patterns of abuse. Police occupational culture is understood to have some distinguishing features that tend towards the widespread disregard for formal rules and the law. These include:

> its sense of mission; the desire for action and excitement, especially the glorification of violence; and Us/Them divisions of the social world with its in-group isolation and solidarity on the one hand, and racist components on the other; its authoritarian conservatism; and its suspicion and cynicism, especially towards the law and legal procedures (Waddington 1999: 287).

In considering the nature and impact of police culture it is important to keep in mind that the culture is not monolithic or immutable and does not exist in isolation from the rest of society (see Chan this volume). There are important divisions and differences in culture and approach within police organisations. Policing involves various degrees of specialisation and these are likely to give rise to a variety of distinct cultures. Differences in police culture also exist between jurisdictions and in the same jurisdiction over time. At another level, individual police exercise varying degrees of agency and may act beyond or against the norms of the prevailing occupational culture. Police leaders and the messages they send influence police culture (Dixon 1999; Chan 1997; James & Warren 1995). History is also significant in shaping the nature and patterns of police violence and abuse. Australia's colonial past, for example, including the police role in overcoming Indigenous resistance to occupation and removing Indigenous children from their families and communities continue to impact on police interactions with Indigenous people (Cunneen 2001).

Other relevant historical factors include Australia's convict past and the partisan role police played in industrial conflict and class conflict over land.

Political cultures are also important in facilitating or discouraging police violence and abuse. A repressive political context fuels police abuse of powers whereas more open democratic governments encourage greater police accountability and respect for the law. Social structure also plays a part in shaping police behaviour. There is also a relationship between the level of social inequality and the degree of impunity extended to police in dealing with those low on the social hierarchy (Green & Ward 2004: 78-79). Analysis and research of police issues needs to be grounded in the particulars of time and place, taking into account a range of relevant variables, while remaining aware of longstanding and widely recognised features of police culture that have been found to be influential in shaping the contours of police conduct.

Remedies

Formally, consistent with Australia's status as a liberal democracy, there are a range of sanctions and remedies for police abuse of police power. However, no precise line can easily be drawn between the day-to-day activities of police and police abuse of powers. Police discrimination in the form of selective law enforcement is hidden in routine and legitimised policing activities so that formal sanctions and remedies are often unavailable. In addition, as Grewcock (this volume) points out, there is 'a disjuncture between the rights that states proclaim to uphold and promote, and the often very limited protection or application of those rights'.

Police abuses that amount to crimes are theoretically open to sanction through the processes of the criminal law. This remedy is however rarely applied because police are 'gatekeepers' and reluctant to enforce the criminal law against fellow officers. When prosecutions are taken against police, police unions almost inevitably provide police defendants with resources well beyond the means of most private citizens. Moreover, the close relationship between police and government means that criminal processes against police are often subject to strong political pressure (Fitzgerald 1989; Wood 1997; Dixon 1999; Finnane 1994: 170-183). Finally, the public perception of police as 'good guys', means juries are often reluctant to convict.

All Australian jurisdictions have formal mechanisms to deal with complaints against police. Typically these involve a combination of police internal investigation overseen or supplemented by external oversight. A number of factors tend to undermine the effectiveness of these mechanisms, including lack of resources, lack of political commitment to substantive police accountability, and police internal solidarity. There is widespread cynicism about the ability of the complaints systems to deliver justice. As one criminal lawyer put it:

> [T]here is not much substance to the [complaints] process ... processes all sound very well and good but when you actually look behind what's actually happening ... the investigations ... just go across the surface (quoted in McCulloch & Palmer 2005: 97).

The police 'code of silence' has long been understood as a problematic feature of police accountability. John Klenig notes:

> An "us" develops and is cultivated that distinguishes itself from the "them" [suspects and the community] ... such solidarity, often characterised in familial terms

manifests itself in forms of loyal support for fellow officers that are sometimes heroic, sometimes foolhardy, and sometimes unconscionable ... It is [a] cover up, the blue code, wall or veil of silence ... The unwillingness of police to speak about excessive force or other abuses of authority not only subverts the process of accountability but probably also contributes to the likelihood of deviance (Klenig 2000: 222-223).

In the face of ineffective complaints mechanisms and the difficulties in bringing criminal charges against police there has been a move towards the greater use of civil actions. These actions are initiated privately and thus outside the influence police exert on the criminal justice system. A number of plaintiffs have successfully sued police and been awarded significant compensation after having had their formal complaints dismissed. However, successful civil actions require considerable material and psychological resources that are available to plaintiffs in only a small minority of cases (McCulloch 2002; McCulloch & Palmer 2005).

Official inquiries, Royal Commissions and, in cases of a death, coronial inquests, also provide potential avenues for police accountability. Each, however, encounter formidable hurdles. Police are a strong and effective political lobby group, generally enjoying a close and mutually supportive relationship with the media. Police are influential in shaping popular ideas about crime and law enforcement so that effective accountability measures are frequently portrayed by police as undermining their ability to fight crime by playing into the hands of criminals. Consequently, robust accountability structures and processes often run afoul of political pressures (Freckelton 1991).

All available remedies provide an inadequate basis for challenging police abuse of powers. However, in a limited number of cases some redress is achieved, and Royal Commissions and coronial inquests have on occasion brought to light patterns of police abuse that led to significant reforms. History demonstrates that pressure for change instigated through diverse legal, media and political strategies can lead to positive changes in police behaviour but can often take many years to achieve and are inevitably subject to challenges and set backs.

Case Study: fatal police shootings in Victoria

The events and circumstances surrounding a spate of fatal shootings by police in Victoria from the late 1980s through to the mid 1990s provide a useful case study in police use of force, police culture, accountability and reform. Fatal shootings by police reside at the extreme end of police use of force and power with consequences that are irreversible. Police shootings are the single most controversial policing issue in Victoria over past decades. While other state police forces have been involved in shooting controversies, Victoria stands alone in terms of sheer numbers. In 1994 the then Chief Commissioner wrote:

There have been an extraordinary number of fatal shootings by police officers in this state. I believe we have reached the point where we must reconsider our position and reassess the impact that this level of force has on the relationship that we have with the community (quoted in McCulloch 2001: 92).

Fatal shootings by Victoria Police became a major public issue with a sharp escalation in the number of such shootings in the late 1980s. In the two years between 1987 and 1989 Victoria Police fatally shot 11 people, compared with only 10 fatal police shootings in the previous 13 years. The number of fatal shootings by police in Victoria was also disproportionate with those in other states. Between 1984 and 1995 the Victoria Police shot and killed just over twice as many people as all other police forces in Australia. In this 11-year period there were 35 police shooting fatalities in Victoria compared to 34 in other states and territories. In the first nine months of 1994 alone, there were twice as many fatal police shootings in Victoria as in the previous six years in New South Wales (McCulloch 2001: 100). In addition, between 1990 and 1995 police in Victoria shot and killed seven people with histories of mental illness, compared with five such shootings in all other states and territories combined (McCulloch 2001: 100).

Controversy over fatal shootings by police in Victoria was fuelled not only by the statistics but also by the circumstances of some of the shootings. In two cases police were suspected of planting firearms on the deceased to support self-defence claims. There was also suspicion that two men shot and killed by police were executed as pay back for the murder of two police constables in 1988. In a number of instances the deceased were shot in the back or from the rear. On three separate occasions police claim to have mistaken another object for a firearm. In one instance, knife wounds suffered by a police officer, allegedly caused by the deceased before he was shot, were, according to some expert opinion, self-inflicted. Two eye-witnesses to one fatal police shooting denied police claims that the deceased was wielding a knife in each hand when she was shot (McCulloch 2001: 108-109).

Suspicion surrounding the legality of some fatal shootings was heightened by the inadequacy of the investigations carried out by police. Senior police frequently made comments supporting officers involved in fatal shootings soon after the shootings. Typically within a few hours of a shooting senior police declared the shootings justified despite little or no investigation having taken place. In addition, the media, relying on information from police, frequently carried misinformation about the circumstances of the shootings, omitting problematic facts and including information, much of it false, which put the deceased in the worst possible light (McCulloch 1996, 2001: 109).

Over time, however, families of the deceased, along with legal, community, and church groups succeeded in creating pressure for reform. A special series of coronial inquests was established in 1990. Public concern peaked in September 1994 with the fatal shooting of an Indigenous woman with a history of mental illness. She was shot four times, including three times in the back. Public anxiety was such that the Chief Commissioner and the Minister for Police wrote an open letter to the public stating that:

> For the Victoria Police the issue of police shootings has led to a massive rethink on the handling of operations ... The concerns of the Victorian community about police shootings have been heard by Victoria Police (quoted McCulloch 2001: 100).

The 1993 decision by the Victorian Director of Public Prosecutions (DPP) to charge 10 Victoria Police and one former officer over the fatal shootings of two men demonstrated that police cannot always rely on being above the law. Subsequent events, however, highlight the difficulties involved in using the criminal law against police. Within 12 months of announcing the charges, the DPP was embroiled in a major dispute with the state government over moves to undermine his independence. Police displeasure over the shooting-related charges was a major factor in precipitating the government's action. Changes to the DPP's position eventually prompted his resignation. His replacement dropped the charges against all but three of the police officers and significantly scaled down the prosecution. The police officers eventually tried over the killings were found not guilty (McCulloch et al 1994; McCulloch 2001: 110-111).

It was not only the legality of the police shootings, however, that was at issue but also their necessity. Police are obliged to use only minimum force against offenders and suspects, unlike the military who may use overwhelming force to defeat or kill an enemy. A significant proportion of fatal shootings in Victoria involved members of the Special Operations Group (SOG). The SOG is a paramilitary group that incorporates military philosophy, training and weapons into law enforcement. SOG training is geared towards teaching members how to shoot first and survive armed confrontations, rather than how to avoid confrontation and risk to life wherever possible. Paramilitary groups tend to cultivate an extreme version of traditional police culture, placing a premium on physical strength and group solidarity. The police sense of mission, danger and social isolation are all heightened in the ranks of the SOG, where all but the fittest, strongest and most highly motivated are excluded (McCulloch 2001: 116-149). The high fatal police shooting toll in Victoria between late 1980 and mid 1990 is best explained by the integration and normalisation of SOG philosophy and tactics into everyday policing. This normalisation occurred on a number of levels but most specifically through the elevation of former members of the SOG to force-wide firearms training positions so that confrontational military style of firearms tactics became accepted as 'best practice'. As a result of this training police became confident shooters but gained no countervailing confidence in less lethal alternatives (McCulloch 2001: 150-173).

Delivering his finding into the series of fatal shooting inquests in 1994 the Coroner maintained that the:

> policy of the Victoria Police Force and its SOG accepts ... the use of force, forced entry, consequential firearms confrontation, consequential instinctive use of police firearms with legal justification, consequential personal risk to police members exposed to a person with a gun and consequentially and ultimately condones shooting by police members with legal justification (quoted in McCulloch 2001: 148).

Eventually in the mid 1990s Project Beacon was implemented to retrain police in firearm's use. The Project aimed to balance communication, conflict resolution and incident planning with firearms and defensive tactics training. It succeeded in reducing the rate of fatal shootings (McCulloch 2001: 101-102). This experience is similar to that in the United States where intense public criticism over fatal shootings by police translated into reforms and a decline in the number of shootings by police (Green & Ward 2004: 81). While the reforms were largely positive some were problematic. The focus on reducing resort to firearms created an opportunity for the introduction of capsicum spray as a standard police weapon. Although the spray was originally justified as an alternative to firearms it is mainly used in situations where firearms would never be used; it is in some cases fatal, and it is itself prone to abuse. Since its introduction in Victoria it has been adopted by police throughout Australia (McCulloch 2000).

The Victorian reforms in the police approach to firearms were underlined and reinforced by the appointment of Australia's first and, to date, only female Chief Commissioner in 2001. The new Chief Commissioner heralded a move away from the crime fighting model that underpins confrontational styles of policing towards more community oriented policing embracing social cohesion and enhancing rights as key aims (Victoria Police 2001-2002: 5; Prenzler 2004: 306). While the influence of paramilitary policing in Victoria was reigned in as a result of firearms reforms and consolidated with a change in policing philosophy the integration of military styles of policing into everyday policing is an issue that needs to be understood as part of a broader trend.

Counter-terrorism policing

The development of a national counter-terrorism framework in the 1970s formed the basis for the incremental integration of national security into law enforcement. The integration of national security into law enforcement provided the platform for the introduction of higher levels of force into policing and a shift in philosophy away from a focus on individual offenders towards pre-empting perceived threats by groups constructed as enemies.

Australia, like other western democracies, had until this point maintained a strict demarcation between national security and law enforcement. Under Australia's constitution and democratic traditions, the military were responsible for external defence and the police were responsible for internal security. Part of the national counter-terrorism framework included the establishment of paramilitary counter-terrorism units, like the SOG, in state police forces in the mid 1970s (McCulloch 2001: 68-91). These units straddled the line between the police and military, blurring the distinction between the two organisations (Jefferson 1990; Kraska & Kappeler 1997).

Despite the strong social tradition against the use of the military in internal defence or law enforcement and the original designation of paramilitary groups as counter-terrorist groups, the paramilitary police groups were subsequently used in a wider range of police operations and spread their influence, in Victoria at least, through involvement in the training of other state based police. During the three decades up to the end of the 20th century, the paramilitary groups became normalised into state police forces, creating a platform for increased integration and links between the police and the military, including joint training, exercises and detailed contingencies plans for the use of the military in internal defence (McCulloch 2001).

Policing post-9/11

Changes to Australia's counter-terrorism framework post-9/11 have extended the integration of law enforcement into national security in ways that are likely to reinvigorate and extend the influence of paramilitary policing. Community policing has been adopted throughout Australia as a reform (Australasian Police Ministers' Council 2005: 1-3). While community policing is difficult to define, it is broadly understood to encompass a variety of arrangement that involve non-coercive engagement with the community under the auspice of programs such as partnership policing, neighbourhood policing, reassurance policing and problem-orientated policing (Edwards 2005: 79; Seagrave 1996: 6). Writing about the challenges counter-terrorism potentially poses to community policing, Murray (2005: 348) maintains that:

> The threat of terrorism that exists today will test the resolve of police commissioners who choose to retain community policing as a dominant policing philosophy. In this new environment, there is no doubt the effectiveness of community policing will be challenged and some will rationalise it away as being too soft to match the so-called 'war against terror'.

The counter-terrorism legal framework also threatens to intensify coercive and discriminatory styles of policing and undermine already inadequate police accountability. Police powers have been greatly expanded under the counter-terrorism legislative framework. New powers are aimed principally at preventing terrorism by anticipating the risk of terrorism (see for example, McCulloch & Carlton 2006). This development amplifies the already established trend in relation to risk-based crime control policies (O'Malley this volume). Counter-terrorism laws have shifted policing focus even further away from investigating crime towards monitoring and disrupting the activities of local 'suspect communities'. Before 9/11, Lucia Zedner (2000: 210) wrote:

> Whereas traditional modes of punishment focused attention on the individual wrongdoer, on the determination of their guilt and on punishment, attention is now increasingly turned to a target population of potential wrongdoers. The means by which this population is identified is wholly unscientific, relying on class prejudice and drawing on questionable presumptions about people's lifestyles and habits.

Ideas and stereotypes about 'race', religion and ethnicity fuel attempts to identify and pre-empt the risk of terrorism. There has been little headway made in efforts to develop predictive behavioural or characteristic profiles for counter-terrorist purposes. In the absence of meaningful indicators that correlate statistically with terrorist conduct, 'race', ethnicity and/or religion are being used as proxies for risk and used as the basis for a wide range of law enforcement decisions (Goldston 2006). In 2005, the Police Federation of Australia requested new legislation to indemnify police against civil lawsuits for using racial profiling under new counter-terrorism laws (Kearney 2005). While racial, religious and/or ethnic profiling is ineffective and even counter productive in identifying potential terrorists, similar to selective law enforcement, such profiles reflect and reinforce popular preconceptions about what and who represent a threat, advancing the criminalisation of those ethnic and religious minorities stereotyped as terrorists.

Intelligence is particularly important in predicting and pre-empting threats and risks. Evidence is gathered to investigate crime and bring offenders to trial. Intelligence is gathered in order to predict risk and as the basis for extrajudicial police action. The contemporary counter-terrorism framework blends intelligence with evidence and security with law enforcement in unprecedented ways. Police coercive powers are now linked to intelligence. Post-9/11 there has been a substantial increase in powers to police and intelligence agencies which have the effect of expanding opportunities for overt and covert surveillance, monitoring and searching (Lyon 2003).

The Australian Security Intelligence Organisation (ASIO) now has unprecedented coercive powers to question and detain. Under these new powers people can be compulsorily detained and questioned even if they are not suspected of any crime, let alone terrorist activity. The secrecy surrounding ASIO's operations means that these powers come with few of the usual oversights or remedies that accompany regular police powers. Providing a secret intelligence agency with coercive powers means Australia for the first time has 'secret police', of the kind more often associated with totalitarian regimes (McCulloch & Tham 2005).

Recently enacted counter-terrorism preventive detention and control orders radically expand police powers beyond the remit of the traditional criminal justice processes. Under these new powers police can detain people and restrict their movements and activities for extended periods of time without evidence of any criminal activity and without trial and conviction. Intelligence, which may amount to no more than innuendo, gossip or suspicions fuelled by animosity or prejudice, and which is not subject to rigorous testing in open court, is the basis for the exercise of these new police powers (Lynch & Williams 2006: 41-58).

Expanded police powers to prevent terrorism are promoted as a reasonable balance of liberty and security in light of new threats. The threat that is addressed however is only partial in that it ignores or downplays a number of significant risks. The first of these is the risk born by 'suspect communities'. Coercive police action based on fallible intelligence will result in false positives where people innocent of any wrongdoing are subject to police powers including various levels of force and coercion. These false positives will not be spread randomly throughout the population but will instead cluster in 'suspect communities' where the bulk of police attention is focused. Pre-emptive counter-terrorism policing and some of the risks that it animates were demonstrated in the killing of Brazilian Jean Charles de Menezes after the London bombings in July 2005. Falsely suspected on the basis of faulty intelligence of being a suicide bomber, he was gunned down by police on the London underground on his way to work (McCulloch & Sentas 2006). His killing highlights the reality that while risks are speculative police coercion and force is immediate, non-negotiable and sometimes fatal.

Some argue that the balance between liberty and security is in reality a 'proposal to trade off the liberties of a few against the security of the majority' (Waldron 2003: 196). The issue however is more fundamental that this. The liberty versus security equation fails to take into account the risk that accompanies alienating 'suspect communities' through pre-emptive police action. Such communities are less likely to share vital information about potential or suspected threats with police. Beyond this, police coercion may play a part in fuelling a new generation of risks by increasing support for political violence and recruitment to terrorist causes (Hillyard 2005; Cole 2003:189-197; Lyons 2002). Security policing based on social exclusion ultimately makes everybody less secure.

Conclusion

Critical criminology pays close attention to the genesis and dynamics of police abuse of power, recognising that no clear line can be drawn between the normal everyday practices of police and those activities that are formally understood as abuse of power. Formally illegal police abuse of power, like other state crimes, is responsible for a range of significant harms that are largely denied and rarely responded to or analysed as crimes. Examining and analysing the dynamic of police violence and abuse and the responses to it inevitably proves revealing not only in terms of policing but also in relation to the political, social and economic terrain in which policing takes place. Selective law enforcement has been integral in perpetuating divisions based on 'race', ethnicity, class, and gender. It succeeds in obscuring the extent and nature of the harms perpetrated by powerful actors and obscuring the extent to which police violence and abuse contribute to the insecurity, suffering and the diminished life chances of those often already struggling on the margins of society.

Counter-terrorism policing formalises the self fulfilling prophesy of selective law enforcement and criminalisation by extending and consolidating the coercive policing attached to notions of what and who constitute risk. If as O'Malley (this volume) argues, 'risked based policies in crime control have shifted the burden of risk from victims to offenders', then counter-terrorism policing shifts the risk from *imagined* victims 'us' to *imagined* offenders 'them'. The integration of national security into law enforcement redraws and fortifies the imaginary border between the community to be protected and those they are to be protected from.

It is worth however heeding the caution against 'catastrophic forecasts' related to transformations in justice and modes of policing based on risk (Zedner quoted in O'Malley this volume). Because policing is intimately connected to politics and society it is not immutable or inevitable. Family violence and sexual assault are policed differently today because of longstanding campaigns by feminists to improve the position of women and to recognise these crimes against women as 'real crimes'. The police shootings toll in Victoria was ultimately reduced because the community rejected such events as a reasonable price for 'law and order'. Similarly in the 'war on terror' there is evidence in Australia and internationally of growing recognition of the myriad human costs in terms of proliferating insecurities for targeted communities and the broader community that arise from creating 'suspect communities' in the 'war on terror' (Innes 2006). Critical criminologists in their research and understanding of policing are working to articulate these costs in an effort to move beyond practises of security based on social exclusion so that ultimately 'our' security is not based on the insecurity and suffering of the 'other' (see Burke 2001).

References

Australasian Police Ministers' Council 2005, *Directions in Australasian Policing: 2005-2008*, November 2005, Australian Police Minister's Council, Canberra.

Blagg, H & Wilke, M 1995, *Young People and Police Powers,* Australian Youth Foundation, Sydney.

Burke, A 2001, *In Fear of Security: Australia's invasion anxiety,* Pluto Press, Sydney.

Chan, J 1997, *Changing Police Culture: policing in a multicultural society,* Cambridge University Press, Melbourne.

Cole, D 2003, *Enemy Aliens: double standards and constitutional freedoms in the war on terrorism,* The New Press, New York.

Cunneen, C 2001, *Conflict Politics and Crime: Aboriginal communities and the police*, Allen & Unwin, Sydney.

Dixon, D (ed) 1999, *A Culture of Corruption: changing an Australian police service* Hawkins Press, Sydney.

Edwards, C 2005, *Changing Police: theories for 21st century societies,* Federation Press, Sydney.

Finnane, M 1994, *Police and Government: histories of policing in Australia,* Oxford University Press, Melbourne.

Fitzgerald, G 1989, *Report of the Commission of Possible Illegal Activities and Associated Police Misconduct,* Queensland Government Printer, Brisbane.

Freckelton, I 1991, 'Shooting the Messenger: the trial and execution of the Victorian Police Complaints Authority', in Goldsmith, A (ed), *Complaints Against Police: the trend towards external review,* Clarendon Press, Oxford.

Goldston, J 2006, *Ethnic Profiling and Counter-Terrorism: trends, dangers and alternatives,* Paper to Anti-Racism and Diversity Intergroup, European Parliament, 6 June 2006.

Green, P & Ward, T 2004, *State Crime: governments, violence and corruption,* Pluto Press, London.

Hillyard, P 2005, *The 'War on Terror': lessons from Ireland,* <www.ecln.org/essays/essays-1.pdf>.

Human Rights and Equal Opportunity Commission (HREOC), 1991, *Report of the National Inquiry into Racist Violence in Australia,* Australian Government Publishing Service, Canberra.

Innes, M 2006, 'Policing Uncertainty: countering terror through community intelligence and democratic policing', 605(1) *The ANNALS of the American Academy* 222.

James, S & Warren, I 1995, 'Police Culture', in Bessant, J, Carrington, C & Cook, S (eds), *Cultures of Crime and Violence: the Australian experience,* La Trobe University Press, Bundoora.

Jefferson, T 1990, *The Case against Paramilitary Policing,* Open University Press, Philadelphia.

Kearney, S 2005, 'Police Alarm on Racial Profiling', *The Australian,* 27 September.

Klenig, J 2000, 'Police Violence and the Loyal Code of Silence', in Cody, T, James, S, Miller, S & O'Keefe, M (eds), *Violence and Police Culture,* Melbourne University Press, Melbourne.

Kraska, P & Kappeler, V 1997, 'Militarizing American police: the rise and normalization of paramilitary units', 44 *Social Problems* 1.

Lynch, A & Williams, G 2006, *What Price Security: taking stock of Australia's anti-terror laws,* UNSW Press, Sydney.

Lyon, D 2003, *Surveillance after September 11,* Polity Press, Cambridge.

Lyons, W 2002, 'Partnerships, Information and Public Safety: community policing in a time of terror', 25 *Policing: an international journal of police strategies & management* 530.

McCulloch, J, Connellan, G & Isles, A 1994, 'Putting the Politics back into Prosecutions', 19(2) *Alternative Law Journal* 78.

McCulloch, J 1996, 'Blue Murder: press coverage of fatal police shootings', 29 *Australian and New Zealand Journal of Criminology* 102.

McCulloch, J 2000, 'Capsicum Spray: safe alternative or dangerous chemical weapon?', 7 *Journal of Law and Medicine* 311.

McCulloch, J 2001, *Blue Army: paramilitary policing in Australia,* Melbourne University Press, Melbourne.

McCulloch, J 2002, 'Civil Actions Against police', in Prenzler, T (ed), *Corruption and Reform in Australian Policing,* Federation Press, Sydney.

McCulloch, J & Palmer, D 2005, *Civil Litigation against Police by Citizens between 1994-2002,* <www.aic.gov.au/crc/reports/200102-19.html>.

McCulloch, J & Tham, J 2005, 'Secret State, Transparent Subject: the Australian Security Intelligence Organisation in the age of terror', 38(3) *Australian and New Zealand Journal of Criminology* 400.

McCulloch, J & Carlton, B 2006, 'Pre-empting Justice: suppression of financing of terrorism and the "War on Terror"', 17(3) *Current Issues in Criminal Justice* 397.

McCulloch, J & Sentas, V 2006, 'The Killing of Jean Charles de Menezes', 32 *Social Justice* 92.

Murray, J 2005, 'Policing Terrorism: a threat to community policing or just a shift in priorities?', 6(4) *Police Practice and Research* 347.

Prenzler, T 2004, 'Chief Commissioner Christine Nixon, Victoria: Australia's first female Police Chief', 5(4/5) Poli*ce Practice and Research* 301.

Reiner, R 1992, *The Politics of the Police*, Harvester & Wheatsheaf, New York.

Scutt, J 1990, *Women and the Law: commentary and materials*, The LawBook Co, Sydney.

Seagrave, J 1996, 'Defining Community Policing', 15 *American Journal of Police* 1.

Skolnick, J & Fyfe, J 1993, *Above the Law: police and the excessive use of force*, The Free Press, New York.

Tombs, S & Whyte, D 2003, 'Scrutinizing the Powerful: crime, contemporary political economy, and critical social research', in Tombs, S & Whyte, D (eds), *Unmasking the Crimes of the Powerful: scrutinizing states and corporations*, Peter Lang, New York.

Victoria Police 2001-2002, *Annual Report*, Melbourne.

Waddington, PAJ 1999, *Policing Citizens*, UCL Press, London.

Waldron, J 2003, 'Security and Liberty: the image of balance', 11 *Journal of Political Philosophy* 191.

Wood, JRT 1997, *Final Report of the Royal Commission into the NSW Police Service Vol 1: Corruption*, RCNSWPS, Sydney.

Zedner, L 2000, 'The Pursuit of Security', in Hope, T & Sparks, R (eds), *Crime, Risk and Insecurity*, Routledge, London.

18

POLICE CULTURE: A BRIEF HISTORY OF A CONCEPT

Janet Chan

Introduction

Over time every occupation develops its own set of knowledge, expertise, ways of working, rituals, vocabulary, sensibilities and even body language. These special modes of operation, language and traditions are often loosely referred to as the 'culture' of a particular occupation. In the criminal justice system, one group of workers – the public police – has been singled out for attention in criminology and the term 'police culture' is frequently used as shorthand for the occupational culture of police officers. This fascination with police culture has a great deal to do with the role and special powers of police officers and the negative publicity police culture has received. The culture of other professionals within the criminal justice system – judicial officers, lawyers and correctional officers – though equally worthy of attention, has simply not been the subject of as much research and writing.

In this chapter, I will provide a brief history of the concept of police culture and explain why it has become an important issue. For this I will draw on the key literature that has discussed police culture in the past and introduce some recent thinking and research on the subject. In the final section, I will discuss the implications of this new understanding of police culture for critical criminology.

Features of Police Culture

Early accounts of police culture originated from ethnographic studies of routine police work, usually by academic researchers (for example, Skolnick 1966; Ericson 1982, 1993) and occasionally by former police officers (for example, Holdaway 1983; Young 1991). Readers should be aware, however, that these accounts are almost always based on *street-level* police officers in Western democracies, usually English-speaking countries, and are therefore not readily generalisable to police performing other duties or those working in non-Western, developing or post-conflict nation states (see Brogden & Shearing 1993 and Marks 2005 for analyses of South African police cultures).

Researchers have identified a number of key features of police culture. Skolnick (1966) suggests that police have a distinctive 'working personality'; as a group they have developed special rules, customs, values, perceptions and judgements that guide them in their work (Skolnick & Fyfe 1993). Manning and Van Maanen (1978) see police culture as consisting of rules of thumb, a special language, and a set of shared values and customs that underpin how officers relate to each other and to the public. Police culture also encompasses a host of basic assumptions about the role of the police and judgements about people (Manning 1978).

Reiner's (2000: ch 3) review of the literature summarises the characteristics of police culture as follows. Police often have a sense of mission about their work: they see themselves as the 'thin blue line' between order and chaos. They are also 'adrenalin addicts', often delighting in the thrills of action and chase. Many have developed a cynical view of their social environment, a constantly suspicious attitude, and an isolated social life with a strong sense of solidarity with other police officers. Police also tend to categorise the public into the 'rough' and the 'respectable'. Police are usually conservative in politics and morality; their culture is sexist and prejudiced against ethnic minorities. Police also hold a pragmatic view of police work, which discourages innovation and experimentation.

Another well-known aspect of police culture is the apparent 'code of silence' and solidarity among police officers when faced with allegations of misconduct (Westley 1970). The code, according to Skolnick and Fyfe (1993: 110), is typically enforced 'by the threat of shunning, by fear that *informing* will lead to exposure of one's own derelictions, and by fear that colleagues' assistance may be withheld in emergencies' (emphasis in original). Officers interviewed in Chan, Devery and Doran (2003: 259) gave vivid accounts of how this code worked:

> [A]n officer who complained against another police is regarded as 'dangerous' because he or she could get others into trouble. The initial fear has more to do with not wanting to be punished for 'stuffing up' (making mistakes), but it evolves into a form of solidarity and a strategy of ostracism against those who make complaints. ... [T]he consequences of 'dobbing in your mate' are such that the complainant, even if not ostracised outright, would always carry the stigma and fellow officers would not 'stick their neck out for you'.

The masculine culture of police forces was taken for granted by early studies, since most officers at that time were male. The gradual increase in the proportion of female officers in recent decades has not, on the whole, made much difference to this masculine culture. Even with the passage of anti-discrimination laws and the introduction of equal employment opportunity policies in many jurisdictions, policing is still generally regarded as 'a man's job' (Appier 1998; Heidensohn 1992; Martin 1999). Doran and Chan (2003) describe how female recruits in the longitudinal study implicitly accepted that physicality was an essential part of police work, so that even though they expected to receive equal treatment as male recruits when they first joined the police, over time many saw male protectiveness of women in the job as 'only natural' and sexist jokes as 'harmless fun' that both sexes engaged in.

There is a well-recognised distinction between the 'street cop culture' and the 'management cop culture' (Reuss-Ianni & Ianni 1983). 'Street cops', or operational officers at the street level, often see management as being out of touch with the reality of policing, while 'management cops' are concerned with making the police more professional, efficient and responsive. Police officers interviewed in Chan et al (2003) told researchers that they felt the need to protect each other against the police organisation, a need that grew out of the fear of getting into trouble for minor mistakes and a sense of cynicism against management. One consequence of the fear of mistakes and lack of trust in management is the development of a 'cover your arse' approach to work (Van Maanen 1978; Chan et al 2003).

Police culture is often regarded as the product of the demands of police work. Skolnick (1966) sees the 'working personality' as a response to the danger of police work, the authority of the police constable, and the pressure to be productive and efficient. Reiner (2000) similarly suggests that the 'cop culture' has developed as a way to help police cope with the pressure of police work. For example, police officers' sense of solidarity with each other comes from their need to be able to rely on the support of their workmates in dangerous or difficult situations. Similarly, officers interviewed in Chan et al (2003: 250) said that working in the police was 'like being in a family', but the bond between officers were stronger than family bonds because 'only other police understand what you go through at work'. As a result, officers developed a strong sense of trust in their fellow police, a trust they regarded as essential for teamwork.

In the same vein Van Maanen (1978) suggests that police cynicism is developed over time after arbitrating numerous disputes among citizens who regularly try to shift blame on others. Police also develop a hard 'shell' to protect themselves from the 'misery and degradation' they regularly experience while 'doing society's dirty work' (1978: 120). Police officers interviewed in Chan et al (2003:255) similarly mentioned the need to develop a 'shell' or a front to cope with the pain and abuse of the job and to manage their emotions in order not to 'end up a basket case'.

Police culture is said to be similar across jurisdictions. Referring to studies in the United States, Europe and Asia, Skolnick and Fyfe (1993: 92) observe that the 'fundamental culture of policing is everywhere similar … [since] the same features of the police role – danger, authority, and the mandate to use coercive force – are everywhere present'. However, there is an abundance of research evidence that cultural differences exist between police forces (Reiner 2000; Wilson 1968), between police officers at different rank (Chan 1997; Reuss-Ianni & Ianni 1983), in different work roles (Foster 2003) and with different orientations to the job (Reiner 2000; Muir 1977; Shearing 1981).

Police culture is also said to show a 'remarkable stability' over time: in spite of repeated reforms, the tightening of controls, the introduction of new technologies, and the recruitment of better educated officers, the 'old habits and traditions' of street level policing has 'survived largely intact' (Manning & Van Maanen 1978: 267). Nevertheless, elements of police culture have been vulnerable to change over time. For example, advances in information and communications technology have dramatically changed aspects of the structure and culture of policing (Ericson & Haggerty 1997; Chan et al 2001). Similarly, major reforms in police accountability can weaken the 'code of silence' but reinforce the 'cover your arse' culture (Chan 2007).

Linking culture with misconduct

Why has police culture been an issue in criminology? Simply put, the main reason is that police culture has often been linked with police misconduct and corruption. In

Australia, the Fitzgerald Inquiry in the late 1980s first linked police culture to the toleration of police corruption. The Inquiry found that within the Queensland Police Force at the time, there was a culture of 'contempt for the criminal justice system, disdain for the law and rejection of its application to police, disregard for the truth, and abuse of authority' (Fitzgerald Report 1989: 200). Fitzgerald (1989: 202-203) emphasised that the 'unwritten police code' was a 'critical factor in the deterioration of the Police Force': 'The police code ... requires that police not enforce the law against other police, nor co-operate in any attempt to do so, and perhaps even obstruct any such attempt'.

Fitzgerald (1989: 211) also suggested that new recruits who joined the police were often socialised into the police culture and as a result they became part of the 'brotherhood', protecting corrupt cops and condoning illegal behaviours:

> Naturally, after a very short time in the Police Force, young people lose any sense of perspective on the culture of which they have become part. Fellow police and police work define their self-image, their attitude to society and their place within it. Peer pressure becomes overwhelming and is supported by other factors.

Police racism is another issue that has been linked to police culture. Because police have enormous discretionary powers in their work – powers to stop, question, move on, search and arrest people – their values and attitudes, ways of working and the assumptions they hold (in other words, their culture) can affect how the law is enforced. In Australia, there have been concerns about the over-policing and over-representation of Indigenous people in the criminal justice system (Human Rights and Equal Opportunity Commission (HREOC) 1991; Cunneen & Robb 1987), harassment of young people from ethnic minorities and Aboriginal communities (Youth Justice Coalition of New South Wales 1990; HREOC 1991; O'Neill & Bathgate 1993), instances of violent or intimidatory police practices against young Aboriginal and ethnic youths (HREOC 1991), as well as differential treatment of Aboriginal children by the juvenile justice system (Luke & Cunneen 1995). Although the underlying issues can be complex, discriminatory practices and over-policing may be a direct result of the structural and cultural organisation of police work (see Chan 1997).

Police culture is often regarded as an obstacle to police reform, though there is no suggestion that misconduct is involved. Often reforms are resisted or subverted because officers simply carry on as before, ignoring new laws or procedures introduced to improve police practice. Manning and Van Maanen (1978: 267) have long observed that 'there are powerful means available within the occupation that act to systematically discourage innovation while they encourage the status quo'. Brogden and Shearing (1993: 96) similarly noted that 'police culture has been commonly depicted as the major impediment to [South African Police] transformation' in post-apartheid South Africa.

Is Police Culture a useful concept?

A focus on culture has the distinct advantage of not limiting our understanding of police conduct by resorting simply to psychological and individualistic explanations. For example, a cultural explanation of police corruption would steer away from the 'bad apple' theory and look for telltale signs in the working habits, values and ethos of police officers that may breed or condone corruption. For example, the Mollen Report (1994: 1-2) referred to the police culture, rather than individual corrupt officers, as a key factor in understanding the extent of police corruption in New York City:

> What we found is that the problem of police corruption extends far beyond the corrupt cop. It is a multi-faceted problem that has flourished in parts of our City not only because of opportunity and greed, but because of a police culture that exalts loyalty over integrity; because of the silence of honest officers who fear the consequences of 'ratting' on another cop no matter how grave the crime; because of wilfully blind supervisors who fear the consequences of a corruption scandal more than corruption itself; because of the demise of the principle of accountability that makes all commanders responsible for fighting corruption in their commands; because of a hostility and alienation between the police and community in certain precincts which breeds an 'Us versus Them' mentality; and because for years the New York City Police Department abandoned its responsibility to insure the integrity of its members.

Similarly, a cultural explanation of police racism would not simply rely on identifying individual officers who are racially prejudiced. Rather, it would broaden the search for explanations to discriminatory language, values and behaviour that are routinely used and accepted by police officers as a group.

Thus, police culture provides a broader perspective for understanding police practice and police malpractice, but like other cultural explanations, the use of police culture to understand police practice can be quite limited. This is because the term 'culture' is often used in a static and functionalist sense. For example, a standard definition of organisational culture given by an eminent organisational theorist is as follows:

> [Culture is] a pattern of basic assumptions – invented, discovered, or developed by a given group as it learns to cope with its problems of external adaptation and internal integration – that has worked well enough to be considered valid and, therefore, to be taught to new members as the correct way to perceive, think, and feel in relation to those problems (Schein 1985: 9; emphasis removed).

Therefore, according to this standard definition, culture is something that has been developed over a long period of time; it serves a particular function (internal integration and external adaptation) and is taught to the next generation of workers, so that it is likely to remain the same unless there are sudden and dramatic changes in the internal and external environment.

However, policing is an occupation that is experiencing a great deal of social, cultural and technological change. With the globalisation of security threats, advances in communications and biotechnology and the phenomenal growth of private policing, the stability of police culture can no longer be taken for granted. Even the transmission of police culture from one generation to the next is not a straightforward or predictable task, especially when the police organisation and its environment are undergoing major changes (Chan et al 2003).

Cultural explanations also present problems for policy-makers and managers. If culture is something embraced by members of a group and the glue that binds them together, it can be very difficult to change because it is a 'deep phenomenon' (Schein 1985). Attempts at cultural change do not always yield the intended consequences. In fact, cultural explanations are usually flawed because they tend to downplay the agency of members of the group even though individual officers often exercise judgement in deciding what they want to do (Fielding 1988; Chan et al 2003). Of course, there are group dynamics involved and members do often strive to be accepted and respected by others in the group. But police culture is a defence mechanism and a support system developed by police themselves so that they can carry out their work; it is not something imposed from above or externally (see Chan et al 2003).

So in many ways police culture is not a very useful concept for explaining police conduct or misconduct, although the term has had a long history of usage and is a succinct way of capturing values, norms, and perspectives within a relatively homogeneous group. An analogous situation can be found in our general use of the concept of culture. For example, 'Chinese culture' is often used as a shorthand for designating certain traditions, values, rituals, beliefs and preferences, but anyone who knows the history of China and Chinese people would be quick to point out that there is not a single, monolithic Chinese culture. Not only does it vary by geographical location and history, Chinese culture encompasses many ethnic subcultures and is evolving and recreated continuously in a globalised world, so that increasingly the term has very little relevance as an indicator for a distinct set of values and customs. Police culture may be similarly losing its usefulness as a concept if the occupation continues to change and diversify.

New thinking on Police Culture

Even though the term police culture may be becoming less useful, the underlying phenomenon of the formation and transmission of shared values, norms and skills among occupational groups such as police is still important and worthy of further study. In searching for a more useful way of thinking about police culture (or indeed any occupational culture), I have found it fruitful to explore the conceptual tools of the French sociologist Pierre Bourdieu whose theory of practice appropriately combines considerations of the structural context of policing with the institutionalised ways of seeing, thinking and doing within an occupation (for a full discussion see Chan et al 2003; see also Shearing & Ericson 1991 for an excellent alternative conceptualisation).

Bourdieu introduces two important concepts: the *field* and the *habitus*. A field is a social space of conflict and competition, where people struggle to establish control over specific power and authority. Central to the concept of field is the notion of *capital*. There are various forms of capital that operate in different social fields. These include economic capital, cultural or informational capital, social capital which relates to connections and membership in groups, and symbolic capital which is the form other types of capital take on when they are regarded as legitimate (Bourdieu 1987: 3-4). A simple way to think about a field is to compare it to a game where players possess tokens of different colours representing different types of capital. Players' relative force in the game, their position and strategic orientation depend on the volume as well as composition of their tokens. They can play to increase their capital or they can play to change the rules of the game; thus the field can also be a field of struggle (Bourdieu & Wacquant 1992: 98-100). In policing, the field reflects the social, political and legal capital available to police — both *individual* resources such as rank, experience, physical strength, skills, knowledge, discretion, autonomy, information, connection and reputation; and *organisational* resources such as promotional opportunities, public support, budget allocation, legal powers and political independence.

Habitus is a system of 'dispositions' that integrate past experience and enable individuals to cope with a diversity of unforeseen situations (Wacquant 1992: 18). People acquire these dispositions either individually, through family and the education system, or as a group, through organisational socialisation. These dispositions include assumptions, knowledge, skills, and values as well as physical and emotional attributes. It is a 'feel for the game' that people develop; it enables an infinite number of 'moves' to be made in an infinite number of situations. In policing, the habitus embodies what police officers often refer to as 'commonsense' (see Manning 1997) and what is commonly known as 'policing skills' (see Brogden et al 1988).

The importance of this framework lies in Bourdieu's observation that the habitus and the field function fully only in relation to each other. Habitus generates strategies that are coherent and systematic, but they are also 'ad hoc because they are "triggered" by the encounter with a particular field' (Wacquant 1992: 19). The relation between field and habitus operates in two ways: on the one hand, the field *conditions* the habitus which is created by the constraints and necessities of the field; on the other hand, habitus *constitutes* the field as it provides the cultural frames for making sense of the field (Bourdieu & Wacquant 1992).

A good illustration of the relationship between habitus and field is found in the socialisation of new police recruits (see Chan et al 2003). Experienced police tend to take their habitus for granted, so that they act almost instinctively because 'when habitus encounters a social world of which it is the product, it is like a "fish in water"' (Bourdieu & Wacquant 1992: 127). When new recruits join the police, however, they carry with them a habitus that is a product of the field they previously inhabited. In their initial encounter with the police, recruits feel like a 'fish out of water', but over a period of time, in order to reduce their sense of alienation and anxiety (Schein 1985), consciously or unconsciously they learn to develop a feel for the 'game' played by their peer groups. When the field itself is changing, however, the socialisation process is much more unpredictable and fluid because the occupational habitus is itself unstable (Chan et al 2003).

Conclusion: implications for critical criminology

This way of understanding police culture has a number of implications for a critical criminology that seeks to engage in social theory to effect social change and criminal justice. First of all, the new framework recognises that police culture is not something internal to the police – it exists within a field of policing, where officers compete for resources or capital. It is the 'game' played in each field that generates a particular kind of habitus or cultural/bodily knowledge. Thus, political conditions (Finnane 1990; Henry 1994), public opinion (Skolnick and Fyfe 1993), legal rules (Dixon 1997), markets for illegal goods (Mollen Report 1994), supervision styles (Van Maanen 1983), leadership and management policies (Chan 1997), technologies (Chan 2003) all have a hand in shaping the policing habitus.

Secondly, this formulation does not assume that police culture is the same everywhere or unchanging over time. There is also no reason to stereotype police culture as uniformly or even predominantly negative. As researchers and police officers themselves have pointed out, police culture can be positive, and there is much scope for cultivating a professional police culture (Chan et al 2003). This was the approach taken by the Wood Royal Commission which, compared with the Fitzgerald Inquiry, showed a much more sophisticated and nuanced understanding of police culture: 'It is essential ... that the solidarity and mutual support which are central to the culture be turned around in support of a goal of integrity and profes-sionalism' (Wood Report 1997: 214).

Thirdly, conceiving police culture in the context of habitus and field provides a theory of cultural change. At the simplest level, if the field of policing changes then the habitus will also change because it is a product of the field. There is therefore scope for improving police practice through reform strategies that shift the weight of what is regarded as valuable capital, for example, recruitment, training, law reform and governing structures. Again, the Wood Royal Commission is a good example of taking seriously the need to change the field when reforming the police; its recom-mendations cover a wide range of strategies including a major overhaul of the governing and accountability structure; reform of legal, administrative and manage-ment systems; restructure of training and education; and the monitoring and audit of the implementation of reforms (Wood Report 1997).

Finally, this framework explains why police reforms do not always lead to pre-dictable or intended outcomes. Bourdieu (2000) has suggested that when the field changes, the adjustment of the habitus is usually incremental and contingent, not mechanical. This helps us understand why cultural change is so difficult – why, in spite of the increased recruitment of women (Martin 1980; Doran & Chan 2003) and black officers (Wilson et al 1984; Cashmore 1991), changes in technology (Chan 2003) and accountability structures (Chan 2007), certain features of police culture seem to have changed little. The lesson for criminal justice policy-makers is that not all changes in the field will result in changes in practice or culture. Some changes have little real consequences since officers find that they can continue to play the 'game' the way they used to do without problem. Some officers are unable to adjust to the new 'game', either through incompetence or inflexibility, and so they either play the new game badly or they decide to quit. In practice, policy changes usually involve a bundle of initiatives, some more effective than others depending on the complexity of the problem they are trying to address.

Police culture is one of a few concepts that have successfully found their way from academic research to policy discourse. The concept may have become less use-ful and relevant as the field of policing continues to change into a more diverse and pluralised network of regulatory agents, but the underlying social and justice iss-ues remain as important as ever. This short history of police culture as a concept should send a warning that the term 'culture' can obscure more than it reveals about the characteristics of a group, be they police officers or community members. Bourdieu's conceptual framework reminds us that dispositions (culture) and posi-tions (status) are always connected and can only be understood in relation to each other.

References

Appier, J 1998, *Policing Women: the sexual politics of law enforcement and the LAPD*, Tem-ple University Press, Philadelphia.

Bourdieu, P 1987, 'What Makes a Social Class? On the theoretical and practical existence of groups', 32 *Berkeley Journal of Sociology* 1.

Bourdieu, P 2000, *Pascalian Meditations,* Polity Press, Cambridge.

Bourdieu, P & Wacquant LJD 1992, *An Invitation to Reflexive Sociology*, Polity Press, Cambridge.

Brogden, M, Jefferson, T & Walklate, S 1988, *Introducing Policework,* Unwin Hyman, London.

Brogden, M & Shearing, C 1993, *Policing for a New South Africa,* Routledge, London & New York.

Cashmore, E 1991, 'Black Cops Inc', in Cashmore, E & McLaughlin, E (eds), *Out of Order: policing black people,* Routledge, London.

Chan, J 1996, 'Changing Police Culture', 36(1) *British Journal of Criminology* 109.

Chan, J 1997, *Changing Police Culture: policing in a multicultural society,* Cambridge University Press, Melbourne.

Chan, J 2003, 'Police and New Technologies', in Newburn, T (ed), *Handbook of Policing,* Willan Publishing, Cullompton.

Chan, J 2007, 'Making Sense of Police Reforms', 11(3) *Theoretical Criminology* 323.

Chan, J, Brereton, D, Legosz, M, & Doran, S 2001, *e-Policing: the impact of information technology on police practices*, Criminal Justice Commission, Brisbane.

Chan, J with Devery, C & Doran, S 2003, *Fair Cop: learning the art of policing*, University of Toronto Press, Toronto.

Cunneen, C & Robb, T 1987, *Criminal Justice in North-East New South Wales*, Bureau of Crime Statistics and Research, Sydney.

Dixon, D 1997, *Law in Policing: regulation and police practices*, Clarendon Press, Oxford.

Doran, S & Chan, J 2003, 'Doing Gender', in Chan, J, Devery, C & Doran, S (eds), *Fair Cop: learning the art of policing,* University of Toronto Press, Toronto.

Ericson, R 1982, *Reproducing Order: a study of police patrol*, University Of Toronto Press, Toronto.

Ericson, RV 1993, *Making Crime: a study of detective work*, Second Edition, University of Toronto Press, Toronto.

Ericson, RV & Haggerty, K 1997, *Policing the Risk Society,* University of Toronto Press, Toronto.

Fielding, N 1988, *Joining Forces: police training, socialization, and occupational competence,* Routledge, London.

Finnane, M 1990, 'Police Corruption and Police Reform: the Fitzgerald Inquiry in Queensland, Australia', 1 *Policing and Society* 159.

Fitzgerald Report 1989, *Report of a Commission of Inquiry Pursuant to orders in Council,* Commission of Inquiry into Possible Illegal Activities and Associated Police Misconduct, Brisbane.

Foster, J 2003, 'Police Cultures' in *Handbook of Policing*, Willan Publishing, Cullompton.

Heidensohn, F 1992, *Women in Control? The role of women in law enforcement,* Clarendon Press, Oxford.

Henry, V 1994, 'Police Corruption: tradition and evolution' in Bryett, K & Lewis, C (eds), *Un-Peeling Tradition: contemporary policing,* Macmillan, Melbourne.

Holdaway, S 1983, *Inside British Police: a force at work,* Blackwell, Oxford.

Human Rights and Equal Opportunity Commission (HREOC), 1991, *Racist Violence*, Report of the National Inquiry into Racist Violence in Australia, AGPS, Canberra.

Luke, G & Cunneen, C 1995, *Aboriginal Over-Representation and Discretionary Decisions in the New South Wales Juvenile Justice System,* Juvenile Justice Advisory Council of NSW, Sydney.

Manning, P 1978, 'The Police: mandate, strategies, and appearances', in Manning, P & Van Maanen, J (eds), *Policing: a view from the street,* Goodyear, Santa Monica & California.

Manning, P 1997, *Police Work: the social organization of policing,* Second Edition, Waveland Press, Prospect Heights.

Manning, P & Van Maanen, J (eds) 1978, *Policing: a view from the street,* Goodyear, Santa Monica & California.

Marks, M 2005, *Transforming the Robocops: changing police in South Africa,* University of KwaZulu-Natal Press, Scottville.

Martin SE 1980, *Breaking and Entering: policewomen on patrol,* University of California Press, Berkeley.

Martin, SE 1999, 'Police Force or Police Service? Gender and emotional labor', 561 *Annals, AAPSS* 111.

Mollen Report 1994, *Commission Report: Commission to Investigate Allegations of police corruption and the Anti-Corruption Procedures of the Police Department,* City of New York.

Muir, WK 1977, *Police: street corner politicians,* University of Chicago Press, Chicago.

O'Neill, S & Bathgate, J 1993, *Policing Strategies in Aboriginal and Non-English Speaking Background Communities,* Final Report, Northern Territory Police, Winnellie, NT.

Reiner, R 2000, *The Politics of the Police,* Third Edition, Oxford University Press, Oxford.

Reuss-Ianni, E & Ianni, F 1983, 'Street Cops and Management Cops: the two cultures of policing', in Punch, M (ed), *Control in the Police Organisation,* MIT Press, Cambridge.

Schein, EH 1985, *Organizational Culture and Leadership,* Jossey-Bass, San Francisco.

Shearing, C 1981, 'Deviance and Conformity in the Reproduction of Order', in Shearing, C (ed), *Organizational Police Deviance,* Butterworths, Toronto.

Shearing, CD & Ericson, RV 1991, 'Culture as Figurative Action', 42 *British Journal of Sociology* 481.

Skolnick, J 1966, *Justice without Trial,* John Wiley & Sons, New York.

Skolnick, J & Fyfe, J 1993, *Above the Law: police and the excessive use of force,* The Free Press, New York.

Van Maanen, J 1978, 'Kinsmen in Repose: occupational perspectives of patrolmen', in Manning, P & Van Maanen, J (eds), *Policing: a view from the street,* Goodyear, Santa Monica & California.

Van Maanen, J 1983, 'The Boss: first-line supervision in an American police agency', in Punch, M (ed), *Control in the Police Organization,* MIT Press, Cambridge.

Wacquant, LJD 1992, 'Toward a Social Praxeology: the structure and logic of Bourdieu's sociology', in Bourdieu, P & Wacquant, L (eds), *An Invitation to Reflexive Sociology,* Polity Press, Cambridge.

Westley, WA 1970, *Violence and the Police: a sociological study of law, custom and morality,* MIT Press, Cambridge.

Wilson, D, Holdaway, S & Spencer, C 1984, 'Black Police in the UK', 1(1) *Policing* 20.

Wilson, JQ 1968, 'The Police and Crime', in Manning, P & Van Maanen, J (eds), *Policing: a view from the street,* Goodyear, Santa Monica & California.

Wood Report 1997, *Royal Commission into the New South Wales Police Service: Final Report,* NSW Government, Sydney.

Young, M 1991, *An Inside Job,* Clarendon Press, Oxford.

Youth Justice Coalition of New South Wales 1990, *Kids in Justice,* Youth Justice Coalition of NSW, Sydney.

19

GIVING VOICE: THE PRISONER AND DISCURSIVE CITIZENSHIP

David Brown

Introduction

When you (the reader) think of a prisoner, is the image you conjure up based on direct experience, for example from having been in prison or from visiting someone you know in prison, or from visiting a prison as part of an educational course? Or from discussions with family, friends, neighbours, workmates and others who have been in prison or who know people who have? Or is it derived from a media source such as a television show (*Prisoner* if you are older or *Prison Break* or *Oz* if younger), a movie such as *Chopper* or *The Shawshank Redemption*, a documentary, a play or a novel? Is the prisoner in your mind a man or a woman, black or white? Do you conceive of the prisoner as an 'outsider', someone who is strange, other, dangerous? Do you think that people are sent to prison *as* punishment or *for* punishment?

The answers individual readers might give to such questions will depend on the sources of information about prisons and prisoners to which you have been exposed; on the way you read or interpret such information; and on your general political dispositions and social and cultural sensibilities regarding issues of crime and punishment, which in turn will be related in some way to the wider historical, political and cultural context, prevailing attitudes and the available repertoire of accounts. What this chapter will argue is that one of the tasks of a critical penology is to stress the importance of hearing and listening to the 'voices from below', the voices of prisoners, in answering questions about prison and prisoners, about crime and punishment, such as those above. This is not to assert some sort of empiricism or essentialism that we can only know 'the truth' about a particular experience, institution or phenomenon, if we have ourselves 'been there', experienced it at first hand. One did not need to go to South Africa under apartheid to know that it was wrong and to speak out against it. Nor is it to assert that prisoners' accounts have some privileged authenticity or veracity which allows them to trump accounts of those whose knowledge is obtained from sources other than prison experience or whose prison experience is formed from non-prisoner subject positions (cf Foucault 1977; Howe 1994).

The importance of listening to prisoners' accounts

It is important to listen to prisoner accounts of their experiences for the reason that as all accounts are in various ways *partial*, both in the sense of incomplete and of expressing a preference for a particular position, efforts to achieve a fuller understanding of a phenomenon such as the prison experience will be enhanced. This is even more the case where a range of exclusionary forces and practices of secrecy prevent or hinder the expression and circulation of their voices. In situations where 'normal' access to the forms of circulation of expression, to the ability to take part in acts of what I have elsewhere called, 'discursive citizenship' (Brown 2002a: 323) in a democratic polity, are routinely restricted or prevented, it is more important than ever that these suppressed voices be heard. This applies not only to prisoners; the voices of other groups or individuals who face difficulties in gaining access to the means of communication and who suffer some form of exclusion, segregation, disability or stigma, are similarly muted in comparison with those of the 'primary definers' who tend (not always successfully) to set the terms and parameters of debate, muted even in comparison with the citizen-caller to talkback radio.

Another reason why a critical criminology and penology should look to and learn from prisoners' accounts is to prevent or curtail institutional abuses of power. For as the recent histories of a range of institutions from the prison, the hospital, the school, the juvenile or refugee detention centre, the aged care home, to the church and the family, have shown, abuses in the form of neglect, brutality, bullying, physical and sexual violence, tend to flourish in situations of secrecy and unequal or asymmetrical power relations, in situations where the accounts of the abused are ignored, discounted or suppressed, or have no means of circulation. In short, the greater the ability of excluded groups to partake in a discursive citizenship, the lesser the risk of institutional abuse occurring or of continuing unabated.

Consider, for example, the question posed by Justice Nagle in his Royal Commission Report on New South Wales Prisons in 1987, after setting out what he described as a 'regime of terror' (Nagle 1978: 134) inflicted on 'intractable' prisoners at Grafton gaol: 'how could a system built on such brutality and savagery continue unchecked for thirty-three years?' (1978: 144). One answer to this question is because prisoners' accounts of what happened were suppressed, and if and when they received some circulation, were met by untruthful denials by the Corrective Services Department and the Minister and were discounted as the fabrications of 'criminals' who lacked veracity by virtue of their status or identity.

The extent to which accounts of prisoners can be discounted, not by an impartial investigation of the particular claims but by a blanket denial based on an assumption that the moral status of 'criminal' or 'prisoner' necessarily precludes veracity, is an indication of the strength or weakness, of a specific democratic political culture. A political culture in which lack of veracity is presumptively assigned on the basis of the status or identity of the claimant (for example, identities such as 'criminal', 'prisoner', 'unlawful non-citizen' and 'terrorist') is a political culture lacking in a key safeguard against the abuse of power, a political culture prey to the corrosive effects of the politics of exclusion, fear and demonisation. Whether as individuals we are concerned or not with particular issues such as the treatment of prisoners or asylum seekers, they indirectly affect us all in that the health and well-being of a democratic polity depends in part on the prospects of, as EP Thompson (1980: 167) put it so succinctly, 'the bringing of power to particular account'.

In the interests of promoting the voices of prisoners, this chapter will examine some of the sources and forms through which those voices might be heard and some of the issues they might raise. First, a brief bibliographic note, followed by observations on the uses to which prisoner's accounts might be put, most obviously as an antidote to the sanitised prison of official discourse. There follows a discussion of prison riots as a form of expression, a proto political 'voice', with particular reference to the widespread prison disturbances of the 1960s and 1970s across a number of countries. For it was at this point that links between prisoners and prison movement organisations and the 'new' critical criminology and penology was forged, links given theoretical force in Mathiesen's *Politics of Abolition* (1974) and Foucault's *Discipline and Punish* (1978). The issue of alliances are central to the strategies of prison struggle and the chapter notes some of the problems with Mathiesen's specifications for organisation among the 'expelled' and suggests that the most appropriate strategy for prison struggle is that around maximising the conditions under which prisoners can exercise their political and discursive citizenship. The media and the law are central to this task so a discussion of prisoners as 'mediated' and 'legal' subjects follows. Finally, the chapter briefly examines the 2006 total disenfranchisement of prisoners from voting in federal elections and the successful High Court challenge to this disenfranchisement mounted by Indigenous Victorian prisoner Vicki Lee Roach, assisted by lawyers working pro bono.

Prisoner writing

Prisoner writing is an obvious, but often little acknowledged source of knowledge about prisons, prisoners and penality. On an international stage the best-known accounts from prison literature are those of writers whose work is seen as having significant literary merit (see Davies 1990) such as Jean Genet, Fyodor Dostoevsky, Alexander Solzhenitsyn, Oscar Wilde and Primo Levi, or political significance, such as Antonio Gramsci, George Jackson, Peter Kropotkin, Alexander Berkman, and Victor Serge. In Australia in the literary genre there is the leading convict novel, Marcus Clarke's *For the Term of His Natural Life* (1874), and the novels, plays and poetry of Peter Kocan, Jim McNeil, Ray Mooney, Robert Adamson, Kevin Gilbert and many others too numerous to list. A recent literary addition, which has reached an international audience and is about to be made into a film, is Gregory Robert's *Shantaram* (2003).

But it is important to recognise the value in a range of less overtly literary or political autobiographical accounts such as convict accounts of life in the prisons of the penal settlement through to more recent prison writings. In the most recent addition to the genre, Bernie Matthews in *Intractable* (2006) describes how access to a typewriter in Katingal, proved to be the tool by which he dug himself out of the prison system and changed his career from armed robber to award winning journalist, thus escaping the fate of most of the men dubbed by *The Daily Telegraph* 'The Brutes of Katingal'. Matthews' work is but one example of the genre of prisoner autobiographical literature that is an important and neglected resource in penology. Such literature might be used in a range of ways: to effect personal change and desistance, to argue for penal and criminal justice reform, to expose abuses, miscarriages and injustice; as a resource in prisoner literacy and education programs; in the training of prison administrators and prison, probation and parole officers (Nellis 2002); and in literature, law, criminology, penology and criminal justice educational courses.

The role of prisoner accounts in challenging official discourse

Prisoner writing provides a valuable antidote to the sanitised prison of official discourse. Edney provides an excellent example, comparing the 'official' history of Pentridge Prison and H Division in particular, as recounted in Lynn and Armstrong (1996) with accounts provided by prisoners of the same period and events (O'Meally 1979; Eastwood 1992; Mooney 1997; Roberts 2003). In Lynn and Armstrong's account the violence and disorder of H division which led to the establishment of the Jenkinson Inquiry is attributed largely to outside causes, including 'recalcitrant prisoners, inadequate prison infrastructure, and insufficient resources, outside social forces, intrusion of norms from the legal system and an influx of young prisoners' (Edney 2006: 366, summarising Lynn and Armstrong 1996: 156-158). What is missing in such accounts, but evident in the prisoner literature, is the sense of the 'systematic and entrenched' nature of 'a culture of brutality and violence' as a 'working philosophy' (2006: 367) of H Division and the agency of prisoners engaged in collective action by way of riots and strikes in response to the violence deployed against them. Edney concludes by highlighting the gulf between the official and prisoner accounts, warning of the dangers of 'acquiescence to official accounts of prison history as the indubitable truth' (2006: 377).

Without hearing from prisoners we are left with the sanitised prison of official discourse. John Pratt in *Punishment and Civilisation* (2002) examines prisoners' accounts of their conditions, particularly food, clothing, personal hygiene and language, recounted in autobiographies and memoirs. This discussion provides in part a contrast, in part confirmation, of the official accounts provided by way of inquiries and official reports (some 1300 in all) on which the book is based. Pratt (2002: 121) argues that:

> There are two very different versions, then, of 'the truth' about prison life. On the one hand, we have official penal discourse. Here, prisons came to function as they should in a civilised society: there were to be no gratuitous and barbaric punishments – these had been left in the past – the gags, the floggings, even bread and water diets towards the end of the period had been removed from the prison agenda; ... On the other hand, we have the very different story that the prisoners had to tell. In their accounts, continuous themes of deprivation and degradation characterise prison life; reforms might even introduce new privations and torments.

By and large Pratt suggests that historically it was the authorities' accounts that were typically accepted as true while prisoner's accounts of deprivations, mistreatment and complaints were routinely denied.

The expressive function of prison revolts in the 1960s and 1970s

Social historians such as Rude (1964) and Thompson (1963, 1993) have explored the 'moral economy' of the crowd or mob, and the expressive, proto political function of riots and disturbances as expressions of moral indignation (Owen 2006) among the disenfranchised, which were listened to by the rulers. Prison riots can be analysed in similar terms as an expression of grievances and a sense of injustice (Woolf 1991; Sparks & Bottoms 1995), a 'giving voice' to concerns which have been ignored or silenced, in a way that is known will attract media, public and official attention (Scraton et al 1991; Sim 1991, 1994; Carter 2001), what Bree Carlton (this volume) calls 'institutional text'. While the subsequent official response is often to attempt to portray the events as individual acts of wanton violence and damage by a small number of criminal trouble-makers, the success of such portrayals is not necessarily guaranteed, as illustrated by inquiries such as the Nagle inquiry in New South Wales prompted largely by the riot at Bathurst in 1974 and the Woolf inquiry in the United Kingdom, by the riot at Strangeways in 1990. One of the crucial measures of the success of particular inquiries is their ability to establish a rough approximation of 'the truth' about the causes of riots (Hancock & Liebling 2004: 100). A key condition for this 'truth-telling' capacity to be fulfilled, is the recognition that prisoners' accounts must be heard and, given their cloistered state, practical mechanisms of access, communication and representation adopted to ensure this (Brown 2005: 45-49).

A wave of riots took place in prisons across the United States, United Kingdom, Europe, Australia and elsewhere in the 1960s and 1970s as part of a more generalised movement of anti-institutional revolts in psychiatric hospitals, schools, and universities and the emergence of new political subjects: second wave feminism, black power and land rights, the gay movement and the hippy trip. Prison movement groups such as RAP and PROP in the United Kingdom, GIP in France and the PAG in Australia, some with abolitionist philosophies, supported the increased prisoner militancy and drew media and public attention to bashings and brutality. In particular cases the riots spawned Royal Commissions of inquiry, which often verified prisoners' accounts and grievances and made recommendations for substantial penal reform.

Critical criminologists, lawyers, students and others played a key role in building a variety of social movements around prison and criminal justice issues in this period, answering Becker's (1967) 'Whose side are we on?' question in unequivocal terms. I have elsewhere described the 'engaged character of Australian critical criminology' (Brown 2002b: 96-101) with particular reference to the alliances formed between critical criminologists and the prisoners' movement. In the New South Wales context a group of academics, lawyers and students, schooled in Taylor, Walton and Young's *The New Criminology* (1973), Mathiesen's *The Politics of Abolition* (1974) and later Foucault's *Discipline and Punish* (1978), worked closely with prisoners and ex-prisoners in agitating for the Nagle Royal Commission into prisons and in drafting a major abolitionist submission to that inquiry (see generally Zdenkowski & Brown 1982; Findlay 1982; Vinson 1982).

Alliance building and prisoner subjectivity

The issue of alliance building is crucial to an engaged and critical criminology, and it is here that certain weaknesses in Mathiesen's influential *The Politics of Abolition* became apparent (Brown & Hogg 1985). Mathiesen (1974: 173) places considerable emphasis on the fact that prisoners are unproductive, leading to the central strategic understanding that 'a necessary condition for organisation among the expelled is to alter the very grounds for their being expelled: their lack of contribution'. This is to be overcome by linking up with those groups on the outside that have a key role in productive relations and an interest in changing society, namely the radical part of the working class, with whom prisoners 'have concrete interests in common'. Prisoners' organisations on the outside are to provide the necessary connecting link, for the prison struggle is dependent and derivative in relation to the major locus of power and struggle in production.

Such an analysis asserts 'a priori agents of change', and 'privileged points and moments of rupture' (Laclau & Mouffe 1985: 178-179) and an underlying relation of unity waiting to be realised. But subject positions can no longer be constituted a priori according to particular privileged locations or essential subjectivities; social movements derive their progressive character through their discursive constitution and prisoners are plural, not unified subjects, unities being a matter of construction, not attribution based on location. Further, difficulties emerged in practice in differentiating 'negative' reforms, which opposed the underlying tenets of the prison and thus were to be supported and 'positive' reforms, which strengthened the prison leading to incorporation (Brown & Hogg 1985: 71-73). Similar difficulties beset the principle of 'voluntariness', which was to determine the correct attitude to 'alternatives'. It became increasingly apparent both that reform measures could not be 'specified or evaluated a priori by reference either to some positive/negative calculus or to some general theory of law, state, capital, legitimation, legal right etc' and that 'voluntariness' was an inadequate concept through which to think the specific nature of regulatory conditions (1985: 73).

Foucault's *Discipline and Punish* (1978: 30), in its rejection of a conception of power as merely negative constraint emanating from some central location, appeared to offer a recognition of the diverse and dispersed struggles of prisoners in their 'minute material details', 'revolts at the level of the body, against the very body of the prison', contesting 'its very materiality as an instrument and vector of power'. However Foucault's generalisation of Bentham's panopticon into an all encompassing 'carceral' or 'disciplinary society', tended to diminish the significance of prison struggle in favour of ceaseless resistance to disciplinary power.

What might be rescued from the abolitionist heritage is the emphasis on the 'unfinished', not as in Mathiesen, as a basis for a strategy of 'abolition' of the established order, for this ignores the productive and dispersed nature of power, conceiving it as 'located in specific institutions as a property to be possessed and wielded and thus in the final instance destroyed' (Brown & Hogg 1985: 71), but as a never ending struggle to participate in the processes of becoming, becoming visible as human subjects and contesting the conditions of subjectivity in and through which that humanity is constructed and denied. Such struggles are dispersed, their progressive potential and character are not guaranteed and derive not from whence they come, but from their discursive constitution and articulation (Laclau & Mouffe 1985: 169) and in particular their reflexive capacity to assert human value, including the human value of victims of criminal acts. In this formulation, prison struggle is essentially a struggle over participation – participation in the processes through which criminalisation is transacted, adjudication and punishment conducted, subject identities formed and a discursive citizenship exercised.

Prisoners as 'mediated' subjects

As particular identities and subjectivities are less and less fixed and more and more fluid, increasingly transacted through media, so prisoners' relationship with and access to media become more and more important. Media treatment of prisons has tended to fluctuate between sensationalist exploitation of public fears and fascination with notorious prisoners and their crimes, reformist critiques of prison conditions, and largely ignoring prison issues. A current political measure of the success of prison administrators and politicians is that prisons are kept off the front page of the tabloids in a version of 'no news is good news', a result secured by an increased emphasis and resources devoted to security, the prevention of escapes and a tight policy of internal administrative control of media access to prisoners and prisons. Bentham's 'principle of lesser eligibility' that prison conditions must always be kept below those of the honest poor has a continued pertinence in media accounts of prisoners enjoying 'motel conditions' and particular notorious prisoners having access to electric hot water jugs and televisions.

While it is always possible to point to examples of sensationalist and exploitative media treatment of some prison issues and the notoriety of particular prisoners, radical accounts which focus only on exploitation do less than justice to the diversity of media treatment and its importance as a vehicle for humanising even the most hated and deviant. As Catherine Lumby (2002: 105) argues, following John Hartley (1996), it is in 'the interaction between popular media products and their audiences that political, social and cultural debate is produced' so that 'the focus is less on whether a given media report or program accurately or even positively 'represents' the prison system but on whether prisoners are able to achieve a high enough level of visibility to establish their membership of an increasingly mediated public sphere'. The issue becomes in these terms, that of securing greater media access by and to prisoners for all forms of media, especially the 'new media', so that prisoners can speak for themselves and most importantly 'personalise and humanise issues' (Lumby 2002: 112). Central to this are the media produced by prisoners and prison movement organisations such as Justice Action, which in 2005 initiated a court action seeking to require the NSW Department of Corrective Services to distribute an election issue of their newspaper *Framed* on the grounds that its prohibition was an illegitimate infringement of the implied constitutional right of freedom of political communication and participation (see Redman et al 2008).

Prisoners as legal subjects

Such legal actions seeking to utilise the forums of the law and the judicial process, highlight the limited protections for prisoners available in law in the Australian context. Edney (2001: 8) has argued that the 'hands off' doctrine, expressed most clearly by Dixon CJ in the case of *Flynn v The King* (1949) 79 CLR 1, that the courts should be wary of recognising prisoners as legal subjects because to do so would shift management of the prison from prison administrators to the courts, in the process undermining prison authorities and opening the floodgates, became 'progressively untenable over time … due to its disturbing implication that there existed an important area of social concern beyond the jurisdiction of the law'. The 'prisoners as outlaws' approach was undermined by the findings of inquiries such as Nagle in New South Wales (1978) and Jenkinson in Victoria (1973) after riots and disturbances at

Bathurst and Pentridge, giving rise to a qualified legal 'retrieval' of prisoners' rights in the 1960s and 1970s, a judicial move to conceive of prisoners as legal subjects given their 'unique and vulnerable position' (2001: 10). However Edney (2001) argues that a new form of 'hands off by stealth' was later achieved by the courts giving deference to the judgment and expertise of prison administrators.

> After a detailed review of the authorities Groves (2001: 20) concludes that:
> Judicial decisions on the interpretation of correctional legislation have not yielded principles by which the decisions of prison officials may be subjected to rigorous scrutiny by the courts in applications for judicial review. Legislative attempts to grant rights to prisoners have also provided few clear benefits to prisoners.

The limited jurisdiction of the Human Rights and Equal Opportunity Commission 'prevents that body from operating as an effective grievance mechanism for prisoners' (see also Minogue 2002) and the effects of international instruments such as the *International Covenant on Civil and Political Rights* (1976) have been slight, Groves (2001: 21) arguing that judicial attitudes present a 'significant obstacle', for Australian courts have proved 'extremely reluctant to draw on international instruments in the interpretation of correctional legislation'.

Feudal conceptions of prisoners as 'civilly dead', far from being consigned to history as part of Elias' 'civilising process' have undergone somewhat of a revival or refurbishment in Australia, evident in the decision on the case of *Dugan v Mirror Newspapers Limited* (1979) 142 CLR 583, and in a host of recent exclusionary practices: in the 2004 and 2006 federal disenfranchising legislation; in State provisions restricting prisoner access to victims compensation for injuries suffered in prison; in the *Civil Liability Act* 2002 (NSW) and subsequent amendments which 'substantially removes any effective redress for negligence or abuse by prison authorities and other prisoners' (Morrison 2007: 9); in longstanding exclusions in most jurisdictions from jury service; in post release disabilities suffered by those with criminal records such as gaining insurance; and in attempts to deny male prisoners access to medical services in order to store sperm when undergoing potentially debilitating surgery; to mention but some. In 'popular' discourse, notions of civil death follow prisoners out of prison on release, a recent *Daily Telegraph* editorial justifying the continued media harassment of parolee, John Lewthwaite, with the observation that 'by his crime, he made himself a permanent outcast, a pariah. Normal people don't want him near them'.[1]

The attempted complete removal of prisoner franchise

The contemporary revival of civil death and forfeiture notions, under the rubric of 'breach of the social compact' was evident in attempts by the Howard federal government to completely remove serving prisoners from the franchise in federal elections, taking the position back to before federation (for the history of prisoner voting entitlements see Fitzgerald & Zdenkowski 1987; Orr 1998; Ridley-Smith & Redman 2002; Davidson 2004; Brown 2007; Redman et al 2008). Notably absent from government contributions to the 2004 and 2006 debates was any reference to the importance of the franchise as a manifestation (indeed under the *Electoral Act*, a

---

1   *The Daily Telegraph*, 'Child Killer to stay "outcast"', 5 September 2007; and for a range of views of 'penal populism' and 'the new punitiveness' see Pratt et al 2005; Pratt 2007.

'duty') of citizenship, a basic human right, and a mechanism of participation in a democratic polity. It was left largely to an independent country-based MP, Peter Andren, and to the leader of the Greens, Senator Bob Brown, to raise these broader arguments. For Andren, 'the right to vote – to have a say in who governs the country and even, at a state level, who runs the prisons – is a basic human right. As a right, it is not something that should be taken away by politicians' (Hansard, House of Representatives 10 August 2004). For Bob Brown:

> The whole basis of the respect for the rule of law rests on the participation of citizens through the democratic selection of their representatives making the law. How will prisoners subject to this feudal concept of civil death have respect for the law if they are banned from participating in its formation? One has to remember that it is our job to encourage people to take part in society, to feel empowered to be in society and to feel they have a role in society – not to take away that role (Hansard, Senate 12 August 2004).

The relative silence of Australian law-makers on these questions highlights weaknesses in theories of citizenship. Many such theories 'are strong on affirmations of equality, freedom and participation, but weak in that they fail to provide an explicit and concrete account of how citizenship, how membership of a political or civic community, is acquired and lost' (Brown 2002a: 324-325). The debate over prisoners' rights make such failures seem particularly acute: citizenship theory feels abstract and rhetorical when set against a popular and political discourse in which the 'forfeit' argument plays strongly to disqualify or dis-entitle prisoners from full citizenship. Vaughan's (2000: 26) characterisation of prisoners as 'partial' or 'conditional' citizens is a more accurate rendering of their actual sociological and political situation 'than the either/or of universal citizen/non-citizen outlaw'. It also calls attention 'to the fluid and unfinished nature of the prisoner's status and ability to participate in public discourse as a fully fledged democratic subject; a subject in the process of becoming' (Brown 2002a: 322).

The 2006 prisoner disenfranchisement was subject to challenge in the Australian High Court in June 2007 by Vickie Lee Roach an Indigenous woman prisoner in Victoria (*Roach v Electoral Commissioner and The Commonwealth of Australia* [2007] HCA 43). Vickie Lee Roach has completed a Masters degree in prison, is hoping to start a PhD and is active in prison based education programs and in mentoring other prisoners. In an open letter read on ABC Radio National's (2007) *The Law Report* she wrote:

> The one inescapable fact is that at any given time there are approximately 20,000 prisoners in this country, and 99% of these will be released eventually. For most of us, re-entry to society will come sooner rather than later. For many, during the term of whichever government will be elected later this year. Excluding us from the democratic process while we are in prison, however short our stay might be, implies we have forfeited our right to political participation, not just for the duration of our term of imprisonment, but for however long it might be until any subsequent election. I believe this serves only to further alienate us from society and ensures that the exiting prisoner feels no connection, commitment, or loyalty to his or her community, and may therefore not feel bound to respect its laws or social mores.
>
> As an Indigenous woman and a survivor of the stolen generation, I also believe the issue of voting rights is especially important to the Aboriginal com-

munity. If you consider that we make up 22% of Australia's prison population, while only 1% of the general population, and with those of us in prison being a large proportion of our total number, taking away our right to vote effectively silences yet again the political voice of Aboriginal people.

Conclusion

Vickie Lee Roach's words highlight the fluid and never ending historical struggles over the politics of imprisonment and penal reform and over the political and citizenship status of prisoners. Her appeal to us is as a prisoner, an Indigenous woman and a political subject, seeking to exercise a discursive citizenship by voting, by undertaking education courses in prison, by mentoring other prisoners, by engaging in legal challenge and public debate. In August 2007, the High Court handed down orders upholding her claim that the 2006 disenfranchising legislation was invalid, but upholding the 2004 legislation, so that prisoners serving less than three years can vote, a partial re-enfranchisement, a victory for Vickie Roach, her legal team and prisoners in general. In a poignant illustration of both the limits of the decision and the fragility of human rights protection in Australia, Vickie Lee Roach did not regain the vote as she is serving a four-year sentence. She was a bystander in the 2007 federal election, silenced in the fundamental act of political communication involved in voting. But the silencing effected by electoral disqualification will be partial only. It will be partial because voting is only one (albeit central) way in which she seeks to communicate, exercise her discursive citizenship, and express her fundamental human value as a person who, despite being imprisoned, seeks to participate in the public realm.

The disenfranchisement will also be partial only, because the legacy of critical criminology and penology has armed us with some of the means to resist the silencing of prisoners as discursive subjects and the broader politics of exclusion of which it is but a part. Foremost among those means is a disposition to listen to the varied and various voices of prisoners and assist in their circulation. To return to the series of questions that began this chapter and add another one, how do we all, as individuals, as members of communities, as citizens, as voters, as a society, answer Vickie Lee Roach's final appeal to us: 'Who cares if prisoners have the right to vote?'.

References

ABC Radio National 2007, *The Law Report*, 12 June, <www.abc.net.au/m/lawreport/stories/2007/1945622.htm>.

Becker, HS 1967, 'Whose side are we on?', 14(3) *Social Problems* 239.

Brown, D 2002a, 'Prisoners as Citizens', in Brown, D & Wilkie, M (eds), *Prisoners as Citizens*, Federation Press, Sydney.

Brown, D 2002b, '"Losing my religion": reflections on critical criminology in Australia', in Carrington, K & Hogg, R (eds), *Critical Criminology*, Willan Publishing, Cullompton.

Brown, D 2005, 'Commissions of Inquiry and Penal Reform', in O'Toole, S & Eyland, S (eds), *Corrections Criminology*, Hawkins Press, Sydney.

Brown, D 2007, 'The Disenfranchisement of Prisoners', 32(3) *Alternative Law Journal* 132.

Brown, D & Hogg, R 1985, 'Abolition Reconsidered', 2(2) *Australian Journal of Law and Society* 56.

Brown, D & Wilkie, M 2002, *Prisoners as Citizens*, Federation Press, Sydney.

Carter, KW 2001, 'The Casuarina Prison Riot: official discourse or appreciative inquiry?', 12 *Current Issues in Criminal Justice* 363.

Clarke, M 1874 [1997], *For the Term of His Natural Life*, republished by Oxford University Press, Oxford.

Davidson, J 2004, 'Inside Outcasts: prisoners and the right to vote in Australia', *Current Issues Brief No 12 2003-04*, Australian Parliamentary Library, 2, <www.aph.gov.au/library/pubs/CIB/2003-04/04cib12.pdf>.

Davies, I 1990, *Writers in Prison*, Basil Blackwell, Oxford.

Eastwood, E 1992, *Focus on Faraday and Beyond*, Coer De Lion, Melbourne.

Edney, R 2001, 'Judicial Deference to the Expertise of Correctional Administrators: the implications for prisoners' rights', 5 *Australian Journal of Human Rights* 1.

Edney, R 2006, 'Contested Narratives of Penal Knowledge', 17(3) *Current Issues in Criminal Justice* 362.

Findlay, M 1982, *The State of the Prison*, Mitchellsearch, Bathurst.

Finnane, M 1997, *Punishment in Australian Society*, Oxford University Press, Melbourne.

Fitzgerald, J & Zdenkowski, G 1987, 'Voting Rights of Convicted Persons', 11(1) *Criminal Law Journal* 11.

Foucault, M 1977, 'Intellectuals and Power', in Bouchard, DF (ed), *Language, Counter-Memory, Practice*, Cornell University Press, Ithaca.

Foucault, M 1978, *Discipline and Punish*, Pantheon, New York.

Groves, M 2001, 'International Law and Australian Prisoners', 24(1) *UNSW Law Journal* 17.

Hancock, N & Liebling, A 2004, 'Truth, Independence and Effectiveness in Prison Inquiries', in Gilligan, G & Pratt, J (eds), *Crime, Truth and Justice*, Willan Publishing, Cullompton.

Hartley, J 1996, *Popular Reality*, Arnold, London.

Howe, A 1994, *Punish and Critique: towards a feminist analysis of penality*, Routledge, London.

Jenkinson, KJ 1973, *Report of the Board of Inquiry into Allegations of Brutality and Ill Treatment at HM Prison Pentridge*, Victorian Government Printer, Melbourne.

Laclau, E & Mouffe, C 1985, *Hegemony and Socialist Strategy*, Verso, London.

Lumby, C 2002, 'Televising the Invisible: prisoners, prison reform and the media', in Brown, D & Wilkie, M (eds), *Prisoners as Citizens*, Federation Press, Sydney.

Lynn, P & Armstrong, G 1996, *From Pentonville to Pentridge: a history of prisons in Victoria*, State Public Library, Victoria.

Mathews, B 2006, *Intractable*, Pan Macmillan, Sydney.

Mathiesen, T 1974, *The Politics of Abolition*, Martin Robertson, London.

Minogue, C 2002, 'An Insider's View: human rights and excursions from the Flat Lands', in Brown, D & Wilkie, M (eds), *Prisoners as Citizens*, Federation Press, Sydney.

Mooney, R 1997, 'Bluestone Shadows', *The Sunday Age*, 14 September.

Morrison, A 2007, 'The Duty of Care to Prisoners', 81 *Precedent* 8.

Nagle, J 1978, *Report of the Royal Commission into New South Wales Prisons*, NSW Government Printer, Sydney.

Nellis, M 2002, 'Prose and Cons: offender auto/biographies, penal reform and probation training', 41(5) *The Howard Journal* 434.

O'Meally, W 1979, *The Man They Couldn't Break*, Unicorn Books, Melbourne.

Orr, G 1998, 'Ballotless and Behind Bars: the denial of the franchise to prisoners', 26 *Federal Law Review* 55.

Owen, JR 2006, 'Moral Indignation, Criminality, and the Rioting Crowd in Macquarie Fields', 18(1) *Current Issues in Criminal Justice* 5.

Pratt, J 2002, *Punishment and Civilisation*, Sage, London.

Pratt, J 2007, *Penal Populism*, Routledge, London.

Pratt, J, Brown, D, Brown, M, Hallsworth, S & Morrison, W (eds) 2005, *The New Punitiveness*, Willan Publishing, Cullompton.

Redman, R, Brown, D & Mercurio, B 2008, 'The Politics and Legality of Prisoner Disenfranchisement in Australian Federal Elections', in Ewald, A & Rottinghaus, B (eds), *Democracy and Punishment: international perspectives on criminal disenfranchisement*, Cambridge University Press, New York.

Ridley-Smith, M & Redman, R 2002, 'Prisoners and the Right to Vote', in Brown, D & Wilkie, M (eds), *Prisoners as Citizens*, Federation Press, Sydney.

Roberts, G 2003, *Shantaram*, Scribe Publications, Carlton North.

Rude, G 1964, *The Crowd in History: a study of popular disturbance in France and England 1730-1848*, Lawrence & Wishart, London.

Scraton, P, Sim, J & Skidmore, P 1991, *Prisons Under Protest*, Open University Press, Milton Keynes.

Sim, J 1991, '"We are not animals, we are human beings": prisons, protest, and politics in England and Wales 1969-1990', 18(3) *Social Justice* 107.

Sim, J 1994, 'Reforming the Penal Wasteland: a critical review of the Woolf Report', in Player, E & Jenkins, M (eds), *Prisons After Woolf: reform through riot*, Routledge, London.

Sparks, R & Bottoms, AE 1995, 'Legitimacy and Order in Prisons', 46(1) *British Journal of Sociology* 45.

Taylor, I, Walton, P & Young J 1973, *The New Criminology*, Routledge, London.

Thompson, EP 1963, *The Making of the English Working Class*, Vintage Books, Middlesex.

Thompson, EP 1980, *Writing by Candlelight*, Merlin Press, London.

Thompson, EP 1993, *Customs in Common: studies in traditional popular culture*, New Press, New York.

Vaughan, B 2000, 'The Civilizing Process and the Janus-Face of Modern Punishment', 4(1) *Theoretical Criminology* 71.

Vinson, T 1982, *Wilful Obstruction*, Methuen, Sydney.

Woolf, Lord Justice 1991, *Prison Disturbances*, April 1990, HMSO London.

Zdenkowski, G & Brown, D 1982, *The Prison Struggle*, Penguin Books, Melbourne.

20

Understanding Prisoner Resistance: Power, Visibility and Survival in High-Security

Bree Carlton

The organisation of collective and individual resistance against authority is integral to understanding the political and volatile dynamics of imprisonment (Bosworth & Carrabine 2001: 501). Since the inception of the prison, prisoners have resisted and transgressed disciplinary structures through numerous tactics such as refusal and non-compliance, subversion, unauthorised communication with other prisoners and the outside world, hunger strikes, 'no-wash' protests, industrial action, letter writing, campaigning, undergoing official complaints processes, legal action, barricades, fires, riots and escaping (Cohen & Taylor 1972; Zdenkowski & Brown 1982; Scraton et al 1991; Rodriguez 2006). Indeed, any attempt to trace the historical origins of punishment and reform in Australia necessitates consideration of the transformative impacts of resistance from below upon contemporary disciplinary regimes, penal structures and practice (Finnane 1997), and some attention has previously centred on the way prisoner rights movements in the 1960s and 1970s have provided vital opportunities for positive reform and change in penal policy and practice (Vinson et al 2004).

This chapter provides a historical examination of the nature and occurrence of resistance in high-security prisons specifically, with reference to the Pentridge Prison Jika Jika High-Security Unit in Victoria. Critical to this discussion is the context in which high-security prisons were devised as an official solution to managing prisoner non-compliance in the 1960s and 1970s (Fitzgerald 1977; Zdenkowski & Brown 1982; Ward & Churchill 1992; Rodriguez 2006). Officials hoped that through the application of hi-tech security devices, sophisticated architectural design, complex managerial and disciplinary strategies, physical and psychological control over prisoners could be maximised. However, experience suggests that such regimes have worked to exacerbate the disorder they were supposed to prevent. In high-security pre-existing tension and conflict are often magnified by the psychological effects and pressures associated with extended periods of lockdown, social isolation, sensory deprivation and unaccountable power structures integral to the management of the institution (Fellner & Mariner 1997; Haney & Lynch 1997;

Rhodes 2004). While highlighting official imperatives and the drive to manage resistance, this chapter is centrally concerned with documenting and analysing challenges posed by prisoner resistance. In the context of institutional shortcomings and failings, prisoner resistance has been used to justify the intensification and escalation of 'security'.

This chapter provides an examination of the official discourses and political contexts that have fortified and given rise to the continuing project of prison securitisation and the increasing use of modern high-security. The case study section considers prisoner resistance in Jika Jika in order to demonstrate how high-security conditions can work to exacerbate extreme and violent forms of resistance. By analysing and documenting resistance in Jika Jika, it is possible to illuminate subjective accounts of power, visibility and survival in high-security, an institution traditionally shrouded in secrecy and hidden from public view. However, it is critical to begin by providing a broad conceptual framework to understand the nature of institutional resistance in its various forms.

Conceptualising power and resistance as institutional text

Domination and subordination are defining forces underpinning the operation of power and institutional structures in prison. Both Foucault (1991a) and Ignatieff (1978) have addressed the historical shift away from public spectacles of punishment centred on the body towards privatised and institutionalised punishments directed at the mind. The prison emerged as a dominant form of punishment in the 18th and 19th centuries and while it was intended by reformers to create a more humane system of punishment, its ultimate impact on those sentenced to life imprisonment, was to emulate the result of death (Dayan 2002: 13).[1] Such an experience is tantamount to civil death. In place of physical mistreatment, torture or death, a newly sentenced prisoner's civil status in organised society is subject to total destruction (Dayan 2002). In this way, prisoners are remoulded and defined by the institution that asserts and maintains ownership of their incarcerated identities and bodies (Pugliese 2002).

This is essentially a process of institutionalisation and disempowerment; a symbolic exertion of state power that moves beyond the physical confines and realities of imprisonment (Scraton et al 1991). Such a process inevitably renders the prisoner invisible to the outside world and fosters the maintenance of institutional secrecy. It is this experience of disciplinary power that provides a critical backdrop for the occurrence of resistance in prison.

Prisoner resistance comprises a key avenue for challenging and negotiating disciplinary power in prison. For many prisoners resistance serves as a bargaining tool and a means of resolving the 'crisis of visibility' (Carter 2000: 365). For others it serves as a vehicle for self-expression or a way of venting feelings of frustration and desperation. For most, the act of resistance depending on its form is a key com-

---

1   The origins of the prison are strongly associated with the birth of industrial capitalism; liberalist ideologies and the idea of individual rights; the American Revolution, and resistance to English and European colonial power in Asian and African regions. Early reformers intended the prison to impose an institutional regime of religious self-reflection and reform, while others such as Jeremy Bentham advocated it as a system of total surveillance to internalise productive labour habits (Davis 2003).

ponent of short and long-term survival (Cohen & Taylor 1972). It is also acknowledged that gendered and racialised experiences of disciplinary power in prison generate distinct motivations and modes of resistance (Bosworth 1999; Rodriguez 2006; Pugliese 2002). The experiences of political prisoners in regional conflicts such as Northern Ireland and South Africa for example, have also provided very different conditions for the generation of resistance in those institutional structures and contexts (McKeown 2001; Corcoran 2006). Having acknowledged such differences, this chapter focuses specifically on resistance as a product of high-security, arguing that the oppressive psychological and physical realities of such conditions effectively compound prisoner experiences of disempowerment and feelings of loss of control, thus evoking more extreme, desperate and sometimes violent measures of resistance. It is within such a context that the prisoner's mind and body come to comprise renewed sites of struggle upon which the institutional dynamics of disciplinary power and resistance are played out.

Resistance in prison cannot be conceived as an isolated occurrence or attributed to the actions or pathologies of 'disturbed' individuals. It must be considered as part of a system and more specifically a political product of institutional power relations and conditions. The oppositional and reactive forces of disciplinary power and resistance comprise a fierce institutional dynamic of struggle further heightened by the physical and psychological pressures of the oppressive regime and environment. Central to Foucault's work is the notion that power is not static but determined by a complex flow of varying sets of relations and structures that change with circumstances and time (Foucault 1991b 81; Danaher et al 2000: xiv). According to Foucault, power does not solely function for negative, repressive or coercive purposes. He argues it is productive in that it produces resistance to itself (Foucault 1991a). Therefore, where there is power, there also exists the constant threat and occurrence of resistance.

While Foucault acknowledges the productive relationship between power and resistance, theorist Michel de Certeau (1984) focuses on the threat of resistance and provides a deeper exploration of its potentialities and occurrence in practice. De Certeau characterises resistance as the 'obverse' of power. More specifically, he argues resistance comprises the 'tactics' and corresponding weapons of the dominated or powerless (de Certeau 1984). Resistance in a high-security prison requires the subversion and use by prisoners of already existing disciplinary strategies or topographies of power to achieve their ends. As de Certeau observes:

> [T]he weapons of the weak are those which already exist as strategies of the strong ... the powerful in any given context can tabulate, build, and create spaces and places, while the relatively powerless can only use, manipulate and divert these spaces (cited in Cresswell 1996: 164).

The dynamic of power and resistance in prison can be thus characterised as a productive and reactive relationship wherein the 'strategies' of the powerful comprise direct responses to the 'tactics' of the powerless and vice versa. Moreover, an escalation or intensification of discipline and control often results in the emergence of correspondingly extreme forms of resistance (Rhodes 1998: 286). Such a correlation is pertinent to the hidden dynamics of high-security or management units for intractable prisoners. As this chapter argues, while they are designed to suppress opportunities for resistance, heightened disciplinary spaces effectively invite and magnify disorder.

Managing resistance: a historical and political continuum

The institutional dynamics that give rise to resistance need to be situated within historical contexts. This discussion is pertinent given the post-9/11 push towards securitisation in Australian prisons. High-security units are perennially sanctioned on the basis of the violent and dangerous identities of prisoners held within (Scraton et al 1991; Sim 1994, 2004; Rodriguez 2006; Davis 2005). Such risks are reinvented and repackaged each time a new facility is on the agenda. Presently the focus rests with terrorism and high-security units have been advanced domestically and internationally to house convicted terrorists and terror suspects in the 'war on terror' (Davis 2005; Gordon 2006: 42-59).

In Australia, officials warn that the increasing number of individuals in prison for terrorist related offences is producing internal security risks that could extend beyond prison walls. State prison authorities and the Australian Federal Police (2006) in particular have raised concerns about what they represent as moves by extremists to radicalise and recruit in prison (Australian Federal Police 2006). They argue such activity has led to a growth in terrorism beliefs and the involvement of individuals in gang and terrorist activity and pose security threats that could extend beyond prison walls. Such concerns have led to a proposed program of 'de-radicalisation' in prisons (Australian Federal Police 2006; ABC News Online 2007; AAP 2006), the construction of 'super-prisons' with increased systems of surveillance, security and control, and the development of an exclusive 'AA' high-security classification rating reserved for those already held in restrictive high-security conditions for terrorist-related offences in all Australian states (NSW Parliament 2005; Human Rights Law Resource Centre 2006).

While focused on threats to national security, current concerns must be recognised as part of an ongoing official drive towards securitisation and the management of prison order. Official concerns about 'risk' represent powerful justificatory drivers for the implementation of draconian policies and practices in criminal justice, and a perennial vindication for tighter management and security in prison (Sim 2004: 128). Violent resistance and non-compliance in prison are officially attributed to the 'risk' posed by individuals and in particular the prison system's 'worst of the worst'. Official explanations attribute disturbances to individual management and security problems and effectively divert any focus from systemic or material concerns such as prison conditions (Scraton et al 1991: 65). By focusing on criminal pathologies the authorities present powerful justifications for increased security, the use of segregation, punishment cells and high-security or control units.

Modern high-security units can be seen as a primary official response to prisoner rights movements, politicisation, disorder and rebellion experienced in prisons across western democratic states in the 1960s and 1970s (Fitzgerald 1977; Churchill & Vanderwall 1992). Such 'new generation' prisons combine hi-tech security devices, sophisticated spatial and managerial strategies with social isolation (Davis 2003: 50). They have been characterised as the 'penultimate synthesis of technology and space in the service of social control and dehumanisation within the prison' (Shaylor 1998: 387). Heightened institutional security and secrecy, physical separation of prisoners and guards, hi-tech monitoring equipment, constant surveillance, electronic controls, pastel colours, bullet proof glass, a sealed interior environment, sensory deprivation and overload, limited prisoner 'privileges', constant cell searches by specialist security squads and open-ended sentences are all hallmarks of modern high-security (Funnell 2006; Haney 2003; Haney & Lynch 1997; Human Rights Watch 1999). In high-security, technologies are mutually reinforcing, giving new meaning to prisoner experiences of 'total confinement'. In these units, prisoners have been routinely subjected to excessive levels of force including forced cell extractions, discharge of electronic stun devices, chemical sprays, shot guns with rubber and real bullets and the use of psychotropic drugs for pacification (Gordon 2006: 50).

Australia's first high-security units, namely the Katingal Special Security Unit in New South Wales and Jika Jika were in the 1970s developed in line with international standards and trends (Inquest Transcript 1988-1989b: 445). Most pertinent to these trends was the increasing use of segregation and classification systems operating on the principle of separating recalcitrant prisoners from the majority. In 1966 the landmark Mountbatten report into British prisons marked the beginning of a new era in prison security (Mountbatten 1966). Authorities commissioned the report following a series of sensational escapes by notorious high-security prisoners (Fitzgerald 1977: 49). Most significant was Mountbatten's recommendations that a centralised classification system determine the security risk of all prisoners from highest to lowest, and that prisoners classified high-security be centrally detained within single 'Alcatraz-type' segregation units (Fitzgerald 1977: 51-52). The Mountbatten Report signified a repressive shift from 'treatment' and 'rehabilitation' within penal policy back to 'control' and 'security' (Fitzgerald 1977: 50). The increasing implementation of segregation principles during this time has been criticised as fostering the widespread use of high-security units as 'prisons within prisons' (Fitzgerald 1977). In Australia the use of punitive segregation and development of high-security units developed as a retributive response by officials to the growing movement of prisoner rights and specific events such as the 1974 Bathurst riots in NSW and widespread unrest and rioting in Pentridge Prison Victoria (Zdenkowski & Brown 1982).

In addition to segregation, high-security also formed the basis for the application of pseudo-scientific principles and practices of 'behavioural modification' and 'adjustment'. These rose to prominence through an era of disturbing psychological experimentation and strategies designed for the purposes of counter-insurgency, interrogation and political imprisonment in the cold war period (McCoy 2006; Gordon 2006; Physicians for Human Rights 2005; Lucas 1976). During this time, research in the fields of psychology, particularly cognitive science, revealed the powerful potential of manipulating human behaviour and the devastating impacts of sensory deprivation and prolonged isolation on the human psyche (McCoy 2006; Physicians for Human Rights 2005). Other research highlighted the impact of sleep deprivation, the administration of psychotropic drug and electroshock treatments, 'special' behavioural adjustment incentive programs and social isolation (McCoy 2006; Ryan 1992: 83-109; Fitzgerald 1975). Much of this research and 'expertise', gleaned from the imprisonment and interrogation of political dissidents in Northern Ireland, South Africa, Russia, East Germany and Korea, was applied in domestic prison systems in the 1960s and 1970s to deal with prisoner subversion and non-compliance (Ryan 1992; Fitzgerald 1977; Lucas 1976: 153-167).

These technologies are officially neutralised as painless spatial and psychological methods to achieve prisoner control, and are legitimated by professional discourses associated with security, punishment and incarceration (Rodriguez 2006: 148-149). However, whether the methods used are overtly physical or psychological, 'the intent is to apply stress to the individual in such a way that normal psychological functioning and defence mechanisms break down and the victim becomes amenable to behaviour manipulation' (Lucas 1976: 156). In this sense psychologically geared methods of control are devised to curb independent thinking, to 'break' and 'remould' difficult or recalcitrant prisoners into a state of conformity and compliance; and to 'silence and destroy' those concerned with their rights (Rodriguez 2006; Ryan 1992).

It is critical to recognise how criminal stereotypes and the institutional criminalisation of dissent have served to justify the use of draconian methods and technologies of control in prison. The uses of high-security or control units must be therefore considered as systems devised to ensure total control over long-term prisoners identified and cast by the authorities as unruly and dangerous. However, experience suggests the nature of power structures in high-security and the stringency of conditions have achieved little in terms of managing disorder. Rather, as the case study of the Jika Jika High-Security Unit demonstrates, such conditions have magnified the institutional struggle over control, exacerbating extreme forms of disorder, violent confrontation and crisis.

Case Study: resistance in the Jika Jika High-Security Unit

Prisoner disturbances are often examined through the lens of official discourse and represented as manifestations of individual disciplinary or management problems and security concerns rather than as comprising a direct product of material conditions, institutional power structures and practices. In this way prisoner actions are stripped of their meaning and legitimacy. They are often dismissed as the result of drug-induced, hysterical, violent and threatening behaviour and regarded as confirming the individual pathologies of those confined as beyond rehabilitation and redemption (Scraton et al 1991).[2] As argued above, this provides an ongoing powerful impetus for security crackdowns and harsher punishments. For this reason the following section prioritises prisoner accounts of resistance. Such impressions stand in stark contrast to official assurances that Jika Jika was a secure, efficient and humane solution for housing high-risk prisoners. To consider acts of resistance in the absence of this context would be to overlook the impact and experience of institutional power while confirming simplistic images associated with criminality, violence, dangerousness and lack of social value. Most importantly it is through the characterisation of prisoner acts of resistance out of context, as 'animalistic', 'mad' or 'violent' that attention is inevitably directed away from the violence associated with methods of institutional discipline and control in high-security.

In October 1987, prisoners in the Pentridge Prison Jika Jika High-Security Unit (hereafter 'Jika') built a barricade and lit a fire to draw attention to conditions. The fire resulted in the deaths of five prisoners and the Jika's closure as a high-

---

2   In prison most violence cannot be unquestioningly characterised as resistance. In high-security personality clashes, ongoing vendettas and the frequent incidence of physical confrontation and violence are fundamental to daily institutional life and relationships. Jika Jika specifically was defined by a predatory, masculine culture of violence that is present in all male prisons. While recognising the predominance of such a culture, violence and domination in prison must be understood not as a pathological manifestation of abnormal otherness but part of the normal routine which is sustained and legitimated by institutional power structures and the wider culture of masculinity (Sim 1994; Scraton et al 1991).

security prison. Jika was constructed to house and manage the system's 'worst' prisoners. However, despite the emphasis on technology and efficiency, the complex was fraught with entrenched management problems, internal conflict and disorder. Between 1980 and 1987 there were multiple escapes, assaults, murders, prisoner campaigns, protest actions barricades, fires, hunger strikes, acts of self harm, attempted suicides and prisoner allegations of misconduct and brutality by prison staff (Prison Reform Group 1988; Inquest Transcript 1988-1989a; Inquest Transcript 1988-1989b). During this time, the Victorian prison authorities sought to deflect attention from the acute level of crisis within. They attempted to neutralise prisoner campaigns, presenting publicised incidents as individual disturbances and reinforcing the violent nature of prisoners. Each act of aberrant behaviour or breach of security was systematically represented and used to fortify justifications for tighter security, stricter discipline and ultimately longer periods spent in high-security. Conversely, Jika prisoners publicly challenged these official views while heightening individual and collective campaigns of non-compliance. However the price paid for this was an ever expanding sentence in high-security, the ongoing denial of prison 'privileges' and in some cases serious bodily harm and death.

Resistance within high-security is pervasive, subversive, and requires prisoner ingenuity. It incorporates a broad variety of actions and attitudes. While many prisoners resisted the Jika regime, many did not perceive their actions as ideological or political.[3] In Jika, transgressive acts often served simple needs such as letting off steam or creating a situation to break the monotony of the daily routine. In this respect, 'counter-conduct' in prison can often be characterised as much by anger, rage, exploitation and injustice as by pleasure, play and boredom (Bosworth & Carrabine 2001: 507). It is therefore important to distinguish between acts of resistance and unintentional or intentional acts of transgression.

Transgression is judged or defined by those who react to it, while resistance rests on the intentions of the actor(s) (Cresswell 1996: 23). This is illustrated through prisoner actions in Jika, where daily regimes and routines were unselfconsciously subverted and defied. Rather than stemming from broader political objectives (although sometimes they did), these everyday actions can be characterised as reflexive and unselfconscious; organic responses and strategies to survive the stringencies of lockdown. These included heated exchanges between prisoners and prison officers and prisoner refusal in many forms (Inquest Transcript 1988-1989a: 694-710). While not intentionally political to begin with transgressive acts provide 'potentials' for resistance, in that the moment a reaction or response is drawn from the institution, the meaning of the act correspondingly transforms, providing new possibilities for future struggle (Cresswell 1996: 23).

The transformative potential of transgressive resistance is illustrated through unauthorised modes of communication engaged by Jika prisoners. These conversations, dubbed by the authorities as 'Jika talk', were based on codes of sign language

---

3   While prisoner disobedience and rebellion constituted an essential part of the daily routine in Jika, it is also recognised that not all prisoners resisted. Prisoners with partners, wives and children often adapted to and accepted the system in order to retain contact with the outside world, while others chose not to challenge the system for their own personal reasons. The prisoner accounts used have emerged as those of active prison campaigners who have specifically sought to get information out about their experiences, conditions, views and actions. This chapter therefore represents a very specific experience of resistance in the high-security wing of Jika.

used to converse across the bulletproof glass divides separating unit 'sides' (Inquest Transcript 1988-1989b: 2024). One prisoner stated that prisoners believed Jika was electronically bugged with listening devices, so anything of any great importance was said via sign language (Inquest Transcript 1988-1989b: 1106). While 'Jika talk' was used to organise collective protests such as the 1987 fire in secrecy, it often served as a general method of communication (Inquest Transcript 1988-1989b: 2141). 'Jika talk' comprised a basic survival tool in that it enabled a medium for prisoner conversation to occur unmonitored by prison officers and other hi-tech surveillance devices. It also enabled prisoners to sustain a sense of collectivism despite the conditions and pressures of lockdown.

Resistance tactics in Jika are characterised by the following categories of 'self-protecting', 'campaigning', 'escaping', 'striking', and 'confronting' (Cohen & Taylor 1972: 134). Perhaps most critical to the Jika experience is 'self-protective' tactics, which encompass a range of refusals to cooperate with prison staff, prisoner intransigence and challenges to rules. Self-protective resistance also refers to the use of intellectual engagement or 'mind building', where prisoners use study as a coping mechanism to make sense of their own experience and assert themselves. This is accompanied by a rise in self-consciousness and realisation of the individual self 'against' the institution rather than 'within' it (Cohen & Taylor 1972: 138).

Self-protective tactics can be illustrated through various forms of refusal and constituted a fundamental non-violent basis for passive resistance by Jika prisoners (Inquest Transcript 1988-1989a: 694). Prisoners refused food, medication and prison officer orders. They also engaged in campaigns of disobedience, holding competitions as to how many charges one could accumulate. It was reported that prisoners 'would constantly come out on muster with one shoe on, or a singlet on, or a shirt on backwards, bed unmade or stay in bed while [officers] were trying to do requests' (Inquest Transcript 1988-1989a: 711).

Self-imposed loss of privileges (LOP) was an additional response by prisoners to the arbitrary cancelling visits or confiscating various privileges such as activities equipment, televisions or radios by prison staff with little or no explanation. Self-imposed LOP involved the refusal of 'privileges' and comprises a self-conscious form of buying out of or 'resigning from the system' (Interview 2004). Overall, self-protective tactics in Jika comprised retaliatory responses by prisoners who sought to exert control in their interactions with prison officers by 'upping the ante', welcoming the prospect of retribution and demonstrating they remained unbroken by the system (Interview 2004).

'Campaigning' is a related mode of fighting back that involves prisoners formalising complaints about conditions into professional individual and collective campaigns (Cohen & Taylor 1972: 140). The role of 'campaigning' is particularly significant to Jika as many of the emerging prisoner accounts and experiences were products of ongoing campaigns by prisoners considered 'trouble-makers' by officials (Inquest Transcript 1988-1989b). If an incident occurred where a prisoner was intimidated, abused or threatened, unit prisoners kept diaries and records documenting events. In some units mutual support was provided between prisoners on upcoming legal trials or reclassification, along with other grievances. These same prisoners lobbied collectively for a public inquiry or Royal Commission into conditions and allegations of brutality within Jika. They lobbied staff for legal and educational materials. They painted, drew pictures and political cartoons and composed poetry and writings about their experience. They wrote letters to family members, friends, prison advocates, legal representatives, and journalists about conditions inside. They smuggled out unauthorised information and produced and circulated prisoner publications detailing their experience and concerns. Many made formal complaints to the Ombudsman and some prisoners pursued human rights litigation against the Department (Inquest Transcript 1988-1989b). Some of these men, still in the prison system, continue with this work in different institutional contexts nearly 20 years on.

'Escaping' involves prisoners physically transgressing the bounds of the institution. In 1983, four prisoners caused the authorities great embarrassment when they broke out of Jika. While before this period the complex was officially celebrated as 'escape-proof', the four easily eluded prison officer supervision, expensive video surveillance, microwave technology and the razor wire fences lining the compound. They remained at large for over two months (Inquest Exhibit 183 1988-1989b).

'Striking' refers to modes of resistance such as hunger strikes designed to attract outside attention and humanitarian responses. External support and exposure were critical for high-security prisoners who had no access to the media to publicise conditions. Between 1986 and 1987 in Jika there was a series of individual and collective hunger strikes. A number of prisoners participated in a collective hunger strike during March and April in 1986 and this resulted in the granting of some small concessions such as the provision of carpet mats on the cell concrete floors (Interview 2004).

As argued above, while heightened forms of disciplinary control and the tightening of security are designed to suppress resistance, in reality they have the effect of exacerbating extreme forms of disorder and violent confrontation. 'Confronting' tactics signify a last-resort willingness to take chances in a powerless situation (Cohen & Taylor 1972). These acts are largely collective and include barricades, violent attacks on staff, prisoners 'cracking-up' and engaging in cell and property destruction, sieges, hostage taking and fire. When publicised, such disturbances are attributed to a subversive and troublemaker minority when in reality they are indicative of deeply systemic problems and crises. Such activity peaked in Jika during 1987 and was exacerbated by official retributive responses to prisoner resistance. Prisoners reported security crackdowns, the arbitrary denial of privileges, abusive force and 'special treatment' were frequently directed at noncompliant prisoners. Moreover, resisting prisoners perceived they were singled out, intimidated and threatened by staff (Prison Reform Group 1988). Jika prisoners argued their 'confronting' responses were amplified by official refusals to address grievances in a manner that extended beyond the implementation of retributive disciplinary crackdowns.

A mode of reactive non-compliance associated with high-security is bodily resistance. Such acts comprise a response to definitive and open-ended sentences in extreme conditions of isolation. Bodily resistance takes place in both collective and individual circumstances and involve actions such as the 'bronze-up' (the smearing and throwing of excrement), no wash protests and self-mutilation. Through the use of their bodies, Jika prisoners engaged in forms of resistance over which the authorities and prison officers had no control. While prisoner self-harm was reported to take place readily, there is too little publicly available documentation to establish its prevalence in Jika (Prison Reform Group 1988). However, a regularly recorded example of bodily resistance was the prisoner bronze-up. In Jika, the bronze-up involved prisoners collecting their own faeces and smearing it throughout the cell areas (Prison Reform Group 1988; Interview 2004; Inquest Exhibit 18 1988-1989b). Not only did it create a hygiene risk to staff and other prisoners; the act of smearing aggravated non-participating prisoners because of the discomfort associated with the smell within non-ventilated and confined areas. The bronze-up served as an effective bargaining action for prisoners due to the fact the authorities could not prevent its use.

Bodily resistance involves the symbolic subversion of power structures imprinted on the prisoner's body by processes of institutionalisation. When all avenues for rebellion are removed and prisoners experience the full effects of total confinement, they quickly discover that their bodies, the very ground of the panoptical relation, are its potential undoing (Rhodes 1998: 287). Forms of bodily resistance are essentially desperate vehicles for resisting when other external paths have been removed. Acts such as self-mutilation can also result in a temporary reprieve from conditions when prisoners are transferred to hospital. Most importantly, bodily resistance presents an avenue for prisoners to assert self-determination and control over their imprisoned bodies.

The experience of power and resistance in Jika illustrates that the avenues open to prisoners to air grievances and complaints are severely limited. The forms of resistance discussed above must be conceived as a desperate product of material conditions and power structures experienced by prisoners in high-security. The tendency of officials and staff to respond reactively to prisoner non-compliance through the escalation of discipline and control only serves to fuel institutional dysfunction, crisis and harm. This was certainly the case in Jika and matters escalated in 1987 with a series of violent incidents, the protest fire and deaths.

Conclusion

While it is clear that prisoner resistance and transgression led to an increased dynamic of institutional struggle in Jika, such actions are distinct from other direct instances of resistance self-consciously or collectively geared by prisoners to defend prisoner rights, raise awareness and publicly challenge the legitimacy of the institution. In this way, resistance in Jika marked a decisive progression that exacerbated the potentials for resistance within the distinct topographies of power integral to high-security. This progression responded directly to the changing functions and exertions of disciplinary power. As the regime became increasingly unaccountable, restrictive and coercive, prisoner actions in turn echoed such extremities, drawing attention from the outside and thus making prisoners and their plights increasingly visible, if only temporarily.

There is a dangerous dynamic that can develop in prison when discipline and security are maintained by forcible methods that exceed acceptable legal boundaries. As the case study of Jika demonstrates, the deployment of forcible methods and continuing exertions of unaccountable power within the restrictive context of high-security merely serve to build mutual resentment and antagonism while leading to the occurrence of serious abuses, violent outbursts, riots and a descent into general crisis. It was this dynamic that led to the barricade, fire and deaths in 1987.

Control and security based solutions do not address in any meaningful way problems produced by systemic, material conditions. They serve only to further entrench existing conflict and crises that are subsequently addressed through a further escalation of security and retributive responses. The prison regime requires and produces 'institutional crises as a premise for its constant revision and reinvention of technologies of domination' (Rodriguez 2006: 146). This is the self-fulfilling prophecy of security, which is linked to the official project of managing resistance.

This chapter has sought to demonstrate that resistance within institutional settings is integral to understanding the political and volatile dynamics of imprisonment. Central to this discussion are the official discourses and political contexts that have given rise to the increasing official drive towards prison securitisation. While prisoner rights movements of the 1960s and 1970s acted as a temporary trigger for reform and change, this chapter has examined the ways resistance has also served as a precursor for prison securitisation, namely the reproduction and proliferation of high-security as a measure to suppress and manage resistance.

A focus on resistance and its impacts on institutional dynamics, particularly within the sealed world of high-security, provide a critical space for the subjective exploration of the prison experience. The development of critical frameworks to analyse and understand prisoner actions as products of a system, provides an alternative counter-discourse to the predominant official focus on prisoner dangerousness, risk and violence that underpins the retributive shift towards securitisation. This can only serve to open up much needed rational debate about the costs of high-security while providing potential and opportunities for reform.

References

AAP 2006, National Media Release, 'Seminar to address radicalisation in prisons', 24 July, <http://afp.gov.au/media_releases/national/2006/seminar_to_address_radicalisation_in_prisons>.

ABC News Online 2007, 'Islam used as camouflage for prison gangs', 22 April, <www.abc.net.au/news/newsitems/200704/s1903490.htm>.

Australian Federal Police, July 2006, *National Media Release: seminar to address radicalisation in prisons*, Australian Federal Police Media, Canberra.

Bosworth, M 1999, *Engendering Resistance: agency and power in women's prisons*, Aldershot, Dartmouth.

Bosworth, M & Carrabine, E 2001, 'Reassessing resistance, race, gender and sexuality in prison', 3(4) *Punishment and Society* 501.

Carter, K 2000, 'The Casuarina Prison Riot: official discourse or appreciative inquiry', 12(3) *Current Issues in Criminal Justice* 363.

Churchill, W & Vanderwall, JJ (eds) 1992, *Cages of Steel: the politics of imprisonment in the United States*, Maissoneuve Press, Washington.

Cohen, S & Taylor, L 1972, *Psychological Survival: the experience of long-term imprisonment*, Penguin Books, Middlesex.

Corcoran, M 2005, *Out of Order: the political imprisonment of women in Northern Ireland 1972-1998*, Willan Publishing, Cullompton.

Cresswell, T 1996, *In Place/Out of Place: geography, ideology and resistance*, University of Minnesota Press, Minnesota.

Danaher, G, Schirato, T & Webb, J 2000, *Understanding Foucault*, Allen & Unwin, Sydney.

Davis, AY 2003, *Are Prisons Obsolete?*, Seven Stories Press, New York.

Davis, AY 2005, *Abolition Democracy: beyond empire, prisons and torture*, Seven Stories Press, New York.

Dayan, J 2002, 'Cruel and Unusual: parsing the meaning of punishment', in Pether, P & Sarat, A (eds), 5(2) *Law-Text-Culture* 7.

de Certeau, M 1984, *The Practice of Everyday Life*, translated by Rendall, S, University of California Press, Los Angeles.

Fellner, J & Mariner, J 1997, *Cold-storage: super-maximum security confinement in Indiana*, Human Rights Watch, New York.

Finnane, M 1997, *Punishment in Australian Society*, Oxford University Press, Oxford.

Fitzgerald, M 1975, *Control Units and the Shape of Things to Come, Radical Alternatives to Prison Publications*, London.

Fitzgerald, M 1977, *Prisoners in Revolt*, Penguin Books, Middlesex.

Foucault, M 1991a, *Discipline and Punish: the birth of the prison*, Penguin Books, Middlesex.

Foucault, M 1991b, 'Questions of method', in Burchell, G, Gordon, C & Miller, P (eds), *The Foucault Effect: studies in Governmentality with two lectures by and an Interview with Michel Foucault*, University of Chicago Press, Chicago.

Funnell, N 2006, 'Where the Norm is Not the Norm: Goulburn Correctional Centre and the Harm-U', 31(2) *Alternative Law Journal* 70.

Gordon, A 2006, 'Abu Ghraib: imprisonment and the war on terror', 48(1) *Race and Class* 42.

Haney, C & Lynch, M 1997, 'Regulating Prisons of the Future: a psychological analysis of supermax and solitary confinement', XXIII *New York University Review of Law and Social Change* 4.

Haney, C 2003, 'Mental Health Issues in Long-Term Solitary and 'Supermax' Confinement', 49(1) *Crime and Delinquency* 124.

Human Rights Law Resource Centre 2006, *Submission to UN High Commissioner for Human Rights regarding conditions of detention of unconvicted remand prisoners in Victoria, Australia*, Human Rights Law Resource Centre, Melbourne.

Human Rights Watch 1999, *Red Onion State Prison: super-maximum security confinement in Virginia*, Human Rights Watch, New York.

Ignatieff, M 1978, *A Just Measure of Pain: the penitentiary in the Industrial Revolution*, Columbia University Press, Columbia.

Inquest 1988-1989a, *Unpublished transcript of proceedings and exhibits at Coroner's investigation into the death of Sean Fitzgerald Downie*, State Coroner's Office, Melbourne.

Inquest 1988-1989b, *Unpublished transcript of proceedings and exhibits at Coroner's investigation into the deaths of James Loughnan, David McGauley, Arthur Gallagher, Robert Wright and Richard Morris*, State Coroner's Office, Melbourne.

Interview 2004, conducted with ex-Jika Jika prisoner Peter Reed, 15 May.

Lucas, WE 1976, 'Solitary Confinement: isolation as coercion to conform', 9 *Australian and New Zealand Journal of Criminology* 153.

McCoy, A 2006, *A Question of Torture: CIA interrogation from the Cold War to the War on Terror*, Metropolitan Books, New York.

McKeown, L 2001, *Out of Time: Irish Republican prisoners Long Kesh 1972-2000*, Beyond The Pale Publications, Belfast.

Mountbatten 1966, *Report of the Inquiry into Prison Escapes and Security*, HMSO Home Office, London.

NSW Parliament 2005, *Report of Proceedings, General Purpose Standing committee No 3, Inquiry into the Department of Corrective Service*, 8 December.

Physicians for Human Rights 2005, *Break Them Down: systematic use of torture by US forces*, Physicians for Human Rights, Washington.

Prison Reform Group 1988, 'Jika Jika Revisited: a collection of prisoner writings', *The Doing Time Magazine*, Prison Reform Group, Melbourne.

Pugliese, J 2002, 'Penal Asylum: refugees, ethics, hospitality', 1(1) *Borderlands e-journal*, <www.borderlandsejournal.adelaide.edu.au/vol1no1_2002/pugliese.html>.

Rhodes, L 1998, 'Panoptical intimacies', 10(2) *Public Culture* 385.

Rhodes, L 2004, *Total Confinement: madness and reason in the maximum-security prison*, University of California Press, Berkley.

Rodriguez, D 2006, *Forced Passages: imprisoned intellectuals and the US prison regime*, University of Minnesota Press, Minneapolis.

Ryan, M 1992, 'Solitude as Counter-Insurgency: the US isolation model of political incarceration', in Churchill, W & Vanderwall, JJ (eds), *Cages of Steel*, Maissoneuve Press, Washington.

Scraton, P, Sim, J & Skidmore, P 1991, *Prisons Under Protest, Crime, Justice and Social Policy Series*, Open University Press, Milton Keynes.

Shaylor, C 1998, 'It's like living in a black hole', 24(2) *New England Journal of Criminal and Civil Confinement* 385.

Sim, J 1994, 'Tougher than the rest? Men in prison', in Newburn, T & Stanko, E (eds), *Just Boys Doing Business? Men, Masculinities and Crime*, Routledge, London.

Sim, J 2004, 'The victimised state and the mystification of social harm', in Hillyard, P, Pantazis, C, Tombs, S & Gordon, D (eds), *Beyond Criminology: Taking Harm Seriously*, Pluto Press, London.

Vinson, T, Cunneen, C, Baldry, E, Collins, B & Brown, D 2004, 'The Nagle Report: 25 years on symposium' (Collection of Articles), 16(1) *Current Issues in Criminal Justice* 93.

Zdenkowski, G & Brown, D 1982, *The Prison Struggle: changing Australia's penal system*, Penguin Books, Ringwood.

21

RISK, PUNISHMENT AND LIBERTY

Mark Brown

*We are not born equal; we become equal as members of a group
on the strength of our decision to guarantee ourselves mutually
equal rights.*

Hannah Arendt, *The Origins of Totalitarianism* (1951)

Introduction

This chapter is concerned with three phenomena of utmost importance to our time:
the rise of 'risk' thinking; the recrudescent idea of existential dangers immanent in
certain types of offender; and the uncertain status of liberty rights in contemporary
western democracies. The chapter demonstrates how all three are linked and how the
discourses of risk and danger as they are articulated in contemporary penal politics
have come to place citizens' liberty rights, commonly regarded as basic and inalienable, on an increasingly unstable footing.

Such rights were of paramount concern to Hannah Arendt, the German-Jewish
political philosopher who, in the aftermath of the Holocaust, wrote about the genesis
of totalitarianism in the twin evils of anti-Semitism and imperialism. Arendt's analysis of illiberal and totalitarian rule provides lessons for us today that we would
ignore at our peril. Chief among these must be that the political rights of suspect
minorities – in her case, of Jews, Gypsies and mental defectives in 1930s Germany –
may be easily dispensed with, appearing, as it were, a cheap and wholly reasonable
exchange for the greater good of the wider society. Through abrogations that initially
barely register notice, we may move quite quickly toward a much more fundamental
collapse of politics and morality that undermines the basis of civilised society.

Arendt (1951, 1963) traced the conditions and processes that allowed a class of
people, the Jews of Europe, to be stripped of their citizenship rights, to be placed
outside law, to be deemed 'stateless persons' and finally to be regarded as superfluous and warranting extermination. In her account of the trial of Eichmann, the SS
officer accused of masterminding the Final Solution, Arendt coined the term 'the
banality of evil'. Eichmann showed little evidence of being a monster and indeed
little malevolence of spirit. And his conscience, so intricately examined during the
trial, and through which Arendt by extension discusses the conscience of the German people, was far from being void. Rather, the acceptance by Eichmann and the

wider population of the need to make the Reich *Judenrein* (free of Jews and pure in blood) came through a series of small steps in which each increment – the formation of Jewish lists, the exclusion of Jews from certain jobs, limitations on currency transactions, restrictions on movement or migration, the identification of Jews by special signs (the yellow star), together with the high position of those supporting the necessity of these steps – progressively separated European Jews from the political community by membership of which, as Arendt (1951: 382) notes in my opening quotation, we 'guarantee ourselves mutually equal rights'.

In this chapter I want to make the case that recent developments in the penal sphere which bring together the age-old grammar of danger with a new science of risk represent a particularly potent and toxic combination that is corrosive to democratic rights and values. Arendt's (1951: 567) work is valuable for the light it sheds on the mechanics and meaning of the 'many intermediate stages' by which this is achieved. Her work should also make us vigilant to what she terms the 'strong temptations' (Arendt 1951: 592) that exist to solve social problems by recourse to strategies of domination.

I wish to argue that society's current fixation with the dangers posed by child sex offenders, when grafted to the utopian dream of a calculus that would render their behaviour predictable, provides the conditions which authorise the first small steps, many of which have already been taken in the case of sex offenders, by which individuals are forced outside political community, into a position as secondary citizens, thus narrowing their liberty rights and eroding the foundation upon which our democratic citizenship has been founded. The twin notions of risk and danger are central to the machinery by which this has been achieved and so the first section of this chapter will briefly point to the place of these ideas in the penal process. Part two will then consider a case study, examining a series of recent Australasian initiatives aimed at protecting society from people who have sexually offended against children. Finally, I will draw out some of the key lessons of Arendt's analysis of totalitarian rule, suggesting that in our determination to stamp out the risks and dangers presented by child sex offenders we have begun to move down the path toward illiberal government.

Risk and danger

The French sociologist Robert Castel (1991) has described a radical shift in social thinking and practices, one he characterised as a movement 'From Dangerousness to Risk'. The new strategies, he argued, 'dissolve the notion of a subject or a concrete individual, and put in its place a combinatory of factors, the factors of risk' (1991: 281). The idea of the demise of dangerousness is now widely held, both in the theoretical circles within which Castel moves and in the technical literature on offender assessment (for example, Steadman 2000).

The dangerous offender

Dangerousness, as it has classically been thought of, and as Castel (1991) imagines it, is something attaching to the person. A statement such as 'this offender should not be released because he is dangerous to himself and others' typifies this presumption that danger is embodied in the individual. Naturally, the sorts of things by which individuals are felt to present a threat change over time, so the idea of dangerousness also reflects social and cultural conditions and anxieties and, at different times, moves forward and back between the idea of dangerous individuals and the idea of 'dangerous classes'. Moreover, the idea of dangerousness is always a two-part classification, or what Castel (1991: 283) terms a 'deeply paradoxical notion', because it implies both a quality immanent to the individual and a probability that the feared action will come to pass.

Risk and reoffending

This probability element is what we refer to as risk and criminologists have tried since at least the 1920s to identify the characteristics of offenders that would help predict whether or not they will reoffend. The factors found to be predictive of further offending we term 'risk factors' and so 'risk' itself, as the term is understood in the penal system, refers to the probability that an individual will at some point in the future reoffend in some specified way.

Castel's insight was that the radical expansion in the use of risk assessment would produce a paradigm shift in the way we think about and work with offenders. The risk factors so crucial to these calculations of risk, far from describing the attributes of a distinct or knowable person, are instead merely an array of what Castel (1991: 288) terms 'heterogeneous elements'. Their value, therefore, lies not in the sense of learning who the person is as a person, but that they 'construct the objective conditions of emergence of danger' (1991: 289). Mary Douglas (1992) attributes the new attraction of risk as a concept to its connection with scientific precision. Thus, she suggests, for things that threaten us '*danger* would once have been the right word', but plain *danger* does not have the aura of science or afford the pretension of a possible precise calculation' (1992: 25, emphasis in original).

Another attraction of risk, Douglas (1992) suggests, is that it pretends an analysis that is purely calculative and thus free of political or cultural weight. Of course, this is nonsense. To begin, the array of 'heterogeneous elements' referred to by Castel (1991) is heterogeneous by the fact that it includes factors both endogenous and exogenous to the individual. Risk assessment is concerned with the distribution of such factors across a population: it is a 'science' of population rather than a science of 'the person' or of 'the human condition'. As such, many features of the social environment, including social or cultural mores and by-products of social structural variables (such as poor education associated with social deprivation) become inscribed in the calculative mechanisms of assessment tools. But although such tools sweep together both individual and environmental factors to produce a collection of 'risk factors', both the ascription of risk and the interventions this triggers are located at the level of the individual.

Treatment and risk management thus emerges as a raison d'être of contemporary penal practice. In Castel's (1991: 289) view, this creates 'a vast hygienist utopia' in which all are deemed in some measure deficient (even the mildest offender is still only 'low' risk) and planners are given the almost unchallengeable right to intervene under a rubric of prevention. Any casual examination of contemporary correctional systems will bear out most parts of this depiction: risk assessments are now routinely applied to almost all offenders, whether before sentence or on entry to community or custodial corrections. The risk classification offenders receive plays a large role in

255

determining eligibility for non-custodial sanctions and, if placed on such a sanction, determines the level and intensity of supervision.

The calculation of offender risk is thus now one of the key movements around which the penal system and penal work is routinised. This observation has prompted writers like Feeley and Simon (1992, 1994) to suggest the emergence of a New Penology wherein penal work is structured around the classification, control and management of offender risk and in which the old subject of penal power, a moral actor whose guilt, remorse, reasons for offending and so on structured punishment and penal practice, has been replaced by a technocratic system for the management of risky populations.

An alternative view

These massive shifts toward risk-based practice, while transforming the penal system in important ways, have not entirely effaced the notion of dangerousness and the dangerous offender. Indeed, the idea continues to have force thanks to its implicit relationship with existential threats to self and community, links that Douglas (1992) suggests place it together with sin and taboo as signalling key decision points in the rules and mores that underpin community solidarity. Viewed together with her earlier analysis of the concepts of purity and defilement (Douglas 1966), dangerous offenders may be also understood as those who present peculiar threats to a society through risk of defilement. Both Hacking (2003) and Pratt (2005) have suggested that it is precisely the threatened defilement of children – an uncontested symbol of purity in most societies – that gives contemporary outrage against child sex offenders such potency. In contexts such as this the ideas of risk and danger come together, combining an identified existential threat with a calculative modality that offers the possibility of quarantining it. Further still, these notions of risk and danger have eclipsed the discourse of punishment – of who should be punished and to what degree – to emerge into a new field of hygienist social defence: the monitoring and internment of 'suspect' citizens.

Case study: sex offender monitoring and preventive confinement

In the past decade moral panic over child sexual abuse has reached a level that, while perhaps not unprecedented, has been of sufficient force to unleash a wave of extremely punitive and illiberal measures designed to promote 'community safety'. In the main, these new measures aim to protect children by keeping at bay the threats posed by high-risk or dangerous offenders through programs of post-sentence monitoring or confinement. Some Australasian jurisdictions already have laws for the preventive detention of dangerous offenders. Preventive detention is essentially the imposition of an indefinite sentence of imprisonment for the purposes of public protection, wherein the public interest over-rides the normal guiding principle that punishment should remain proportionate to the nature and gravity of the crime. A long debate in the 1980s over the merits of preventive detention for dangerous offenders (see generally Floud & Young 1982) was rekindled in Australia by the cases of Garry David in Victoria and Gregory Kable in New South Wales when in each case special legislation was used to ensure their continued confinement at the close of a finite sentence.

This experiment in post-sentence confinement came to nought, however, as Garry David died in prison and the New South Wales legislation was struck down as unconstitutional by the High Court in the case of *Kable v Director of Public Prosecutions (NSW)* (1996) 189 CLR 51. However, by the end of the 1990s in the United States, post-sentence confinement had become an established feature of crime control through the use of civil commitment statutes, or what are otherwise termed Sexually Violent Predator laws.

Australian State governments have taken their cue from the US and followed suit. In June 2003 Queensland's *Dangerous Prisoners (Sexual Offenders) Act* came into force. There now exists a small literature on the Act (see for example, Gray 2005), and the case of *Fardon v Attorney General (Qld)* (2004) 210 ALR 50, in which the constitutionality of Robert Fardon's indefinite preventive confinement under the Act was upheld by the High Court. In 2006 both Western Australia and New South Wales responded, promulgating legislation that provided for post-sentence detention and/or extended supervision orders under the *Crimes (Serious Sexual Offenders) Act* 2006 (NSW) and the *Dangerous Sexual Offenders Act* 2006 (WA). By 2007 Victoria also was well under way to its own post-sentence confinement scheme, which is likely also to be targeted toward sexual offenders generally. Each of these schemes provides for long periods of post-sentence confinement – ranging from indefinite detention in Queensland and Western Australia to five-year (extendable) detentions in New South Wales and the mooted Victorian scheme.

These confinement schemes may also be buttressed by arrangements for the long-term supervision and monitoring of offenders in the community. New Zealand and Victoria both have quite draconian versions of such schemes and it is on these two pieces of legislation that I wish to concentrate, not simply because alongside the confinement schemes they represent a considerable undermining of citizens' liberty rights, but because by their nature they will be applied to a much larger population of individuals.

Victoria

Victoria's serious sex offender monitoring legislation was rushed through the Legislative Council in a single day on 24 February 2005. This legislation, the *Serious Sex Offenders Monitoring Act* 2005, provides for extended supervision orders of up to 15 years to be placed upon child sex offenders who have completed a finite sentence of imprisonment. The Act as passed provides for limitations to be placed on an ex-offender's movement, place of work, residence and contact with certain classes of people (principally children), and further provides for mandatory assessment and if necessary treatment, as well as electronic monitoring, the imposition of a curfew and restrictions upon activities, such as use of the internet. Incredibly, the Act also provides that a person, once registered, may be directed to 'reside at premises that are situated on land that is within the perimeter of a prison' (s 16(3A)). In order to qualify for this scheme, sex offenders must have been imprisoned for one of a long list of mainly child sex offences (though bestiality also is included) and, following an assessment of risk and other relevant matters, a Court must be satisfied 'to a high degree of probability' that the individual would commit another relevant offence if extended supervision were not imposed.

These are extraordinary restrictions upon the life and liberty of people who are by all other measures free citizens. Briefings provided to parliamentarians estimated that as many as 80 to 100 sex offenders per year would be eligible to come under monitoring. The debate on the key issues raised by this sort of legislation was mild to say the least, and there was wide bipartisan support for the measure (Hansard 2005). Both sides accepted the premise that children represent a special class worthy of protection and that offences against children constitute a form of behaviour so egregious that almost any measure against it would prove acceptable. 'Child-sex offenders', it was argued by the government, 'commit extraordinary crimes, and as such must be subject to extraordinary measures' (2005: 21). The Bill, it was said, must be seen as 'an unusual step that is to apply in unusual circumstances' (2005: 22). In this climate, the idea of liberty rights rapidly evaporated. This occurred in two ways. To begin, the rights of those who have committed sex offences against children were treated as essentially frivolous: the Minister shepherding the Bill noted that while 'there are all sorts of issues about one's rights after serving one's sentence', the 'special obligation' of protecting children 'warrants whatever [restrictions are necessary] in relation to the supposed rights of offenders' (2005: 36). Once offender rights had been framed as subsidiary to those of other citizens, discussion turned simply on whether due process was followed to ensure that only those who were high-risk, and thus could fall under the provisions of the legislation, would be captured: protections were therefore provided first for establishing and then for reviewing assessments of risk to ensure people are not incorrectly classified. Civil liberties, in other words, attach only to those members of the community who fall outside the class of high-risk sex offenders and so care must be taken to ensure people are not incorrectly classified.

The Victorian case illustrates very neatly the way notions of risk and danger work together to justify penal measures that significantly erode the liberty rights of a class of citizens. The danger to children acts as a kind of leitmotif for existential threats to community and, in the face of such a threat, their protection must know no bounds. Further, the existence of a scientific literature on child sex offenders underwrites the 'vast hygienist utopia' (Castel 1991), providing the logic and tools whereby these risks may be identified and eliminated. Unfortunately, as Wood and Ogloff (2006) have observed, the Victorian Parliament proceeded on the highly contentious assumption that high-risk sex offenders could indeed be accurately identified. Yet, as research summarised by Wood and Ogloff shows, reoffending rates often are very low, sometimes as low as 6% for certain types of child sex offences. Moreover, while the language of risk speaks of 'high' or 'medium-high' risk, carrying with it images of imminent, impending threat, the base rates that underlie these may sometimes be no more than a 12% chance of reoffending within five years. The capacity of current prediction methods to predict what an offender will do is thus distinctly limited. 'Whilst the few most empirically validated and widely used tests show promise, they are far from predicting with the accuracy mandated in [the Act]' (2006: 188).

The Victorian case also illustrates the implicit expansive tendency of utopian hygienist schemes. Together the opposition Liberal and National parties argued strongly that the legislation should not be limited just to child sex offenders, as a class, for they were themselves part of a larger class of dangerous offenders requiring post-sentence monitoring. The offence of rape, in particular, became central to the debate: why should the legislation capture an offender who rapes a 17-year-old young woman, but exclude the rapist of an 18 year old? Further, could not the elderly also be regarded as a group within the community to whom, like children, special protection was owed? The opposition lamented the pity that 'this legislation had [not] been more vigilant in its opportunity to address more broadly the prospect' of extending post-sentence supervision to these two additional classes (Hansard 2005: 31). Thus, any sense that child sex offenders might constitute some kind of singular 'special class' is dispelled.

New Zealand

The New Zealand legislation providing for extended supervision orders (ESO) is similar to its Victorian counterpart in its broad approach and features: it provides for long term (up to 10 years) monitoring of child sex offenders judged to be at risk of further offending of a similar type. However, the scheme, introduced by the *Parole (Extended Supervision) Amendment Act* 2004 goes further in some important ways. It is retrospective in nature, meaning that offenders who at the time at which it came into effect were essentially free citizens, having completed a finite sentence and having been released back into the community, could be made subject to its provisions. Furthermore, the scheme allows for the penal confinement of an 'offender' – as those subject to the Act are described – for up to 12 months under home detention. It was this penal character of the scheme and the availability of retrospectivity that forced the New Zealand Attorney-General to conclude that its provisions 'constitute a prima facie infringement of [the retroactive penalties and double jeopardy provisions] of the Bill of Rights Act' (cited in *Belcher v Chief Executive of the Department of Corrections* [2007] 1 NZLR 507 at [31]). In 2006 the New Zealand Court of Appeal heard an appeal by Joseph Belcher against being placed under an extended supervision order. The circumstances of the case and the judgment of the court shed important light on the operation of the scheme and the latitude courts are prepared to grant executive power in the face of special threats. At the time the ESO was imposed, Belcher had been living freely in the community for three and a half years and his appeal against the ESO rested on two factors related to this. First, he argued the ESO constituted retrospective double punishment and so breached the Bill of Rights. Second, he argued the evidence of risk did not substantiate a declaration against him. In an interim judgment, the court concluded in respect of the first issue that an ESO 'amounts to punishment and thus engages ss 25 and 26 of the *New Zealand Bill of Rights Act* 1990 [NZBORA]' ([2007] 1 NZLR 507 at [49]) and as such 'the ESO legislation is inconsistent with NZBORA' (at [57]). However, since the Crown's argument in this area had been so poor, the court asked the Crown to reconsider and return with proper argument on the issue. In the event, no formal declaration of inconsistency was made, a decision supported by the New Zealand Supreme Court when the case later went to appeal (*Belcher v Chief Executive of the Department of Corrections* [2007] NZSC 54).

Yet the court was much more confident of its capacity to rule on the issue of risk. Here three matters were at issue: applying group data (of reconviction rates) to individual cases, the importance of ideographic (individuating) factors, and the timing of reoffending.

Evidence was presented by the appellant, Belcher, that while the risk assessments used were roughly accurate in separating groups of offenders, within the appellant's group it was impossible to say whether any one member would reoffend or not. Furthermore, since reoffending rates were not high (only 28% after five years, or 43% at 10 years), the prediction at best amounted to chance. Since the Crown had proffered no information that was specific to the appellant, there was no reason to believe he should not be within the non-reoffending membership of his group. This view, the appellant argued, should be bolstered by the fact that the appellant had been a free member of the community for a lengthy period after his fixed sentence.

The court was not swayed by this argument and two factors appear to weigh heavily in its reasoning. First, its construal of public risk was extraordinarily broad, more so even considering the consequences for otherwise free citizens: '[T]he risk of relevant offending', it concluded, should be 'both real and ongoing and one that cannot sensibly be ignored having regard to the nature and gravity of the likely re-offending' ([2007] 1 NZLR 507 at [11]). Thus, once a picture of possible outcomes has successfully been painted – those threats to children around which the legislation is drafted – the demand for predictive accuracy is lowered to the point of 'real and ongoing', something statistical risk factors seem capable of establishing on their own. Second, the court appears to have given considerable deference to the presumed rights of government to make laws on public policy grounds ([2007] 1 NZLR 507 at [34]), something which would condition courts' interpretation of matters like substantiveness of public risk, and that warranted the rather unusual step of reserving a judgment of inconsistency with the NZBORA.

The New Zealand case seems to indicate that whether risk is treated as a kind of folk concept (as in Victoria) or in a more technical fashion (as in New Zealand, where risk instruments are used and their interpretation debated), it functions principally as a shorthand for perceived or imagined dangers and it is this sense of danger – the defilement of children – that drives concern for technical matters like probability of offending, or the liberty rights of citizens, into a secondary and subservient position.

None of this should be to say, however, that the problems of child sex offending are not real, nor that the risks of repeat offending by some individuals are insignificant. Rather, it is to point out that solutions to social problems need to be more than simply practical solutions, they must also be just solutions (Floud & Young 1982). It is for this reason that the Court of Appeal's acceptance of group-based reoffending data seems distinctly unjust, for, to paraphrase Floud and Young, justice demands that evidence of dangerousness include more than simply evidence that a person belongs to an at-risk group, it demands that that the evidence of dangerousness be specific to this person, something that requires a model of individual causation over and above the simple identification of common risk factors.

Dangerous offenders: between liberty and civil death

To close this chapter I wish to consider the problems of risk, punishment and liberty through a return to the work of Arendt and a consideration of the way societies may accept and participate in the unwinding of rights and the imposition of what historically has been termed 'civil death' upon certain of their own members.

The seductions of domination and the problem of superfluous people

Arendt (1951) predicted that the era of totalitarian rule had passed, but that the seductions of domination would remain. For that reason her descriptions of illiberal government should serve as 'the politically most important yardstick for judging events of our time' (1951: 570). And so, regardless of political stance, do new developments serve the purposes of domination or not?

The case studies presented in this chapter, wherein discourses of risk and danger combine to justify the emergence of a new, second-class citizen, one who is monitored, confined, restricted in activity and movement, appear to do just that. But what is it about the peculiar risks posed by the sex offender that make this kind of response thinkable or reasonable? And why, as critical criminologists, should we look to the work of an historian and political theorist for guidance? Does not criminology already possess sufficient tools for the analysis of this 'problem'? And why, if our problem is so anodyne as the monitoring and confinement of a few nasty sex offenders, should we look to the origins of the Holocaust – of all things – for guidance? The answers to these questions will, I hope, become apparent here. But I may preface this discussion with Arendt's own recognition that although her main concern was the history and fate of Jews, the logics, strategies and objectives that provided for their sequestration and designation as superfluous 'sub-humans' were by no means limited to the 'Jewish problem' alone. Here I wish to mention just three of these factors in connection with the 'sex offender problem': first, the logic of utilitarian solutions; second, the strategy of camouflage; and finally, the objective of killing 'the juridical person in man' (Arendt 1951: 577).

Utilitarian logic

Under the logic of utilitarian solutions, governments are inclined to solve their most pressing social, political or economic problems on the principle of self-interest and its extension, the notion of a 'greater good'. Arendt (1951: 568) describes this as underwriting the 'nihilistic principle that "everything is permitted"', a principle grounded in notions of 'common sense' and reflected quite clearly in the language of parliamentary debate on Victoria's sex offender legislation noted above. If sex offenders, carrying within them as they do the potential to offend again, may be subject either to removal from society (through preventive confinement) or to lockdown within it (through monitoring), they no longer retain the capacity to act – whether for good or ill – as free citizens. As such they are removed, by at least one step but maybe more, from the political community of free citizens and become, to one degree or another, superfluous to the wider society; not needed by it, nor valued within it. Once a group is thought superfluous, the 'test' for their good versus the greater good is unlikely to find in their favour.

Strategies of camouflage

But even in times of exception it is difficult simply to remove a whole class of people from society. For that to occur requires the strategy of camouflage and this strategy, as the analogy suggests, is delicately patterned and thus difficult to pick against its background of social and political debate and policy. Four features emerging from Arendt's analysis seem particularly pertinent.

First is the tactic of gradualism, or 'intermediate stages'. These are the small, often seemingly innocuous changes that set up the structure of the larger policy. Australasian governments have initially fought hard to maintain the boundaries of this policy of penal confinement and monitoring: it applies only to child sex offenders. Yet even before the ink was dry on Victoria's monitoring law, extensions to other classes of criminal (adult rapists) and victim (the elderly) were being mooted. Moreover, in another sphere, anti-terror legislation has made provision for a similar set of restrictions to be placed on terror suspects. And elsewhere, the rights of asylum seekers to access Australian law have been removed (see Poynting and Pickering this volume).

Second is the argument of necessity. Despite evidence to the contrary (Wood & Ogloff 2006), discussion of child sex offenders in both New Zealand and Victoria was premised upon arguments that they were at higher risk of reoffending than other offenders. Together with images of impending dangers to children – their defilement by unrestrained monsters – this creates a situation where even unpleasant or unjust measures may be reframed. As Arendt (1963) illustrates by reference to Himmler, the Reich's architect of psychological persuasion, conscience may be assuaged by the use of language – here, for instance, we discuss 'high-risk' offenders, when in fact we may be talking about groups with reoffending rates as low as 6% – and through the tactic of reversing burdens. In the latter case, we talk not of the terrible burden of confinement or monitoring upon offenders, but of the terrible burden that protection of children places upon us who must devise and allow such schemes.

Third is the establishment of categories and then of exceptions. The function of the latter is to confirm the validity of the former. Thus, by debating why adult rapists could not reasonably be included in a monitoring scheme, Victorian parliamentarians implicitly recognised the principle that removing the liberty rights of others – in this case child rapists – was a valid and reasonable strategy. All debate that follows over 'who is in' and 'who is out' of the scheme reinforces the validity of the scheme per se. It was the acceptance of the validity of such difference and hierarchy of worth, argues Arendt (1963: 131) that 'had been the beginning of the moral collapse of respectable Jewish society', for it indicated an acceptance that some had more right to live than others. Moreover, the creation of hierarchies of worth and the placement of certain individuals into a second-class citizen status creates the problem known in political philosophy as the issue of distant strangers: what ethical obligations do I in fact have to those outside my own political community?

Finally, the strategy of camouflage works through elementary appeal. Not only do strategies of domination provide a tempting solution for governments, they may also prove tempting to citizens who, Arendt (1951: 592) suggests, are liable to view 'instruments for making men superfluous … as much of an attraction as a warning'. Part of the attraction lies in their common sense solution to practical problems, a yearning for which Arendt locates in the same fears about risk and security that O'Malley describes in this volume. This was the sort of person, Arendt (1951: 448) writes, 'who in the midst of the ruins of his world worried about nothing so much as his private security'. The strategy of camouflage ensures that illiberal strategies of domination work their way into a society, as it were, undercover, patterned across different domains with various and shifting justifications, requiring of us extra vigilance to their sometimes beguiling attractions.

Objective: effacing the bearer of rights

All of these factors come together in the key objective of domination: the killing of the juridical figure, the bearer of rights. Such killing has a long history and is commonly referred to as civil death. Perhaps the clearest modern example is the case of detainees at Guantanamo Bay: the Unites States government has devised a status 'illegal enemy combatant' that leaves them outside US civil or criminal jurisdiction, contentiously beyond the reach of international law and the Geneva Convention, and thus subject only to the rules of the victor. The Nuremberg Laws of 1935 introduced the first exclusions from German citizenship: henceforth Jews would no longer be full citizens (Reichsburger) but instead subjects of the German state (Staatsangehorige). Though current developments in Australasia have not yet introduced such formal distinctions of status, it is clear there nevertheless exists a diminished status for individuals who, having committed no crime, have been made subjects of penal confinement or monitoring. The point of removing rights, as the historical case in Germany or contemporary case in Guantanamo Bay well illustrates, is to efface civil status and the capacity for independent action.

Arendt (1951: 374) seems to have captured the confusion of the New Zealand Court of Appeal in the face of this new means by which rights could be withdrawn when she writes thus: 'Jurists are so used to thinking in terms of punishment, which indeed always deprives us of certain rights, that they may find it even more difficult than the layman to recognise that the deprivation of legality, that is of all rights, no longer has a connection with specific crimes'. If we are not yet at the point of observing the withdrawal of all rights we might nevertheless pause to consider what rights remain for a Queenslander who, having committed no further offence, finds himself subject to indefinite penal confinement. Or a New Zealander, living freely in the community for three and a half years, who now finds himself subject to a 10-year extended supervision order.

Conclusion

This chapter has attempted to provide a critical criminological analysis of risk in the contemporary penal domain. While it has been common in both theoretical and technical writing to posit a demise of dangerousness in the face of the new calculative modality of risk, I have attempted to show here how the two notions are far from mutually exclusive. In fact, not only may they work together – playing off dystopian images of existential threat against the offer of a predictive technology to solve the crisis – but their combined force may be greater than the parts alone. This is illustrated, I suggest, by the emergence of a whole new realm of penal confinement and monitoring that has been untied from the traditional association between distinct crimes and accompanying punishments. In the contemporary penal sphere the logics and practices of risk have thus become bifurcated. On the one hand risk is routinised in the antiseptic procedures of courts, community correctional centres, parole boards and the like. On the other, 'high-risk' offenders emerge as a special class, which, when combined with the discourse of dangerousness push at the boundaries that have in the past constrained the clamour to effect public protection through the removal of individual liberties.

In the case studies presented here I have sought to show how child sex offenders have become one of the first such classes (along with terror suspects and asylum seekers) to find themselves caught within this new machinery of control. Yet the possible significance of these developments is difficult to interpret if we rely only upon a criminological analytic and so it is for this reason that I have introduced Hannah Arendt's work on totalitarian and illiberal rule. Aside from the details of her case studies, her work contains important lessons about vigilance, personal political responsibility and the fragility of what we might presume to be our 'inalienable' individual rights in the face of state power. It is perhaps fitting then to close this chapter with her salutary reminder to those who would stand by as others' rights are removed: 'politics', she writes 'is not like the nursery; in politics obedience and support are the same' (Arendt 1963: 279).

References

Arendt, H 1951, *The Origins of Totalitarianism*, Schocken Books, New York.

Arendt, H 1963, *Eichmann in Jerusalem: a report on the banality of evil*, Penguin, London.

Castel, R 1991, 'From Dangerousness to Risk', in Burchell, G, Gordon, C & Miller, P (eds), *The Foucault Effect: studies in governmentality*, University of Chicago Press, Chicago.

Douglas, M 1966, *Purity and Danger: an analysis of the concepts of pollution and taboo*, Routledge, London.

Douglas, M 1992, *Risk and Blame: essays in cultural theory*, Routledge, London.

Feeley, M & Simon, J 1992, 'The New Penology: notes on the emerging strategy of corrections and its implications', 30 *Criminology* 449.

Feeley, M & Simon, J 1994, 'Actuarial Justice: the emerging new criminal law', in Nelken, D (ed), *Futures of Criminology*, Sage, London.

Floud, J & Young, W 1982, *Dangerousness and Criminal Justice*, Heineman, London.

Gray, A 2005, 'Standard of Proof, Unpredictable Behaviour and the High Court of Australia's Verdict on Preventive Detention Laws', 10 *Deakin Law Review* 177.

Hacking, I 2003, 'Risk and Dirt', in Ericson, RV & Doyle, A (eds), *Risk and Morality*, University of Toronto Press, Toronto.

Hansard 2005, Parliamentary Debates, Legislative Council Fifty-Fifth Parliament, First Session: 24 February 2005, Victorian Government Printer, Melbourne.

Pratt, J 2005, 'Child Sexual Abuse: purity and danger in an age of anxiety', 43 *Crime, Law and Social Change* 263.

Steadman, H 2000, 'From Dangerousness to Risk Assessment of Community Violence: taking stock at the turn of the century', 28 *Journal of the American Academy of Psychiatry and Law* 265.

Wood, M & Ogloff, RP 2006, 'Victoria's Serious Sex Offender Monitoring Act 2005: implications for the accuracy of sex offender risk assessment', 13 *Psychiatry, Psychology and Law* 182.

22

PENAL POPULISM AND THE CONTEMPORARY ROLE OF PUNISHMENT

John Pratt

It is important to respond to those who commit crime with punishment – otherwise the criminal law loses its authority (Durkheim 1893). We should thus expect to find a strong relationship between levels of crime and levels of punishment – the latter following trends in the former. However, current developments in modern society, particularly in the Anglophone world, illustrate that the relationship between crime and punishment is a weak one. From what had seemed to be the inexorable growth of crime for most of the post-war period, in many modern societies all indicators (crimes recorded by the police, victim surveys, and so on) now suggest that crime has been in significant decline from the early 1990s. However, as this has taken place, punishment levels have *increased*. Most spectacularly, the rate of imprisonment in the United States has increased from 110 per 100,000 of population in the late 1970s to 750 in 2007. Elsewhere, the escalation began to take place from the mid 1990s, that is, after the decline in crime had begun. In New Zealand prison rates have increased from 128 per 100,000 of population in 1995 to 186 in 2006; in England from 99 to 148 over the same period; and in Australia from 96 to 125. Even countries previously known for their low rates of imprisonment are experiencing this phenomenon. In the Netherlands, for example, the imprisonment rate has increased from 66 to 128.[1]

Why should this be happening and what is it telling us about the contemporary role of punishment? What I want to argue in this chapter is that this trend is the product of a crucial change in the axis of penal power in modern society. For much of the modern era, penal policy was developed by governments in conjunction with the 'criminal justice establishment', notably civil servants, the legal community, academics and penal reform groups. However, from the early 1990s, *penal populism* has been increasingly influential on policy development. By penal populism, what I am referring to is the way in which policy is increasingly likely to be determined by governments in conjunction with those who claim to speak on behalf of the public (law and order lobbyists, talkback radio hosts, the popular press, and so on). In such

---

1   These statistics are taken variously from Christie (2003), Garland (2001) and the website of the International Centre for Prison Studies, King's College, University of London.

ways, 'ordinary people' are no longer left out of policy making, but instead they, or more likely those who claim to speak on their behalf, have become important definers of its quantity and intensity. The chapter will sketch in the way in which the parameters of punishment in modern society have been reconfigured as a result of these changes. It will then explore the reasons for the emergence of these populist tendencies, using New Zealand as case study. While it is acknowledged that this is not necessarily a uniform trend, it will demonstrate that the role of punishment in such societies is to reassert the moral authority of a weakened central state (Garland 1996), in addition to sanctioning crime.

The privatisation and bureaucratisation of punishment

In the early part of the 19th century, prisons were holding places for those awaiting the sentence of the court rather than a court sentence in their own right. Punishment was at this time, as Foucault (1979) has vividly illustrated, targeted at the body of offenders and performed in public, whether this be in the form of executions, floggings, maimings, stonings, and so on. These corporeal sanctions had the ability to draw local communities together against criminals who were projected as their common enemy. In addition, the elaborate rituals associated with the death penalty – it was not enough to simply put offenders to death, they might also be decapitated after hanging, their entrails torn out and their bodies displayed on gibbets – symbolised the power and authority of the sovereign over the lives of their subjects. At the same time, while punishment could be used to mutilate and destroy in these ways, it could also be used for economic and imperial purposes in the form of transportation to the colonies.

By the 1860s, though, transportation had virtually come to an end, as had nearly all the 'spectacles of suffering' (Spierenburg 1984) that the corporeal punishments constituted. The death penalty had been available in England for over 200 offences at the beginning of the 19th century; after 1861 it was, for all intents and purposes, available only for murder. Furthermore, public executions had by now been largely abolished. The riotous carnivals that these had become were no longer appropriate to the industrial age, where order, routine and precise timekeeping were essential. In addition, the changing structure of modern democratic society gave increasing political power to middle class elites. While executions remained popular with the general public, the latter viewed these scenes with revulsion (Gatrell 1994), as with other raucous public events such as fairs and sporting contests.

After the abolition of *public* executions, the death penalty continued to be further sanitised and used progressively more sparingly (Pratt 2002). After the Second World War, there were only a handful of executions each year in respective Australian states and New Zealand. The death penalty was no longer thought to have a legitimate place in the penal repertoire of the civilised world by governments and the criminal justice establishment. Notwithstanding continuing high levels of public support for its retention, it was abolished in the Anglophone countries in the period from the mid 1950s to the mid 1970s. At this time governments were prepared to assume a strong leadership role in penal policy development, in accordance with the growing authority of the central state at this time: 'it is not our business to wait for public opinion on such an important issue', one speaker in the Canadian debate on abolition in the federal parliament proclaimed in 1975 (Pratt 2002: 32).

With the demise of transportation and corporeal sanctions, imprisonment became a punishment in its own right. Contrary to the importance given by Foucault (1979) to Jeremy Bentham's prison blueprint – the panopticon (only a handful of which were ever built) – Pentonville model prison, opened in 1843, became the most important influence on subsequent 19th century prison building (Pratt 2002). While the panopticon was designed to be managed by the private sector and open to the public, Pentonville and its successors were managed by state bureaucracies. As a result, an administrative veil was drawn across the prison. Prisoners became detached and removed from the world beyond it, unknowable to the general public and transformed into mythical monsters, a status which being behind prison walls gave them, those walls being a firm dividing line between citizenship and non-citizenship in modern society. Once imprisoned, the public became largely indifferent to what happened to them.

This indifference allowed the criminal justice authorities to put what eventually came to be their paternalistic, elitist and liberal stamp on the administration of prison life. During the course of the 20th century, prisoners came to be seen as victims of misfortune or social inequalities. With the development of the post-war welfare state in particular, it was thought that there was a duty in the prisons, as in the rest of society, to provide expert assistance for prisoners, both in relation to correcting their individual deficiencies and at the same time ameliorating the disadvantageous social conditions which were thought to have contributed to their criminality. Again, public sentiments on crime and punishment were ignored altogether or treated with disdain: 'one cannot be unaware that the body of assumptions underlying the common talk of common people are not the assumptions on which contemporary prison administration is based' (Fox 1952: 137).

Instead, under the prevailing axis of penal power, penal policy was meant to be determined on a rational, efficient and humanitarian basis. Penal excesses should be avoided; those who were punished should still be treated with dignity and respect, away from public view and scrutiny; and punishment should be finite and certain in duration. In just the same way that elite opinion, at least, was repulsed by the death penalty, so too was there repugnance at indeterminate prison sentences. As with the death penalty, these indeterminate sentences were associated with totalitarian societies where they were used extensively as a political strategy against 'enemies of the state' (Pratt 1997). In post-war democratic societies, these provisions rapidly fell into disuse (Bottoms 1977). More generally, it was thought that the sentence of imprisonment should be used restrictively, and that prison conditions should be liberalised as far as possible. That these remained, in reality, a long way short of these standards, as a voluminous prisoner biography literature testifies (Pratt 2002), does not undermine the formal expectations of what prison conditions *should* be like, as countless official reports in the mid-20th century confirm. Those societies, which most closely conformed to these standards, the Scandinavian countries and the Netherlands, were thought to be the leaders of modern penal development.

A new axis of penal power

Since the 1970s, a new axis of penal power has emerged: one that is framed more around the relationship between governments and the general public, with a reduced role for the criminal justice establishment in policy development. Previous public indifference has given way to demands for involvement and consultation at various levels in penal affairs. This has also meant that issues of crime and punishment, instead of being determined behind the scenes by government experts, have become very public matters. To demonstrate their affinity with what are assumed to be the expectations of the general public, politicians are likely to validate commonsense understandings that crime is increasing, when in reality it has been in decline; that sentences have been too lenient when prison levels have been rising; that the criminal justice system favours offenders at the expense of victims; and that it is the criminal justice establishment which has engineered such a travesty. New laws have thus been designed to 'rebalance the criminal justice system', as Tony Blair (commenting whilst British Prime Minister) put it, since 'there is a huge and growing gap between the criminal justice system and what the public expects from it' (BBC News, 23 June 2006). To address these 'justice gaps', victims' rights have been enhanced in most jurisdictions. Victims may thus be able to make representations to parole hearings and in the sentencing court, and they may be notified of the release of some categories of prisoners, particularly sex offenders.

In addition to regular invocations of public opinion to justify policy development, we find the use of political mechanisms such as plebiscites and referenda, which provide for more direct injections of public sentiment in this area. For example, in the New Zealand general election of 1999, there was a 91.75% vote in favour of the following citizens initiated referendum: 'should there be a reform of our criminal justice system placing greater emphasis on the needs of victims, providing restitution and compensation for them and imposing minimum sentences and hard labour for all serious violent offences?'. Notwithstanding its inherent contradictions, breaches of human rights and inconsistencies, the non-binding referendum was very influential on subsequent penal legislation, which, inter alia, prescribed much longer prison sentences for some groups of offenders (Pratt & Clark 2005).

If this seems an exceptional, although not unique,[2] demonstration of public mood and a government's subservience to it, the effects it has produced are characteristic of this new axis of penal power. That is to say, dramatically rising rates of imprisonment and deteriorating prison conditions, sometimes deliberately as in parts of the United States, sometimes as the incidental product of prison overcrowding that this new punitiveness has brought about. We also find a range of new 'dangerousness' legislation designed to keep in custody those who are thought to be too dangerous to be released, even if this brushes to one side long established conventions against indefinite punishments and double jeopardy. Most of the United States now has sexual predator laws. These allow for the indefinite civil detention of those so judged (some form of 'mental abnormality' and a conviction for sex crime establishes this) *after* they have served a finite prison term.

But it is not simply that punishment has become more punitive. It is also more *visible*, notably in England, New Zealand and the United States. Chain gangs have re-appeared in the latter, alongside public shaming penalties (for example, sex offenders have to wear a t-shirt advertising their crimes (Garvey 1998)). In Britain, those subject to anti-social behaviour orders can be publicly 'named and shamed'. Similar practices can be found in New Zealand. Shopkeepers advertise local undesirables in

---

2   The use of public ballots to introduce penal laws is very common in the United States and three strikes laws, sexual predator legislation and community notification laws have their origins in this way.

their windows; the police circulate local communities with details of prisoners returning home and so on. In both these societies, there have also been regular outbreaks of vigilante activities, as if in demonstration of the weakness of the central state authority and the lack of respect it now commands from sections of its population (Johnston 1996).

Having said this, it also needs to be recognised that, outside of the United States where the death penalty was reintroduced in 1976, this new punitiveness has not led to any resurrection of punishments to the human body. While, until recently at least, public opinion consistently favoured the restoration of the death penalty, politicians have been firm in their resistance to this. Indeed, abolitionism has been institutionalised in the rights and duties of governance demanded by supra-national entities such as the European Union. Abolitionism is one of its preconditions for membership. Even in the United States, there are indications that support for it may be declining, as well as its use.[3] This is also true of other abolitionist countries[4] and, in reality, there is no prospect whatsoever of it returning to the rest of Western society in the foreseeable future.

However, the United States does lead the way – a new leader of Western penal development – in providing a much more severe penal language in which a good part of public and political debate about punishment is now encased: phrases such as 'zero tolerance', 'life means life', 'truth in sentencing', 'three strikes and you're out' (that is, three convictions lead to mandatory imprisonment irrespective of the gravity of the crime) and 'sexual predators' which regularly feature in this globalised discourse (Franko Aas 2005) all began their life in this country. Notwithstanding the absence of any *direct* policy transfer from the US to similar Anglophone countries (Jones & Newburn 2006), these transparent slogans have become emblems of the way in which popular commonsense should order the criminal justice system, in contrast to the opaque and muddled expertise of the criminal justice establishment.

Explaining the rise of penal populism

Of course, populism is not the only influence on penal development at the present time, but it is perhaps the most significant one (Pratt 2006a). What is it, then, that has brought about the reconfiguration of penal power, which has allowed populism to flourish? There would seem to be five main causes. The first relates to the decline of deference; a rejection by much of the general public of the hitherto unquestioned acceptance of authority or establishment figures and the values they represent. Nevitte (1996) argues that this has been the natural consequence of the success of post-war social reforms which raised the living standards of the whole population – to the effect that those in positions of power by virtue of wealth and privilege would no longer be viewed as the social superiors of the rest of society, and allowed to govern, unquestioned, as they had done previously. This has had a significant impact

---

3   There were 98 executions in the United States in 1999, the highest since the reintroduction of the death penalty in 1996. In 2005 there were 60. Public opinion in the United States was 61-29 in favour of the death penalty in 1997; in 2004 it was 50-46. Statistics available at <www.death penaltyinfo.org/article.php?scid=73&did=1029>.

4   In a TV New Zealand opinion poll in 2004 only 33% supported the reintroduction of the death penalty, down from 67% in 1998.

on the rise of penal populism in so far as it can transform the relationship between governments and their civil service, fundamentally weakening the ability of the latter to keep penal policy within their own exclusive grasp and determination. Instead, it can be left vulnerable to whatever external influences populist politicians choose to ally themselves with when developing policy. Furthermore, the authority of criminal justice officials has been diminished. Judges and magistrates, for example, are regularly thought to be 'out of touch' or 'from another planet' and so on by the public and some politicians (Hough 1996). Without the barrier of deference that used to be placed in front of such influences from outside of the criminal justice establishment, commonsense concepts such as 'three strikes' and 'life means life' have been allowed to become normative values of sentencing systems.

Secondly, there has been substantial evidence in many modern societies of a decline in trust in politicians and existing political processes (Pratt 2006a). While the venality of some politicians may have contributed to this, it seems to be more generally derived from the perceived inability of politicians and existing political processes to respond to the needs of 'ordinary people', the key constituency from which populism draws its support. In countries such as Britain and New Zealand, this disillusionment set in during the 1970s when the inflexibilities of welfare bureaucracies and strategies seemed to block their aspirations (Garland 2001) while simultaneously favouring such unworthy members of society as 'dole bludgers' and 'scroungers'. The subsequent shifts to a neo-liberal polity in these societies provided a much greater sense of personal freedom and choice but at the same time removed many state-provided safety nets for those who then made the wrong choices – leading to societies which are strong on individualism but weak on social bonds and interdependencies.

Simultaneously, the impact of globalisation has weakened the authority of sovereign states. As a result, at a time when governments no longer seem to be in control of events because of their vulnerability to external organisations and forces, we find a greater citizen involvement in politics itself, in the form of single-issue pressure groups and more fickle and unpredictable electoral support. This is no longer tied to rigid class hierarchies but instead flirts with politicians of whatever shade who are prepared to speak to these matters.

Thirdly, ontological insecurity. During the development of modern society, one of the ways in which individuals had been able to guard against existential anxiety was 'by developing a framework of ontological security of some sort, based on routines of various forms. People handle dangers and the fears associated with them in terms of the emotional and behavioural formulae which have come to be part of their everyday behaviour and thought' (Giddens 1991: 44). However, it is clear that many of the conditions necessary for such formulae are no longer in place: so many of the pillars of stability and security that had been built up during the development of modern society have crumbled away. Tenured employment has all but disappeared; family life has been shattered by divorce and marriage has given way to more transient cohabiting practices; there have been declines in church attendance, trade union membership and various other forms of community involvement (Fukuyama 1995; Putnam 2000). Personal security was put in jeopardy as a result of the seemingly inexorable rise in crime, especially during the 1970s and 1980s. This became one of the most obvious indicators that the social order was breaking down, that the authority of the criminal law and of the state itself was being wilfully disregarded and where governments, whatever their political colour, seemed to have no control over such events.

In these respects many citizens will be more likely to put their trust and support in those populist organisations and political movements which claim to have the solutions to such problems: magical, common-sense solutions usually based on invocations of some golden period in the past when social stability and order seemed secure. In these ways, the growth of punitive sentiments is characteristic of these more general concerns about a perceived decline in social cohesion rather than the reality of crime dangers. The more social cohesion seems to be unravelling, the more strident will be the calls for more severe punishments – as a way of restoring the authority of the criminal law and of providing consensus and uniformity (Tyler & Boeckmann 1997).

Fourthly, the role of the media. Although crime has been in decline since the early 1990s, there is clear evidence (van Kesteren et al 2000) to suggest that most people still think that crime is increasing. This is because, in the changing nature of social relations in the modern world, most people are likely to elicit their knowledge of such events from vicarious rather than direct sources: they will rely primarily on the mass media rather than their neighbours and family for news of such events. In these respects, crime reporting confirms common-sense assumptions that crime is out of control even though all the gauges of it may demonstrate the opposite (Jewkes 2004). The dimensions of the problem are enlarged through the media's over-emphasis on crime news while the immediacy of its threat is increased, making it seem one that is acute, requiring drastic action. At the same time, changes in the structure of the media, particularly the popular media, which have been brought about by the impact of deregulation and new information technology have accelerated this tendency. News reporting and current affairs programs have had the time allocated to them reduced while their content has been simultaneously simplified. For example, in relation to the United States, the CBS flagship current affairs program, *Sixty Minutes*, Fallows (1997: 57) found that:

> [O]f the nearly 500 stories between 1990 and 1994, more than one third were celebrity profiles, entertainment industry stories, or exposés of petty scandals. Barely one fifth of the stories concerned economics, the real workings of politics, or any other issue of long-term significance.

In addition, through the impact of new information technology, ordinary people are increasingly provided with the opportunity to make, report and comment on the news themselves, ensuring that broadcasting elites no longer have exclusive control of knowledge and information about crime and other matters. The development of talkback radio has accelerated these moves towards mass participation in news making and opinion-forming. Such programs are usually hosted by 'entertainers' or 'personalities', rather than journalists, who nonetheless present their shows as legitimate forums for serious consideration of political events and issues. But, unlikely to have specialist knowledge or training themselves, they then fall back on common-sense as a way of understanding these matters and by so doing reaffirm the common-sense world views of their listeners.

Fifthly, democratisation has provided the opportunity for the emotive experiences and opinions of ordinary people rather than detached objective expert analysis to become the framework through which crime and punishment is understood. Victimisation is seen as a particularly authentic expression of this new mode of knowledge. The harm that has been inflicted on victims is seen as harm inflicted on the rest of society, justifying the much greater penal severity that spokespeople for such victims demand. Indeed, victimisation has assumed an iconic status in populist discourse. The way in which particular laws have been named after crime victims ('Megan's Law' is the most obvious example[5]) becomes a way of honouring them and memorialising them. Equally, victims of crime who fight back in defence of their family or property when it seems that the criminal justice authorities cannot provide this assistance, may become popular heroes: they become another emblem of the way in which the interests of such 'ordinary people' have been overlooked or dismissed by the criminal justice establishment. In these respects, the British *Crime and Disorder Act* 1998 which introduced controversial anti-social behaviour legislation[6] was described by the then Home Secretary as 'a triumph for democratic politics – in truth a victory for local communities over *detached metropolitan elites*' (Hansard, HOC 8, April 1998, vol 370, emphasis added).

In such ways, a large-scale insatiable sense of fear and anxiety has developed over this period, with a yearning for security and certainty, which has always proved to be elusive as new risks and dangers reveal themselves, but which the state can no longer provide guarantees against. This has come about partly through political choices, in the shift from welfare to neo-liberal polities, which insist that individuals, not the state, insure themselves appropriately. And partly because globalisation and the rise of supra-national entities weaken the state's remaining authority. As a result, at a time when central state governance has been contracting and no longer claims to have the solution to all the difficulties we are likely to face, populist demands are generated for a strong, central state that *can* provide remedies to what seem to be our biggest dangers. Crime and punishment issues can seem the most easily solvable of these when common-sense knowledge, based on anecdotes, memories and folklore begins to displace scientific rationalities and expertise as the mode of knowledge through which such matters are formally addressed.

Case study: New Zealand

These, then, are the ideal-type conditions in which populism flourishes. New Zealand has enjoyed something of a 'full house'. Not only is this a society where elites and establishment forces have always enjoyed little deference, for various historico-cultural reasons (Pratt 2006b), but, in addition, in 1984 it moved almost overnight from being the most regulated Western society to the most deregulated. For a decade thereafter, politicians of both Right and Left insisted that 'there was no alternative'.

Notwithstanding the ways in which such economic restructuring has turned New Zealand into a more market-driven, cosmopolitan and heterogeneous society, it has also led to a collapse of faith in establishment politicians amidst the growth of wide ranging insecurities and anxieties that this dramatic shift in governance has

---

5   This was the first of the United States community notification laws, introduced in California in 1993 after the murder of Megan Kanka by a recidivist sex offender.

6   The legislation is controversial because it is a hybrid measure: it imposes civil sanctions for anti-social behaviour that can then be backed up with criminal sanctions if breached.

brought about. As a response to this disenchantment, politicians agreed to change the electoral system in 1996 from 'first-past-the post' to proportional representation with, as well, the availability of non-binding citizens' referenda (Pratt & Clark 2005). In such ways, it was thought that public opinion and sentiment would have more influence on policy development than had previously been allowed. Some of the most obvious outlets for these sentiments relate, of course, to crime and punishment issues. As such, fringe parties, which have law and order as one of their central issues, have been formed and have been able to gain leverage for these matters when becoming junior partners in the inevitable coalition governments that this electoral system leads to. Furthermore, extra-establishment law and order lobby groups (in particular the Sensible Sentencing Trust (SST) which was formed in 2001), have campaigned to keep law and order issues in the public spotlight in the aftermath of the 1999 referendum.

The rise to prominence of this organisation was assisted by the deregulation of the new media in this country. Since the late 1980s, its national broadcasting company (TVNZ) – originally developed along the lines of the BBC – has for all intents and purposes become a commercial channel, far more dependent than before on advertising for its revenue source. Since the late 1980s it has also had to compete with private terrestrial television channels and satellite television. As a result, law and order has become a regular theme in its news programs because of its inherent ability to 'shock, frighten, titillate and entertain' (Jewkes 2004: 3). At the same time, this reconstituted medium demands that those who provide opinions on these issues do so in the form of commonsensical sound bites rather than lengthy and opaque analysis. SST spokespeople have been well suited for this (see Pratt & Clark 2005) and in addition, in the run up to the 2002 general election organised two well-publicised marches, which substantially increased their public profile. These were intended as remembrance rallies for the victims of violent crime. Many of the marchers at the rallies carried handmade wooden crosses, some bearing the names of murder victims. Members of Parliament from the main political parties, as well as government ministers, attended the rallies and addressed the marchers in the penal language that was expected of them in these surrounds ('life should mean life, no parole'; 'there's no reason for parole'). Academics and others who offered opinion elsewhere that opposed such representations of public sentiment and its legitimacy were personally attacked in the media. Even Governor General and former High Court Judge Dame Silvia Cartwright was angrily criticised by prominent opposition Members of Parliament for being anti-populist when she made the comment 'prisons don't work' while opening the Crime and Justice Research Centre at Victoria University.

Judges, though, in the aftermath of the election, certainly followed the new penal direction that had been demanded. Indeed, they had earlier been warned by the Labour Justice Minister to take note of public sentiment and expectations when sentencing. They risked losing their discretion and autonomy if they did not: 'public opinion does not take kindly to being ignored, particularly when there is a suspicion it is being dismissed arrogantly' (Goff 2000: 1). The Labour/Alliance government (1999-2002) then initiated a Judicial Complaints Process to oversee the appointment, monitoring and disciplining of judges: '[the Justice Minister] said a worryingly large number of people no longer have full confidence in the justice system' (Goff 2000: 1). Since then, record lengths of imprisonment have been set, judges taking the view that 'society's attitude to violent crime has moved on since [a 1995 case], as have sentencing levels' (*R v Bell* [2003] NZCA 188). It is against this background that the rate of imprisonment in this country has continued to accelerate, notwithstanding declining crime figures.

Overall, then, penal populism has been able to make such a dramatic impact in this country because the central state lost much of its authority to govern in the aftermath of economic restructuring. The changes in the electoral system in the mid 1990s are reflective of this and have since allowed for much more populist input to penal policy. Meanwhile, other developments that were a consequence of restructuring, such as the reconfiguration of TVNZ, have provided the means by which populist forces have been able to capture and change penal policy debates.

Conclusion

While New Zealand is an exemplar of the effects penal populism *can have*, there is no inevitability to this. In countries such as Canada and Finland, penal populism has made no impact at all. In the former, this seems to have been primarily because its political leaders – certainly at federal government level – have been determined not to follow the United States example (Meyer & O'Malley 2005). At the same time, the Canadian democratic structure provides a firm barrier against populist influences. This consists of federal and provincial systems of government, with each tier having its own penal bureaucracy. In addition, responsibility for penal affairs is divided between federal and provincial governments: the former maintain penitentiaries, housing all those offenders serving sentences of two or more years; the latter maintain gaols for those serving less than two years. Penal authority is thus both diffused and at the same time a long way removed from the agitations of any local law and order associations. Before these can make any headway they have to pass through successive layers of government and bureaucracy, a considerable test of endurance for what are usually loosely held together coalitions. As a result, the Canadian rate of imprisonment, one of the highest in the OECD at 120 per 100,000 of population around 1980 has not only remained stable thereafter but declined to 105 in 2007 (statistics taken from Government Printer and website of the International Centre for Prison Studies, King's College, University of London).

There is a marked contrast here between the political systems in Canada and New Zealand. The latter country has a unicameral system of government and only one penal bureaucracy. This allows for a much clearer demarcation of penal power and also provides the possibility for much more direct access to governments by populist organisations (Pratt & Clark 2005). The Canadian system of government also differs in these respects from that of the United States. There, crime and punishment issues are likely to be given much greater attention at state level, where there is greater jurisdiction over these matters, but rather less in other areas of government, allowing again for greater local influence of law and order lobby groups.

With regard to Finland, its rate of imprisonment declined from 200 per 100,000 of population in 1950 to 55 in 1998 (in 2007 it was 68). It has been able to achieve this primarily because of high levels of trust in politicians and the criminal justice establishment. This level of trust has not occurred by accident but has been historically embedded. Trust in the legal profession came about because of the strong belief developed in the 19th century in legal structures and written law as guarantees of Finnish autonomy. Finland at that time was part of the Russian

Empire, with the status of a self-ruling Grand Duchy. In addition, artists and intellectuals played an important part in strengthening Finnish national identity from this time. The 'debt of honour' that this has led to has since become an entrenched feature of the culture of that country. Wandering around the capital city, Helsinki, one finds many statues of intellectuals, economists, artists and musicians, with streets and parks named after them. This is a further example of the way these qualities are celebrated and respected in this country, in contrast to the veneration of ignorance over intellect that is associated with populism. As a consequence, there is still a coalition of interest in this country between political elites and intellectuals: rather than being seen as alien outsiders, the ideas of the latter are valued and are influential on policy development.

Furthermore, trust and tolerance have been cemented into Finnish society through the development of universal welfare state provision, rather than this serving as a residual safety net as in most of the Anglophone world. If welfare is understood in the latter more restricted and stigmatic way, it is likely to find few allies when neo-liberal governments cut it back and transfer responsibility for its provision from the state to the private sector. In Finland, in contrast, the inclusive model of state welfare provision provides high levels of stability and security and allows it to act as a shock absorber at times of dramatic social change. The state's guarantee of wellbeing also extends to crime victims. It compensates them and then attempts to recover this from their offenders. Under these circumstances, victimisation is depoliticised. There is little of the sense of disenchantment and disillusionment that exists in those societies where populism has become a powerful influence on penal development.

Ultimately, however, populism thrives where the central state weakens and loosens its authority over the governance of everyday life. When this happens, individuals, instead of assuming responsibility for their own risk management, demand enhanced protection from the state against the insecurities that constantly seem to be pressing in on them. The state itself can offer little in return, though, constrained as it is by the imperatives of economic restructuring, and weakened as it is by globalisation and the rise of supra-national organisations. The exception to this has been in the area of crime and punishment. By giving way to expressions of public sentiment and what passes for public opinion here (there is no populist health policy or pension policy, for example), the new punitiveness that has been unleashed becomes a way of bolstering a fraying social order and consensus. In addition to sanctioning crime, this has become the contemporary role of punishment in many modern societies.

References

BBC News 2006, 'Blair attacks the justice gap', 23 June, <http://news.bbc.co.uk/1/hi/uk_politics/5108158.stm>.

Bottoms, AE 1977, 'Reflections on the Renaissance of Dangerousness', 16 *Howard Journal of Criminal Justice* 70.

Christie, N 2003, *Crime Control as Industry*, Martin Robertson, London.

Durkheim, E 1893, *De la Division du Travail Social*, translated by Simpson, G 1964, *The Division of Labor in Society*, Free Press, New York.

Fallows, J 1997, *Breaking the News*, Vintage, New York.

Foucault, M 1979, *Discipline and Punish: the birth of the prison*, translated by Sheridan, A, Penguin Books, Harmondsworth.

Fox, L 1952, *The English Prison and Borstal System*, Routledge & Kegan Paul, London.

Franko Aas, K 2005, 'The Ad and the Form: punitiveness and technological culture', in Pratt, J, Brown, D, Hallsworth, S, Brown, M & Morrison, W (eds), *The New Punitiveness: trends, theories, perspectives*, Willan Publishing, Cullompton.

Fukuyama, F 1995, *Trust: the social virtues and the creation of prosperity*, Free Press, New York.

Garland, D 1996, 'The Limits of the Sovereign State: strategies of crime control in contemporary society', 36 *British Journal of Criminology* 445.

Garland, D 2001, *The Culture of Control*, Oxford University Press, New York.

Garvey, S 1998, 'Can Shaming Punishments Educate?', 65 *University of Chicago Law Review* 733.

Gatrell, VAC 1994, *Hanging Tree: execution and the English people*, Oxford University Press, Oxford.

Giddens, A 1991, *Modernity and Self-Identity*, Polity Press, Cambridge.

Goff, P 2000, 'Public Opinion and the Judiciary', <www.beehive.govt.nz/Print/PrintDocument.aspx?DocumentID=6912>.

Hough, M 1996, 'People Talking about Punishment', 35 *Howard Journal of Criminal Justice* 191.

International Centre for Prison Studies, King's College, University of London, <www.prisonstudies.org>.

Jewkes, Y 2004, *Media and Crime*, Sage, London.

Johnston, L 1996, 'What is Vigilantism?', 36 *British Journal of Criminology* 220.

Jones, T & Newburn, T 2006, 'Three Strikes and You're Out: exploring symbol and substance in American and British crime control policies', 46 *British Journal of Criminology* 781.

Meyer, J & O'Malley, P 2005, 'Missing the punitive turn? Canadian criminal justice, 'balance' and penal modernism', in Pratt, J, Brown, D, Hallsworth, S, Brown, M & Morrison, W (eds), *The New Punitiveness: trends, theories, perspectives*, Willan Publishing, Cullompton.

Nevitte, N 1996, *The Decline of Difference: Canadian value change in cross national perspective*, Broadview Press, Ontario.

Pratt, J 1997, *Governing the Dangerous: dangerousness, law, and social change*, Federation Press, Sydney.

Pratt, J 2002, *Punishment and Civilization: penal tolerance and intolerance in modern society*, Sage, London.

Pratt, J 2006a, *Penal Populism: key ideas in criminology*, Routledge, London.

Pratt, J 2006b, 'The Dark Side of Paradise: explaining New Zealand's history of high imprisonment', 46 *British Journal of Criminology* 541.

Pratt, J & Clark, M 2005, 'Penal Populism in New Zealand', 7 *Punishment and Society* 303.

Putnam, RD 2000, *Bowling Alone: the collapse and revival of American community*, Simon & Schuster, New York.

Spierenburg, PC 1984, *The Emergence of Carceral Institutions: prisons, galleys, and lunatic asylums, 1550-1900*, Erasmus Universiteit, Rotterdam.

Tyler, T & Boeckmann, R 1997, 'Three Strikes and You Are Out, But Why? The psychology of public support for punishing rule breakers', 31 *Law and Society Review* 237.

van Kesteren, JN, Mayhew, P & Nieuwbeerta, P 2000, *Criminal Victimisation in Seventeen Industrialised Countries: key-findings from the 2000 International Crime Victims Survey*, The Hague: Ministry of Justice, WODC.

PART V

FUTURE DIRECTIONS IN CRITICAL CRIMINOLOGY

23

RESISTING A 'LAW AND ORDER' SOCIETY

Russell Hogg

Introduction

In 1979 Stuart Hall (1980: 3) described the 'drift into a "Law and Order" society' in Britain as 'a deep and decisive movement towards a more disciplinary, authoritarian kind of society'. For Hall, the change did not involve a move towards an autocratic state, an abandonment of the 'normal' institutions of liberal democracy. Rather the very prominence of law and order signalled a shift *within* the liberal institutional repertoire, away from its consensual towards its coercive pole, away from its social, welfare and integrative functions towards an intensification of its controlling, disciplinary and criminalising functions. The general thesis has since been applied to other western societies.

This chapter will further describe the thesis, consider evidence supporting the trend towards a law and order society and rehearse some of its core features. It will then consider in broad outline some other trends that do not exactly invalidate the thesis, but which complicate it somewhat. They also highlight important points of potential resistance and contestation. In the final section more recent developments are briefly examined, notably the so-called 'war on terror', which has sealed a developing process where local and global have become increasingly inter-connected in the contemporary politics of law and order. This presents new challenges.

The drift towards a 'Law and Order Society'

In *Policing the Crisis – Mugging, the State, and Law and Order* (1978), Hall and his colleagues provided an analysis of the roots and character of the economic, social and political changes affecting Britain in the 1970s. In particular, they highlighted the manner in which law and order had become centrally implicated in these changes and the popular and political responses they elicited (Hall et al 1978).

The book was a landmark contribution to critical criminology. It analysed an important moment of transition in society and demonstrated a certain prescience about what was to come, given that it pre-dated the governments of Margaret Thatcher and Ronald Reagan. Equally it marked a shift in the critical criminology project itself. The 1960s and 1970s was a period of radical optimism – the era of the 'new left', the anti-war and student movements, struggles against colonialism and racism, second wave feminism, gay sexual liberation, anti-psychiatry and prison abolition movements. Reflecting the climate of the times, new deviancy theorists and critical criminologists sought a new and radical politicisation of questions of crime and control. As it happened, the politicisation occurred but not in the way they anticipated. It was presided over, not by graduates of the new left, but the students of Friedrich von Hayek and Milton Friedman (Cohen 1996).

Margaret Thatcher (British Prime Minister 1979-1990) and Ronald Reagan (US President 1981-1989) were the key political figureheads in what proved to be a broad and enduring reconfiguring of politics in the 'advanced' capitalist democracies. The entry of terms like 'Thatcherite' and 'Thatcherism' into the everyday political vocabulary is a reminder that she conferred her name on a new governing doctrine as well as a government. Above all else these labels signify the overthrow of the social democratic consensus that had evolved in various forms from early in the 20th century (for an account of this shift in Australia see Kelly 1994). Instead of the hoped for leftward shift, these politicians led and symbolised a decisive move towards a new model of free market capitalism, which was further entrenched by the implosion of eastern bloc socialism in the late 1980s and the advance of globalisation in the 1990s. The new right sought to *free* the market, but when it came to other domains the hallmark of the new conservatism was not liberation, but discipline: 'free economy and the strong state' (Gamble 1988; Hall & Jacques 1983).

Critical criminology has since undergone a diversification, if not fragmentation, of its project(s). This reflects trends within progressive social movement politics more generally and the destabilisation of any fixed or straightforward polarity between 'left' and 'right'. The politicised nature of the crime question has remained and, along with it, the spectacle of a rather vociferous electoral politics of law and order largely conducted as a contest over who can deliver tougher measures of control: more coercive powers, more police, more prisons (Downes & Morgan 2002; Hogg & Brown 1998). Gone are the days when a United States Attorney-General could write a book on crime in which he argued that:

> The basic solution for most crime is economic – homes, health, education, employment, beauty. If the law is to be enforced – and rights fulfilled for the poor – we must end poverty. Until we do, there will be no equal protection of the laws. To permit conditions that breed antisocial conduct is our greatest crime (Clark 1971: 28).

Hall's analysis was conceptually framed by Gramsci's (1971) theory of hegemony. Gramsci argued that hegemony reflected the distinctive nature of capitalist rule in the west, namely its heavy reliance upon ideological and moral leadership and the construction of consent, rather than on coercive domination. Hall depicted the new conservative politics of law and order as part of a *hegemonic* struggle in response to the crisis facing Britain in the 1970s. Ordinary citizens were recruited to its agenda by linking popular anxieties about rising crime and moral decline to the need to strengthen the state in its traditional coercive functions whilst reining in social welfare and Keynesian economic management. The themes played across a range of other issues – including education, the family, welfare, trade union power, race and immigration – and often drew links between them. A new 'commonsense' about crime (Hogg & Brown 1998) and a new moral consensus on the need for a punitive crack down on offenders and other troublesome groups was constructed. Rehabilitation and welfare, the penal rhetoric correlating with social democratic hegemony, gave way to punishment and control. 'Zero tolerance', 'three strikes and you're out', 'truth in sentencing' are now globally familiar slogans that exemplify the new penal rhetoric. They resonate with, as they actively cultivate, punitive popular feeling, setting the tone and direction of new, more draconian crime policies.

The general thesis of *Policing the Crisis* has held a central, if often unacknowledged, place in critical criminological work. Analysis has been progressively shorn of its neo-marxist theoretical baggage but the development and application of concepts like 'authoritarian populism' (Hall 1980), 'penal populism' (Bottoms 1995) and the 'new punitiveness' (Pratt et al 2005) reflect attempts to generalise and refine the central idea that crime control has undergone an expansion and intensification in late modern societies.

Others have argued that the 'law and order society' thesis over-states and over-generalises the degree of 'dystopic' rupture (Zedner 2002), that it focuses unduly on developments in punishment to the exclusion of change (and continuity) in other parts of the control apparatus (Hinds 2005, 2006) and that it makes insufficient allowance for the 'volatile and contradictory' character of developments in the crime control field (O'Malley 1999; Brown 2005).

Others still have traced how crime policy transfer occurs between societies and the impact of globalisation on crime control. The global 'war on terror,' drug trafficking, unauthorised people movements and border security, have given impetus to new forms of transcarceral cooperation and practice and a crime control discourse that begins to blur established distinctions between domestic law enforcement and national security (see Findlay and Pickering this volume).

This brief overview does less than justice to the range, depth and quality of critical scholarship and debate on these questions. It suffices to convey a sense of their complexity and the absence of agreement as to what is, in fact, happening, let alone how to analyse it and how to resist it.

Some developments appear to clearly exemplify the drift into a 'law and order society'. I will briefly consider three of the more important ones before turning to other developments that suggest the landscape of contemporary crime and social control is more varied and contingent than this thesis, standing alone, suggests. I will argue that it is not fruitful to conceive of resisting the drift into a law and order society with measures and programs from 'outside' this landscape. Rather meaningful strategies of resistance must necessarily recognise, analyse and engage the possibilities given by present conditions.

Punitiveness: the return of the prison

The principal marker of the drift to a more authoritarian society is usually taken to be the progressive expansion of western criminal justice systems, especially their prison systems. In simple quantitative terms the trend is undeniable. From the 1970s there has been a veritable explosion in prison populations and rates throughout the world. The United States led the way. Its imprisonment rate began to rise earlier off an already higher base and more rapidly than that of other countries. The United States prison population underwent a four-fold increase in 20 years from half a million in 1980 to almost two million by 2000. It currently has an imprisonment rate in excess of 700 per 100,000 adult population (Indyk & Donnelly 2007: 9). Most other English-speaking countries and most of the European world also experienced dramatic increases if not on the massive scale of the United States. Between 1984 and 2005 Australia's imprisonment rate almost doubled from 88 to 163 per 100,000 adult population (Australian Institute of Criminology 2007).

Populism: the return of the people

The 'law and order society' thesis involves much more than quantitative claims about imprisonment rates however. The more critical issue is what rising incarceration rates reflect about the changing character of the political order and the place of law and order within it. Central to this is the idea that crime and punitiveness have been assuming a more important role in the politics, governing practices and legitimacy of liberal democratic states, corresponding to the simultaneous erosion of social democratic values and institutions.

Changes in the structure of economies and communities and in patterns of family and individual life in the last quarter of the 20th century brought with them new and pervasive uncertainties for many people and growing electoral volatility, disaffection and mistrust in major political, social and economic institutions.

In times of insecurity, popular fears, particularly those centred on crime, have become an increasingly important currency of political power. These fears are tapped, or frequently stirred, and political remedies and reassurance is then offered, often in the form of tough, symbolically powerful doses of punitiveness.

Tough measures are seen to be necessary to 'restore public confidence' in government, law and the criminal justice system. This populist mantra appeared in New South Wales in the 1988 election, one of the first in which law and order dominated as an electoral issue (Hogg 1988c). 'Truth in sentencing' and building new prisons were seen to be the necessary panacea to public mistrust. Imprisonment rates quickly shot up, as did new prisons to contain the growing numbers. The trend has continued ever since, although there is little to suggest that public confidence in the justice system has increased or that crime fears and concerns have diminished as a consequence. However, the failure of tough law and order policies to yield the promised results has led to no rethink of their efficacy, no sense that perhaps public insecurities have deeper roots. Rather failure only seems to confirm one thing: that policies are not tough enough and punitive efforts need to be redoubled.

Offenders have become scapegoats for a range of ills besetting society. Some in particular (like child sex offenders) are singled out for special public condemnation and punitive treatment. Law and order populism gives voice and validation to common feelings (anger, hostility, fear and revenge) and seeks to channel inchoate insecurities against well-defined outsider groups. Crime policy becomes symbolic. Measures are more important for what they *say* than what they *do*.

Crime has acquired a novel political salience and a 'new axis of penal power' has emerged around it (see Pratt this volume; Pratt 2002; also see Garland 2001). Populist crime policy is increasingly produced in transactions between the most politicised element within the executive (political leaders, political staffers, pollsters and media advisors) and the tabloid media. Professional knowledge and opinion, research and evidence are marginalised. The experts – judiciary, public servants, and academics – are ignored or more frequently derided as remote and out of touch with community problems and sentiments (Garland 2001: 7). Politicians and their inner coterie of advisers, pollsters and media/marketing experts appeal above the heads of the political establishment (parliament, party, public service, the 'elites' and 'special interests') to the fabled 'silent majority', those who know what it is to live in fear. Sound-bite formulae and press headlines like 'zero tolerance' and 'three strikes and you're out' best reflect the tone and fruits of law and order populism.

Victimology: the return of the victim

Central to populism has been the return to visibility of the crime victim:

> The interests and feelings of victims – actual victims, victims' families, potential victims, the projected figure of 'the victim' – are now routinely invoked in support of measures of punitive segregation ... Laws are passed and named for victims: Megan's law; Jenna's law, the Brady bill ... The new political imperative is that victims must be protected, their voices must be heard, their memory honoured, their anger expressed, their fears addressed ... The victim is now, in a certain sense, a much more representative character, whose experience is taken to be common and collective, rather than individual and atypical. Whoever speaks on behalf of victims speaks on behalf of us all ... this vision of the victim as 'Everyman' has undermined the older notion of 'the public' (Garland 2001: 11).

In keeping with Garland's analysis it has become a commonplace of election campaigns in New South Wales for major political parties to surround themselves with high profile victims and victim organisations. Talkback radio hosts and tabloid media selectively narrate victim experiences as representative of the deepest insecurities afflicting everyday life. There is also a growing tendency to confer civic status on private tragedy and personal loss, commemorating it in ways (laws and public monuments, for example) hitherto reserved to honour events of national public significance (like national self-sacrifice in war) or acts of exceptional personal heroism.

The victim of populist discourse is commonly the ideal-typical victim (Christie 1986), individuals *like us*, or especially our children, wives, elderly parents: respectable, innocent, vulnerable types. *Others* – for example, asylum seekers fleeing torture, disappearances and other human rights abuses – do not necessarily qualify. Indeed they can be subject to the most pitiless treatment. Membership of the community of victims is not therefore open to all who have suffered. Sympathy for the victim who is one of *us* has a flip side that is often defensive, insular and inclined to overlook or deny the suffering of others (Lee 2007).

Resisting the drift to a 'Law and Order Society'

> With misdeeds as with domination, with capitalisms as with sciences, what we need to understand is the ordinary dimensions: the small causes and their large effects (Latour 1993: 125).

The implication in many of the early critical writings on the drift to a 'law and order society' was that resistance required a hegemonic, popular democratic strategy of the Left. For a time the 'Left Realist' project gave criminological expression to this outlook (Matthews & Young 1992; Hogg 1988b). These days critical analysis within criminology proliferates but pretensions to offer a unifying banner are less common (cf Scheerer 2000). The political-intellectual projects that even vaguely approximate it – like feminism, human rights criminology and, more recently, the restorative justice movement – still tend to be more focused on specific domains of discourse, policy and practice than grand narratives and the broad sweep of transformative political change.

This retreat from visions of transformative change was underscored by the progressive, ultimately complete, discrediting of 20th century models of actually existing socialist societies. New political fronts and fault lines – like nationalism, the environment, gender, globalisation, sexuality, religion and human rights – have since cut across old class divisions and the bipolarity of left/right. For many, the new path to enlightenment involves a more modest and experimental attitude:

> [A] turn away from all projects that claim to be global or radical. In fact we know from experience that the claim to escape from the system of contemporary reality so as to produce the overall programs of another society, another way of thinking, another culture, another vision of the world, has led only to the return of the most dangerous traditions (Foucault 1997: 126).

Democracy as well as populism

The populist strain within law and order discourse in countries like Australia, Britain and the United States is undeniable. But Mick Ryan (2005) has argued we need to also recognise that popular engagement with public policy and political responsiveness to popular demands (be it in relation to penal policy, the environment, or any other issue) is part of a long term, broadly democratic and irreversible shift in the political culture of western countries. A long-term process of de-subordination has been under way. Trust and deference with respect to major, once authoritative, institutions – political, industrial, economic, religious – have eroded. Populism is one manifestation of this. Care is needed, however, not to conflate all popular engagement with *populism*.

Nor should it be forgotten that pressure for greater public scrutiny and accountability in relation to criminal justice (especially prisons and policing) originated with movements that advanced progressive reform agendas (Zdenkowski & Brown 1982). These efforts were invariably driven by the desire to expose abuses and policies (violent prison regimes like that in Grafton in New South Wales and police 'verballing' of suspects in custody) that were sustained by a broadly passive, deferential culture in which the rule of administrators over closed institutional worlds was mostly undisturbed by outside scrutiny. In the past the rhetoric relating to the governance of 'deviant' populations may have been more benign, but the practice was often brutal and discriminatory.

Ambiguity and complexity can also be seen in other developments, including the advent of victim-centered policies and the victim movement. Paying greater heed to the interests and needs of crime victims is hardly retrograde in itself. Many victim support measures are laudable and long overdue. Exposing and addressing the hidden victimisation of some groups – women, gays, ethnic and racial minorities, institutionalised populations – are amongst the significant and progressive achievements of contemporary crime politics. Victim discourse may often be exclusionary and exploitative in character, but it is contestable, as these examples make clear.

New forms of accountability

Criminal justice policy has also been increasingly exposed to forms of public scrutiny other than those driven by mass media and appeals to punitive populism. Since the 1970s a whole new government apparatus has developed, variously called the audit or national integrity branch of government. It includes human rights commissions, ombudsman, statistical and research bureaux, auditors-general, corruption commissions, inspectorates and other watchdog agencies. Some of this machinery initially developed as part of a progressive drive in the 1970s for greater public accountability over expanding state functions and powers, but it has lost little of its impetus under the influence of the neo-liberal emphasis on performance monitoring and efficiency. It may not seem all that radical or ideologically inspiring but the achievement in institutionalising greater public transparency and providing important safeguards against a repetition of past patterns of institutional power abuse should not be dismissed.

'Neglected features of contemporary penal systems'

In the rush by new conservatives to embrace the free market – to downsize government, reduce social expenditure and impose market disciplines on public services – law and order was one area that was to be spared the razor. Yet it turned out to be otherwise. Law and order was not immune from demands for greater efficiency, performance measurement and market pressures. In fact concerns with inefficiencies, costs, court delays and the like have been a perennial feature of criminal justice debates for many years.

This needs to be set against the fact that the progressive expansion of the role of criminal justice over the entire course of the 20th century was an integral feature of the growth of the regulatory-welfare state. This produced penal developments that were widely 'neglected' by criminologists, including the proliferation of summary offences, the growth in reliance upon non-custodial sanctions and the expansion of regulatory controls (Bottoms 1983; Hogg 1988a; Braithwaite 2003). The trend has not abated. Even as imprisonment rates increased and governments talked tough on crime, they continued, less visibly, to push a growing proportion of cases from higher to lower courts (with their more limited sentencing powers) and extend the use of non-court alternatives. Major areas of crime and criminal justice have been de-dramatised and subject to a new parsimony, presenting a contrast with the punitive, expressive measures associated with law and order populism.

Crime prevention, managerialism and privatisation

More recently, personal and community safety have, like other services, been subject to a kind of privatisation in which citizens, households, corporations, organisations, and communities are encouraged to assume greater responsibility for their own security, alone and in conjunction with government agencies and private security providers. This has seen most western governments embrace crime prevention as a major policy area, promoting the delegation of responsibility for personal and community safety, multi-agency partnerships and an increased role for the private sector and for technologies of surveillance (like saturation use of closed-circuit television). Coupled with the growing privatisation of public spaces – walled housing estates, shopping malls, recreational parks – security concerns and measures have become increasingly embedded in the urban environment and urban design, creating new forms of social and spatial exclusion and new strategies of surveillance-based control (For a critical excavation of the future of urban social control see Mike Davis's (1992) now classic study of Los Angeles).

Many see in such developments a managerial trend within criminal justice and social control, part of a more general developing neo-liberal logic within late modern western polities (see O'Malley this volume). At the same time the stress on 'whole-of-government' approaches, on shared public/private provision and on audit and reflexivity in relation to crime prevention and control opens up new arenas of contestation and new opportunities for progressive change. Control of knowledge and debate has to a degree been wrested from the criminal justice bureaucracies that have in turn been increasingly required to respond more creatively to their own problems and to the assertive demands of a plurality of active constituencies.

New visions of justice

New theories and visions of justice have arisen in this ferment with a real and practical purchase on change and reform, including ideas and measures around restorative justice (conferencing, circle sentencing), therapeutic justice (drug courts) and problem-solving justice (see Daly et al 2006). Of course, particular measures call for specific, critical scrutiny. Nevertheless these developments signal the availability of alternatives to the slide into a law and order society. In the spirit of Latour's (1993) injunction we would do well to reject an older, crippling critical attitude which was inclined to see the practical political purchase of any reform as counting against it, as evidence even that it must be part of some 'net-widening' or other malign control strategy.

From law and order to national security:
a nation of victims?

In Australia's federal system, the administration of justice is primarily a state responsibility and law and order issues have been largely played out in state/territory politics. This is changing. Crime is emerging as a major national political issue. Transnational crimes like drug trafficking, cyber crime (especially internet pornography) and people trafficking have increasingly drawn the Commonwealth into the crime debate. The 2001 national election saw the identification of a new transnational danger: the asylum seeker arriving on Australian shores in people smugglers' boats. This further galvanised the developing national politics of law and order that linked internal with external fears (see Poynting and Pickering this volume).

Ordinary criminal threats to the community have increasingly been fused with dangers to national security. Law and order has become progressively merged with the defence of the nation. This metamorphosis in law and order discourse was sealed by the attacks on New York and the Pentagon on 11 September 2001 and the subsequent terrorist attacks in Bali, Madrid, London and elsewhere. Following 9/11, global terrorism has been constructed by the political/media axis as the new spectral threat besetting the nation, a threat in which geo-political and local dangers are deeply enmeshed. We are told the danger is existential, a threat to the very nation, its way of life and its values. There is a 'clash of civilizations'. The danger does not emanate from a foreign state or invading armies. Rather in the everyday pedagogy worked by some politicians and the tabloid media we are warned that the threat is in our midst: 'Middle Eastern' youth who flaunt their defiance of Anglo-Australian values, imams who refuse to preach in English, Islamic leaders who fail to loudly condemn extremism (an impossible ask where most media simply fail to report voices of moderation), Islamic modes of dress, Islamic attitudes to women and the list goes on. The mundane, visible signs and artefacts of social, cultural and religious difference are increasingly framed by terrorism, recasting them as security threats.

In keeping with the nature of the danger said to be confronting the nation, a vast new apparatus of executive powers has been instituted and is constantly being augmented. It is 'transcarceral' in the dual sense that it both integrates law enforcement and national security powers *within* Australia and establishes new cross-border strategies and cooperative arrangements involving the executive agencies of *different* states. This includes states with appalling human rights records. In the most disturbing of these arrangements, the rendition programs of the United States Central Intelligence Agency (CIA), the west has 'outsourced' torture and repression to its allies in the 'war on terror'.

Australia, we are told by the political authorities, is *especially vulnerable* to terrorism. This is not solely or even primarily because of the likely scale of any possible terrorist attack. Indeed most defence experts in Australia and internationally dispute that terrorism is a strategic threat to societies or states like Australia, although they agree that it is a not insignificant threat to individuals. In place of this traditional, strategic conception of risk, however, the Australian Government suggested *our* vulnerability derives (amongst other things) from 'the very high value our society places on human life'.[1] We are more fearful and the threat is more urgent because we share an acute sensitivity to the value of human life (although apparently not a sensitivity that encompasses all human lives, as the folly of Iraq shows). The threat to the nation is constructed not from the potential mass loss of life or impact on our institutions, but only by conflating the polity with the projected subjective feelings and fears of its citizens: we have a special collective vulnerability because we are special. As Joanna Bourke (2005) has argued in the British context, this way of defining the terrorist threat nurtures 'a national identity of victimhood'.

It fuses elements from law and order discourse with the 'unreasoning fearfulness' that has driven a powerful strain within Australian nationalism (Renouf 1979). The crime-fearing subject (Lee 2007) meets the fearful nation, infusing the drift to a 'law and order society' with defensive nationalist anxieties. As a national community of putative victims we are encouraged to see ourselves as 'a trauma society' (Bourke 2005). And, as Bourke observes, 'the status of victim serves to depoliticize our responses' and blinds us to others' suffering.

In this changed international environment criminology is challenged to look beyond its more traditional and familiar focus on domestic crime debates and issues.

Conclusion

Once again, although these are deeply disturbing developments there are also hopeful signs of change and paths for resistance. In the 1970s Julia and Herman Schwendinger (1975) argued the case for a human rights-based criminology, in which

---

1   This was the argument advanced by the Government in the High Court in *Thomas v Mowbray* in response to a constitutional challenge to its control order regime (See: [2007] HCA Trans 76 (20 February 2007) at p 7).

international human rights standards would govern the definitions of crime and the research agendas of criminologists. This would turn attention to the human rights violations of states and other powerful actors and to problems of institutionalised racism and sexism and other forms of discrimination. At the time the development of global and regional human rights machinery was making slow progress. The idea of a radical human rights criminology attracted academic interest, but it was probably widely regarded as having little immediate purchase on political change.

The ground has since shifted with major advances in global and regional enforcement regimes and human rights jurisprudence. The abrogation of the sovereign immunity of political leaders for gross human rights abuses as in the case of the erstwhile Chilean dictator, Augusto Pinochet, the establishment of ad hoc international tribunals to deal with crimes against humanity in countries like the former Yugoslavia, Rwanda and Sierra Leone, the creation of the permanent International Criminal Court and the proliferation of national truth commissions to grapple with human rights abuses of past regimes are all signs of this advance.

There has been a corresponding expansion over the same period in the network of non-government agencies involved in aid, peace, human rights and other areas of international work, what Keane (1996) calls a 'new politics of civility' (also see Ignatieff 1998; Human Security Centre 2005; Scheerer 2000). Notwithstanding concerted government media management and abundant uncritical media coverage and framing of issues and events in the 'war on terror', the very 'promiscuity' of contemporary communications media unleashes sources of information and supports spaces for debate and contestation that are impossible for governments to control (Ignatieff 1998: 11). Witness the speed with which images of the Abu Ghraib prison abuses entered global channels of communication, shifting public attitudes and altering the terms of the political debate about the invasion of Iraq and the 'war on terror'. Closer to home the shift in popular opinion and the political debate concerning David Hicks' detention in Guantanamo Bay is a further example of the instability of official, hegemonic representations and their vulnerability to popular, democratic challenge (even on the favoured conservative political terrain of national security) (Sales 2007).

Finally it is possible to detect convergences between global and local forces in the shaping of new visions and models of justice. Concepts – like justice, truth, reconciliation, restoration – that are central to the way human rights and peacekeeping criminology has addressed crime, violence and conflict in societies torn by large scale racial, ethnic, colonial and other divisions turn out to also have a political purchase at the domestic level, in contemporary debates on crime policy and the reform of local policing and justice structures in stable democratic societies like Australia. A reason for this is that stability often belies the reality of deep division and injustice, which is sublimated in everyday violence, crime, conflict, and the administration of criminal justice.

These are amongst the tools available to resist the local and global drift to 'a law and order society', and, even more worrying, the increasing fondness of some political leaders for augmenting the domestic forces of law and order with the trappings of military power, a move signalled by the Australian Prime Minister's attempt in mid-2007 to portray bold and decisive national political leadership by deploying the Australian army to restore law and order in remote Indigenous communities. It is to be hoped that the choice is not as stark as one between a growing civilisation of power and its growing militarisation. Critical, politically engaged inquiry and debate may do its part to prevent it from becoming so.

References

Australian Institute of Criminology 2007, *Australian Crime: facts and figures 2006,* AIC, Canberra.

Bottoms, A 1983, 'Neglected Features of Contemporary Penal Systems', in Garland, D & Young, P (eds), *The Power to Punish: contemporary penality and social analysis,* Heinemann, London.

Bottoms, A 1995, 'The Philosophy and Politics of Punishment and Sentencing', in Clarkson, C & Morgan, R (eds), *The Politics of Sentencing Reform,* Clarendon Press, Oxford.

Bourke, J 2005, 'Politics of fear blinds us all', *Guardian Weekly,* 7-13 October.

Bourke, J 2006, *Fear: a cultural history,* Virago, London.

Braithwaite, J 2003, 'What's wrong with the sociology of punishment?', 7(1) *Theoretical Criminology* 5.

Brown, D 2005, 'Continuity, rupture, or just more of the "volatile and contradictory"? Glimpses of New South Wales' penal practice behind and through the discursive', in Pratt, J, Brown, D, Brown, M, Hallsworth, S & Morrison, W (eds), *The New Punitiveness: trends, theories, perspectives,* Willan Publishing, Cullompton.

Christie, N 1986, 'The Ideal Victim', in Fattah, E (ed), *From Crime Policy to Victim Policy: reorienting the justice system,* Macmillan, London.

Clark, R 1971, *Crime in America: observations on its nature, causes, prevention and control,* Pocket Books, New York.

Cohen, S 1996, 'Crime and Politics: spot the difference', 47(1) *British Journal of Sociology* 1.

Daly, K, Hayes, H, & Marchetti, E 2006, 'New Visions of Justice' in Goldsmith, A, Israel, M & Daly, K (eds), *Crime and Justice: a guide to criminology,* Third Edition, LawBook Co, Sydney.

Davis, M 1992, *City of Quartz,* Vintage, London.

Downes, D, & Morgan, R 2002, 'The Skeletons in the Cupboard: the politics of law and order a the turn of the millennium' in Maguire, M, Morgan, R & Reiner, R (eds), *The Oxford Handbook of Criminology,* Third Edition, Oxford University Press, Oxford.

Foucault, M 1997, 'What is Enlightenment?' in Lotringer, S & Hochroth, L (eds), *The Politics of Truth,* Semiotexe, New York.

Gamble, A 1988, *The Free Economy and the Strong State: the politics of Thatcherism,* Macmillan, London.

Garland, D 2001, *The Culture of Control,* Oxford University Press, Oxford.

Gramsci, A 1971, *Selections from the Prison Notebooks,* edited and translated by Hoare, Q & Nowell-Smith, G, Lawrence & Wishart, London.

Hall, S 1980, *Drifting into a Law and Order Society,* Cobden Trust Human Rights Day Lecture 1979.

Hall, S, Critcher, C, Jefferson, T, Clarke, J & Roberts, B 1978, *Policing the Crisis: mugging, the state and law and order,* Macmillan, London.

Hall, S, & Jacques, M (eds) 1983, *The Politics of Thatcherism,* Lawrence & Wishart, London.

Hinds, L 2005, 'Crime Control in Western Countries 1920 to 2000' in Pratt, J, Brown, D, Brown, M, Hallsworth, S, & Morrison, W (eds), *The New Punitiveness: trends, theories, perspectives,* Willan Publishing, Cullompton.

Hinds, L 2006, 'Challenging Current Conceptions of Law and Order', 10(2) *Theoretical Criminology* 203.

Hogg, R 1988a, 'Criminal Justice and Social Control: contemporary developments in Australia', 2 *Journal of Studies in Justice* 89.

Hogg, R 1988b, 'Taking Crime Seriously: Left Realism and Australian criminology', in Findlay, M & Hogg, R (eds), *Understanding Crime and Criminal Justice*, LawBook Co, Sydney.

Hogg, R 1988c, 'Sentencing and Penal Politics: current developments in New South Wales', *Proceedings of the Institute of Criminology No 78, Sentencing*, University of Sydney, New South Wales.

Hogg, R & Brown, D 1998, *Rethinking Law and Order*, Pluto Press, Sydney.

Human Security Centre 2005, *War and Peace in the 21st Century*, Human Security Report, <www.humansecuritycentre.org> .

Ignatieff, M 1998, *The Warrior's Honour: ethnic war and the modern conscience*, Chatto & Windus, London.

Indyk, S, & Donnelly, H 2007, *Full-time Imprisonment in New South Wales and other Jurisdictions: a national and international comparison,* Judicial Commission of NSW, Sydney.

Keane, J 1996, *Reflections on Violence*, Verso, London.

Kelly, P 1994, *The End of Certainty: power, politics and business in Australia*, Revised Edition, Allen & Unwin, Sydney.

Latour, B 1993, *We Have Never Been Modern*, Harvester Wheatsheaf, Cambridge.

Lee, M 2007, *Inventing Fear of Crime: criminology and the politics of anxiety,* Willan Publishing, Cullompton.

Matthews, R, & Young, J 1992, *Issues in Realist Criminology*, Sage, London.

O'Malley, P 1999, 'Volatile and contradictory punishment', 3(2) *Theoretical Criminology* 175.

Pratt, J 2002, *Punishment and Civilization*, Sage, London.

Pratt, J, Brown, D, Brown, M, Hallsworth, S & Morrison, W, (eds) 2005 *The New Punitiveness: trends, theories, perspectives*, Willan Publishing, Cullompton.

Renouf, A 1979, *The Frightened Country*, Macmillan, South Melbourne.

Ryan, M 2005, 'Engaging with Punitive Attitudes Towards Crime and Punishment: some strategic lessons from England and Wales', in Pratt, J, Brown, D, Brown, M, Hallsworth, S & Morrison, W (eds), *The New Punitiveness: trends, theories, perspectives*, Willan Publishing, Cullompton.

Sales, L 2007, *Detainee 002: the case of David Hicks*, Melbourne University Press, Melbourne.

Schwendinger, H & Schwendinger J 1975, 'Defenders of Order or Guardians of Human Rights?' in Taylor, I, Walton, P & Young, J (eds), *Critical Criminology*, Routledge & Kegan Paul, London.

Scheerer, S 2000, 'Three Trends into the New Millennium: the managerial, the populist and the road towards global justice' in Green, P & Rutherford, A (eds), *Criminal Policy in Transition*, Hart Publishing, Oxford.

Zdenkowski, G & Brown, D 1982, *The Prison Struggle: changing Australia's penal system*, Penguin Books, Ringwood.

Zedner, L 2002, 'Dangers of Dystopias in Penal Theory', 22(2) *Oxford Journal of Legal Studies* 341.

24

Understanding Restorative Justice Through the Lens of Critical Criminology

Chris Cunneen

Introduction

There is an uneasy relationship between critical criminology and restorative justice. On the one hand, restorative justice is a story of optimism, reform and social change. Yet it also demonstrates a tendency to work within traditional criminal justice systems and whilst doing so, fails to challenge the exclusionary processes of criminalisation. This chapter explores some of the tensions between restorative justice and critical criminology – it is a critique of restorative justice within the context of the unfulfilled possibilities that restorative justice might hold.

Restorative justice can be defined in a number of ways including as a process, or as a set of values or goals, or more broadly as a social movement seeking specific change in the way criminal justice systems operate. A frequently cited definition is that restorative justice 'is a process whereby parties with a stake in a specific offence collectively resolve how to deal with the aftermath of the offence and its implications for the future' (Marshall 1999: 5). This definition emphasises the process requirement that all parties have an opportunity to be heard about the consequences of the crime and what needs to be done to restore victims, offenders and the community. Other definitions emphasise the values and goals of restorative justice rather than the process. The core values are said to be healing relationships between all parties involved, community deliberation rather than state-centred control of decision-making, and non-domination.

The roots of restorative justice can be found in a range of different approaches in criminology and law emerging during the 1960s and 1970s and provide a context for the contemporary development of restorative justice as akin to a 'social movement'. These origins include the development of 'informal' justice, including victim-offender mediation. In addition a number of intellectual traditions supported the development of restorative justice, including European critical traditions of abolitionism, religious traditions stressing reconciliation and healing, and in North America, Australia and New Zealand those who stressed the values of Indigenous cultures and dispute resolution processes in 'pre-state' societies (Daly & Immarigeon 1998; Pavlich 2005).

In practice, restorative justice has varied significantly both in process and in the extent to which core values and goals are met. Restorative justice covers a range of practices that might occur at various points within the criminal justice process, including pre-court diversion, processes working in conjunction with the court including at the point of sentencing, and post sentencing with prisoners. We can see examples of restorative justice in victim-offender mediation, in family group and youth justice conferencing, and in sentencing circles. We can also see claims to restorative justice as a principle in post conflict and transitional justice settings such as the South African Truth and Reconciliation Commission. In addition there are a range of areas outside the criminal law where restorative justice practices have been used including workplaces, schools and child protection matters. There is a wide literature on the processes of restorative justice (for recent examples, see Johnstone & Van Ness 2007; Sullivan & Tift 2006). In addition, there have been numerous evaluations of restorative justice programs in New Zealand, Australia, the United Kingdom, Europe and North America (for summaries, see Strang 2001; Luke & Lind 2002). It is not the purpose of this chapter to review either the process or evaluation literature.

In its more critical manifestations, restorative justice theory has provided a critique of key conceptualisations and institutions of the criminal justice system. It provided the possibilities for challenging the discourses of criminalisation and punishment. It decentred the notion of 'crime' to the extent that categories of 'harm', 'conflict' and 'dispute' replaced the state's exclusive definition of criminal behaviour. It rethought the relationship between victim, offender and community, and in particular challenged the idea that the rights and interests of the victim and offender were diametrically opposed in a 'zero sum' relationship. In regard to penality, restorative justice presented itself as a 'third way' between just deserts and rehabilitation.

Yet restorative justice can also be seen as a discourse which is consonant with neo-liberalism to the extent that it focuses on the 'active' responsibility of individual subjects: the responsibility of the offender for the particular crime and the responsibility of the victim to participate in a process to restore their losses. Further the process itself rejects a key role for the state and privileges ownership by the community (O'Malley 2006: 221-222). A key argument in this regard is that restorative justice practices have developed within, and helped to create bifurcated criminal justice systems, which increasingly distinguish access to restorative justice programs on the basis of recidivism and risk.

Critical perspectives on restorative justice have emerged from a number of avenues. For the purposes of this discussion, these arguments may be grouped as neo-marxist, postmodernist and poststructuralist, feminist, postcolonial and liberal. These critical perspectives are broad. Not surprisingly, there are intersections and overlap in their application to restorative justice. These critiques cover various points relating to the role of the state and its agencies, concepts of globalisation and community, relations of class, 'race', ethnicity and gender, and questions about the rule of law, legal principles and appropriate process. Fundamental to these critiques are questions of power and resistance and modes of punishment within neo-liberal regimes.

The state role in restorative justice processes

A major neo-marxist critique of restorative justice emerged at the same time as new restorative justice practices, particularly in juvenile justice, were being formulated in the early 1990s (see for example, White 1994). This critique revolved around the relationship between restorative justice and the state. In particular the developing state-directed control of restorative justice appeared to undermine the more radical potential of restorative justice. Neo-marxists were concerned that the claims of restorative justice embodied both a profound naiveté about the nature of politics and a sanguine view of state power. As White (1994: 187) argued, restorative justice:

> accepts at face value the liberal democratic notion that the state is somehow neutral and above sectional interests, that it operates for the 'common good', and that it is an impartial and independent arbiter of conflicts.

From a neo-marxist perspective, there has been little recognition by restorative justice proponents of the move over the past two decades from a social state to a more repressive state as part of the ascendancy of neo-liberal politics. The withdrawal from responsibility in areas of health, education and welfare, and the shift towards modes of governance through privatisation, and individual and community responsibilisation have all had profound effects on the role of the state in crime control. Similarly, the class-based impact of unemployment and marginalisation, particularly among young people, poses very real problems for restorative justice practice – especially if that practice is built on a presumption of individualised responsibility for crime and restoration. What the neo-marxist critique demands is that restorative justice respond seriously to these broader social and economic issues and that it be able to deal constructively with the various 'hidden injuries' of class including alienation from school and work, homelessness, drug abuse and marginalisation.

A further concern, particularly in Australia and New Zealand, is the failure to understand the complexity of the relationship between colonised peoples and colonial/postcolonial states. There is little recognition that the state and particularly its criminal justice agencies are not seen as legitimate by Indigenous peoples in settler states. A state-sponsored restorative justice program may well be viewed with suspicion and seen as another imposed form of control which undermines existing Indigenous modes of governance. There is the added political and historical irony to this, given that restorative justice proponents, particularly during the 1990s, defined their activities as consonant with, and drawing inspiration from Indigenous cultures (Cunneen 1997; Blagg 1997).

Policing

A major issue stemming from the relationship between restorative justice and the state has been policing and criminalisation. In many jurisdictions the police exercise significant discretionary powers over restorative justice programs. For example, police can determine access to youth justice conferencing programs, and play a key role in the operation of the conferencing process and subsequent agreement. The centrality of the police role is especially problematic given concerns over the inappropriate exercise of police discretion, the dominance of police or other professionals over other conference participants and the lack of accountability of police (White 1994; Cunneen 1997). The expanded police role in restorative justice programs has led to greater police powers. In most jurisdictions the increased role of police has not been accompanied by any further accountability or control over police decision-making (Blagg 1997). At the same time there have been significant legislative extensions of police powers in Australia, particularly in relation public order offences (see Brown et al 2006; McCulloch this volume). These greater powers have the effect of bringing more people into all areas of the criminal justice system, including those deemed 'restorative'.

Indigenous peoples, and racial and ethnic minorities may have good reason to be sceptical that police are independent arbiters in the process of restorative justice. There is the danger that minority youth will be classified by police as 'unsuitable' for restorative justice schemes particularly if they have prior offending histories or are deemed uncooperative (Cunneen & White 2007).

Restorative justice processes need to effectively critique inappropriate and racist policing and broader processes of criminalisation. Policing and the criminal justice system has a determining role in constituting social groups as threats and in reproducing a society built on racialised boundaries. The process of criminalisation constitutes 'a significant racialising discourse' (Keith 1993: 193), from which restorative justice is not immune. If restorative justice lacks the ability to critique increases in police powers, public order interventions over minor offences or the discriminatory use of stop and searches, then it is nothing more than another regulatory device used in the service of power. It becomes simply a mode of governance that facilitates and further legitimates state intervention.

Punishment

Restorative justice reaches into longstanding debates about the nature and purpose of punishment. Daly and Immarigeon (1998) question whether restorative justice is indeed contrary to retributivist or rehabilitation models of justice or combines elements of these approaches. More significantly, restorative justice programs have been introduced within a framework of greater emphasis on individual responsibility, deterrence and incapacitation. As other writers in this book have argued (for example, Pratt, Hogg) there has been a significant intensification of punishment over the past decades – at the same time as restorative justice practices have been introduced. Thus there may be elements of restorative justice, retribution, just deserts, rehabilitation and incapacitation all operating within a particular jurisdiction at any one time.

Discussions of postmodern penality are useful in contextualising the place of restorative justice in contemporary fields of punishment. Pratt (2000), for example, has discussed the return of public shaming, and the resurfacing of a premodern penal quality. He also notes the development of other phenomena that would seem out of place within a modern penal framework including boot camps, curfews and the abandonment of proportionality (2000: 131-133). O'Malley (1999) has discussed the 'bewildering array' of developments in penal policy including policies based on discipline, punishment, enterprise, incapacitation, restitution and reintegration – policies which are mutually incoherent and contradictory. However, much of the discussion around a postmodern penality has centred on the movement of penal regimes towards the prediction of risk: the development of 'techniques for identifying, classifying and managing groups assorted by dangerousness' (Feeley & Simon 1994: 173).

The emphasis on actuarialism, the prediction of risk and policies of incapacitation are not contradictory with the way restorative justice practices have developed, rather they can be seen as complementary strategies put in place within single systems of justice. Indeed risk assessment becomes a fundamental tactic in dividing populations between those who benefit from restorative justice practices and those who are channelled into more punitive processes of incapacitation through being refused bail, or facing mandatory supervision or imprisonment. The modes of assessing risk are increasingly accomplished through a variety of 'weak' and 'strong' risk predictive mechanisms from a simple recognition of prior criminal record through to the application of specifically designed risk assessment tools.

We can see these processes operating more clearly in the context of a greater *bifurcation* of existing justice systems. For example, in Australia conferencing models have been introduced in a context where juvenile justice systems are increasingly responding to two categories of offenders: those defined as 'minor' and those who are seen as serious and/or repeat offenders. Minor offenders benefit from various diversionary programs such as conferencing schemes. Serious and repeat offenders, on the other hand, are classified ineligible for diversionary programs and are dealt with more punitively through sentencing regimes that are more akin to adult models.

Further, these processes of bifurcation have been intensifying over the past decade particularly with changes in bail legislation, which have dramatically increased remand numbers among adults and juveniles, and greater restrictions on eligibility to diversionary programs such as youth conferencing.

Globalisation

Globalisation has the effect of imparting preferred models of capitalist development, modernisation and urbanisation (Findlay 1999). In this context, globalisation increasingly demands particular forms of capital accumulation, as well as associated social and legal relations both within and between nation states. At first glance this may seem irrelevant to the localised claims of restorative justice. Yet discussions around globalisation should alert us to the need to situate the growing interest in restorative justice within the shifting boundaries of relations within and between the first world and the third world. This is particularly the case when much restorative justice talk presents itself as an alternative narrative on justice, as something outside the justice paradigms of retribution, deterrence and rehabilitation, and as a form of resolving disputes which is 'non-Western'.

Little attention has been paid to whether restorative justice can be seen as much as a globalising force as traditional western legal forms. The potential to over-run local custom and law is as real with restorative justice as it is with other models built on retributivism or rehabilitation (Cunneen 2002). The risk is that restricted and particularised notions of restorative justice will become part of a globalising tendency which restricts local justice mechanisms in areas where there is a demand to 'modernise' (Findlay 1999; Zellerer & Cunneen 2001: 251). Thus actual localised customary and non-state practices for resolving disputes and harms will be replaced by what the West understands to be restorative justice – and we can see examples of this in Australia where Aboriginal customary processes are seen as less legitimate than state-sanctioned forms of restorative justice such as conferencing. Alternatively traditional forms of localised justice may be forced to respond to crimes they were never designed to deal with (for example, the gacaca local dispute processes in Rwanda dealing with genocide) in the interests of broader appeals to restorative justice (Iffil 2007).

Reparations and transitional justice

Another tendency of globalisation is the expanding role of restorative justice in dealing with matters of transitional justice, state crime and the gross violation of human rights. There is a growing literature that considers the importance of reparations for historical injustices and the potential links between reparations and restorative justice (Cunneen 2006; Findlay & Henham 2005). Internationally there has been growing acceptance that governments acknowledge and make reparations to the victims of human rights abuses, as well as widespread acceptance of the principle of reparations. Reparations have significant potential overlap with the goals of restorative justice, and have been articulated as such for example in the South African Truth and Reconciliation Commission (Cunneen 2006).

Part of the globalising tendency is the introduction of specific processes for responding to state violations of human rights, and can be seen in the work of organisations like the International Centre for Transitional Justice (ICTJ) in New York. The ICTJ provides advice and models for the establishment of truth and reconciliation commissions. The concern is that these processes for restorative justice are ones that become imposed, partly in the interests of the West to resolve conflict in a particular way, and without local and organic links to the particular society.

Community

Pavlich (2005) notes that within restorative justice discourses the absolute existence of 'community' is assumed. Community appears as the 'spontaneous and voluntary collective domains that constitute the foundations of civil society' (2005: 97). Community is not a natural set of relations between individuals, nor a natural social process lying at the foundation of civil society. Communities are always constructed on the broad terrain of history and politics. Radical critiques provide a multilayered understanding of the problematic relationship between community and state. Basic to this understanding is a concern that the notion of community presents a harmonious view of social and political relations, which masks conflict, power, difference, inequality and potentially exploitative social and economic relations.

The postmodernist understanding of restorative justice has questioned the implicit consensual notions of civil society and community. Pavlich (2001) argues that 'community' is also fundamentally about *exclusion*. 'The promise of community's free and uncoerced collective association is offset by a tendency to shore up limits, fortify a given identity, and rely on exclusion to secure self-preservation' (2001: 3). Such a vision of community is only a short step away from the 'gated' community of the wealthy excluding the poor; the community of interest generated by power and prestige. 'Community' can easily spill over into class, cultural and racial purity, xenophobia and racism (Bauman 1998). Indeed the problem is that restorative justice can become what it opposes: a practice which closes, limits and excludes individuals, rather than reintegrates.

Another point of departure in radical critique is to question the claim that restorative justice provides an avenue for 'the community' to take back from the state the ownership of the problem of crime. From feminist perspectives the problem has been that the state has never adequately criminalised crimes of violence against women. To the extent that we can discuss 'community' in this context, we may well find that 'community' reflects the patriarchal relations which provide for the acceptance of violence against women. Rather than providing a barrier and safeguard against offending, it may provide social and cultural legitimation for violence.

From a postcolonial perspective, colonial policies were directly responsible for the destruction and reconstruction of 'community' in the interests of the coloniser. Many contemporary Indigenous communities were created directly as a result of colonial government policies of forced relocations. Further, contemporary racial and ethnic minority communities within first world metropoles are specifically created under conditions determined by neo- and post-colonial relations which influence the nature of immigration and post-immigration experiences (Cunneen & Stubbs 2002). History and contemporary politics have shaped both Indigenous and post-war immigrant communities. What then does 'community' mean for minority people in these situations and how does it impact on relations with the police, the criminal justice system and the state more generally?

Neo-marxist and governmentality critiques of neo-liberalism also identify the current tendencies towards the responsibilisation of individuals, families and communities and the preference towards 'governing at a distance'. Pavlich (2005: 97) notes that the 'community' of restorative justice is essentially constituted by the state which designs, creates, funds and staffs the restorative justice project. It provides authority and legitimacy to the 'community' that then participates in the restorative justice project. Such a community is not independent of state agency.

Gender

Perhaps the most sustained critique of restorative justice has come from feminists who have emphasised the lack of understanding of power relations embedded in crimes against women. Feminist arguments have been particularly important in relation to the problems of applying restorative justice practices to domestic violence. The starting point in this critique is that domestic violence is a particular type of crime and that the fundamental priority of any type of intervention must be to ensure the physical protection for victims, usually women and children (Stubbs 1997, 2002).

Thus restorative justice needs to be able to deconstruct generalised notions of crime: the nature of domestic violence is specific. The violence is not a discrete act between two individuals who are unknown to each other. Rather the violence may be part of a number of gendered strategies of control including various forms of behaviour and coercive tactics. The violence itself may be part of a patterned cycle of behaviour which includes contrition. Furthermore, there are social and cultural dimensions that give meaning and authorisation to the violence and constrain women's options in response (Stubbs 2002: 45). We cannot assume that actors marshalled together for a restorative justice conference will be capable of reflecting the necessary support for victims who are in a structurally disadvantaged position.

Indeed, the basic premise of restorative justice, that the harm between victim and offender is to be repaired, must be questioned as an outcome sought by women seeking intervention, support and protection against violence (2002: 51).

There is also no particular reason to suspect that restorative justice practices will privilege or indeed give a voice to minority women or respond adequately to different groups of women who experience differing levels of violence. In Australia, for example, the homicide rate for Indigenous women is 10 times that of other women. Other minority women also have variable rates, for example, Filipino women's homicide rate is five times the general rate for other women in Australia (Cunneen & Stubbs 2002). These differences directly reflect the gendered outcomes of colonial and postcolonial conditions. Having said that, it is also worth noting that colonised women's appalling experience with western criminal justice interventions may lead them to see restorative justice as a potential avenue for better outcomes (Nancarrow 2006).

Liberal critique and legal process

Many criminal justice activists have expressed disquiet over aspects of restorative justice programs. Often these criticisms are aimed at specific restorative justice practices and might be broadly characterised as critiques based on liberal arguments centred around the rule of law and equality before the law. The concerns can be distinguished from those of critical criminologies to the extent that they assume with a certain level of 'tweaking' the process can be rectified.

Yet these concerns also represent the protection of basic rights and values that critical criminologists would also seek to uphold. They include concerns over abuse of due process; absence of procedural rights and protections; excessive, disproportionate or inconsistent outcomes and so forth (see for example, Warner 1994: 142-146). These concerns include the potential undermining of defendant's rights at the investigatory, adjudicatory and sentencing stages of the criminal justice system.

At the investigatory stage, the lack of independent legal advice, pressures to admit an offence to obtain the presumed benefit of diversion and the avoidance of a criminal record, and the lack of testing of the legality of police searches, questioning and evidence gathering may compromise outcomes. Furthermore, the pressure to admit an offence means that issues relating to *mens rea* (the defendant's mental fault) and legal defences are not considered by the court.

A related concern is that the outcome from a restorative justice program may be more punitive than might be expected if the normal sentencing principles of consistency, proportionality and frugality were applied. There is also potential to ignore the basic human rights principles relating to children and young people: upholding the primacy of the best interests of the child and rehabilitation when sentencing and making other decisions affecting children and young people.

The establishment of conferencing and other restorative justice procedures can introduce the potential for net widening. In particular, young people may become subject to conferencing procedures for behaviour which would have previously been regarded as too trivial to warrant official intervention (Polk 1994: 133-135). Whether this emerges as a problem in particular jurisdictions will to some extent depend on the specific legislative and policy framework within which the restorative justice procedures operate. For example, legislative criteria determining use, and checks and balances over referral and other official decision-making may act to minimise the potential problem. In an effort to provide a framework for improving conferencing for young people, the Australian Law Reform Commission (1997: 482) has recommended that national standards for juvenile justice should provide best practice guidelines for family group conferencing.

'Non state' punishment and postmodern hybridity

Restorative justice often lays claim to a pre-modern Indigenous authenticity as part of its search for a 'myth of origin' (Daly 2002). Often the claims, which link restorative justice practices to Indigenous peoples, are trivialising. They disavow the complex effects of colonial policies which have, at various times, sought to exterminate, assimilate, 'civilise', and Christianise Aboriginal peoples. They also disavow the complexity and variations in Indigenous dispute resolution mechanisms (Zellerer & Cunneen 2001: 246-247).

The search for origins of restorative justice in Indigenous traditions has provided an important rhetorical tool to distinguish restorative justice traditions from modern state-centred systems of punishment. It has been partly a story about what the West has lost. The broad argument is that over the longer period of human history the state assumed the function of punishment only relatively recently and that, previously, societies functioned well with restorative forms of sanctioning. Restorative methods of dispute resolution were dominant in non-state, pre-state and early state societies: individuals were bound closely to the social group and mediation and restitution were primary ways of dealing with conflict. Further, these pre-modern, pre-state restorative forms of sanctioning can still be found practised in Indigenous communities today.

There are simple dichotomies underpinning this story of restorative justice: non-state sanctioning is restorative (and, conversely, state imposed punishment is not) and Indigenous societies and pre-modern societies do not use utilise retributive forms of punishment as their primary mode of dispute resolution. Yet this simple story distorts the diversity of Indigenous cultures and the variety of sanctions used by Indigenous peoples within their specific cultural frameworks. Not surprisingly, some sanctions are 'restorative', in the sense that a modern proponent of restorative justice would accept, and some, clearly, are not. Indigenous sanctions might include temporary or permanent exile, withdrawal and separation within the community, public shaming of the individual, and restitution by the offender and/or their kin. Some sanctions may involve physical punishment such as beating or spearing.

Rather than a simple dichotomy between a pre-modern, pre-state restorative justice, and the modern state's model of retributive (and rehabilitative) punishment, perhaps a more useful conceptualisation is to see the current developments in restorative justice within a framework of hybridity that is neither pre-modern nor modern. By 'hybridity', I am referring to transformations in punishment, similar to a form of 'fragmented' justice or 'spliced' justice, where traditional legal bureaucratic forms of justice are combined with elements of informal justice and Indigenous justice (Blagg 1997; Daly 2002).

Thinking about restorative justice within the context of hybridity provides us with the opportunity to think through the complexity of the relationship between restorative justice and state-centred punishment. It provides the opportunity to avoid critical criminology's approach to restorative justice falling into a 'criminology of catastrophe' (O'Malley 2000) that is over-determined and leaves little room for contestation, transformation and resistance. In that spirit I offer both a pessimistic and an optimistic view of restorative justice hybridity.

A pessimistic view of restorative justice hybridity

A pessimistic reading of current developments is that in many cases restorative justice programs have been introduced within frameworks emphasising individual responsibility, deterrence and incapacitation. It is an argument that has informed much of this chapter. It is an argument that sees punishment in neo-liberal societies as incorporating a variety of goals and processes from restorative justice to incapacitation.

It is a view of penal policy that emphasises inconsistencies in punishment, but which in their overall effect has seen a substantial increase in more punitive outcomes (see Pratt et al 2005). In this context restorative justice is reduced to yet another penal strategy reserved for those who are deserving, while the 'undeserving' (the homeless, the marginalised, the poor and non-white populations) get what they have always got in ever increasing numbers – gaol.

Statistically robust risk assessment tools used in countries like Canada and Australia (such as the Youth Service Level Case Management Inventory) provide a veneer of science to the sorting of people on the basis of race and class. The focus on individual factors such as age of first court order, prior offending history, failure to comply with court orders, and current offences are all used to predict risk of future offending. A range of socio-economic factors is also connected to risk, including education (such as 'problematic' schooling and truancy) and unemployment. The individual 'risk' factors are de-contextualised from broader social and economic constraints. And so through the miracle of statistics, the most marginalised groups within society reappear as those who offer the greatest risk to 'our' security. Our 'evidence-based' research tells us these are the 'problem cases' unlikely to respond to the opportunities offered by restorative justice, and are fit subjects for more punitive law and order policies.

An optimistic view of restorative justice hybridity

However, there is also an alternative story to hybridity. For example, an optimistic account of the development of restorative justice hybridity might be found in recent developments in Indigenous justice. There is potential to create new positive forms of hybrid justice which are consistent with the principles of restorative justice. New spaces can be created wherein Indigenous communities have opportunities to formulate and activate processes derivative of their own particular traditions, and where scepticism about state-imposed forms of restorative justice can be replaced with organically connected restorative justice processes that resonate with Indigenous cultures (Cunneen 2007).

This vision of restorative justice where hybridity and cultural difference can be accepted is emancipatory in a broader political sense, whereby restorative justice is not only a tool of criminal justice; it is a tool of social justice. In this example, hybridity can involve a re-imagining of new pathways and meeting places between Indigenous people and the institutions of the coloniser – a place where the institutions of the coloniser are no longer taken for granted as normal and unproblematic, where the cultural artefacts of the colonisers (the criminal justice system) lose their claim to universality. In this context, restorative justice provides an opportunity for decolonisation of our institutions and our imaginations and a rethinking of possibilities (Cunneen 2002).

One brief example of these hybrid developments is the expansion of Indigenous courts[1] which allow the local Indigenous community to become more actively involved in the sentencing process and, as a result, introduce new ideas about what might constitute an appropriate sentence for an offender. In this sense, community involvement opens the sentencing process up to influences beyond the ideas of criminal justice professionals. This is particularly important for Aboriginal communities who have generally been excluded from legal and judicial decision-making. The courts typically involve Aboriginal elders or community group members sitting on the bench with a magistrate. They speak directly to the offender, expressing their views and concerns about offending behaviour and provide advice to the magistrate on the offender and about cultural and community issues. Offenders might receive customary punishments or community service orders as an alternative to prison. Importantly, appeals to restorative justice in this context provide an avenue for opening up the justice system to greater Indigenous control. It is an opportunity to reconfigure the justice system with different values, different processes and different sets of accountability.

Conclusion

This chapter has outlined some of the key issues that have emerged in critiques of restorative justice. Finding answers to these criticisms is an important part of developing restorative justice practice and theory in a way that is sensitive to issues of social justice and political transformation. It is important to recognise that many progressive political activists see restorative justice as a preferable policy alternative to more punitive criminal justice approaches. The question is whether restorative justice can actually live up to their expectations.

As critical criminologists we need to ask whether the vision for reform for restorative justice proponents coalesces with other social and political movements. For example, do feminist interests in the protection of women, or Indigenous interests in promoting self-determination, or anti-racist organisations in reforming the criminal justice system, or neo-marxist interests in social justice match the aims of restorative justice? Does restorative justice assist in meeting the aims of these social and political movements? Will the racism, sexism and class-based interests and biases of the criminal justice system be removed, modified or left untouched by restora-

---

1   The courts are titled after local Indigenous names such as Koori Courts (Victoria), Murri Courts (Queensland) and Nunga Courts (South Australia). New South Wales has adopted the Canadian circle sentencing model for Indigenous people in that state.

tive justice? Indeed, will greater bifurcation of justice systems serve to compound existing oppressions?

Blagg (1998, and this volume) has discussed the need to open up and imagine new pathways and meeting places in justice systems. He refers to this as the 'liminal spaces' where dialogue can be generated, where hybridity and cultural difference can be accepted. A context of hybridity may be a useful way of considering contemporary developments, where new forms of doing justice are being developed which merge the restorative with new democratising practices. To this extent restorative justice might pose an unrealised promise that still has considerable opportunity for development. That development, however, depends on the establishment of a critical reflexivity about the relationship of restorative justice to other forms of power. While some offenders and victims may be restored, there is also a dark side to a developing hybridity. Restorative justice has also found itself a partner to a greater emphasis on individual responsibility, deterrence and incapacitation.

References

Australian Law Reform Commission 1997, *Seen and Heard: priority for young people in the legal process*, AGPS, Canberra.

Bauman, Z 1998, *Globalization: the human consequences*, Columbia University Press, New York.

Blagg, H 1997, 'A Just Measure of Shame', 37(4) *British Journal of Criminology* 481-501.

Blagg, H 1998, 'Restorative Visions and Restorative Justice Practices: conferencing, ceremony and reconciliation in Australia', 10(1) *Current Issues in Criminal Justice*, 5.

Brown, D, Farrier, D, Egger, S, McNamara, L & Steel, A 2006, *Criminal Laws*, Federation Press, Sydney.

Cunneen, C 1997, 'Community Conferencing and the Fiction of Indigenous Control', 30(3) *Australia and New Zealand Journal of Criminology* 292.

Cunneen, C 2001, *The Impact of Crime Prevention on Aboriginal Communities*, New South Wales Crime Prevention Division and Aboriginal Justice Advisory Council, Sydney.

Cunneen, C 2002, 'Restorative Justice and the Politics of Decolonisation', in Weitekamp, E & Kerner, H-J (eds), *Restorative Justice: theoretical foundations*, Willan Publishing, Cullompton.

Cunneen, C 2006, 'Exploring the Relationship between Reparations, the Gross Violations of Human Rights, and Restorative Justice', in Sullivan, D & Tift, L (eds), *The Handbook of Restorative Justice: global perspectives*, Routledge, New York.

Cunneen, C 2007, 'Reviving Restorative Justice Traditions', in Johnstone, J & Van Ness, D (eds), *The Handbook of Restorative Justice*, Willan Publishing, Cullompton.

Cunneen, C & Stubbs, J 2002, 'Migration, Political Economy and Violence Against Women: the post immigration experiences of Filipino women in Australia', in Freilich, JD, Newman, G, Shoham, SG & Addad, M (eds), *Migration, Culture Conflict and Crime*, Aldershot. Ashgate.

Cunneen, C & White, R 2007, *Juvenile Justice: youth and crime in Australia*, Oxford University Press, Melbourne.

Daly, K 2002, 'Restorative Justice: the real story', 4(1) *Punishment and Society* 55.

Daly, K & Immarigeon, R 1998, 'The Past, Present and Future of Restorative Justice: some critical reflections', 1(1) *Contemporary Justice Review* 21.

Feeley, M & Simon, J 1994, in Nelken, D (ed), 'Actuarial Justice: the emerging new criminal law', *The Futures of Criminology*, Sage, London.

Findlay, M 1999, *The Globalisation of Crime: understanding transitional relationships in context*, Cambridge University Press, Cambridge.

Findlay, M & Henham, R 2005, *Transforming International Criminal Justice*, Willan Publishing, Cullompton.

Iffil, S 2007, *On the Courthouse Lawn*, Beacon Press, Boston.

Johnstone, J & Van Ness, D (eds) 2007, *The Handbook of Restorative Justice*, Willan Publishing, Cullompton.

Keith, M 1993, 'From Punishment to Discipline', in Cross, M & Keith, M (eds), *Racism: the city and the state*, Routledge, London.

Luke, G & Lind, B 2002, 'Reducing Juvenile Crime: conferencing versus court', *Crime and Justice Bulletin*, No 69, New South Wales Bureau of Crime Statistics and Research, Sydney.

Marshall, T 1999, *Restorative Justice: an overview*, Home Office, London.

Nancarrow, H 2006, 'In Search of Justice for Domestic and Family Violence: Indigenous and Non-Indigenous Australian Women's Perspectives', 10(1) *Theoretical Criminology* 87.

O'Malley, P 1999, 'Volatile and Contradictory Punishments', 3(2) *Theoretical Criminology* 175.

O'Malley, P 2000, 'Criminologies of Catastrophe? Understanding criminology on the edge of the new millennium', 33(2) *Australian and New Zealand Journal of Criminology* 153.

O'Malley, P 2006, 'Risk and Restorative Justice: governing through the democratic minimisation of harms' in Aertsen, I, Daems, T & Robert, L (eds), *Institutionalizing Restorative Justice*, Willan Publishing, Cullompton.

Pavlich, G 2001, 'The Force of Community', in Strang, H & Braithwaite, J (eds), *Restorative Justice and Civil Society*, Cambridge University Press, Cambridge.

Pavlich, G 2005, *Governing Paradoxes of Restorative Justice*, Glasshouse Press, London.

Polk, K 1994, 'Family Conferencing: theoretical and evaluative concerns', in Alder, C & Wundersitz, J (eds), *Family Conferencing and Juvenile Justice: the way forward or misplaced optimism?*, Australian Institute of Criminology, Canberra.

Pratt, J 2000, 'The Return of the Wheelbarrow Men', 40 *British Journal of Criminology* 127.

Pratt, J, Brown, D, Brown, M, Hallsworth, S & Morrison, W 2005, *The New Punitiveness: trends, theories, perspectives*, Willan Publishing, Cullompton.

Strang, H 2001, *Restorative Justice Programs in Australia*, A Report to the Criminology Research Council, Australian Institute of Criminology, Canberra.

Stubbs, J 1997, 'Shame, Defiance and Violence against Women: a critical analysis of "communitarian" conferencing', in Bessant, J & Cook, S (eds), *Violence Against Women: an Australian perspective*, Sage, Thousand Oaks.

Stubbs, J 2002, 'Domestic Violence and Women's Safety: feminist challenges to restorative justice', in Strang, H & Braithwaite, J (eds), *Restorative Justice and Family Violence*, Cambridge University Press, Cambridge.

Sullivan, D & Tift, L (eds) 2006, *The Handbook of Restorative Justice: global perspectives*, Routledge, New York

Warner, K 1994, 'Family Group Conferences and the Rights of Offenders', in Alder, C & Wundersitz, J (eds), *Family Conferencing and Juvenile Justice: the way forward or misplaced optimism?* Australian Institute of Criminology, Canberra.

White, R 1994, 'Shaming and Reintegrative Strategies: individuals, state power and social interests', in Alder, C & Wundersitz, J (eds), *Family Conferencing and Juvenile Justice: the way forward or misplaced optimism?* Australian Institute of Criminology, Canberra.

Zellerer, E & Cunneen, C 2001, 'Restorative Justice, Indigenous Justice and Human Rights', in Bazemore, G & Schiff, M (eds) *Restorative Community Justice: repairing harm and transforming communities*, Anderson Press, Cincinnati.

25

TOWARD CONSTITUTING A CRITICAL CRIMINOLOGY FOR RURAL AUSTRALIA

Garry Coventry and Darren Palmer[1]

Recently I was talking to a journalist about country Australia and he asked if I was afraid of One Nation. I replied no, I was not afraid of One Nation, the political entity, but I was afraid of Australia becoming two nations (Anderson 1999).

John Anderson, Deputy Prime Minister at the time, addressed how rural and regional Australia was being left behind and had lost the recognition of their contribution to nation building, so that a 'sense of alienation ... is deep and palpable in much of rural and regional Australia today', estimable through consideration of social indicators, including depression, alcoholism, youth suicide, youth unemployment and 'the tragic circumstances in which many Aboriginal families exist'. Anderson raised two broad foundation themes for this chapter about a critical criminology project for rural Australia: the effects of global economic and social change on rural and regional Australia; and the concern that Australia was fracturing along an urban/rural divide.

Our task is not small, in that we endeavour to canvass the broad spectrum of critical criminology as it applies to different landscapes beyond the urban. By necessity, we need to embrace this broader framework. We mostly use the term 'rural' throughout this chapter but are mindful of the fact that this landscape includes remote, rural and regional centre communities. These communities have distinct issues regarding social harm and social justice; key matters that require a critical criminological agenda to address on local, regionalised and global scales. The argument presented here is that criminology, in and of rural areas, must challenge state agency formulations of the problem of crime, responses to crime (or lack thereof) and the imposition of centrally developed urban models or programs.

We propose that an alternative agenda is required, whereby locally developed and owned initiatives are enhanced. These should not succumb to the criminology *numbers game*: that crime *is* more of a problem than previously recognised, and that exposure of *hidden crime* is used to generate a 'law and order' agenda to control 'failing' individuals, families or other sub-groups, as if this is the provenance for

---

1   We wish to acknowledge the research assistance by Diane Solomon Westerhuis at James Cook University.

shaping a better future for rural Australia. What is needed, instead, are initiatives fundamentally informed by the principles of social justice and human rights, and community empowerment. Further, they need to be inclusive through engaging with situated knowledge of the local, and directed at contesting both notions of social harm and responses to such harms implemented in various communities. As Currie (2007: 176) argues more generally 'the public presence of a vocal and influential criminology has never been more critical' and, we suggest, is of vital importance for rural critical criminology in Australia. Until recently, the public presence of criminology in rural communities has generally been *ad hoc* and not part of a systematic program focused on a rural criminology project (Wiles 1999).

To further explore a rural agenda we address three key issues: has rural criminology been a neglected area of study and, if so, why? Secondly, how can we begin to theoretically explore the interconnectedness of the rural, national and global domains? Finally, what are some of the key issues that confront a rural criminological project?

Has rural crime been neglected by criminology?

We accept that crime and crime control are generally imagined as an urban problem and, until the past few years, criminological research has done little to challenge and displace this view in Australia (Scott et al 2007), North America (Weisheit & Donnermeyer 2000) and Britain (Yarwood 2001). Cogently, Girling et al (2000) have labelled rural-based research the *terra incognita* of criminology.

Pointedly, there have been earlier calls to the criminological community to engage with rural research (Clinnard 1944). Some 20 years later, Chambliss (1964) reminds us of the original laws of vagrancy and the extent to which rural workers were targets of criminalisation if they were deemed to be idle. Vagrants were seen to be disreputable and outsiders – either marginal to or threatening to the needs of a developing industrialisation. Criminalisation of the idle continues into the present. Prisons are full of those considered to be superfluous to the economic and social arrangements of the state – 'the new dangerous classes' to the economy (Irwin 2005).

Considering the precariousness of Indigenous peoples and their marginality to the mainstream economy there is a striking similarity between how Indigenous people are criminalised today and early vagrancy laws. Exclusion from processes and practices of the modern state relates to Indigenous peoples' placelessness and disadvantage. Their plight within the urban environment and beyond is one of economic and social exclusion (Hogg 2005). Their *place*, outside the urban environment, is usually seen to be apart from the 'gated' suburbs and cities of globally based consumption. In Queensland, the situation of most Indigenous Australians being *superfluous* to mainstream economic relations is exacerbated by the application of various laws to regulate space (Havemann 2005).

The Howard Government did much to undermine the development of independent Indigenous institutions and undermine Indigenous family structures (Hogg 2005). The electioneering for the 2007 Federal Government was a matter of public importance for many of these communities. This institutional dismantling creates problems with '[l]inking communities vertically to resources, power and authority' (Karstedt 2007: 152). This undermines effective crime prevention and enhanced community capacity, which requires the ability of individuals, groups and communities to reach up through local, State/Territory and national agencies and structures to express rights and make requests via transparent processes (Karstedt 2007: 152). In targeting reductions of Indigenous employment funding and welfare payments, governments have portrayed Indigenous communities as facing a 'national emergency' and in need of interventions that override the processes and procedures that apply to the remainder of the Australian population. Without employment opportunities and sensitivities to the long history of the deleterious effects of criminal justice practices in Indigenous communities, we have concerns that the Federal Government (notwithstanding the November 2007 change in government) could use the Northern Territory, and beyond, as a new kind of vagrancy ground. The reforms in employment and welfare policies and programs could well see the drift of 'the idle' from more remote areas to regional centres where they are likely to remain marginalised and seen as a criminal justice problem.

Beyond these specific issues it is clear that a rural critical criminology needs an historical appreciation of what factors shape the 'patterning of knowledge production and acquisition' (Manning 2005: 24). Perhaps, little rural criminology has occurred due to occidental images and assumptions about orderliness in rural communities (Hogg & Carrington 2003, 2006). However, an alternative account of the relative absence of rural criminology, and an account that is important for the development of rural criminology, is to use a 'truncated version of the sociology of knowledge' (Manning 2005: 24). This requires a particular emphasis on the history of the institutionalisation and development of Australian criminology and the absence of considerations of rurality in that history. Further, we comment on definitional issues that bedevil criminology, other disciplines and institutions that criminological research relies on for much quantitative baseline data (for instance, the Australian Bureau of Statistics).

Criminological history

To understand the relative, though not absolute absence of rural criminology, it is vital to canvass social, structural and institutional dimensions of criminological history and practice (Garland 2002).

In the 1950s, criminology was introduced as a university 'discipline' in Melbourne and Sydney (O'Malley & Carson 1989), but was quickly consumed by the task of its need to embrace internal institution building and the development of international networks. At the same time, a range of key criminology/criminal justice issues was simultaneously being addressed through activism (Finnane 2006). While urban crime rates were purportedly increasing up until the late 1960s there was little in the way of a solid Australian institutional basis for criminology (O'Malley & Carson 1989), in general, let alone for rural criminology.

As criminology struggled to cement itself within the architecture of university and policy domains, the call to its administrative dimensions to focus on meeting agency-defined needs on the control and prevention of crime became more demanding, followed soon by the rise of 'law and order' political campaigns in the late 1970s and into the 1980s (Hogg & Brown 1998). With limited criminology research staff, the struggles over institution building and the pressing problems of crime and urban change, there was much to be done about criminological issues closer to home – literally in terms of where criminologists generally lived and where their employing institutions were located – in the major urban centres.

If this partially explains the 1950s-1980s period, what accounts for the subsequent and continued limited criminological interest in rural communities? We suggest that this is related to how criminology has been organised in Australian universities and how the tertiary sector itself was organised. Put simply, it is only since the post-Dawkins reforms of the late 1980s that regional universities started to be more than a very minor criminological presence in the tertiary sector. These universities have corporate missions that emphasise rural and regional engagement, including two universities having established rural research centres involving criminological research (University of New England (UNE) and Charles Sturt University). It is in these institutions that we can identify an emerging key group of researchers and research networks shaping the shift in the criminological gaze towards rural criminological research and policy (see Barclay et al 2007).

We need to be careful in distinguishing between a rural criminological project and research on rural issues of criminological interest. The former has been more limited than the latter. Beyond the research identified above, historical studies have certainly provided significant analyses of rural crime (see McQuilton 1979; Sturma 1983). Further, we need to be wary about the view that criminologists (and others) have an 'arcadian perspective on rural life and rural communities' as an explanation for the relative absence of rural criminology (O'Connor & Gray 1989: 167). What academics produce in research publications is largely structured by institutional factors alluded to above, as well as related issues concerning funding for rural crime research and the ability to spend significant time in rural locations to conduct research (Cunneen & Robb 1987; Cunneen et al 1989). Cunneen and his colleagues' work is instructive of our larger point: they engaged in several years of rural research and developed the social networks and institutionalised relations that fostered and sustained their rural research. It can be argued from this body of work that building these relationships is necessary, but we are arguing explicitly that entrenching these relations – social, structural and institutional – is essential to further a critical rural criminology. It is this larger criminological project that the recent studies by Hogg and Carrington (2006) and Barclay et al (2007) have sought to stimulate.

In other words, we are pointing to the broader historical development of criminology as part of a plausible and important explanation for a relatively limited rural criminological project. This is important both as providing an additional account of the lack of rural criminological studies historically, and as pointing to the need for institutionalised networks for the future enhancement of rural criminology.

Data and definitions

Another factor shaping the limits of rural criminology concerns 'data issues', to which we would add 'definitional' issues, as they are inter-related. Despite the introduction of national time series data in 1993 there are still barriers to the conduct of some forms of criminological research. While crime statistics might break the imagery of the 'rural idyll' of low crime (Dingwall & Moody 1999: 3), a critical agenda needs to be about much more than the inadequacy of officially recorded crime and its collation. As Hogg and Carrington make clear, crime statistics are 'necessarily limited … ways of representing crime for certain governmental, social and intellectual purposes' (2006: 54) and thus are 'proxy measures that render certain aspects of the social reality of crime and violence amenable to particular, albeit limited, forms of analysis' (2006: 59).

The 'discovery' of rural crime poses its own difficulties. We need to be vigilant about the possible drift towards a *criminology-by-numbers*, a kind of technical administrative criminology that is keen to find new fields of the 'dark figure' of crime to generate research and policy action. All crime in all locations, whatever the metrics, has inclusions and exclusions, moral and normative implications, and specific historical, economic and political dimensions that have shaped the construction of place, race, class and gender relations that inform the nature of crime and reactions to it in the specific context under examination. Thus, we need to ensure that the power and authority to identify the problem must go beyond the *crime-is-a-problem* approach by being sensitive to the above-mentioned dimensions that pertain to any locality. The current 'national emergency' in the Northern Territory is precisely an example of such an approach: crime is a problem, identify hidden offending, and locate the response within a 'disaster management' framework in a manner that avoids any of the complexities indicated above.

Related to the 'data deficit' dilemma there have been significant difficulties in precisely defining what 'rural', 'remote' and 'regional' mean in economic, cultural, political and social terms. While criminology is now increasingly seeking appropriate working definitions for the study of rural crime, there will not be an easy solution found in current statistical measures.

An example of the complexities and importance of these data/definitional problems and their importance for policy development can be seen in the Commonwealth plan for the reform of policing remote Indigenous communities (Valentine 2007). The report used the accessibility/remoteness index of Australia (ARIA, based on distance from population centres) to determine remoteness and then assesses 'Implied Police Numbers Required'. Of note, crime data were not part of the analysis due to unavailability. In other words, on an issue of such significance as the provision of policing resources there was an inability to be able to draw on available data on remote crime to inform policy development. Leaving aside the limits to these types of data, we can only concur with Carrington (2007: 43) 'that there are data comparability and collection issues requiring the attention of researchers and policy makers'.

The global and the local

Notwithstanding the limits on rural research and the problems with definitions and data collection, we now turn our attention to contemporary research themes and future prospects for the development of a rural critical criminology.

The contrast between rural and urban crime has usually been seen as one of degree; that rural crime was different in nature and less prevalent than urban crime. However, this is changing as studies of *traditional* rural crimes such as cattle duffing and farm crime are being supplemented with the examination of 'new' harms such as environmental crime, water theft, the illegal dumping of waste, desecration of rock art and illegal fishing (see Beirne & South 2007). These broad areas are opening up new issues in rural criminology, described by White (2007) as 'green criminology', which to us includes not only crimes against the environment but also the criminalisation of people protesting against environmental damage.

Further, critical studies of rural criminology can be found in research linked to globalisation, in cases where democratically unaccountable transnational institutions override the interest of marginalised communities and/or in cases of environmental crime. Edwards (2005), for example, warns that in studies of transnational organised crime excessive focus on the cross-border feature of organised crime networks overlooks the transformation of local environments and structures by processes of globalisation. The *Mining Ombudsman Annual Report 2003*, for example, details community complaints of human rights abuses and environmental degradation arising from the overseas operations of Australian mining companies (MacDonald & Ross 2003). Further, Croall (2005: 238) suggests that such impacts of globalisation are 'inherently criminogenic', given local crimes of resistance to domination by others.

Perspectives on rural crime

Clearly, a range of criminological perspectives has emerged in recent years seeking to understand the nature of crime in rural communities. For instance, micro-place theories (Donnermeyer 2007), social control (Carcach 2001) or social disorganisation (Jobes et al 2004) have been central themes in rural criminological research. Carcach (2001), for example, found that the social disorganisation model, developed for urban communities, provides an adequate explanation for the variation of crime rates among rural localities of Australia. More recently, Woodhouse (2006) provides a substantial link to critical thinking by examining the explanatory value of social capital[2] as a means of understanding comparative crime rates and attitudes in two rural Queensland locations. Scott et al (2007: 1) describe Australian rural crime research as unique, pointing out that Australian crime 'outside the city is not so much spatialised as racialised', while conversely in the United States this 'racialisation' appears in relation to inner-city crime.

Two recent publications have done much to establish a research agenda for rural criminology. Barclay et al (2007) provide wide-ranging theoretical and research ideas regarding the context of crime and criminal justice in rural Australian communities. Further, Hogg and Carrington (2006) set a broad agenda challenging key assumptions about crime: both rural *and* urban. While their empirical research is limited to New South Wales, the study has broader application by raising key issues: that research should be sensitive to localised historical and cultural contexts; that the general *modernisation* thesis that associates violence with urban areas (that is, as a society modernises and urbanises it shifts from the benign relationships of rural communities to a more violent one) should be challenged by framing an understanding of rural crime within a broader 'rural crisis'; and, that a more critical assessment of the alleged broader civilising processes associated with modernisation (see Elias 1978; Putnam 1993) should be developed. What is needed, as Hogg and Carrington (2006) suggest, is a more nuanced understanding of the *civic contexts* of the different *rurals*. It is only by understanding rurality as more than 'a discrete physical region fixed in time and space' and, instead, as being culturally constructed through enactment and reproduction of (always contested) meaning (2006: 6) that we can hope to fashion a critical rural criminology. Moreover, this enhances our capacity to resist the pressure of 'law and order' agendas and direct our attention towards the means of cultivating trust and legitimacy within these communities and between them and state agencies.

---

2   In simple terms, 'social capital' refers to the levels of communal associations, trust, and cohesiveness. The literature on social capital is extensive and reviewed by Woodhouse (2006).

More generally, the broad brush of theories of globalisation and its effects need to be linked to the local context: 'security, identity and subjectivity of people anywhere can only be disclosed, grasped and rendered intelligible *somewhere*' (Girling et al 2000: 10, emphasis in original). This indicates the need to develop a research agenda that is alert to broader global shifts (for instance the 'risk society', Giddens 1998) while engaged with the specificity of place.

Localised projects are of utmost importance. At the very least, these kinds of research projects have potential to provide social policy and program markers for critical criminology. To explore this further, we raise 'securitisation' and 'policy transfer' as two key developments that offer considerable scope for elaboration, refinement and comparisons in rural locations. These were selected because there has been little commentary on such matters for rural communities and they demonstrate the reach of policies and programs from global and national centres to rural Australia.

Securitisation

'Securitisation', in part, refers to dramatisation of threats as challenging *our way of life* and framing this dramatisation in a manner that creates imperatives, making change 'both urgent and inevitable' (Loader 2002: 135). Analysis of securitisation of urban environments has been well covered in the literature (see Graham 2004) but absent in its application to rural and remote areas.

Major rural and remote industries are increasingly engaged in efforts to protect against perceived threats of terrorism and other global risks/crimes, whereby the global comes to inhabit and shape the local. For instance, regional ports and off-shore facilities have been subject to post-9/11 securitisation under the *Maritime Transport and Offshore Facilities Security Act 2003*. This legislation mandates risk assessments and security plans for compliance approval from the Office of Transport Security (Commonwealth of Australia 2006). Further, the 'remote' waters off the north coast of Australia were a particular target for government intervention, with the Federal Government committing $388.9 million in 2006 to enhance maritime security against people smuggling, illegal fishing, drug smuggling, and transnational crime including terrorism. Securitisation has also had an impact on regional airports through the spread of technology such as the introduction of closed-circuit television, metal detectors and security/risk management training (Commonwealth of Australia 2006).

More generally, we need to explore how various behaviours are positioned as threatening 'our' way of life in rural communities. As Woodhouse (2006: 16) has recently identified, in some communities 'people are accepted as long as they don't misbehave', where misbehavour is conduct, including crime, committed by the *others* – people seen to be outsiders such as itinerant rural workers, Indigenous peoples or newcomers from urban centres. We do not claim that these examples empirically prove the reach, forms, processes and techniques of securitisation in rural areas but rather suggest that there are particular operations of securitisation in such areas.

Future research in rural areas could focus on how and the extent to which social problems are dramatised as threats to particular characterisations of rural life and how these processes shape the nature of responses. A *national emergency* approach, as is currently being played out in the Northern Territory, is certainly an example of securitisation: a multi-faceted problem that has been recognised historically is reconceptualised as an emergency where the imperative to act – urgently and unilaterally *on* communities – outweighs the need for deliberation *with* communities and is thus likely to generate 'radical insecurity' *within* communities (Kaplan 2003: 90).

Policy transfer

The second theoretical issue we wish to raise pertains to policy transfer. This refers to the transfer of knowledge about different policies and related administrative and institutional arrangements from one time and/or place to another time and/or place (Newburn 2002). There are two key aspects to this research that require attention. First, there is the concern to unravel precisely what is actually transferred. Newburn and Jones (2007) argue it is more the symbolic – terminology and rhetoric – than the substantive technologies and techniques. Secondly, analyses of why policies travel, in the first place, are needed.

Currently, policy transfer literature is largely concerned with transfer across nations such as *Atlantic crossings* (Newburn 2002). But, consideration needs to be given to both internal transfer within the nation state or sub-national levels (particularly important in federated states), as well as policy transfer between urban and rural communities and between rural communities themselves. In particular, research should be directed at two issues: the content and impact of these policy transfers, and; secondly the very origins of policy development within local contexts. The latter requires a critical analysis of rural and remote policy histories, including 'the ways in which local political cultures and the activities of key political actors serve to initiate, reshape, mediate or resist policy ideas and innovations that travel across' geographic boundaries (Jones & Newburn 2006: 782).

Finally, we add that the information communication revolution – part of the broader globalisation at play – enhances the capacity of rural communities to access information, for example, on various criminal justice initiatives and practices around the world. For instance, Karstedt (2007) recounts a remote community from the Amazon River seeking information from the London Metropolitan Police on successful crime prevention and policing strategies. Likewise, there is considerable interchange of crime prevention program information that is channelled across communities by the Australian Crime Prevention Council and Australian Institute of Criminology (AIC). It is not simply a matter of documenting this process but critically analysing the extent to which what is transferred fits the 'cultural, socio-political, and in particular institutional context' of recipient communities (Karstedt 2007: 147).

Futures for criminology in rural areas

We argued earlier that there is some reason for optimism around a critical rural criminology with the establishment of research centres in regional institutions. Two further issues need to be addressed: engagement and institutional practice.

Engagement with rural communities is vital. For this to occur, we need to ensure that *local* or *spatial* elements of urban-oriented studies are considered in rural, remote and regional communities. In doing so, we need to ensure the local is no longer essentialised as a homogenous 'rural' Australia. Future research must examine the nature of specific problems in the local context of regional, national and global dimensions to social harms in a manner that recognises the confusion, uncertainty, hostilities, conflicts and suspicions that are involved in any analysis of the complexities of crime (Girling et al 2000).

While *institutional practice* is being developed by the new rurally engaged research centres, we need to *hard-wire* community involvement practices into the design of criminology course content, recognising that research and curriculum are not mutually exclusive. Here we draw on our own experience, and that of our colleagues, where we seek civic engagement to ensure the 'dissemination, synthesis and communication is woven into … the education of graduate students' via research partnerships that view the partner agencies 'not just as *passive* consumers of research but as partners in a real sense' (Currie 2007: 187, emphasis in original) involved in framing research questions and research implementation.[3]

From this brief overview we argue that crime and justice in rural Australia is a broad arena ripe for study. Theory, politics, programs and practices are research tasks of considerable magnitude, which require skilful handling. The following non-exhaustive areas of research (not prioritised), in addition to broader issues raised throughout this chapter, offer considerable scope to define a trajectory for rural critical criminology:

- Policing, discretion and an assessment of various forms of Indigenous policing (Cunneen 2001; Blagg & Valuri 2004);
- Sentencing in rural courts (Douglas 1992);
- Vigilantism, particularly racially based forms (Hil & Dawes 2000);
- Pervasive violence and its foundations in poverty (Donnermeyer et al 2006);
- Alcohol and drug abuse problems (Donnermeyer et al 2002);
- Socio-spatial research and the extent to which *remoteness* impacts on access to social services, social relations and social control practices (Clare et al 2006);
- Economic and social globalisation of the planet, and the accompanying degradation of place and people (Hannigan 2006);
- Economic and cultural constructions of identity and relationships to crime and justice (Hogg & Carrington 2006); and
- Comparative studies within and across jurisdictions (Woodhouse 2006).

These topics, albeit brief, are proposed as ways of structuring critical criminology in rural communities. Further, many of these issues could be addressed in ways that examine the extent to which community empowerment occurs. Finally, in cases where interventions occur, questions of sustainability – in institutional, economic, social and environmental terms – require attention.

Concluding comments

The institutionalisation of developing research networks and concomitant outputs toward a rural criminological project is promising. Further, the introduction of rural research centres, criminology conferences specifically directed at rural crime (AIC/

---

3   In undergraduate criminology courses at James Cook and Deakin Universities, we have introduced a team research project/internship element that requires students to collaboratively undertake critical work in local community or agency settings to examine an issue of mutual interest. Both groups actively engage in forging a commensurate, reflective research partnership to enhance the student experience and the agency's need for knowledge regarding program and/or further research data requirements.

UNE 1999; AIC 2001, 2007) and more recent key research publications (Hogg & Carrington 2006; Barclay et al 2007) suggest that the time for criminological practice with sensitivities to, and a 'thick' understanding of, issues concerning rural, remote and regional communities might very well be coming of age.

Dowling (2005: 767) might be right in suggesting that Australian researchers are well placed to conduct and publish research that is 'simultaneously local and global'. It remains to be seen whether this is enough to operate as a 'replacement discourse' (van Swaaningen 1999: 2) to undercut both the dominant imagery of rurality as being absent of crime or the alternative law and order impetus that seems to have developed a hold on the collective imagination of contemporary Australia. Therein lies a fundamental task for critical criminology: the need to challenge this imaginative framing of rural crime 'through analytic and synthetic research, and *disseminating* that work to a broader and potentially more efficacious audience than ourselves' (Currie 2007: 180, emphasis in original). We have argued above that recent developments suggest the significant impact that rural criminology can have for the communities themselves, for a critical social foundation for policy development, for enrichment in criminological research and a for more equitable and just Australian society. But for this to occur through a critical lens requires analyses of the exclusions, power and authority relations, guided by a reflexive research practice.

References

Anderson, J 1999, 'One Nation or Two? Securing a future for rural and regional Australia', Address to the National Press Club, Canberra, 17 February, <www.ministers.dotars.gov.au/ja/speeches/1999/as01_99.htm>.

Australian Institute of Criminology/University of New England 1999, *Crime in Rural Communities: the impact, the causes, the prevention*, 1 March, Armidale.

Australian Institute of Criminology 2001, *The Character, Impact and Prevention of Regional Crime*, Townsville, 1-3 August.

Australian Institute of Criminology 2007, *Improving Community Safety: lessons from the country and the city*, Townsville, 18-19 October.

Barclay, E, Donnermeyer, J, Scott, J & Hogg, R (eds) 2007, *Crime in Rural Australia,* Federation Press, Sydney.

Beirne, P & South, N 2007, *Issues in Green Criminology: confronting harms against environments, humanity and other animals*, Willan Publishing, Cullompton.

Blagg, H & Valuri, GM 2004, 'Aboriginal Community Patrols in Australia: self-policing, self-determination and security', 14(4) *Policing and Society* 313.

Carcach, C 2001, *Issues in the Study of Regional Crime: implications for crime prevention and control*, paper given at The Character, Impact and Prevention of Crime conference in Regional Australia, Townsville.

Carrington, K 2007, 'Violence and the Architecture of Rural Life', in Barclay, E, Donnermeyer, J, Scott, J & Hogg, R (eds), *Crime in Rural Australia,* Federation Press, Sydney.

Chambliss, W 1964, 'A Sociological Analysis of the Law of Vagrancy', 12 *Social Problems* 67.

Clare, J, Morgan, F, Ferrante, A & Blagg, H 2006, 'Research Note: Assessing Relative Rates of Indigenous Family Violence: using existing quantitative data and a triangulation methodology to identify rural areas in greatest need of additional legal services', 18(1) *Current Issues in Criminal Justice* 170.

Clinnard, M 1944, 'Rural Criminal Offenders', 50(1) *The American Journal of Sociology* 38.

Commonwealth of Australia 2006, *Protecting Australia Against Terrorism 2006: Australia's National Counter-Terrorism Policy and Arrangements*, Department of Prime Minister and Cabinet, Canberra.

Croall, H 2005, 'Crime Against the Environment', in Sheptycki, J & Wardak, A (eds), *Transnational and Comparative Criminology in a Global Context*, Glasshouse, London.

Cunneen, C & Robb, T 1987, *Criminal Justice in North-West New South Wales*, NSW Bureau of Crime Statistics and Research, Sydney.

Cunneen, C, Findlay, M, Lynch, M & Tupper, V 1989, *The Dynamics of Collective Conflict*, LawBook Co, Sydney.

Cunneen, C 2001, *Conflict, Politics and Crime: Aboriginal communities and the police*, Allen & Unwin, Sydney.

Currie, E 2007, 'Against Marginality: arguments for a public criminology', 11(2) *Theoretical Criminology* 175.

Dingwall, G & Moody, S (eds) 1999, *Crime and Conflict in the Countryside*, University of Wales Press, Cardiff.

Donnermeyer, J, Barclay, E & Jobes, P 2002, 'Drug-related Offences and the Structure of Communities in Rural Australia', 37(5) *Substance Use and Misuse* 631.

Donnermeyer, J, Jobes, P & Barclay, E 2006, 'Rural Crime, Poverty and Community', in de Keseredy, WS & Perry, B (eds), *Advancing Critical Criminology: theory and application*, Lexington Books, Lanham.

Donnermeyer, J 2007, 'Locating Rural Crime: the role of theory', in Barclay, E, Donnermeyer, J, Scott, J & Hogg, R (eds), *Crime in Rural Australia,* Federation Press, Sydney.

Douglas, R 1992, 'A Different Kind of Justice? Trial and punishment in the rural Magistrates' Courts', 10(1) *Law in Context* 62.

Dowling, R 2005, 'Social and Cultural Geographies of Australia', 6(5) *Social and Cultural Geography* 767.

Edwards, A 2005, 'Transnational Organised Crime', in Sheptycki, J & Wardak, A (eds), *Transnational and Comparative Criminology in a Global Context*, Glasshouse, London.

Elias, N 1978, *The Civilizing Process*, Pantheon, New York.

Finanne, M 2006, 'The ABC of Criminology: Anita Muhl, JV Barry, Norval Morris and the making of a discipline in Australia', 46(3) *British Journal of Criminology* 399.

Garland, D 2002, 'Of Crime and Criminals: the development of criminology in Britain', in Maguire, M, Morgan, R & Reiner, R (eds), *The Oxford Handbook of Criminology*, Oxford University Press, Oxford.

Giddens, A 1998, *The Third Way: the renewal of social democracy*, Polity Press, London.

Girling, E, Loader, I & Sparks, R 2000, *Crime and Social Change in Middle England: questions of order in an English town*, Routledge, London.

Graham, S (ed) 2004, *Cities, War and Terrorism: towards an urban geopolitics*, Blackwell, London.

Hannigan, J 2006, *Environmental Sociology,* Routledge, London

Havemann, P 2005, 'Denial, Modernity and Exclusion: Indigenous, placelessness in Australia', 5 *Macquarie Law Journal* 57.

Hil, R & Dawes, G 2000, '"The Thin White Line" Juvenile Crime, Racialised Narrative and Vigilantism, North Queensland Study', 11(3) *Current Issues in Criminal Justice* 308.

Hogg, R & Brown, D 1998, *Rethinking Law and Order*, Pluto Press, Sydney.

Hogg, R & Carrington, K 2003, 'Violence, Spatiality and Other Rurals', 36(3) *Australian and New Zealand Journal of Criminology* 293.

Hogg, R 2005, 'Policing the Rural Crisis', 38(3) *Australian and New Zealand Journal of Criminology* 340.

Hogg, R & Carrington, K 2006, *Policing the Rural Crisis,* Federation Press, Sydney.

Irwin, J 2005, *The Warehouse Prison: disposal of the new dangerous class,* Roxbury, Los Angeles.

Jobes, P, Barclay, E, Weinand, H & Donnermeyer, J 2004, 'A Structural Analysis of Social Disorganisation and Crime in Rural Communities in Australia', 37(1) *Australian and New Zealand Journal of Criminology* 114.

Jones, T & Newburn, T 2006, 'Three strikes and you're out: exploring symbol and substance in American and British crime control policies', 46(5) *British Journal of Criminology* 781.

Kaplan, A 2003, 'Homeland Insecurities: reflections on language and space', 85 *Radical History Review* 82.

Karstedt, S 2007, 'Creating Institutions: linking the "local" and the "global" in the travel of crime policies', 8(2) *Police Practice and Research* 145.

Loader, I 2002, 'Policing, Securitization and Democratization in Europe', 2(2) *Criminal Justice* 125.

Macdonald, I & Ross, B 2003, *Mining Ombudsman Annual Report 2003*, Oxfam Community Aid Abroad, Victoria.

Manning, P 2005, 'The Study of Policing', 8(1) *Police Quarterly* 23.

McQuilton, J 1979, *The Kelly Outbreak 1878-1880: the geographical dimension of social banditry*, Melbourne University Press, Melbourne.

Newburn, T 2002, 'Atlantic Crossings: "policy transfer" and crime control in the USA and Britain', 4(2) *Punishment and Society* 165.

Newburn, T & Jones, T 2007, 'Symbolizing Crime Control: reflections on zero tolerance', 11(2) *Theoretical Criminology* 221.

O'Connor, M & Gray, D 1989, *Crime in a Rural Community,* Federation Press, Sydney.

O'Malley, P & Carson, K 1989, 'The Institutional Foundations of Australian Criminology', 25(3) *Australian and New Zealand Journal of Criminology* 333.

Putnam, R 1993, *Making Democracy Work: civic traditions in modern Italy*, University of Princetown Press, New Jersey.

Scott, J, Hogg, R, Barclay, E, & Donnermeyer, J 2007, 'Introduction: "There's crime out there, but not as we know it". Rural Criminology – The Last Frontier', in Barclay, E, Donnermeyer, J, Scott, J & Hogg, R (eds), *Crime in Rural Australia,* Federation Press, Sydney.

Sheptycki, J & Wardak, A (eds) 2005, *Transnational and Comparative Criminology in a Global Context*, Glasshouse, London

Sturma, M 1983, *Vice in a Vicious Society: crime and convicts in mid-nineteenth century New South Wales*, University of Queensland Press, St Lucia.

Valentine, J 2007, *An Independent Assessment of Policing in Remote Indigenous Communities for the Australian Government*, Report for the Minister for Families, Community Services and Indigenous Affairs, Canberra.

van Swaaningen, R 1999, 'Reclaiming Critical Criminology', 3(1) *Theoretical Criminology* 5.

Weisheit, R & Donnermeyer, J 2000 'Change and Continuity in Crime in Rural America', in La Free, G (ed), *The Nature of Crime: continuity and change, Criminal Justice 2000*, vol 1, United States Department of Justice, Washington DC.

White, R 2007, 'Green Criminology and the Pursuit of Social and Ecological Justice', in Bierne, P & South, N (eds), *Issues in Green Criminology*, Willan Publishing, Cullompton.

Wiles, P 1999, 'Foreword', in Dingwall, G & Moody, S (eds), *Crime and Conflict in the Countryside*, University of Wales Press, Cardiff.

Woodhouse, A 2006, '"People are accepted as long as they don't misbehave": Exploring the Relationship between Social Capital and Crime in Rural Australia', 16(1) *Rural Society* 5.

Yarwood, R 2001, 'Crime and Policing in the British Countryside: some agendas for contemporary geographical research', 41(2) *Sociologica Ruralis* 201.

26

GLOBALISED CRIME AND GOVERNANCE: THE OUTCOMES FOR UNDERSTANDING INTERNATIONAL CRIMINAL JUSTICE

Mark Findlay

Introduction: the ideologies of globalised crime governance

Jonathon Simon in his recent book *Governing through Crime* (2007) positions the well-developed nexus between crime and governance squarely within the risk/security politics of George Bush's post-9/11 America. In the context of United States home security policy, Simon argues that representations of crime create a domestic control agenda. This serves to focus governance on risk and security. The state employs risk techniques and selective policing of security against the fear which risk generates. The state's monopoly over criminalisation and control through criminal justice determine them as important fields for governance. Criminal justice can be aligned with the family, the school and the workplace as fertile governance arenas.

This chapter takes the interconnection between crime and governance to the level of international relations and globalisation. It argues that as important as crime and control may now be to domestic governance, in a global age of crime/risk and control/security the interconnection between crime and governance offers an insight into the future of international criminal justice. In particular, I propose:

- Crime, and notably recent interpretations by the dominant political alliance of global terrorism, are instrumental in the conceptualisation and the promotion of the new globalisation (risk/security hegemony);
- The crime/control/governance nexus has become a prominent feature of international criminal law and criminal justice developments;
- The governance imperatives of a dominant world order have tended to compromise the delivery and legitimacy of international criminal justice.

Returning to the domestic sphere, Simon (2001-2002: 1053) has identified two metaphorical directions crucial to a particular legislative reliance on crime as governance:

- The rise of the 'street' as the nexus for a war on crime style governance; and as a consequence;
- The extraordinary emphasis this placed on policing in managing virtually all organisations, public and private.

From an international/global as opposed to a national/state-based perspective this chapter augments these directions towards:

- The rise of the 'global community' as the habitas for crime (and eventually control);
- The representation of 'humanity' as the global crime victim; and
- The particularisation of a dominant global political hegemony as 'policing' international security against crime, especially terrorism. The 'streets' to be 'policed' are now populated by the global community and are beyond state jurisdiction, legislation and dominion (Roberts 2005).

Crime, and in particular global terrorism, is more than a problem for global governance. It is also instrumental in the promotion of the 'new' globalisation and 'para-justice' control regimes.[1] Along with the argued utility of crime in global governance, the fear of crime and the valorisation of crime victims are identified as vital forces over the crime/governance nexus. This in turn valorises the state in its 'protection' of such citizens. With international terrorism justifying a risk/security nexus for global governance, criminal justice is both relied upon and contorted for the achievement of violent control agendas.

International crime control has become the discourse of the self-proclaimed 'liberal democratic' interlocutor. The idealised political subject (the 'global community' or 'humanity') is realised through the definition of 'actual' threats, and legitimate responses (Findlay 2007). Presidents and Prime Ministers speak on behalf of victim communities and determine what qualifies as crimes of aggression and crimes against humanity. These political discriminations accord legitimacy to idealised victims and alienate and delegitimise the motivations and actions of those who challenge the dominant political hegemony.

The vast and imagined possibility of victimisation through crimes against humanity, and genocide in particular, motivates military intervention and consequential penal regulation. If the fear of crime and terror as a prevailing threat predetermines global political control agendas, then any dominant hegemony claiming the right to identify the terrorist, and the capacity to protect the citizen will retrieve their political currency, even if this does not progress beyond narrative representation (Findlay 2007). Further, as the recent relationship between global governance and international criminal justice suggests, the fragile legitimacy of dominant political alliances has inspired concurrent resort to para-justice strategies wherein violence and oppression run contrary to the protective limitations which demark conventional justice responses.

---

1   As with 'para-politics', the concept of 'para-justice' has no definitional certainty. Here we are employing the notion to encapsulate those control responses which follow on from proscribed behaviours which in other circumstances might be processed through conventional criminal justice. Violence, intimidation and a denial of due process are characteristic of para-justice. Rather than being dismissed as institutional injustice, para-justice makes claims for institutional and process credibility through the determinations of military tribunals in particular, and justifies excessive responses through the necessities of war.

Accepting the potential for crime to facilitate governance at the state level, this chapter explores the recent and apparent synergy between globalisation, a risk/ security nexus, and the structure and form of international criminal justice and governance, particularly in the context of international terrorism. It also speculates on the tension between the legitimating capacity of international criminal justice as a crucial agency of governance, against the reversion to violent and intimidatory control practices of para-justice.

For criminologists, criminal lawyers, international relations scholars and rights analysts, globalisation offers a critical context in which to explore the congruence of crime, justice and governance. The analytical endeavour, therefore, is to reveal how world political domination and cultural segregation is presently negotiated and neutralised in a problematic and partial justice paradigm. What remains for international criminal justice is the challenge to make accountable future developments in global governance.

Factors leading to the rise of global governance and crime control

The dependencies of global governance on international criminal justice, and in turn on a risk/security environment for globalisation have developed reactively. They are repressive, recursive and regressive. International terrorism has necessitated for the dominant political hegemony a shift away from late-modern economic culturation, and towards a containment model, which relies on criminalisation and justice/control supports (often following military or violent intervention) to counter the challenge of alternative cultural and political alignments.

This evolution has not been without its radical coincidences, or its longstanding antipathies. The destruction on 11 September 2001, grounded in part in the struggle between fundamentalism and the 'liberal' ideologies and perceived economic imperialism of the west, has become the backdrop for a *new age of globalisation*. Crime and control within this transition appear as a process to consolidate political victory for a coalition of dependant states, through an emergent and formal international criminal justice system (Findlay & Henham 2005). Consequentially, the dominant hegemony acquires legitimacy through 'justice' as well as force in the face of violent challenge. The consolidation occurs by positioning religion, economy and morality as the features of the enemy for war discourse. Accordingly, a new set of privileged subjects is defined for government, and an old set of enemies for exclusion. The security of the idealised citizen/victim is the justification for meeting the terrorist risk.

Yet legitimacy is fragile. This hegemony is a loose and negotiated order. It lacks true legislative, juridical or executive authority beyond metaphor or concession. The citizenship it serves is ceded to it rather than democratically included. Its normative foundation has few deep or common cultural roots. It is searching for a framework of governance. The risk/security nexus particularly mirrored in international terrorism has to some extent recently provided this.

The legitimating potential of international criminal justice has, in certain control contexts, been supplemented by the dominant global political alliance, with a para-justice paradigm. The violent and oppressive nature of this second level of 'justice' has challenged the legitimacy of control interventions as a consequence of denying some central justice 'balances' which international criminal justice propounds. The assumed necessity and expediency of para-justice has made the legitimating capacity of international criminal justice more potent and less negotiable.

In the context of para-politics, wherein both organised crime and terrorism are said to have their place, the characteristics of para-justice are predominant in control strategies. The adoption of para-justice by the dominant political alliance in this new phase of globalisation reveals an intriguing intersection between the aims and activations of both political forms.

The conflict language of this dominant political hegemony, and the emergence of its strong military imagery in its control discourse (para and conventional), are paradoxical at a global level. Wars against crime are designed to replace military intervention with criminal justice. While war imagery invokes a simplistic and dominant process of demonisation as a consequence of 'victors justice', systematic measures against the criminalised enemy see international criminal justice as well as military intervention engaging both the moral and political threats which they represent.

Legitimacy is a central theme running through this chapter's analysis of global crime and international governance. As with the distortion or dissolution of crucial justice identifiers endorsed through risk and security, the intersection between international criminal justice and the motivations of global political alliances further impugn the legitimacy of justice and the governance it fosters. The challenge for international criminal justice is to reclaim the separation of powers and thereby the capacity to keep governance just. This will not be achieved simply as a consequence of conflict resolution and peace making. International criminal justice must provide a critical and accountable capacity against which to measure the risk/security confluence in contemporary globalisation.

The 'New' globalisation[2]

In the *Globalisation of Crime* (Findlay 1999) I envisaged globalisation as the 'collapsing of time and space', in a political age where modernisation and materialism promoted common culturation through economic development. The 'new' globalisation considered here takes mass communication as a given and modernisation as the medium for the advancement of international political hegemony. A risk/security nexus, which has emerged from the domination by (and violent challenges to) this hegemony, provides a contemporary international context for both crime control and governance issues. With the present (somewhat limited) legitimating potential of international criminal justice above military intervention in post conflict states (Findlay & Henham 2005: ch 7), the connection between criminalisation and governance is inextricable in a world where legitimacy is violently contested.

It is an age of risk and security. From the perspective of 'liberal' western democracies vying for global hegemony, 9/11 was the crunch point; the apocalypse now. In these scenarios of terrorism lie the seeds of the 'new' globalisation. The radical conflation which was '9/11' complemented long-standing antipathies and ushered in a regime of 'war' against ideology, dominion and a re-definition of global

---

2   For the purposes of this argument I am not critiquing the reality or utility of 'globalisation' as an analytical concept.

citizenship. The restructuring of jurisdiction, standing, citizenship, humanity, community and exclusion, essential for the new age of globalisation, have their justifications and projections in 9/11. Global governance through reaction became the reluctant priority. Battle lines were redrawn. Global crime agendas were re-ordered. Security priorities realigned. States of war were more universalised. Crime victimisation and the legitimate claims to global citizenship were conflated. The fissures of exclusion and inclusion were cut against criminality and victimisation across global communities. Governance became defined by criminalisation and the restoration of global security.

Along with this, the 'risk society' has surpassed modernisation as the organising framework for globalisation. 'Victim communities' identified as at risk were valorised as blameless. They required the intercession and security proffered by the dominant political 'culture', just as 'underdeveloped' and transitional cultures required material advancement through the modernisation imperatives of the dominant economy (Findlay 1999: ch 2).

The common push to a mono-culture in globalisation, similar to earlier mercantile epochs, has had to defer an economic priority in order to address the violent challenges of contesting cultures.[3] Rather than engage with the complexity of this resistance, a methodology of criminalisation is employed by the dominant political hegemony, and the immediate motivations for globalisation become re-defined in response to crime risk, as security/control.

Can globalised crime construct governance?

About governance Foucault suggests that the task of acting on the actions of others (government) is bound up with ways of *reasoning* about governing (Foucault 2000). In the sense of globalised governance within the 'new' globalisation, the dominant political hegemony has tended to define what is *knowable* and 'more importantly to produce truth selectively' (Simon 2001-2002: 1063). This 'truth' has emerged as a by-product of its own strategies of intervention, and their legitimacy through the earlier-argued crime/security nexus. A particular notion of governance has been rationalised both through challenges to international security and 'exclusive' approaches to its restoration.

Therefore, the *ways of reasoning about governing* in the recent global context have in significant measure focused around:

- New emergent crime risks;
- Consequent challenges to international security;
- Actual harm of the global citizen and global communities;
- Requiring a force-based response from the 'democratic' international hegemony;
- Legitimating a particular form of international justice intervention; and
- Repositioning ongoing concepts of sovereignty, citizenship, legal standing and alien attack (Findlay 2007).

---

3   The similarities might be extended in contrast with the militaristic mercantile companies in Asia and the New World, chartered by their sponsoring states to make war, colonise, and deliver criminal justice along with the predominant commitment of wealth creation. None of this however operated in the same atmosphere of internationalisation as we see it today.

The translation of this reasoning through epithets and campaigns such as the 'war on terror' has moved the nexus between crime and governance from the politics of the ideal, into processes whereby criminal justice and the control potentials it offers significantly reconstruct and determine the legitimate interlocutors of global conflict (Findlay & Henham 2005). In fact, global conflict, and the re-institution of post conflict states are in part now dependant on the arena of international criminal justice for legitimate resolution. Resistance through violence, no matter how destructive, is marginalised and relegated by the determination of the criminal liability of its principal perpetrators. The tribunal has become essential to the restoration of governability post-military intervention.

Global governance around a political discourse of the 'war on terror' seems now reliant on risk/security balances. An investigation of the structures which are said to achieve and maintain these balances (morphology) align with and support the central structures and institutions of global governance where globalisation addresses risk (crime) concerns for security (control).

This summarises a passage of crime control and governance within the contemporary international risk/security agenda. To move on and detail the institutions and processes responsible for international criminal justice resolutions of risk would identify further the synergy between justice in this context and identifiers of global governance (Findlay & Henham 2005). These would include, not exhaustively:

- Prevailing constitutional legality;
- 'Supra-national' legislative power;
- A set of rules and regulations for administering criminal liability and punishment;
- A fabric of public and private policing;
- State monopoly over prosecution;
- Power to appoint and authorise judges; and
- Executive responsibility for the nature and duration of penalty.

It is not difficult to determine the separation of powers implicit in this structure, which is said to confirm democratic government. This too holds for the consideration of para-justice responses to crimes such as terrorism:

- Prevailing authority to create and maintain alternative 'legalities';
- 'Supra-national' exclusion of both the perpetrators and the mechanisms for their containment beyond the conventional jurisdiction of the state;
- Extraordinary rules and regulations for administering criminal liability and punishment, which in turn rely on complex discretionary delegations and largely anonymous activation;
- A process of investigation and policing which is covert, cooptive, compulsory and confrontational;[4]
- State monopoly over prosecution, and more importantly when to detain and punish without prosecution;
- Power to sanction and penalise without the confirmation of judicial authority;

---

4   For a discussion of these styles of policing see Findlay and Zvekic (1993), ch 2.

- Enforceability through superior force and through the construction of control 'technologies', plus the clandestine application of terror against terror, torture against aggression;
- Collapsing of military and quasi-judicial powers, and the translation of perpetrators into combatants;
- Executive responsibility for the nature and duration of penalty.

Can crime control determine considerations of risk and security?

Garland (2001) as did Cohen (1985) before him argues that community protection is now the dominant theme of penal policy. The risk here is unidirectional. Crime poses a threat to the security of the individual and the community, therefore the state is obliged to minimise that risk through control. The public supports this. On the other hand:

> In these matters (harsh state control interventions) the public appears to be (or is represented as) decidedly risk-averse, and intensely focused on the risk of depredation by unrestrained criminals. The risk of unrestrained state authorities, of arbitrary power and the violation of civil liberties seems no longer to figure prominently in public concern (Garland 2001: 12).

Garland (2001) says more than that new crime control developments have 'adapted' and 'responded' to the late-modern world and to its political and cultural values. He advances these developments as 'creating that world, helping to constitute the meaning of late modernity' (2001: 194). Along with managing problems of crime and insecurity, he argues, crime control 'institutionalises a set of responses to these problems that are themselves consequential in their social impact'.

Strong messages for the managing of risk and the 'taming of chance' travel through the new institutions of international criminal justice. This leads on to an environment of international governance in which the citizen accepts restrictions of liberty, which would have been intolerable in an era of globalisation outside this risk/security nexus, particularly when democracy was marketed as the ideology of modernisation. Now:

> Spatial controls, situational controls, managerial controls, system controls, social controls, self-controls – in one realm after another, we now find the imposition of intensive regimes of regulation, inspection and control and, in the process, our civic culture becomes increasingly less tolerant and inclusive, increasingly less capable of trust. After a long term process of expanding individual freedom and relaxing cultural and social restraints, control is now being reemphasised in every area of social life – with the singular and startling exception of the economy, from whose deregulated domain most of today's major risks routinely emerge (Garland 2001: 194-195).

Prophetically in the global context, Garland identifies the characteristic of reaction. A new sense of international disorder pervaded the dawn of the 21st century and was accompanied by a renewed interest in global order and world governance. Crucial to governance and order internationally, as seen from the perspective of the dominant political hegemony, was addressing:

- Dangerously inadequate controls;
- Rapidly and violently emergent challenges to the control of that hegemony.

Initial responses were militaristic. But as is always the case, these were unsustainable. Criminal justice has been conscripted to take management of the control of global risk (Findlay & Henham 2005). Of course this is not an exclusive control responsibility, and more violent repression will always be on call in a climate of risk and security where the threat is erratic and incisive. However, international criminal justice is the attractive medium-term response because of its perceived potential to enhance the legitimacy of the dominant political hegemony.

Another important feature of the control profile internationally is the re-definition of 'community' and along with it notions of jurisdiction, citizenship and standing. Emersed in community is the potential both for legitimacy and resistance.

In a recent Australian context, the Federal Government's policy on asylum seekers, and the use of criminal justice to 'protect national boarders', and quarantine citizenship is a case in point. This initially was built on a denial of the discourse of political correctness, which allowed for the re-emergence of racially based migration constructions. 'Boat people' became a threat to national integrity and when they were demonised as willing to sacrifice their children in illegal efforts at entry the Australian electorate got behind a party with tough policies which criminalised what later proved to be refugee determinations

Multiculturalism was an associated victim of government policy, which played the race card in the context of national security and international risk. Cultural integrity was degraded and dismissed as ethnic individualism. There has been a particular focus on Islamic communities and their failure to embrace 'Australian values'; and so it was not difficult to equate the threat beyond with the threat within. Whole communities became the target of crime and control identification because of their 'otherness'; a difference which was synonymous with the cultural stereotyping of international terror. The crime was as much to be one in a culture or religion claimed by the terrorist, rather than evidenced by real risks to security and real threats to sovereignty and citizenship. The application of crime and control to internal rather than international security concerns helped also to endorse exclusive and exclusionist notions of nationhood, citizenship and national identity readily compatible with Australia's place in the dominant political hegemony.

So too, the para-justice processes employed in Guantanamo Bay have received a remarkably tolerant response from the conventional institutions of justice governance in the US, even if not so amongst its alliance partners (Meister 2004; Duffy 2005). Arguably this is due to what Garland identifies as a modification of citizenship and the liberties of the democratic state, in the face of heightened risk, and more problematic global security. Paradoxically we see para-justice compromising freedom for its protection (Clark 2002; Chemerinski 2005).

How does the struggle for legitimacy construct this relationship – contested reasoning for governance?

Predominant and prevailing notions of 'truth' are essential in the struggle over the legitimacy of international governance. Dominant *reasoning* presupposes predominance over 'truth' as a delineator of the government and the governed.

When it comes to considerations of 'truth' in the context of terrorist struggle, the contested nature of truth is obvious if also regularly glossed over. Truth is what the suicide bomber is said to die for and what the military and criminal justice responses are set to protect. Can it be the same truth? If not then its relativity becomes a contested objective of the relationship between terror and 'justice' responses. How is the subjectivity of truth here to be managed beyond the force-based authority and supremacy of victor's justice?[5]

In the terrorism/response context it is not so much the nature of truth but its contest which is the connection. The protection of truth is the common justification for the exercise of violence on both sides. Even violent retaliation against say 'genocide' through terrorism claims its legitimacy against 'guilty' or 'blameworthy' violence where truth is at risk. Yet again the relativity of guilt and blame challenge the advance and democratic dominance of a single 'truth' on which the justice response relies.

'Moral standing' is contested, where responses to terrorism law exclusively claim the legitimate use of violence. Those on the other hand who promote re-integrative techniques as against retribution, to more effectively manage original violence, recognise that restorative justice relies on the context of a supportive community if shaming is to be positively applied to offenders (Braithwaite 1989). Without a supportive context, dependent on a common acceptance of the moral standing of the preferred response, attempts at shaming break down as stigmatic rather than re-integrative. Resort to violence is soon reiterated.

However, in the situation of terrorism/response relationships moral standing is at the centre of the contest for legitimacy. Reflective communities, in which both the terrorist and the justice responses are marketed, may oppose the moral legitimacy of each other. These are communities in part galvanised through resistance to the external and oppositional claims for moral standing.[6]

Particularly damaging to the justice response is the resistance of terrorist 'communities' over the basis of moral standing. Dworking's components of the moral standing of law (determinacy, integrity, coherence and wholeness[7]) are difficult for the violent justice response to export when new institutions and processes of incarceration, interrogation, trial and punishment are directed to the terrorist opponent. These novel entities generally contradict or at least strain some of the central protections which make criminal justice in general fair and 'just'.[8]

How do globalised crime priorities inform the political discourse of globalisation?

As mentioned previously, concepts of crime have traditionally relied on some cultural or jurisdictional situation for their relevance and impact. Implicit in this is the expectation that crime stops at national borders, or at least that it has localised interests.

---

5   There is a need here for a more detailed consideration of Weber's (1947) conditions for the authority of the state.

6   Moral standing as a legal/constitutional claim to legitimate voice is discussed in Winter (1988).

7   For a discussion of these, see West (1999).

8   For a discussion of the detail of these changes in criminal justice in the United States and their impact on due process, see Gross (2002).

The jurisdictional boundaries of crime, however, can only be explained in terms of legal convenience and legislative limits. As piracy, smuggling, abduction, gun-running, and counterfeiting have been crime problems for centuries, so too the laws of individual nations have been powerless to control them.

Transnational crime such as terrorism is new only in its technologies and reach, along with the manner in which law enforcement and international agencies have recently identified it as a priority. Again, the selective political representation of crime is the explanation for such a trend. For instance, as governments realise the potential for criminal enterprise to endanger world market structures, capital transfer, national security, and international transport and communication; crime targets are selected out for cooperative action while others, like environmental degradation on a scale well beyond the harm ever caused through terror attacks, are largely ignored. Strategies have been developed for example, to prevent and prosecute commodity futures fraud and abuses, but an international approach to crimes against the environment is yet to be convincingly settled.

The other difference with transnational crime, represented as a recent problem for globalisation, is the manner in which crime control is reshaped in order to address the difficulties with jurisdiction. Crime control is, in this context, at least a bi-lateral endeavour. However, in many control strategies for transnational crime the bi-lateral efforts are stimulated by globalised representations of crime and control priorities.

It is the threat posed both by terrorism and organised crime motivating local jurisdictions to adopt international control agendas. Normally this would be resisted on the basis of the autonomy of criminal justice as a state domain even in the face of international crime threats (Findlay 1995). By concentrating on representations of organised crime and terrorism, as well as the state response through criminalisation, the local authorities have translated the international significance of crime threat to justify local interventions which may have little real impact within the jurisdiction concerned. It is an example of the impact of internationalism on localised criminal justice policy.

The threat of global terrorism as a challenge to 'legitimate' political ordering has stimulated the development of extra-ordinary control responses in a similar fashion that organised crime justified extra-legal state reactions under threat (Findlay 1999: ch 5). Organised crime and their economies, enterprises and market manipulations were determined, throughout the past century, as challenging legitimate political and economic governance. Further, the application of violence and intimidation by organised crime in its control aspirations were said to require a response in kind by the state. With global terrorism today, the dominant political alliance emphasises the risk of terrorism to legitimate governance and its capacity to compromise the protections of conventional justice to its own ends. Para-justice paradigms are promoted in return and legitimated against the nature of the threat and its own methods of 'governance'.

How does international criminal justice relate to global governance?

New levels of law enforcement cooperation across borders have been fostered in a climate of acute threat and exaggerated retaliation (Viano 1999). By concentrating on the violent and intimidatory behaviours of terrorism, rather than on their organisational structures or expressed motivations, the community is more ready to accept strong medicine to prevent terror in its midst. Interestingly, the state has employed the 'terror' of fear concept to facilitate what might otherwise be law enforcement responses that would meet vocal resistance (McCulloch 2003). Para-justice paradigms gain similar purchase in the strategies for national, regional and global security against the representation of risk, which emphasises the challenge to legitimate governance.

Fear or reality, both justice and governance issues depend on constituencies as well as jurisdiction. For international criminal justice and global governance the focus recently is with 'victim communities'. This notion engages:

- Individual victims;
- The communities of these victims which share their harm;
- When the crime is directed at community cohesion or cultural integrity; and
- When violence is motivated by the destruction of what makes communities or cultures (language, art, religion, family structure etc).

A justification for international criminal justice is crimes against humanity. In this sense 'humanity' has a community or cultural location. Justice should reflect 'humanitarian' concerns in its mandate to protect humanity. Such concerns are only partial, sectarian, or selective in the way contemporary global governance views 'humanity'. Anything outside the legitimate citizenship of the dominant hegemony tends to be removed from the protective ambit of its humanity. The excluded are worthy of destruction rather than protection. The followers receive the patronage so long as they ascribe to the dominant order.

The dominant hegemony in this climate of international terrorism (be it manifested in the genocide of Rwanda, the ethnic cleansing of the Balkans, or the anticipated and illusive weapons of mass destruction in Iraq) has significantly transferred militaristic intervention at least in part to the jurisdiction of international criminal justice. This is a transition that carries with it expectations for global governance and the legitimation on which it depends. But in keeping with the agenda and exclusive instrumentation of this political alliance, the morphology of international criminal justice for this purpose is made reliant on common notions of the crimes against humanity, the legitimate victim communities and the appropriate retributive responses. This has in fact meant that the formal institutions of international criminal justice have presented limited pathways of access, and professionally removed representation which in turn have not well integrated and connected with these communities. The consequence for global governance has been to limit the influence of international criminal justice in restoring post-conflict societies.

But it is not about victims and harm as it is not about governance outside context. Much of what we have explored is at least stimulated by the contest of legitimacy. As international criminal justice transforms to better address the needs of victim communities, then its legitimacy, and its power to legitimate as a crucial component of global governance, will be enhanced.

It would be misleading to suggest, which we do not, that the governance/international criminal justice connection depended on the development of a global interest in the core crimes of genocide, and crimes against humanity. The connection between international criminal justice and global governance is both symbolic and applied. We will leave symbolism aside for another day. In terms of the applied connection, designated and located in a context of global insecurity, the power of international criminal justice in global governance is in recuperating the tattered authority of the dominant hegemony as a consequence of military intervention. And at this level, the justice/governance link is reliant on and determined by the failings of the hegemony as much as the transformational strength and consistency of international criminal justice.

Conclusions: crime, control and governance – the challenge for understanding international criminal justice

The nexus between international criminal justice and global governance is dependant on crime/risk and control/security considerations for world order. In critically analysing this relationship, its potential for conflict resolution and its problematic influences over legitimacy, it is important to avoid simple causal analysis. Good governance is not the incontrovertible consequence of justice resolution in preference say to military intervention. Particular contextual conditions need examination in order that good governance can be anticipated from any selected governance model. In addition, the partiality of governance motivations which presently infiltrate the exercise of tribunal-based justice in particular requires critical analysis so that the recursive effects on international criminal justice might be countered.

Robert's (2005) 'cultural assemblage' well covers the dominant political hegemony, which is currently master of international governance, at least at a formal/ economic level. It has come together largely within projects of regional government. Its claims to the indicia of *government* are as yet fragile and primitive beyond military victory. The international organisations said to house global governance while representative, are without authority, without the support of this hegemony. The legislature, judicial institutions and executive bureaucracies emergent from these international organisations are dependant (particularly in resource terms) on this hegemony. The endorsement and protection of global citizenship currently resides with the hegemony, not in terms of democratic inclusion and representation, but rather through patronage.

Roberts (2005: 1) rightly cautions against rewarding these 'negotiated orders' with the established juridical, legal or jurisdictional order required of the nation state:

> Today, under an onslaught of jural discourse and institutional design, the distinctive rationalities and values of negotiated order, while arguably deserving to be celebrated, are effectively effaced.

The para-justice by-products of these negotiated orders, we suggest, should not simply be dismissed as unjust aberrations. They are in fact demonstrative of the influence of politics over domestic, regional and international criminal justice. International, comparative analysis of justice 'negotiation' under the influence of political domination will reveal the politicised purpose for justice as governance. Further, a return to the normative pre-conditions for international criminal justice will indicate how skewed global governance in its present manifestations may have become (Findlay & Henham (forthcoming 2008): ch 1).

Globalisation invites the discussion of governance in terms such as law, justice, and bureaucracy, without or above the state. For law at least this requires severance from a narrow notion of legislative jurisdiction. In the 'war on terror' discourse there

326

is an invocation to protect 'civilisation' and 'democracy' against violent assault. It is compatible with this celebration of preferred international political paradigms, to view law as 'cosmology'. In this sense law and its institutions are engaged in the enterprise of 'imagining and articulating what we want the social world to be' (Roberts 2005: 6). Law in governance in this sense links the discursive formulation of rules and process to an articulation of preferred world order.

If globalisation even in an age of risk and security retains a commitment towards a single culture (Findlay 1999), the preferred justice is exclusive and not pluralist in its authority, coverage, or outreach. Justice also tends to legitimate oligarchic governance rather than to seek legitimacy from it. This is because the trajectory of international criminal justice (even if not its procedures) is towards a concern for humanity and its communities of victims. This then becomes another ground on which the dominant political hegemony claims the legitimacy of its constituency and their patronage.

The trajectory of international criminal justice sees an intersection between the conventional and the para-justice paradigms for the advancement of hegemonic interests. Interestingly, claims for the predominance of security as the framework of governance are commonly used to justify both conventional and para-justice responses. Where the paradigms depart is around the procedural conditions for justice outcomes, particularly those which are said to give international criminal justice its force in state reconstruction and peace-making (Findlay & Henham 2005: ch 8).

In the context of a security/risk nexus the 'reasoning' of contemporary governance is created recursively. A formative and fragile institutional hegemony legitimises globalised forms of 'truth' through control mechanisms specifically designed to minimise threats to its authority. Hence, although 'libertarian' arguments trumpet justice as an integral element of the democratic credo (and thereby through their application internationally, as indicia of global governance), the reverse seems to represent reality. Bilateral intimidation, regional coercion and military incursion are the preferred international relations.

The reduction of risk (in whose-ever name) is accompanied by a reduction in civil liberties, a denial of plurality, and a marginalisation of civil society. Individual autonomy, so central to the normative politics of the dominant hegemony and their idealised community, is subjugated through the sacrifices required to maintain 'civilisation' and 'humanity'. The institutional control of behaviours, which threaten the political hegemony, is justified in amoral terms – terms that do not rely on any notion of a shared reason, experience or shared value system. In this sense, international criminal justice as the theatre in which the crime/risk-control/security nexus is tested has been profoundly compromised. It is a justice largely unconfirmed by universal moralities. As such, it retains limited legitimacy, and its potential to legitimate wider global governance and conflict resolution while present, will continue to have limited sweep.

Risk and security as threats and needs are procured to essentially justify harsh control, and the only morally coherent basis for global governance they can provide is through a reactive denunciation of those who challenge the hegemony. For instance, in order to justify an extreme punishment response, the violence and violent potential of terrorism is highlighted. However, a moral assessment of terrorism in terms of 'mindless' violence is compromised by any corresponding excessive violence of punishment, particularly where this has consequences for innocent communities, in a 'law of war' scenario. In addition, its 'mindlessness' challenges the deterrent impact of violent punishment, which is offered as the reason for requiring violent punishment.

If they are to stand alongside recognised indicia of governance and claim a more long lasting legitimation, the 'new drivers' for globalised justice should be developed from a renewal of humanistic principles as they find expression in what we have referred to elsewhere as 'communities of justice' (Findlay & Henham 2005: ch 7). To sustain and complement these communities, the foundations for international criminal justice need to rediscover the deeper and more grounded rationality for penality as it is expressed in the sharing of values and experiences over time and place.

In this way the 'contexts of control' within the globalisation project may be more convincingly identifiable as coherent and resilient value systems essential to (and more tolerant of) relative forms of human existence. As such, partial and hegemonic justice will be diminished in its role and will no longer provide either a metaphor for, or structural implementations of justice in global governance. A natural consequence of this transition will be the diminution of the risk/security imperative, leaving international criminal justice to offer a more accessible, heuristic and normatively convincing role in global governance and conflict resolution.

The productive study of international criminal justice will need to recognise, for the purposes of a critical policy capacity, the challenge to justice legitimacy posed through its present inclusion in global governance as currently constructed. The analyst should engage with possible 'new moralities' for international criminal justice that reflects a genuine and unconditional commitment to 'humanity' (Findlay & Henham (forthcoming 2008): ch 1). A new model of international criminal justice which grows from a clearer separation of powers within international legality and governance will provide the analyst with the tools to critique the role of justice in keeping governance just. From this, peace-making and conflict resolution can be disentangled from the partial motivations of political dominion. This trajectory takes the analyst from an interest in crime and governance to a concern for the legitimacy which justice offers global governance only within a framework of accountability and inclusion.

References

Braithwaite, J 1989, *Crime Shame and Re-integration*, Oxford University Press, Oxford.

Chemerinski, E 2005, 'Detainees: wartime security and constitutional liberty', 68(4) *Albany Law Review* 119.

Clark, G 2002, 'Military Tribunals and the Separation of Powers', *Suffolk University Law School Faculty Publications,* Paper 111.

Cohen, S 1985, *Visions of Social Control*, Polity Press, Oxford.

Duffy, H 2005, 'Case Study: Guantanamo Bay detentions under human rights and humanitarian law', in Duffy H, *The War on Terror and the Framework of International Law, Cambridge University Press*, Cambridge, Chapter 8.

Findlay, M 1995, 'International Rights and Australian Adaptations: recent developments in criminal investigation', 17(2) *Sydney Law Review* 278.

Findlay, M 1999, *The Globalisation of Crime: understanding transitional relationships in context*, Cambridge University Press, Cambridge.

Findlay, M 2007, 'Terrorism and Relative Justice', 47(1) *Crime, Law and Social Change* 57.

Findlay, M & Henham, R 2005, *Transforming International Criminal Justice: restorative and retributive justice in the trial process*, Willan Publishing, Cullompton.

Findlay, M, & Henham, R (forthcoming 2008), *Beyond Punishment: the future of international criminal justice*, Willan Publishing, Cullompton.

Findlay, M & Zvekic, U 1993, *Alternative Policing Styles: cross-cultural perspectives*, Kluwer, Deventer.

Foucault, M 2000, 'Govenmentality', in Faubion, J & Hurley R (eds), *Essential Works of Foucault 1965-1984*, New Press, New York.

Garland, D 2001, *The Culture of Control: crime and social order in contemporary society*, Oxford University Press, Oxford.

Gross, E 2002, 'Trying Terrorists; Justification for Differing Trial Rules: the balance between security considerations and human rights', 13(1) *Indiana International and Comparative Law Review* 1.

McCulloch, J 2003, '"Counter-Terrorism", Human Security and Globalisation: from welfare to warfare state', 14(3) *Current Issues in Criminal Justice* 283.

Meister, R 2004, 'The Supreme Court, Guantanamo Bay and Justice Fix-it', *Cornell Law School Berger International Speaker Series,* Paper 4.

Roberts, S 2005, 'After Government? On representing law without the state', 68(1) *Modern Law Review* 1.

Simon, J 2001-2002, 'Governing through Crime Metaphors', 67(4) *Brook Law Review* 1035.

Simon, J 2007, *Governing through Crime: how the war on crime transformed American democracy and created a culture of fear*, Oxford University Press, New York.

Viano, E (ed) 1999, *Global Organised Crime and International Security,* Ashgate, Aldershot.

Weber, M 1947, *Theory of Social and Economic Organization*, translated by Henderson, AM & Parsons, T, Oxford University Press, New York.

West, R 1997, 'Taking Moral Argument Seriously', 74(2) *Chicago Kent Law Review* 499.

Winter, S 1988, 'The Metaphor of standing and the Problem of Self Governance', 40 *Stanford Law Review* 1371.

Index